TOTAL
ESPIONAGE

Other Fonthill books by Curt Riess

The Nazis Go Underground

The Rise and Fall of the Luftwaffe

Joseph Goebbels

TOTAL ESPIONAGE

GERMANY'S INFORMATION AND DISINFORMATION APPARATUS 1932-41

CURT RIESS

FONTHILL

Fonthill Media Limited
Fonthill Media LLC
www.fonthillmedia.com
office@fonthillmedia.com

First published in the United Kingdom
and the United States of America 2016

British Library Cataloguing in Publication Data:
A catalogue record for this book is available from the British Library

Copyright © In this edition, Fonthill Media 2016

ISBN 978-1-78155-451-7

Typeset in 10.5pt on 13pt Sabon
Printed and bound by CPI Group (UK) Ltd, Croydon, CR0 4YY

Contents

Foreword
It Isn't Done With Mirrors

Total war necessitates total espionage. The leadership of a country must be capable of finding out about and calculating the entire force of resistance of its opponents, military and otherwise.

Military espionage which, of course, is only a part of total espionage, has other objects than in times past. The technique of warfare has experienced a radical revolution within the last ten years. That in itself would have meant a decisive espionage problem for the Allies. But far beyond the purely military aspect of the war, there were questions of fundamental importance for a coming war which had to be answered. It was not so much the specialized German deployment plans, but the new principles of tactics about which information had to be gathered; not so much the actual rearmament as the potential rearmament; not so much the capacity of war industry as the capacity of the entire industry which would be mobilized for war. Questions compared to which the objects of espionage between 1914–1918 become of secondary importance.

The Nazis understood early that revolutionizing warfare meant revolutionizing espionage. An Intelligence Service which had been mediocre during the First World War was replaced by one which before and during the Second World War achieved enormous triumphs. The Nazis worked on the basis of total espionage.

The Allies stuck to their old-fashioned and outdated system of espionage. Not the least important reason for the defeat of France is the complete failure of its *Deuxième Bureau*. Of the British Intelligence Service it may be said that it failed because it was hampered by its own government. The old-fashioned but still magnificently functioning apparatus of the British Intelligence Service finally cut loose and soon became a match for the German machine. The British even went further. After a purely defensive beginning, they started to organize in German-occupied territories something very similar to the total espionage of the Nazis—a fifth column against the fifth columns.

The birth and the functioning of the total espionage machine will be described in the following pages. They, therefore, will not contain many exciting stories of beautiful dancers who seduced generals and stole important plans. They will not contain the ever-recurrent story of agent X-22, who, after all, was only small fry, while those who really were behind his actions were never shown to the reader for the simple reason that they were not known to the writer. Some of those stories were probably true stories; but they belong to a past era, the romantic era of espionage.

This book is not a book of stories. It is much more the book of only one story. But it is the story of those higher-ups, of those brain trusts of espionage, of those who never disguise themselves and never carry a false passport for the reason that they hardly ever leave their own offices, let alone their country.

This, then, is the story of the greatest espionage organization of all times; of the apparatus which the Nazis have built up in order to cover the world with a net of total espionage.

Much has been written about Nazi spies, and much of it has been falsification. For some strange reason, the word 'Gestapo' has always fascinated most writers, and this organization, which concerns itself mostly with counterespionage, has been credited with, or rather blamed for, many deeds which other sections of the organization accomplished.

The story of total espionage is the story of an organization working with the precision of a gigantic business enterprise; that does not mean that it is a dry or colourless story. On the contrary, it rather resembles a mystery novel, and a bad mystery novel at that. Once more reality has proved to be more fantastic than our imagination, and the reality of the Nazis is something which no Hollywood script writer could or would allow himself to put down on paper. The public in the United States got a faint idea as to what this reality is like during the New York spy trial of 1938, when it was proved in court that a deserter from the United States Army was preparing to kidnap a general.

There will, no doubt, be some questions as to how I obtained my material. To start with, I may say that it has not been done with mirrors.

Like Will Rogers, I know almost only what I read in the papers. I read my newspapers very carefully, especially the German papers, between 1930 and 1938. As is shown in this book, the Germans have printed a great deal of interesting material throughout those years, especially in their military publications. Anybody could have read them. The Intelligence Services of the Allies unfortunately did not.

Of course, the entire material could not have been collected without the help of collaborators. I had collaborators in Japan, in Germany, in Mexico, and in the Balkans; it is by their request that I withhold their names. But I will here take the opportunity to express my gratitude to a collaborator living in the United States who has done valuable work to make this book possible: Mr Richard Winston.

Finally, certain documents served as a basis; documents from the files of the *Deuxième Bureau* which were saved from Paris; documents which came out of Germany and which in part have already been published in other countries. Also, two men helped by giving some documentary evidence; both of them still belong to the secret service of a European country.

All documents which are discussed in the book have either been inspected by me or by my collaborators whom I trust implicitly. All scenes described have been witnessed by at least one of those who informed me about them. All the facts contained in the book, whether or not they have been published before, have been carefully checked and rechecked.

The difficulty in preparing this book was not the lack of material but the abundance of it. There was also a certain amount of material which could not be used because it might have led to misunderstandings and would possibly have harmed those who are fighting Hitlerism and to whom we are therefore all indebted.

Since this book was first conceived and since actual writing began, almost no day has passed without furnishing new material. This book, the central figure of which is Rudolf Hess, was almost half finished when the news of Hess's flight to Scotland reached us. Then came the expulsion of German consuls, the arrest of the Nazi spy ring, the South American reaction against the activities of Hitler agents, and so on.

New material kept pouring in almost up to the last day of the writing. Even now, with the finished manuscript before me, it seems to me almost necessary to enlarge its scope. However, this shall be left to future editions.

I cannot close without expressing my satisfaction that all the events which in one way or another are related to the material of the book have never contradicted its basic theory; on the contrary, each new event has only been one more confirmation of the conception around which this book was written.

CURT RIESS
New York
October 10, 1941

Introduction to
the 2016 Edition

This text was published immediately *before* the Japanese attack on Pearl Harbor, 7 December 1941. It may therefore be considered as a form of time capsule; a text embodying information and thought—general as well as specific—relating to the espionage facilities of the Third Reich, frozen at the time of publication, at a point when Hitler's Germany was seemingly winning the war. The turning of the tide was to come one year later. Most historians tend to agree that Montgomery's defeat of Rommel at the Second battle of El Alamein; 23 October 1942, followed by the launch *Operation Uranus* by the Red Army on 19 November 1942—during the five-month-long Battle of Stalingrad—formed the point at which Hitler's forces began their retreat. In fact some historians, notably William L. Shirer, the American author of *The Rise and Fall of the Third Reich* considers one of the great turning points was much earlier when Hitler was at a loss at what to do about Great Britain. At the beginning of July 1940 Hitler and all his entourage were convinced that Churchill's Government would accept his 'generous' peace offer. He had not believed that Britain would declare war in the first place in 1939, and now that Germany controlled most of Continental Europe he could not conceive of any possible reason why Britain would not accept his offer and lay down its arms. To his way of thinking it was obvious. Why keep fighting? What for? His famous radio speech of 19 July which he believed would be the clincher worked with the German people but not with the British. The official rejection by the British Government on 22 July came like a cold shower to the Wilhelmstrasse. William Shirer explains:

> In truth neither Hitler, the High Command nor the general staffs of the Army, Navy and Air Force had ever seriously considered how a war with Great Britain could be fought and won. Now in the midsummer of 1940 they did not know what to do with their glittering success; they had no plans and scarcely any will for exploiting the greatest military victories in

the history of their soldiering nation. This is one of the great paradoxes of the Third Reich. At the very moment when Hitler stood at the zenith of his military power, with most of the European Continent at his feet, his victorious armies stretched from the Pyrenees to the Arctic Circle, from the Atlantic to beyond the Vistula, rested now and ready for further action, he had no idea how to go on and bring the war to a victorious conclusion. There is, of course, a reason for this, although it was not clear to us at the time. The Germans, despite their vaunted military talents, lacked any grand strategic concept. Their horizons were limited—they had always been limited—to land warfare against the neighbouring nations on the European Continent.

There was of course another alternative open to the Germans. They might bring Britain down by striking across the Mediterranean with their Italian ally, taking Gibraltar at its western opening and in the east driving on from Italy's bases in North Africa through Egypt and over the canal to Iran, severing one of the Empire's main life lines. But this necessitated vast operations overseas at distances far from home bases, and in 1940 it seemed beyond the scope of the German imagination.

Thus at the height of dizzy success Hitler and his captains hesitated. They had not thought out the next step and how it was to be carried through. This fateful neglect would prove to be one of the great turning points of the war and indeed of the short life of the Third Reich and of the meteoric career of Adolf Hitler. Failure, after so many stupendous victories, was now to set in. But this, to be sure, could not be foreseen as beleaguered Britain, now holding out alone, girded herself with what small means she had for the German onslaught at the summer's end.

Failure, after so many stupendous victories, was now to set in—profound words, but not prophetic, for Shirer was writing long after the war. Shirer knew Germany, he knew the Nazis and understood their mind-set. He had lived and worked in Germany during the era of the Third Reich from 1934 to 1940. Curt Riess did not articulate himself in the same manner, but he was prophetic, for he was writing in 1941, only one third of the way through the war period of the Third Reich. Throughout his book is the common thread of the inevitability of the collapse of the Nazi empire. He details the miracle of Teutonic organization which had created this mammoth web of agents, espionage and information garnering, but even so in his eyes it was doomed to fail.

Why was he writing? Being Jewish and exiled from his native land was clearly one enormous grievance. Furthermore he hated the Nazis and everything they stood for with a passion which comes out in his written work. Undoubtedly he craved for the ending of America's isolationism and the adding of the vast American muscle in the fight against the evil of the Axis. Perhaps he hoped that his enthusiastic sensationalism might add weight in this swaying of opinion. He need not have worried. Just eight weeks after his typescript went to the printer America declared war on Germany.

Curt Riess, an exiled Berliner, was well-educated, well-connected and had many friends remaining in Germany. Through Switzerland and Sweden it was possible to get information out and many individuals did so. How many of these brave souls later perished will never be known. Riess's disingenuous throwaway line that much of the information came from newspapers will have fooled few people, and certainly not the key personnel in German Intelligence. Although living in New York, Riess was in personal danger and it may well be that America's entry into the war and the internment of many Germans saved his life. Curt Riess was indomitable in his opposition to Hitler and he wrote several well-informed and interesting accounts touching upon key background and underlying elements of Nazi activity. The interest and importance of this information was dwarfed by the enormity of the War itself and the post-war chaos which saw Europe divided by the Iron Curtain followed in turn by the onset of the Cold War. Now in the twenty-first century, with growing interest in forensic analysis of events of the 1930s, the re-publication of this text provides a valuable contribution to the studies of Hitler's Third Reich.

Curt Riess was a journalist and the newspaper sensationalist tone comes out throughout the book. It is also fair to say that Riess was not shy about blowing up a rumour or turning a possibility into an outright fact and the reader should be made aware of this. Many of the assertions Riess makes in this book we now know, with the benefit of history, hindsight and the wealth of published material, to be incorrect. There are numerous times in his text where he makes a statement which simply cannot be right or cannot be verified. Where this seems to be the case, comments have been made in the endnotes.

The very nature of espionage implies great secrecy and it was simply impossible for Riess to know all that he makes out to know. Where Riess *does* succeed in his book is in getting the message across about the enormity of Nazi activities around the globe. He bangs the drum, page after page. The reader should therefore 'read between the lines' and not accept all of Riess's facts at their face value. He was writing in the summer heat of 1941 after Hitler's hordes had struck out against Russia. The excesses, the horror, the barbarism of what the Nazis were doing needed to be brought before the public—in this case the American public. The British public did not need to be told, civilians were already experiencing night-time bombing and the armed forces and the merchant marine were suffering considerable casualties from U-boats and the *Luftwaffe*.

Riess likes to make out that the Nazis were failing and that quiet heroism on the Continent among the occupied folk was defeating the Germans and making the Nazi overlordship uncomfortable. Unfortunately this was largely wishful thinking at that time. In the early years of the War it was not as significant as he tries to make out although many people in France, Belgium and the Netherlands did shelter British aircrew. The real success of the British Commandos and of the brave operatives of the Special Operations Executive (SOE) was to come later in the War. Riess also likes to make out that the files of the *Deuxième Bureau* were spirited away by heroic French patriots, but that was not the case. Many of the files did fall into the hands of the Nazis and were taken to Germany. They were later captured by the Russians and taken to Moscow. It was only after the thaw of 1991 that some of the captured papers were returned to France.

Riess was certainly right about the horrific public hangings in Poland, and they continued into 1944. He was also right about the indiscriminate shootings in Czechoslovakia. His book was published before Reinhard Heydrich's assassination but undoubtedly when he heard about the event he would have approved. Heydrich was attacked in Prague on 27 May 1942 by a British-trained team of Czech and Slovak soldiers who had been sent by the Czechoslovak Government-in-exile to kill him in *Operation Anthropoid*. He died from his injuries a week later. Riess would also not have been surprised at the Nazi response. Intelligence falsely linked the assassins to the villages of Lidice and Ležáky. Lidice was razed to the ground; all men and boys over the age of 16 were shot, and all but a handful of its women and children were deported and killed in Nazi concentration camps.

Riess's comments about the American and British intelligence agencies are interesting, but slightly incorrect. Now in the twenty-first century the existence of the British Secret Intelligence Service (SIS), commonly known as MI6, is openly acknowledged, but it was not always so, and certainly not during the Second World War. Riess's references to 'B4' make him sound knowledgeable, but he got the wrong end of the stick. One of his numerous informants must have murmured 'B4' and Riess grabbed it as a nugget to make his book sound more interesting with genuine 'information'. In fact B4 was the branch of the Security Service that was responsible for Soviet counter-espionage and in 1939 it was headed by Kathleen Archer followed by Roger Hollis. Throughout most of the 1920s, the SIS was focused on Communism, in particular, Russian Bolshevism.

The bogeyman of communism remained a key priority for many years and MI6 assisted the *Reichssicherheitshauptamt* Amt IV (usually known as Gestapo) via 'the exchange of information about Communism', as late as October 1937. The *Reichssicherheitshauptamt* (or RSHA) was the infamous organization subordinated to Heinrich Himmler, and it was a branch of the SS organization. From 1939 to 1945, the Gestapo was led by the *SS-Gruppenführer und Generalleutnant der Polizei* Heinrich Müller. The head of the British agency's Berlin station, Frank Foley, described his relationship with Müller's so-called communism expert as 'cordial'. This fact is rather shocking and shows that MI6 had its eye on the wrong ball.

A few people have asked if Riess went 'over the top' in his writings, but it seems he did not. Although some of his conclusions were little better than guesswork, there was substantial truth behind his beliefs, and where he lived in New York was a hot bed of Nazi activity. Analyses of the 1930 Census reveal that there were 350,000 non-Jewish German and Austrian-born immigrants in New York City. Many of the Germans had left at the time of the near chaos and instability of the Weimer Republic and some of them believed that Hitler's Nazi government had restored a sense of pride. They felt that Germany was again a player in the world, and they wanted to do what they could for the Fatherland. A small, if significant minority showed its support for the Nazis by organizing and parading under the banner of the German American Bund. It claimed 17,000 New York (almost all foreign-born) members at its height in 1936 and 1937.

Although Riess's text remains 'frozen', new endnotes have been added to provide fuller information on some of the individuals mentioned and on later events of the Second World War and post-war. In the addition, the captions to the illustrations—a new addition to enhance Riess's text—also provide additional background information.

ALAN SUTTON
January 2016

A Biographical Summary of the Life of Curt Riess

Curt Riess was influential and extremely well-connected, with precisely the right streams of information and background knowledge to write this book. It therefore seems appropriate to provide a short biography of him. Riess, originally Curt Martin Steinam, was born of Jewish-German origin on 21 June 1902 in Würzburg, Germany, the son of Bernhard Steinam, proprietor of a clothes shop, and his wife Jenny Straus. As a young man, Riess studied in Paris, Munich, and Heidelberg, and spent time working as a merchant in both New York and Berlin. On a business trip to the USA he discovered his talent for journalism and decided to pursue a career in the industry. Riess' first journalistic position was for a liberal 12 o'clock worksheet in Berlin, for which he also edited the sports section.

Throughout the 1920s, Riess toured Europe as a reporter and film and theatre critic. The breadth of subjects that he encountered and wrote about in these early years give an indication of the prolific and wide-ranging author he was to become.

In 1933, Riess was forced into exile and emigrated to Paris via Prague and Vienna. A year later, he became the European correspondent for the French newspaper *Paris-Soir*, a position that entailed travelling between New York, Paris, London, and Los Angeles, which enabled him to forge close friendships in Britain and the USA.

Having officially become a U.S. citizen in 1938, Riess settled in Manhattan in 1941 at the age of thirty-nine. From there he wrote for the *Saturday Evening Post*, and contributed articles for *Collier's Weekly* and H. L. Mencken's *American Mercury*. Throughout the Second World War, he was heavily engaged in anti-Nazi activity, serving as a spy, and then, once the USA had joined the Allies, as a specialist in the United States Navy. His final military job was as a war correspondent for the Army, and as such he became well known for his exposure of the moral depravity of Adolf Hitler's regime. Other than *Total Espionage*, another of Riess' great works inspired by the war is his biography of *Goebbels* (also published by Fonthill).

At the end of the war in 1945, Riess returned to Germany and began work on his biography of Joseph Goebbels, minister of Nazi propaganda; it would consume him for three years. The discovery, in late 1946, of Goebbels' diaries from 1942-43 was of significant benefit to Riess, whose biography is based chiefly on detailed first-hand information. The diaries were edited by Riess' friend Louis Lochner.

Riess' prolificacy has rarely been matched among twentieth century authors. In addition to his biography on Goebbels, he also wrote acclaimed books and articles on various prominent contemporaries, including composers Rolf Liebermann and Wilhelm Furtwangler, comic actor and director Charlie Chaplin, and Austrian actress Romy Schneider. Then there were his many journalistic articles and an extensive body of novels, screenplays, and plays. He wrote some of his published work under the pseudonym Peter Brandes.

In 1952, he settled down in Switzerland and married the Austrian actress Heather Marie Hathaway. On 13 May 1993, at the age of ninety, Curt Riess died at Maur, a hamlet outside Zurich. He is buried with his wife in Enzenbuhl cemetery.

PART I
The Revolution of Espionage

COLONEL NICOLAI TAKES A TRIP

Early in June 1932, Colonel Walter Nicolai,[1] retired, left Berlin for Munich, where he was to speak in the Brown House.

This would be his second speech in the Brown House. Three weeks before he had appeared before a small group of SA and SS leaders as a representative of the High Command of the German Army. His subject had been 'Germany in a Future War.' It made a particularly deep impression upon his audience when he stated that Germany must make no declaration of war but must immediately smash the opponent by a tremendous air attack.

Now he was again coming as a representative of the High Command, although officially he was no longer a member of the German Army. But this time his speech was only a pretext. In reality Nicolai was going to Munich to discuss with Nazi leaders there a matter which would be of the utmost importance should the Nazis come to power. And he had no doubt that they would.

And so Colonel Nicolai, retired, took the night express at the Anhalter Station. It is hardly likely that anyone recognized this man with the small, thin, unimpressive face, sharp, piercing eyes, and a slightly upturned nose with sensitive nostrils that quivered as though always on the alert for some scent. The man-in-the-street would not even have recognized his name. It had not appeared in the German Who's Who or in military literature for several years. Only people with excellent memories recalled that Walter Nicolai had been the head of the notorious Bureau IIIB, the head of the High Command's Intelligence Service; that behind the scenes he was the most feared man in Germany, in charge of the whole German espionage system during the World War. But then the World War had taken place a long time ago.

A few days before Nicolai's trip—on 31 May—Herr von Papen had become German Chancellor.[2] Germany was stunned. Heretofore, Papen had been a political nonentity. Among the Junkers and the leaders of heavy industry he was considered a charming conversationalist; in racing circles he was called 'good old Franzi.' But evidently Hindenburg had taken a fancy to the charming raconteur.

Nicolai must have smiled when he heard of the appointment. He didn't think much of Franz von Papen, and he knew him better than most. Franz von Papen had once worked for him.

That had been in January 1914, when young Papen became the military attaché to the German Embassy in Washington. His job was not simply the ordinary job of all military attachés—passive espionage, that is, reporting on the military developments of the United States. He was also supposed to fan the flames of existing unrest in Mexico and distract the attention of the United States from Europe. He worked in collaboration with Captain Boy-Ed, the naval attaché.

When the First World War broke out, Papen went to work. He purchased the Wall Street firm of G. Amsinck & Co. to use as a front. From here he dispatched his agents—sailors from German ships caught in American ports, Irish, and other German sympathizers. Some men were distributed among the most vital strategic points in the United States; others he tried to smuggle into the British Secret Service.

He soon began organizing large-scale sabotage. He sent into the British Secret Service a man named Taylor, whose English was so good as to be conspicuous, and 'Taylor' was revealed to be Papen's adjutant, Horst von der Goltz.[3] Another of his adjutants, Herr von Wedell, who specialized in passport forgery, was also unmasked.

Nicolai was not exactly delighted at the results of Papen's work, and in April 1915 he sent a reinforcement. Captain Franz von Rintelen[4] came to New York via South America on a forged Swiss passport and took over the management of the sabotage division. Papen felt Rintelen's presence as a rebuke and tried to get him out of the way. Within a short time he succeeded.

Herr von Rintelen was living in New York as a British subject named Gibbons, and under this name had started a business on Cedar Street. In the summer of 1915 a letter came to him from Papen, addressed to Captain Franz von Rintelen. The American employees of the firm were naturally startled; Washington was also startled; and in August Rintelen had to leave the United States. To add to his ill luck, the British captured him *en route*; they were in possession of the key to the code which Papen and Boy-Ed used to cable the news of Rintelen's departure to Berlin.

Misfortune continued to dog Herr von Papen's footsteps. In the fall of 1915 his portfolio fell into the hands of the State Department. One of his assistants, Dr Heinrich F. Albert, had 'lost' it in an elevated train. The portfolio contained documents so compromising that Washington demanded Papen's recall. On his return voyage Papen carried other compromising documents, which the British removed from his baggage and sent promptly to Washington.

A checkbook with all stubs attached gave the U.S. Government the names of all the people who had been on Papen's pay roll for espionage and particularly for sabotage. From these counterfoils and other documents, Washington learned that the Germans had spent more than $40,000,000 on sabotage alone; that Papen was directly or indirectly responsible for sabotage in more than forty industrial plants and freight yards, not to mention the forty-seven ships in which bombs had been planted before they left American ports. It was established that he had cost the United States more than $150,000,000 in damage resulting from sabotage. The National Labor Peace Council, an organization created to keep the U.S. out of the war, was revealed as a tool of Papen's, set up and paid by him.

Colonel Nicolai knew that Herr von Papen could never have become Chancellor had his activities as a spy and saboteur in the United States been publicized in Germany. And that had almost happened. The great German publishing house, the Ullstein Co., had been about to publish an account of them, and a great deal of pressure had been necessary to persuade Ullstein to suppress the book. In the discussions with Ullstein during 1930 and 1931 the German Government had given as its official reason the fact that the case concerning German sabotage during the World War was still pending before United States Courts. The German Government had always maintained it was not responsible; but these memoirs of Rintelen would definitely have established the responsibility and Germany would have had to pay.

However, Nicolai, the man behind the efforts to suppress Rintelen's book, had other reasons. He wanted everything that concerned the German Secret Service to remain as obscure as possible.

A tremendous amount of money had been spent in the United States alone—far more than Papen's forty millions—and it had been wasted. Espionage had been concentrated in the hands of the official military attaché (Papen), the very man who was not only in the public eye, but who also naturally was watched by the enemy's spy organization. Clearly, this system was all wrong.

Nicolai and especially Ludendorff had recognized this during the First World War—in fact, even before—and year after year they had urged the expansion of the ridiculously small organization. This was all the more necessary because—as Nicolai wrote later on—the British Intelligence Service was a splendid organization, the French *Deuxième Bureau* was hardly less efficient, and in purely military espionage the Russian spy system under Colonel von Mjassodejoff completely outclassed the German Intelligence Service. These enemy organizations were so competent that (all this by Nicolai's own admission) on 4 August 1914, the British were able to nullify the efforts of almost all the German agents in England. And in France and Russia as well, the German Secret Service was in chaos for more than the first six months of the war.

Nicolai had known of the danger, but he had not been able to get his warning across. Then Germany collapsed; there came the Treaty of Versailles; and the young German Republic ruled out espionage from the first. The Weimar Republic had no desire to prepare for war.

These were difficult days for Colonel Nicolai. Suddenly the War Ministry would have no more to do with him. Even to know Nicolai was compromising. He asked what he should do with his archives, which contained secret documents of importance. Nobody in Berlin wanted the documents. He was advised to burn them. There was a strong possibility that the government, which was opening all archives to clear up the question of war guilt, might even publish his secret documents.

Nicolai could not bring himself to destroy the fruits of so many years' labour. Finally, after weeks in which he was shunted hither and thither, he succeeded in finding a temporary hiding place for his papers. He moved more than 48,000 filing trays to the estate of an East Prussian Junker. But he could not keep them there more than six weeks. Finally Alfred Hugenberg, former Chairman of the Board of Directors of Krupp and now the owner of the Scherl publishing house, offered him the use of rooms there. In the process of moving the filing trays to Berlin, more than three thousand disappeared. It later turned out that a certain Belgian Professor Bullus, who probably worked for the Belgian Secret Service, had stolen them and taken them to Brussels.

And then Nicolai sat and waited. The Republic had no use for him. But he waited anyway. And he did not have to wait too long.

Germany was in ferment. The first Free Corps were organized, which later formed the nucleus of the so-called Black Reichswehr. Nicolai had a hand in the building up of the Black Reichswehr, acting as go-between for Defence Minister Gessler and General Kurt von Schleicher.[5] These two men were officials of the Republic and therefore had to be officially ignorant; Nicolai, on the other hand, no longer had any official position.

Matthias Erzberger, who had signed the Armistice for Germany, was assassinated. He was the first victim in a series of Feme murders which soon came in rapid succession,[6] and perhaps it was only a coincidence that he had been the first and only man to attack Nicolai at the Weimar National Assembly.

Nicolai organized not only the Black Reichswehr. He also organized, though in miniature, a new German espionage system. As early as 1920 he had sent agents into the territory occupied by the Allies to determine the disposition and morale of the armies of occupation.

At the same time he organized a kind of detective agency. It was a queer sort of detective agency, backed by the limitless funds of German heavy industry. Its purpose was to gather material which, when published at the proper moment, would undermine the people's confidence in the Republic.

In spite of these diverse activities, Nicolai must have felt rather frustrated. For he was no longer in the midst of the great international espionage industry. And since the end of the war this industry had been expanding to gigantic proportions—Nicolai was well enough informed to know that. He knew that Russian spies were constantly tapping the telephone lines of the Polish War Ministry. He knew that a certain international spy ring was offering for sale, at a quite reasonable figure, the plans of the newest American weapons. He knew that the *Deuxième Bureau* and the French Naval Intelligence had obtained photographs of all Italian border fortifications and plans of the Italian warships that were being built. He knew that formulae of the newest poison gases and gas shells were being offered on the international spy exchange.

And above all he knew that the *Deuxième Bureau* was carrying on extensive espionage operations within Germany itself; that defeated Germany was swarming with an army of enemy spies.

During these years, and particularly between 1928 and 1932, he spent much of his time with Ludendorff. The friendship between the two men became closer. Ludendorff was at that time writing his book, *Der Totale Krieg (A Nation at War)*—which, however, was not published until 1936.

Ludendorff's main idea was that the First World War had been lost because Germany had not succeeded in organizing the entire population for total warfare and had failed to wage war behind the enemy lines as well as at the front. He wrote a good deal about the importance of propaganda.

Total war required total propaganda, and also total espionage. Although Ludendorff did not actually use the word espionage, he had a very definite conception of what it should be like. And so did Nicolai. His idea bore no resemblance to any previous espionage. Up to now, espionage had undergone developments and improvements, but never any fundamental changes. Now a fundamental change was imperative. A revolution.

A MEETING

The meeting which brought Colonel Walter Nicolai to Munich took place in the home of Captain Ernst Röhm.[7] Among those present were Goebbels,[8] Himmler,[9] Hess,[10] and several of the less important functionaries of the National Socialist Party.

These had met to discuss the organization of a secret police system whose activity would begin promptly after the Nazis came to power—not only within Germany, but abroad also. What they contemplated was a kind of police force for all Europe, for the whole world, if possible.

Röhm was under the impression that he was to be in command of this machine. Apparently Hitler had made some such promise to him. But scarcely had the conference begun, when Röhm found himself relegated to insignificance. It became obvious that he had not a single idea of how to build up this kind of organization. Goebbels, on the other hand, had drawn up detailed plans. Himmler did not say much. But when he did speak, Nicolai realized (as he later wrote in a report to the High Command) that the man knew what he was talking about. Hess said nothing at all.

Throughout the conference the unborn secret police organization—not yet named the Gestapo—was defined as an apparatus to observe and suppress the opponents of the Nazis—to prevent a counterrevolution once the Nazis had come to power. That they thought in such terms is quite natural, for the Nazi Party had always had to contend with intense opposition from the liberal and left parties, and certainly this opposition would not cease of itself after the seizure of power.

Nicolai, however, was not particularly interested in such reasoning. He had come to Munich to discuss espionage. On the other hand, he can be credited with seeing from the first the great possibilities of a secret police as a counterespionage organization.

In his (secret) report on the meeting, Nicolai did not elaborate on his thoughts during those hours in Röhm's apartment. But we need not be mind-readers to imagine that as an old professional spy he must have been amused. Here he was among a roomful of men who were preparing to take over the power in one of the greatest countries of the world. And without consulting his files he knew that most of these leaders of the Nazi Party had once been spies. Hitler himself, after the Armistice, had worked as an informer for the Bavarian police and later, also as an informer, for the Bavarian *Reichswehr*. Hugo Machhaus, the first editor-in-chief of the *Voelkischer Beobachter* (after the newspaper had been acquired by the Nazis), had committed suicide in his cell, shortly before he was to be brought to trial on well-substantiated charges of being an agent of the *Deuxième Bureau*. And at the Neustadt an der Haardt Trial of 1930, evidence had been presented that Joseph Buerckel (later Gauleiter of Austria, and still later Gauleiter of Alsace-Lorraine) had for years been in the employ of the French *Sureté Générale*.

Nicolai knew all this, and he probably knew a good deal more.

Throughout that summer of 1932 and into early autumn, Goebbels and Nicolai met frequently in Berlin. Most of their discussions began with propaganda and ended with espionage. Goebbels remarked that the dividing line between propaganda and espionage was at best hazy. Nicolai was no little amazed when Goebbels frankly admitted that he intended to imitate the Russians.

Goebbels was well informed indeed on some things the Russians were doing. He knew that the Communists had been the first to co-ordinate propaganda and espionage. He knew that Lenin himself was the inventor of total propaganda and total espionage, and that he had even coined the word to describe it: *agitprop*—an abbreviation for agitation and propaganda. Propaganda had meant to Lenin persuasion of the masses, and agitation was the aggressive form of persuasion.

Like Hitler, who admitted as much in *Mein Kampf*, Goebbels was impressed by the Communist methods of propaganda. He assured Nicolai that the Führer had done brilliantly to take over the essentials of their method and apply it to the building of the Nazi Party.

Essentially the cell system was the organization of members and sympathizers of the movement into very small units, both within the country and abroad. This same system was applied not only in the propaganda division of the movement, but in the espionage division as well. The Bolshevists had introduced a fundamental change in Russian military espionage. Their spies no longer sought to obtain information from the army officers of the other countries; instead they devoted themselves to the common man, the recruit, the unimportant clerk in military offices. They worked on him 'ideologically,' that is, they tried first to make him a Communist and then engage him as a military spy. It was an excellent idea. And it soon became evident that a recruit, a general's chauffeur, a stenographer in the War Ministry, or an errand boy who delivered uniforms, often had much more interesting information than the high-ranking officer who in the old days had been plied with champagne by some exotic lady so that she might steal his brief case.

This technique, which the Red Army applied from the very beginning, was simply the *agitprop* theory transferred to military espionage. An industry (an army) was not assaulted at the top, through the manager and owner (general), but from the bottom, through the ordinary factory workers (soldiers). Since 1917 the creation of cells had been the secret of Russian espionage. However, Lenin's early death and the struggle between Stalin and Trotsky, had hindered its being carried to completion.

Goebbels had read a great deal and had written several articles on the new Russian method—at least, as it applied to espionage. He could not tell Nicolai anything new. The German General Staff knew all about Russian methods. For in 1917, before Ludendorff sent Lenin to Russia in a sealed train, certain secret agreements were concluded. Among these was an understanding that a number of German military observers would be permitted to go along. Lenin kept his promise, and as a result some twenty officers of the German General Staff remained in Russia for three years. They returned in 1920, and their reports influenced the establishment of direct relations between the Red Army and the *Reichswehr*. Had a German military espionage system existed at the time, these reports would have completely revolutionized it. There was none then, but Colonel Nicolai personally studied the reports very carefully.

During that meeting in Röhm's apartment in June 1932, one man hardly opened his mouth. This man was Rudolf Hess. To all appearances he was present only as Hitler's observer. This almost colourless man, the secretary and shadow of the Führer, seemed indifferent to the matters under discussion.

This was Nicolai's first meeting with Hess. But of course, he knew all about the secretary of Adolf Hitler. He knew that Hess was born in Alexandria, that he had come to Germany only at the age of fourteen, and that at the outbreak of the war, he had volunteered. After the war he became an extreme Nationalist and Anti-Semite; and it was only through great good luck that he escaped with his life during the period of the Munich Soviet Republic. Nicolai knew that soon afterwards Hess had attached himself to Hitler and had defended his leader during the brawls that characterized most of the Nazis' early public meetings. And he knew that Hess had gone into prison with Hitler. But the taciturn young man had written no books and held no special position within the Party.

Hence, Nicolai must have been all the more surprised—and not only Nicolai—when Hess finally did speak, shortly before the end of the meeting in Röhm's apartment.

He spoke for the first time when someone interrupted Goebbels, who had been explaining how the Secret Police would work and the deadly accuracy of its supervision and the ruthlessness of its blows. The objection was: 'Where shall we find the men for such a marvellous police force?'

Hess had replied—according to Nicolai's report—'If we can't find them, we will make them.'

Later on he said something else. 'Mass basis.'

The words fascinated Nicolai. Mass basis—it was to find such a basis that he had come to the Nazis. The mass basis was what was needed to wage total war, and to organize total espionage. A mass basis meant espionage not only in the military realm, but on all fronts, in all realms of life. Espionage in industry, and intellectual life; spying into the psychology of a whole people, into education, sanitation, medicine—into everything.

Hess said little more that evening. But he mentioned a name. He spoke of his teacher and friend, Karl Haushofer,[11] Professor of Geo-Politics at the

Munich University, where Hess had spent years in studying the Japanese. The Japanese, Hess said, provided excellent examples of espionage on a mass basis.

That was Hess's last word that evening. One wonders if Nicolai, for all his cleverness, realized how great was to be the influence of Professor Haushofer upon the new German espionage. And it is certain that he did not suspect how decisive a part in the great drama of German espionage was to be played by this taciturn Rudolf Hess.

It is more than likely that he was as perplexed as the rest of the Party—including Hitler's intimates—when in December 1932 the Führer appointed Hess Chief of the Political Bureau of the Party, thereby placing him above Göring,[12] Goebbels, and all the others.

ARCHITECT HIMMLER

Röhm was not the one who was assigned to run the Secret Police. The post fell to the man who, like Hess, had scarcely opened his mouth at that meeting where the Gestapo was first discussed, Heinrich Himmler.

His real career stemmed from 1925, when Hitler founded the SS. A number of men had been suggested to the Führer as leader of the SS, and some of them had been given a trial. Finally, Gregor Strasser, at that time still a power within the Party, contrived to place his secretary, Heinrich Himmler, in the position. Under Himmler the SS became more and more a counterpoise to the SA and a bodyguard for Hitler. When the Nazis took power in Germany, Himmler was first made Police Commissioner of Munich. And within a few months—by the end of 1933—he was in command of the whole police power of Germany, with the exception of Prussia.

In Prussia Göring was all-powerful; and he had already established the Gestapo there. Göring wanted to retain this tremendous power in his own hands, or in the hands of one of his men. Inevitably he fell afoul of Frick, the Minister of the Interior, who insisted logically enough that the Secret Police lay within his province. Possibly Himmler benefited indirectly from this dispute. Be that as it may, before long he also had the Gestapo of Prussia under his command.

From here it was but a short step to the concentration of all the police power in Germany within his own hands.

To all appearances Himmler seemed incongruously unfitted for such a job. Born in Munich in 1900 of lower middle-class parents, he seemed as a young man well on his way to becoming a typical *petit bourgeois*. He became a merchant, later a teacher. And he looked the part. His face seemed pleasantly stolid and utterly uninteresting. With his fastidious pince-nez, he was the picture of the perfect schoolmaster.

However, those who knew him well and had seen him at work maintained that this placid, punctilious man was subject to sudden and strange changes. The sleepy eyes behind the pince-nez flared into cold anger; the prim lips would grow thin and cruel. And this man, outwardly cool and business-like, could exercise the most horrible brutality, forming his intelligent but demonic decisions and instantly carrying them into action.

He looked like a poor sort of Chief for a secret police. But he proved to be an expert. Even before Hitler took power, the SS had won the title of the OGPU of the Nazi Party—and indeed the name was not inappropriate. Then after the Third Reich came into being, the Gestapo was quite correctly called a complete plagiarism of the OGPU.

Next to Goebbels, Himmler was the foremost connoisseur of Russian methods in the Nazi Party. But while the great propagandist was concerned mainly with the theory, Himmler studied the practice of the Bolshevists. Men who have talked with him agree that he was as well versed in the organization and procedures of the OGPU (Political State Police Department) as though he had been a guest for years in the building on Lubyanka Square in Moscow.

He read every line that had been published on Lenin's close friend, Felix Djerzhinsky, who after the dissolution of the Czarist Ochrana had founded the Vsesoyusnaya Chresvichaynaya Comisia called for short, Cheka. Djerzhinsky had built the Cheka into a magnificent organization. And Himmler knew of the successor to Djerzhinsky, the invalid Vyacheslaff Menzhinsky, who was head in name only of what had now become the OGPU (*Obyedinennoye Gosudarstvennoye Politicheskoye Upraylenye*), and whose real head was G. Yagoda, Menzhinsky's assistant. Himmler had found out everything there was to know about Volynski, the chief of counterespionage and Sloutski, the chief of the Foreign Division. Like Goebbels and like his Führer, Himmler was always willing to use his enemy's ideas for his own purposes.

Himmler lost no time in expanding on an enormous scale. When the Nazis came to power, there were 138,000 police in Germany. A year and a half later—by the end of 1934—there were 437,000, including 250,000 SS men. By the beginning of the war there were 372,000 SS men within the German police system.

Numerically the Gestapo was insignificant among this army of police. Nevertheless it was the core and the crown of the whole organization. The Gestapo had an unlimited budget and unlimited authority. It could interfere anywhere, investigate anyone, including the police. It could arrest anyone.

By the decree of February 1936 'the orders and business of the secret police' were no longer 'subject to review in the administrative courts.'

This meant that no one except Himmler and, of course, Hitler or his deputy, Hess, could question any decision or act of the Gestapo.

The Gestapo terrorized the entire population of Germany. And since 1936 even the great Göring has given Himmler and his affairs a wide berth. Goebbels had stopped interfering with Himmler long before.

Himmler's first job had been to organize a bodyguard for the Führer. He was still intrusted with this task and he still took it very seriously. For example, when, after the assassination of King Alexander of Yugoslavia in Marseille, it was discovered that a newsreel photographer had filmed the entire assassination, Himmler obtained the film and had it run off hundreds of times to observe how he could best guard Hitler against a similar attempt.

Himmler had begun modestly by organizing a bodyguard for one man; he ended by creating a bodyguard for a great country. For the Gestapo was neither more nor less than that. It was a wall around Germany, closing the country off from the outside.

Naturally it was impossible entirely to prevent departures from a country situated in the centre of Europe, nor would that have accorded with the Nazis' plans for the future. But the traveller could not escape from the Gestapo's relentless vigilance. The Gestapo had drawn up comprehensive regulations for travellers. Before securing a travelling permit a would-be traveller had to fill out yards of questionnaires. He had to explain where he was going and why, whom he intended to visit while abroad, whether he had relatives abroad, what were the political opinions of his relatives.

Travellers were given instructions on how to conduct themselves. They were not allowed to wear insignia or uniforms; as soon as they arrived at their destinations they were to report to the nearest German Consulate, or better still, the nearest office of the Nazi Party. After they returned they had to give detailed accounts of their impressions, of what they had seen and heard, of how they had been treated....

All this bordered on espionage, but at the beginning there probably was no such intent. Rather it was a method for checking up on Germans whom the Gestapo had permitted to escape from prison for a short time. For a prison was what it was. Germany, which had been but a few years before the milling marketplace of foreign spies, was now closed off to the outside world, like Italy, Japan, Russia.

Espionage could no longer be attacked from the rear.

Total espionage might now proceed onwards to total war, its ultimate goal. No one knew that better than Himmler himself. No one else was working so fast or so thoroughly, with such understanding of the problem. Yet he was worried.

Shortly before the outbreak of the war, in a lecture to a group of officers, he declared: 'In the future we shall have not only the military front on land, the naval front at sea, the air force overhead, but we shall have a fourth theatre of war: the home front.'

He had done his utmost to co-ordinate this home front to render it harmless—and still he believed that it would have to be reckoned with. He had built up the best possible organization—and he did not believe it would hold together in wartime.

We have it from a reliable source that Himmler reported to Hitler that in case of war 125,000 more agents would be needed for Czechoslovakia alone. It is not certain that he was granted them. But his insecurity is emphasized by the fact that on 5 September 1939, four days after the war began, he instituted a complete reorganization. He established a Cabinet Council for the Inner Defence of the Reich. This Council comprised fifteen commissioners, all SS officers, who worked in close collaboration with the army and the police.

Heinrich Himmler had lost confidence.

THE END OF THE ROMANTIC ERA

On 30 June 1934, the Gestapo murdered General von Schleicher and General von Bredow. The world assumed that Schleicher had been put out of the way as a man with sufficient following to lead a counterrevolution against Hitler. The murder of von Bredow passed almost unnoticed. Yet the two murders were closely linked. Von Bredow had been the head of the *Reichswehr* military intelligence. In this capacity he had obtained information concerning a man named Adolf Hitler—his activities as an informer in 1919 and 1920. Later on it was whispered in the *Reichswehr* that his spying activities had not been restricted to the German Army and the Bavarian Police, but that he had also worked for the French *Deuxième Bureau*.

Whatever the truth, Bredow had the material and had shown it to his friend Schleicher.

The murder of a man with the international reputation of Schleicher created a stir. But in the *Reichswehr* the excitement was keener over the murder of the espionage chief. To be sure, the *Reichswehr* had learned by this time—Nicolai and Ludendorff were excellent teachers—that espionage as preparation for total warfare could not be an isolated function of the army alone. The army circles were perfectly agreeable to having the secret police assume the job of counterespionage. But they were disinclined to have the Gestapo 'liquidate' their chief of military espionage.

They were ready to co-operate, but they insisted, particularly after 30 June, that there must be an organizational separation between purely military espionage and other—total—espionage functions. Behind the scenes there were many bitter disputes, which lasted until the latter part of 1938. These disputes put Göring in a serious dilemma, for on the one hand he was a high Party functionary and on the other hand he was an army leader.

One of the principal reasons for the enmity between Himmler and Göring was Himmler's tireless scheming to infiltrate Gestapo men into the Army Intelligence Service, and thereby to get control of it. Göring gradually took his stand outrightly as an army man and spokesman for the independence of the army. And in spite of Bredow's murder and the removal of Blomberg and Fritsch, the army finally was victorious in this struggle for independence.

In this struggle, the independence of military espionage was only a minor issue. But it was an issue.

For the time being, Nicolai retired into obscurity. In order to put foreign observers off the scent, Hitler appointed him head of the Institute for the History of the New Germany, which was supposed to rewrite the history of the World War to fit the Nazi doctrine.

Of course, this was only a front. Nicolai did not bother to become a historian. Instead he began to organize a new military intelligence service.

It cannot be determined what proportion of the work was his personally— and what proportion that of close collaborators—in particular his favourite pupil, Eugen Ott,[13] who had served under him during the World War. For some years no official notice was taken of Nicolai. He had no official functions. He was not listed in the army registers. Then again, it was said in informed circles that he had been—retired. A paradoxical situation: a retired colonel who had been retired anew. That was by the end of 1937. It was said also that Lieutenant-Captain Canaris[14] (of whom we shall hear more presently) had taken his place. But as soon as the Second World War broke out—that is, as soon as the Third Reich could cast away all caution in regard to the outside world, Colonel Nicolai was suddenly proclaimed once more the head of military intelligence....

But under whatever name, behind whatever front he worked during those first years of Hitler's regime, documentary evidence proves beyond doubt that he was not idle. He established the division of the German General Staff called 'Foreign Armies'; together with Captain Rolf Kratzer he reorganized the division of 'Counterespionage' (*Spionageabwehr*) which operated from the War Ministry and had branches in every army corps headquarters. Finally he acted as co-ordinator between the intelligence service of the army, the fleet, and later the *Luftwaffe* on the one hand and the Foreign Office on the other hand.

Ever since the First World War, and since his conversations with Ludendorff about total war, Nicolai had known that much had to be changed. The spy whose sole task was to ferret out military secrets had become a sorry anachronism. The new espionage must penetrate not only into military secrets, but into the secrets of industry, politics, must penetrate everywhere. Total espionage.

This meant the end of individual espionage activities. Gone was the romantic era of spying. The days of Mata Hari or Mademoiselle Docteur were a thing of the past; the days of even such spies as Cilly Auslaender and Mme Kalman Lidtke, who but a short time before had been spying for Russia and Poland respectively, were over, too. The subtle tricks, the mysterious drugs, the invisible ink, the trunk with false bottom must be put away; they were museum pieces. Gone were the days of bribes—with somewhat unromantic sums of money—and of seductions; the days when the life of a spy resembled a movie script; the days when the head of the Austrian espionage organization, Lieutenant Field Marshal Urbansky, could write: 'The passion for a woman was responsible for one of the greatest triumphs of the Austro-Hungarian intelligence service: the acquisition of the deployment plans of the Russian army....' That did not imply that all the experience of the past was worthless, outmoded. Nicolai was decided on taking over everything that was still useful. During the First World War, he had found out that the Allied spies in German or German-occupied territory communicated with their central bureaus mainly by air. From 1917 on, English and French agents often parachuted down to their assigned territory, and received their wireless apparatus and other materials by parachute. At the time Nicolai had had no reply to such tactics; his spies were not trained parachutists. In the Second World War he would not be caught napping....

It is both significant and amusing that in weaving his spy web, Nicolai did not trouble to send agents to certain countries. Of Romania and Bulgaria, for example, he said that he could buy everything that was needed when the proper time came. He placed Greece in the same category—a mistake he was later to regret.

The objectives of military espionage are a reflection of the strategy of the war which such espionage is anticipating. If we did not know that the German General Staff had comprehensive plans for the Blitzkrieg by 1934, we might deduce as much from the kind of intelligence service Nicolai was building. The directions he issued implied clearly that the General Staff was interested not so much in the fortifications of enemy countries—for later on the mechanized divisions simply bypassed these fortifications—as in detailed information of the countryside behind the forts—roads, railways, bridges, power stations, etc.

Why the emphasis on public utilities? The reason was not what many experts later asserted, that during war such structures would be left more vulnerable than, say, munition factories. Rather the idea was that destruction of public utilities would be more damaging to the morale of the population than destruction of munition factories. Even in the realm of purely military espionage the idea of total espionage had already left its mark.

During these years the entire espionage system was modernized by Nicolai. The espionage chief recognized that during total warfare large-scale sabotage would be necessary. His problem was to discover methods that would mystify the enemy as to the origin and nature of the sabotage. In other words, Nicolai was in search of foolproof methods of sabotage that could be used over and over again.

Perhaps he considered the invention of a certain Dr Schweber, who in 1914, in New York, had invented a new type of infernal machine. It was very small, shaped like a cigar, and left no traces at all, the apparatus being utterly destroyed in the explosion it caused.

But more than this was needed. And in September 1934, Nicolai established a laboratory in Gross-Lichterfelde, near Berlin, a laboratory which practised the scientific method of sabotage. For every manufacturing process directly or indirectly connected with the production of munitions or other vital war goods, they worked out experimentally a companion sabotage procedure which would reduce to a minimum the risks and the costs of sabotage.

In the latter part of 1931—before Hitler had yet come to power—a so-called expert on espionage spoke in Paris on what chances there were for a revival of German espionage. He declared that it would take from ten to fifteen years, if only because a new organization would have no dependable agents to work abroad and would have to spend years planting such agents.

The expert was altogether wrong. Once Nicolai received the signal to expand, he had all the agents he could use. And they were already firmly established abroad.

Most of them were officers whom the General Staff had sent abroad during the First World War to act as observers, at first in neutral countries and later in Russia and Asia Minor. After the Revolution in Germany, many of them had preferred to remain abroad. Now they offered their services to Nicolai.

Then there were the numerous German officers who had been discharged from the *Reichswehr* because of the disarmament imposed by the Treaty of Versailles. Many of these had gone abroad to train foreign armies. The Chilean and Argentine armies, for example, were trained by German officers. Others had gone to China; Röhm had been in Bolivia. These men, too, were available to Nicolai, and naturally they had access to military secrets which were beyond the reach of the finest spies.

Then there were other officers, who after the Revolution had gone abroad to Spain and to North and South America to seek their fortunes. While many had taken up other professions in order to live, they had never ceased to feel themselves German army officers, and they, too, were now available.

Other army officers had been sent abroad as commercial representatives of heavy industry, particularly of Krupp. After the war Krupp had made some pretence of going into peacetime production, but in reality had set up munitions factories in many foreign countries. It might have been a mere chance that many of the Krupp representatives in key positions abroad were former army officers.

It might have been—but it was not. The *Reichswehr*, Nicolai, and the men around him had urged the captains of heavy industry, the Krupps, Thyssens, Stumms, Voeglers, and others, to employ and send abroad as many former officers as possible. Perhaps they only wanted to give their former colleagues a helping hand. But these men were to prove exceedingly useful.

There were also the two great officers' associations which had been founded shortly after the Revolution: the German Officers' Association (*Deutscher Offiziersbund*) and the Teutonic Officers Association (*Deutschvoelkischer Offiziersbund*). Nicolai and Ludendorff had played active parts in the founding of these associations. And curiously enough, the associations were most assiduous in keeping in touch with the expatriate officers. The associations kept mailing lists of them and transmitted private letters from them (letters which did not always treat of strictly personal affairs) to Nicolai. These officers' associations, working in close co-operation with the *Reichswehr*, sent competent members abroad, to Scandinavia, Spain, the former German colonies in Africa and other countries; the men were subsidized and formed so-called *Stuetzpunkte*—strategic points.

In this connection it is necessary to mention the work of Herr Hanns Oberlindober,[15] who worked rather with Nicolai than under him. Herr Oberlindober had been wounded in the war. Afterwards he had a position in the War Veterans' Aid Society, and when the Nazis came to power he had not only 'co-ordinated' this Society but also taken command of the War Veterans' Associations. It was a touching notion of his to organize trips for war veterans to Belgium and French battlefields and cemeteries. And it was only natural that he should establish contact with English and French veterans' organizations and with the leaders of the French association, in particular Jean Goy, whom in 1936 he invited to attend the Nazi Party Congress in Munich.

Oberlindober was in close touch with tens of thousands of Frenchmen, Englishmen, Belgians, Italians, Czechs, and Poles. Among them was the common bond of war reminiscence, of sentimental talks about the days of their youth. It was highly creditable that these former foes should become good friends; and in sheer friendship they talked about many things that under normal circumstances would have been kept secret.

After all, Oberlindober was no Nazi. At any rate, he repeatedly assured his French and English friends that he was not. He said he was a good German; none of his foreign friends could object to that. For all the war veterans' associations in all countries were more or less nationalistic. So were the older retired officers with whom Oberlindober and his colleagues were on so friendly a footing. And these former officers, never tired of criticizing modern military methods, incidentally revealed a good deal about these methods....

We see, then, that Nicolai had plenty of agents, voluntary and—from among Oberlindober's French and English friends—involuntary agents. He had not selected them. For the time being he had to work with those already at hand. However, a totalitarian spy apparatus could not depend haphazardly upon men who perhaps had a certain talent for espionage. Nicolai had to find ways and means to choose his spies systematically and systematically train them.

Here, too, all the groundwork had been laid. The 'Psychological Laboratory' of the *Reichswehr* seemed made for the purpose. One of its primary tasks had been to establish the main principles for the selecting and training of future spies, and to supervise such selection and education.

The Psychological Laboratory was a product of the idea of psychological warfare—an idea which was not original with the Nazis. For as far back as the World War, the United States Army had had a special Division of Psychology.

The old German army had, after 1916, also experimented with psychology. The first army psychologist was Dr Albrecht Blau. But at that time army psychology was wholly unsystematic, and Ludendorff was convinced that the whole idea was so much nonsense.

After the war Blau resigned *pro forma* from the army. But in reality he remained in close touch with the *Reichswehr*, helped organize the Black Reichswehr, and in 1929 returned to active service with the rank of Major.

Strangely enough, it was in the same year of 1929 that the Psychological Laboratory of the *Reichswehr* opened quarters at Lehrterstrasse 58 in Berlin. The name was deliberately chosen to convey as little meaning as possible and to deceive foreign observers. The *Reichswehr* had set up the

Laboratory at this relatively early stage of German rearmament because it recognized that, with the new weapons and techniques of attack, both officers and men must be selected from entirely new viewpoints.

During the first few years the Laboratory, employing a number of scientists and some 100 *Reichswehr* officers, worked mainly on the problem of selection of tank crews and fliers. In addition it functioned as a central agency for world-wide military information.

Its impressive work, however, did not begin until Hitler came to power and when the German rearmament efforts were no longer concealed. The Laboratory was renamed the Psychological Laboratory of the Reich War Ministry, and thereby officially acknowledged as a military institution. By roundabout ways, especially through the establishment of the German Society for Defence Politics and Defence Science (*Deutsche Gesellschaft für Wehrpolitik and Wehrwissenschaft*), the Laboratory was liberally financed.

Many of the problems considered by the Psychological Laboratory had no connection, direct or indirect, with espionage. But the Laboratory's work tended to further the expansion of German espionage by giving it a systematic, scientific foundation.

Most important of all was the psychology of aptitude-testing, a field where an enormous amount of practical work was done. Thousands of careful analyses were made which included psychoanalysis, graphology, personality study, phrenology, and race theory—a mixture of science and mysticism which nevertheless produced astoundingly effective results. An attempt was made to determine what personality traits were best adapted to each branch of the military. These experiments did not omit the study of psychological prerequisites for the profession of espionage. Aptitude tests for spies, or rather would-be spies, were worked out. Of course these aptitude tests were meant only for men who were to take leading positions in the espionage organizations, men who would command and instruct a large number of agents. The Psychological Laboratory did not pretend to go in for mass production.

Besides these aptitude tests, problems of the actual waging of warfare, past, present, and future, were also handled scientifically. The Laboratory paid special attention to military developments abroad, published detailed maps, and big, thorough studies of the military organizations of all countries.

Even more pertinent for future spies were the courses given by the Foreign Countries Department. An agent who had taken these courses knew more about military affairs in other countries than the army officers of the countries themselves.

During the last years before the war, the Psychological Laboratory expanded to astounding proportions. Whereas in 1933, aside from the heads of the Laboratory, only 200 assistants were employed, by 1936 there were 1,450. At this time the Psychological Laboratory maintained a permanent staff of 200 psychologists. The institution was divided into twenty departments. Throughout Germany it employed or co-operated with some 150,000 persons—scientists, officers, and human guinea pigs who were the subjects of experiments....

At that time reconstruction and modernization of German military espionage had been completed. But the ultramodern precision instrument, which seemed to have been constructed out of thin air, was but a small cog in the vast wheel of the espionage organization—also apparently constructed out of thin air. By 1936 the idea of total espionage had become a reality. All Germany had become a huge spy organism which stretched its tentacles everywhere; which covered the world.

B4 CAN'T CONVINCE BALDWIN

Toward 9:30 p.m. on 11 March 1933, three automobiles of the OGPU drew up to a group of houses in the Moscow suburb of Perlovka; here were situated the three villas of the more important employees and engineers of the British firm of Metro-Vickers. In one of these villas the Vickers directors Monkhouse, Thornton, and Buckel were having dinner.

The British Ambassador's telegram also mentioned a certain 'Lett,' although no one from Latvia was present at this dinner. Perhaps the Ambassador wanted to say something that he could not explain directly....

The OGPU agents arrested Monkhouse and Thornton and then conducted a search of the premises which lasted for five hours. They confiscated many documents, for which they carefully made out receipts, and did not leave until the early hours of the morning.

At the same time a chauffeur, a stenographer, and the secretary of one of the directors were arrested in another villa. Also at the same time the Vickers offices in Moscow were searched and Directors Kushny and MacDonald were arrested. If the OGPU intended to arrest the head and founder of Metro-Vickers in Russia, Mr Rhoden, they had come too late. Mr Rhoden had left for England early that morning.

In the Ambassador's first cables, which came thick and fast every hour, it was emphasized that only so-called private persons—engineers—had been arrested. But Downing Street quickly understood and became very nervous. However, within a few hours the Ambassador had encouraging news. The papers the OGPU had found were quite innocent; apparently a few directors had given small presents to Russian engineers. Of course if the Russians insisted on calling them bribes.... The Ambassador added that he hardly knew the gentlemen; the Vickers people had always avoided associating with the Embassy staff.

But London was not so easily calmed. Downing Street cabled to the effect that trade relations would undoubtedly be seriously impaired. Should anything like a show trial be held, the English public would be up in arms and there would be angry protests in Parliament. But the Russian authorities seemed deaf to these hints.

A few hours later on the same day the Ambassador reported that Monkhouse had been given a hearing and had been forced to admit that he had received information on Russian industries from 'important officials,' which information he had transmitted to England. Thereupon the examining magistrate had informed him that under Russian law this was considered industrial espionage. There was no precise information concerning the charges against or the confessions of Directors Thornton and Kushny. Again and again the Ambassador protested against the holding of a public trial. Meanwhile Thornton was compelled to admit that he had given presents to Russian officials....

After Thornton's confession the Ambassador's reports became plainly disconcerting. He cabled that at the hearings the examination revolved monotonously around the question of whether the accused had acted under instructions from 'other British institutions.' Finally the Ambassador cabled the worst possible news. The Russians knew the Vickers director Richards was a confidential agent of the Intelligence Service.

There was a trial. However, the men were not charged with espionage. The indictment read that Vickers had delivered poor turbines and that Russian engineers and Vickers employees in the electric power plants had been carrying on sabotage.

There was nothing Vickers could do. Perhaps the turbines were poor; but whether they were or not, the men must admit everything; for the word espionage must be kept out of the affair. The accused men had their hands tied; they had not practised sabotage, but they had practised espionage. The Russians attained their end; they held a sabotage trial in which the accused men (and notably the Russians) were willing to confess. It made first-rate internal propaganda. And they had crippled the British Intelligence Service in Russia. Charges against Vickers were dropped and instead the Court concentrated on Director Richards and his past. It established that Richards was an agent of the Intelligence Service, who, behind Vickers' back, had utilized his employees and his network of branches for purposes of military and industrial espionage.

The trial ended with mild sentences. But ten years of work by the British Intelligence Service had been undone.

In London it was understood that the Vickers trial was more than an individual case, that it was symbolic of something more. London realized that the OGPU must have set hundreds, possibly thousands of men on the trail in order to track down a tight organization of eighteen persons which had been built up with infinite care. The affair represented the first contest between the conservative system of espionage, which depended on individual action, and totalitarian espionage which rested on the whole population.

London understood that this was the beginning of a crisis. A crisis in the greatest espionage organization in the world: the British Secret Service.

The men who during the war had made the Intelligence Service an organization admired and feared throughout the world, had long since taken their hands from the helm. Sir Reginald Hall, the legendary Chief of the Naval Intelligence Department, had retired. Sir Basil Thomson had retired. The romantic era of T. E. Lawrence was long dead. And the last great lone wolf, Sidney Reilley, who had operated for years in the Soviet Union, had finally fallen into a trap and never returned.

Now, one of the leading men in the Intelligence Service was Sir George Cockerill.[16] He surrounded himself with secrecy. He never let himself be photographed. He did not want to be talked about. Indeed, it would have been difficult to talk about him, for he was hardly ever seen. He was intimate with only two men—Members of Parliament who heard from him from time to time. These MP's were Duff Cooper[17] and Hore-Belisha.[18]

Then there was Sir Robert Vansittart.[19] He, at least, was frequently seen. He was unusually good-looking, elegant and amusing, and a member of all the best clubs. He wrote poems, dramas, and essays, and occasionally had them published. He was a man with an impressive political career, had been with numerous embassies and legations. Now he was officially attached to the Foreign Office as permanent Undersecretary. Working with him and under him were Colonel Sir Maurice Paschal Allers Hankey and Sir Alexander Cadogan.

The Foreign Office Intelligence Department, which Sir Robert headed, was still the best-informed espionage organization in the world. The Naval Intelligence Department still employed more agents in all parts of the world than any other intelligence service. There were the Board of Trade Intelligence Department, the Colonial Intelligence Department (together with the India Intelligence Department), and finally the almost infallible Counter-Espionage Organization of the Home Intelligence Department, Scotland Yard.

A branch of the War Office Intelligence Department was the SIS, the Special Intelligence Section,[20] which rather hung in mid-air and, like the

Deuxième Bureau, united military espionage and counterespionage. Sir George Cockerill was in charge of this section.

And then, shrouded in mystery, there was Department B4. Even in the various bureaus of the Intelligence Service, B4 was spoken of as little as possible. B4 had offices near the Admiralty Arch. It was a completely hush-hush organization. Almost no one was supposed to know that it existed. B4 could command on request the centralized reports and digests from all the other Intelligences. It was divided into regional offices. Its relations to other Intelligences were roughly those of Scotland Yard to the local English County Police—it was called in on problems that needed co-ordination of all the services or on a great emergency. It was and still is the brain of the British Secret Service.

Sir Robert Vansittart was the first to recognize and call attention to the danger Hitler represented. It was on his initiative that the War Office Intelligence Department began to concern itself more intensively with German rearmament. Early in 1934, when Sir Robert spoke with Prime Minister Baldwin about this, he found to his surprise that the Prime Minister remained quite unconcerned. Baldwin was too delighted by the wave of prosperity that had swept over England to be troubled about anything. Sir Robert took the matter to B4, and this department promptly got to work. The agents of the WOID were asked to submit further reports. These new reports confirmed Vansittart's assertions. Sir Maurice Hankey, the liaison man between Vansittart and the Prime Minister, was sent to Baldwin, but for days he was unable to get an audience.

Here was a strange and novel situation for the British Intelligence Service. It was ancient tradition that the IS worked in closest co-operation with the Government. Organizationally, of course, it was an independent institution, not affected by changes in the Government. But each new Government had always accepted it as trustworthy, whether the heads of the IS were of the same political party as the Cabinet Ministers or were their political opponents.

It was something new in English history for a Prime Minister to pay no heed to his own secret service. And that this should have been so, just when Hitler was preparing the next war, had tragic consequences not only for England but for the entire world.

Finally, when in the late autumn of 1934 the gentlemen from B4 became insistent, Baldwin agreed to study the latest reports of the WOID. His conclusions were odd, to say the least. On 29 November 1934, he declared in the House of Commons:

> I think it is correct to say that the Germans are engaged in creating an air
> force, though I think most accounts given in this country in the press are

much exaggerated.... The figure we have on excellent authority is 600 military aircraft; the highest figure we have, also from a good source, is something over one thousand.... Therefore there is no ground at this moment for undue alarm or panic.

The number of German military planes was thrice Baldwin's estimate. The reports of the Intelligence Service, as was later revealed, had been most accurate. Baldwin had simply laid them aside as 'exaggerated.'

During the following months the IS became more and more uneasy. A terrible danger was approaching with seven-league strides, but it was clear that Baldwin would not be warned.

During this period it is probable that Sir Robert Vansittart had more than one serious talk with his closest friend, Winston Churchill. At any rate, on 20 March 1935, in the House of Commons Churchill raised an uncomfortable question: Might not the German air force have outstripped the British air force by now?

On 4 April Foreign Secretary Sir John Simon had to admit that Adolf Hitler himself had told him that the German air force had reached parity with the British air force. Had Sir John listened to his own secret service, he might have learned that a half year earlier. And he would have realized that the German air force was already three times as strong as the British.

On 9 April 1935, Baldwin was still attached to his own idyllic plans for the future.

By March 1937 the strength of the RAF based at home will be about 1,500 first line machines. This compares with the actual figure of 580 first line machines today and with a total of 840 which we should have reached by March 1937 under the expansion program announced last July....

Baldwin was 'rearming.' But he still was not reading the reports of his Intelligence Service.

Then came the climax.

On 23 May 1935, Baldwin admitted in a debate that the British Government had seriously underestimated Germany's capacity for turning out war planes; moreover he said that the British Intelligence Service had been somewhat ignorant of the progress of German rearmament.

The IS could not very well come out in public and give the British Prime Minister the lie.

But there were a number of men in England's political life who knew how the wind was blowing. Among them were Winston Churchill and Anthony Eden, whom Vansittart kept informed, and Duff Cooper and Hore-Belisha, who received their information from Sir George Cockerill. None of these men viewed the future with optimism.

They could have forgiven Baldwin for putting the blame for his own mistakes on the Intelligence Service. That was simply politics. But there was something worse for which they could not forgive him. That was the fact that Baldwin continued to ignore the reports of his Intelligence Department. Baldwin did not like disagreeable news.

PART II
Maginot Line of Espionage

THE DANGEROUS AGE OF THE *DEUXIÈME BUREAU*

Just before the First World War, and afterwards, till the beginning of this war, many French newsstands carried a certain kind of paper-covered novel costing only a few centimes. They were spy novels. They were written by authors with fancy names, and they were very badly written.

The late twenties in France saw a vogue for spy movies. They continued to appear up until the very last days before the present war. These movies and novels had one thing in common: all these works of art presented at least one scene in which the hero, a French secret-service agent, gave enlightenment in these words to a nice chap who didn't know the first thing about espionage: 'If you see anything suspicious, sit down immediately and write a letter to M. le Chef du *Deuxième Bureau*, Paris.'

The effect of such books and movies has never been calculated. Probably even the officers of the *Deuxième Bureau* knew nothing about the public reaction. All they knew was that most of these ventures were terrible flops—from a purely financial as well as from the artistic point of view. All this must have been annoying to them, since it was the *Deuxième Bureau* which did the financing.

Obviously, it was done under the realization that a big spy organization must have the co-operation of the public. It never was done to give the general public a fancy idea of the exciting and adventurous life of the men who worked in the secret service.

Because it just wasn't exciting. The officers of the *Deuxième Bureau* didn't rush around finding secret doors, unmasking sinister plotters, and taking time off to fall in love with a beautiful girl, preferably an American heiress.

At 8:30 every morning they entered the large building on the corner of the Boulevard Saint Germain and the Rue de l'Université. Though this is only a few minutes from the Place de la Concorde, and therefore in the centre of Paris, very few Parisians knew that here were located the *Services du Deuxième Bureau*. There wasn't much traffic on this part of the Boulevard, and after dark it was practically deserted.

It was a big, solid building, inspiring both confidence and a sense of mystery. It had the mingled atmosphere of an old, honoured administration building, and of a haunted house.

Everything seemed to be quite normal until you entered, and were confronted by a man who sat at a little desk next to the big staircase. He asked your business. You had to fill out a form stating your name and the purpose of your visit. Then another man appeared to take the memorandum away, and if you could have followed him you would have seen him go into one of the offices on the main floor and hand the form to somebody who went through a file or list, comparing what you had written with his own information, perhaps comparing the handwriting with a sample of your handwriting.

Once you were inside, everything looked ordinary enough; there was only one thing to distinguish this building from any administration building. It was a little too quiet. There were never any clerks lounging in the corridors and having a chat. There was never a loud noise, outside or inside the offices. At nine o'clock the officers, who by then had looked over their mail, would meet in a large high-ceilinged room with long windows. The walls were panelled in mahogany. In the middle of the room was a large oval table, with fifteen chairs around it. All officers were in civilian clothes. Finally an elderly man would come in and take the chairman's seat. He was of medium height, with greying hair, close-cropped and bristly, and a rather young face, with pince-nez on his nose.

Entering the room at that time you might have taken the meeting for a conference of the directors of an industrial concern of international scope. For when the men started to discuss the mail it was evident that this mail came not only from all parts of France, but virtually from every country in the world. And it also became evident that each of the men was in charge of one particular country or group of countries.

But that was about all you would have learned. Because even here, in the innermost heart of the *Deuxième Bureau*, the language these men used was extremely guarded. No names were mentioned. They always spoke about 'valuable information,' but never said what information.

The Chairman, Colonel Gauché,[1] had been the chief of the *Deuxième Bureau* for many years. Under him were two assistant chiefs. They were Commandant Perrier and Commandant Novarre, both small men of insignificant appearance. Then came eight *chefs de section*, holding the military rank of commanders and captains, each in charge of one particular country or region. Their names were—not their names. Only the Chief himself knew the real names of the officers with whom he worked, and his real name was supposed to be known only by the War Minister.

There was a special oath for every person working in the *Deuxième Bureau*, binding him to utmost secrecy.

The *Deuxième Bureau* was organized on a regional basis. Each region had a district chief. He was an officer in civilian clothes who hired the agents for his territory and who supervised their activity. His office—*Bureaux Frontiers Militaires*—was always close to some frontier. He had to gather the incoming material, sift it, and send it on to Paris.

Then there were the officers within the traditionally neutral countries. Here, supervising agents were established who gave their men assignments, and condensed and sifted their reports before sending them on. They seldom communicated directly with Paris; a report from one of these agents came via the nearest district chief. There, it was once more sifted and condensed and compared with other reports covering the same or a similar subject. Finally a small pencil mark was put on it. It was either a 'C,' a 'P,' or a 'D.' These letters stood for certain, probable, or doubtful.

This system was extremely dependable and safe. It was also extremely slow.

This, then, was the *Deuxième Bureau*: a dignified, business-like institution operating a little too slowly, perhaps. But the *Deuxième Bureau* was something more, something quite different. It operated, for instance, like this:

Every Tuesday and Thursday, at odd hours of the day, some good-looking, elegantly dressed young men entered the large modern apartment house 44 Rue de Lisbonne. They went up three flights and rang the bell of an apartment with the sign: 'Imports and Exports.' (In Paris it is not unusual for an apartment house to contain offices.) They were guided by an elderly and homely woman secretary into an office with wine-red leather chairs, bookshelves of dark wood on which were piled all sorts of papers, books, magazines, and newspapers in great disorder. There was also an enormous desk between two windows. And behind the desk was M. Lemoine.

M. Lemoine was in the habit of providing these young men with money. In return they were supposed to make the acquaintance of secretaries of foreign consulates and embassies; take them out, show them a good time, get as intimate as possible with them, and finally try to steal passports out of their offices. This trick had worked for many years. Even if the girls found out who the thieves were, they very rarely mentioned the matter. If they made a complaint to the police, the particular young man was found and duly arrested. And the foreign diplomat was informed that the thief was being severely punished. In reality, the young man never stayed in prison more than one or two days.

M. Lemoine was a remarkable man. He was tall and heavy-set, bald but extremely vigorous, intelligent and witty. He was a man-about-town, and you would never have guessed that he was more than seventy years old.

His was a fantastic story. His real name was not Lemoine at all, but Baron Koenig. No, not Baron Koenig, but Herr Korff. No, not Korff, but Stallmann. Anyway, he was a native German, and he had been notorious in pre-First World War Berlin and all over Europe as the best cardsharp on the Continent, a man who never lost unless he tried.

There was finally a trial which, involving as it did some important members of Berlin society, became a sensational affair. Stallmann-Korff-Koenig escaped arrest by fleeing to Paris, where he became Lemoine. During the World War he began to work for the *Deuxième Bureau*, directing most of its activities in Spain. It was even said that it was he who finally broke the case of Mata Hari. He himself, however, always denied it.

His export and import office was a front for traffic in arms. Yes, M. Lemoine was always known in international circles as a prospective buyer of arms. However, he very rarely did buy anything. He bought arms only when there was no other way to find out where they were stored.

The office at 44 Rue de Lisbonne was by no means the only one of this kind. There were, in Paris alone, nine more. Most of them were in the neighbourhood of the stock exchange, disguised as brokerage firms, situated in large office buildings among genuine brokerage firms. Throughout France there were sixty-eight such fronts.

Most of them were used merely to receive people who had offered their services and who were not to be invited to the Boulevard Saint Germain.

Some of these offices were highly specialized. Some, for instance, concentrated exclusively on employees of foreign embassies and consulates in Paris and other big cities. All of them employed at least one Frenchwoman—a telephone operator usually. Other offices specialized in other fields. Their safes contained a great assortment of rubber stamps from various foreign offices and ministries, either stolen or cleverly forged. The supply never ran low.

So many agents had to be provided with so many papers. The operatives of the French secret service were everywhere. They worked in munitions plants, they had shops near armouries, they scrubbed floors in aircraft factories, they spent money in night clubs, they were on good terms with dope peddlers and with prostitutes, they played honorable parts in the reserve officers associations, they lent money to moneylenders, they were in love with the executives of export firms, they engaged the services of private detective agencies, they were clients of translating bureaus which also did occasional work for consulates and embassies, they were the pals of the conductors on international sleeping cars passing through many countries on their way across Europe, they drank in little inns with the drivers of buses connecting frontier villages, they stole maps from museums....

They were everywhere.

They were in Switzerland, in Belgium, and in Holland. In these countries the *Deuxième Bureau* had established business firms which apparently were intent upon selling goods to German concerns. The numerous salesmen of these firms—one in Switzerland alone employed at one time ninety salesmen—had travelled all over Germany for years.

All this was not new. This had been built up partly before the First World War. After the defeat of Germany the *Deuxième Bureau* made not the slightest move to reduce its enormous apparatus outside of France. On the contrary, the French were afraid—with good reason, as events have shown—that Germany might arm again and start a new war.

General Dupont had been in charge of the *Deuxième Bureau* during the last years of the First World War—and done wonders. Nicolai himself declared (in his memoirs) that the *Deuxième Bureau* of this period had some achievements it might well be proud of. For example, the French had succeeded in planting a spy named Henry in the German Headquarters and keeping him there for two years. Another spy operating in the tremendously important counterespionage division, a certain Police Commissioner Waegele, was able almost uninterruptedly to deliver information to the *Deuxième Bureau* until shortly before the end of the war. And afterward he spread an even more powerful and efficient network of spies all over Europe.

It was really an amazing organization General Dupont had built up and the most modern secret service to function up to the early thirties.

And it was just then, at a time when Hitler embarked upon the very thing that the French secret service was sworn to prevent; it was just then, when Hitler started to rearm, when the *Deuxième Bureau* should have shown the utmost speed and efficiency, that it began to slip. And it slipped fast.

They were too sure of themselves.

The long and great tradition of the *Deuxième Bureau*'s successful last ten years had persuaded those in key positions that the French secret service was unbeatable. Ironically enough, they made exactly the same mistake the Germans made after their victory in 1871, when they neglected to modernize their secret service, relying on the superiority of their army. The French now committed the error of relying on the traditional excellence of their secret service instead of modernizing it.

They didn't see what was coming because they didn't want to see. The vital breath of any successful spy system is an aggressive spirit; curiosity in itself is aggressive. The French were no longer aggressive in any sense; even their curiosity was flagging.

In a way, they repeated in the field of espionage the same mistake that they committed in the matter of armament. They became purely defensive. They thought they could hold on to what they had. Without their realizing it, their espionage system, which only a few years before had been operated with infinite imagination and daring, now became static. It became a Maginot Line of espionage.

According to classic principles of military espionage, a spy can work only where there is a secret to be discovered. According to such principles, there were three logical spy centres in France: Paris, Alsace-Lorraine (with Strasbourg, Colmar, and Metz), and the North of France (with its factories and fortifications).

The French secret service watched those logical centres. But that wasn't enough, it wasn't nearly enough.

You could feel the lack very strongly in the Boulevard Saint Germain. You could feel it in dozens of little things, each trivial but each betraying the prevailing spirit of clinging stubbornly to tradition.

There was, for instance, the ridiculous device of the little waiting room reserved for all visitors of whom the *Deuxième Bureau* was not quite sure. Opening from this waiting room was a small closet. In this closet stood a strange apparatus designed like a periscope, which allowed a perfect view of the waiting room. The younger officers didn't think much of this apparatus. They felt that anybody who had gained access to the building under false pretenses and for some sinister purpose, was not likely to betray his true intentions by his expression, even when he thought himself unobserved. However, it was a tradition of the *Deuxième Bureau* to take a good look at any stranger before talking to him. And tradition could not be brushed aside.

Or, there was the more important matter of the radio department in the cellar. It had taken years of the most violent struggle on the part of the younger officers to get a radio department installed at all. And it was much too small: there were too few people to listen in on the code short wave broadcasts which Germany was disseminating to her agents all over the world.

The older officers had their own ideas, some of which were absurd.

There was, for instance, one commandant who was in charge of certain Paris activities. He still imagined that espionage could be practised as it has been practised thirty years before. Every few weeks some beautiful young girl whom he had met in a night club would put in appearance at one of the 'brokerage offices.' The undaunted officer was sure that in each one he had discovered a potential Mata Hari. He spared no money to establish her in an elegant apartment and buy her good clothes. And then nothing happened. The Nazis were somehow never considerate enough to fall in love with these ladies. When the lease was up, the Mata Haris went back to their night clubs. They had, at least, got the dresses.

In their definite distaste for anything modern, the French agents were addicted to the oddest methods. One thing all the agents and spies had to listen to every so often was: 'We want facts. We do not want opinions. We can exercise judgment ourselves.' Or: 'Never mind psychology,' they were told, 'use your eyes.'

And then everything was so slow. When General Dupont had built up his network, speed wasn't necessary. But now it was desperately necessary. Hitler had set the pace by his blitz-manner, and utmost speed was of the essence. It is doubtful if the *Deuxième Bureau* could have matched Hitler's speed had it tried. But it never tried. The time-honoured system of sending everything first to the chief of the district, of having every report checked and rechecked, was not for a moment abandoned.

Maybe more speed could have been achieved had there been more money to spend. France was going through a moderate economic crisis. The budgets of all the ministries were cut. But the budget of the *Deuxième Bureau* was slashed. Let an agent ask for a sum which seemed too high, and he was answered sharply, 'We thought you were a patriot.' There were no fixed rates of pay. Five thousand francs was considered high. Twenty to thirty thousand francs was the maximum, spent only in the most important cases.

Through M. Lemoine, a certain Hungarian chemist came to the *Deuxième Bureau* in December, 1936. He offered to go to Germany and get hold of formulae for the new poison gases which were just then being tested in a laboratory near Mannheim. The man went via Switzerland to Germany, and stayed there for two weeks. He returned with the new secret formulae.

They were not yet known to the French Government chemists and they surpassed everything that had previously been developed in the field of poison gases. The *Deuxième Bureau* was delighted. And the agent was paid five thousand francs.

He left Paris two weeks later on a new mission. He never came back. As a matter of fact, he never even entered Germany. Still, he was able to do business with the Nazis. He sold them the information that he had just sold the secret formulae to the *Deuxième Bureau*. For this he received the equivalent of thirty thousand francs.

As for M. Lemoine, he wasn't paid at all. To be sure, it would have been difficult for any government department to pay him, for he needed too much money. Therefore, the *Deuxième Bureau* entered into an extremely interesting arrangement with him.

M. Lemoine was allowed to exploit his friendly contact with the authorities to make money for himself. His greatest source of revenue was the procuring of French visas for rich foreigners who couldn't get them by legal means. But that wasn't all. M. Lemoine was allowed to sell French passports and French working permits, which at that time were in great demand by foreigners who were in the country illegally.

It wasn't astonishing that M. Lemoine, who, after all, had never been overly scrupulous, should choose this way of making a living. But it was fantastic that the French authorities should countenance it. More grotesque than that: while M. Lemoine used this strange commerce to make money for himself, the whole *Deuxième Bureau* started to use it—not for personal advantage, but to obtain the necessary expense money for the agents, which could not be obtained through appropriations.

Many foreigners were offered visas, working permits, or new passports if they would consent to work for the secret service. It became the usual thing for a foreign agent who complained about not getting any pay, to be told, 'What more do you want? Haven't we furnished you with a passport?'

The *Deuxième Bureau* had sunk to the level of M. Lemoine. Maybe, it wasn't exactly corruption, because the *Deuxième Bureau* did it in the interest of the nation. But in a way it was worse than outright corruption. It meant that the fundamental principles of law and order were turned into a farce.

But there were worse things than money matters to trouble the *Deuxième Bureau*. There was treason right in the midst of the French Army.

On 11 September 1937, two buildings near the Place de l'Etoile in Paris were destroyed by time bombs. Investigations followed. And in November it was finally announced that a plot against the Government had been discovered.

It hadn't taken long for the *Sureté Générale* to find out who was behind the plot: two secret fascist organizations, the UCAD (*Union des Comités d'Action Defensive*) and the CSAR (*Comité Secret d'Action Révolutionnaire*). They also called themselves the *Cagoulards* (the hooded ones) because some of their leaders, when conferring with the rank and file, wore hoods, like the Ku Klux Klan.

The *Sureté* found that the *Cagoulards* had secret arsenals of machine guns, dynamite, etc. all over France, in cellars, garages, warehouses, in concrete dugouts. They easily ascertained that all these arms were of German and Italian make.

The conspirators fought the investigation tooth and nail. They were without any scruples. They assassinated some of the *Sureté* agents who were close on their track.

And then the *Deuxième Bureau* arrested Police Inspector Jean Rakowsky. At first this seemed to have nothing to do with the case. The *Deuxième Bureau* had found out through its agents in Italy that Rakowsky had made an offer to the Italian Secret Police—the Ovra—to sell military secrets on a regular basis. Only when Rakowsky was traced and when an Italian agent, Adrian Grosso, with whom he had dealings, was also arrested, did the connection become clear. Grosso admitted being one of the contact men between the *Cagoulards*[2] and their Italian backers. Rakowsky's job had been to inform the *Cagoulards* of the activities within the police department, to warn those who were about to be arrested, or to make evidence disappear from the files.

Jean Rakowsky was tried. But not on the charge of his activities in the *Cagoulard* affair. He was only tried for his services to the Italian secret service. For had he been brought to trial as a member of the *Cagoulards*, many things would have been aired about the *Cagoulards* which everyone concerned thought were better hushed up.

It was one of the first acts of the Minister of the Interior, Albert Sarraut, at the beginning of 1938, to make this clear to the *Deuxième Bureau*. He was furious that the Bureau had arrested a police inspector who, after all, was one of his men. He told the *Deuxième Bureau* to lay off or the French Army might be badly compromised.

He mentioned to the *Bureau* that more than five hundred army officers were involved in the *Cagoulard* affair, and in the logic of the matter would have to be arrested.

The *Deuxième Bureau* was horrified. However, it had no choice. There is a certain strange code of honour prevailing in professional armies which forbids an officer to expose another officer, even when the other is a traitor. The *Deuxième Bureau* was loyal to that code. Furthermore, with danger of war in the near future, it didn't seem wise to have a tremendous scandal in the army and perhaps a minor civil war just at that time. So, ironically enough, because it was afraid of war, it shielded the fifth columnists in its own ranks. They did not consider that those fifth columnists would be— and incidentally have been—a more deadly danger.

One of those compromised in the *Cagoulard* affair was General Gourand, commander of the Paris garrison. But there was worse yet to come. Also compromised was Colonel Loustaneau Lacan, one of the *chefs de sections* of the *Deuxième Bureau*. The officers of the *Bureau* were grateful when, through the intervention of old Marshal Pétain, a scandal was prevented and Colonel Lacan, instead of being arrested, was merely suspended.

They probably did not know that Lacan was a close friend of Marshal Pétain's. And they were still to learn that the old Marshal was compromised in the *Cagoulard* affair, too.

WHAT PRICE USA?

In 1932, the year that saw the birth of total espionage, the United States was still the only Great Power which possessed neither an espionage system nor a counterespionage system. There were not even proper laws against espionage.

There are a number of explanations for this remarkable state of affairs. The United States was not imperialistic; it had no desire to make conquests and therefore was not military. As for industrial espionage—America had no need of it. No spy could learn from another country anything that America did not already know. American industry was further developed than the industry of any other country.

Of course there was a so-called Secret Service. It was a branch of the Treasury Department and it had jurisdiction over the protection of the President, over currency and narcotics.

And there was, of course, the FBI. The Federal Bureau of Investigation had been established in 1908, but it devoted little of its time to espionage. Its chief concerns were white slavery, and later the enforcement of the National Stolen Property Act. Espionage did fall under the jurisdiction of the FBI But in practice the FBI never meddled with an espionage case unless requested to do so by the Army or the Navy.

There were also a Naval Intelligence Bureau and an Army Intelligence Bureau, and there were military attachés to the American embassies who reported what they were permitted to see, just as the military attachés of all other countries. The Intelligence Bureaus were little more than paper organizations. If an arrest had to be made, the case had to be turned over to local police agencies until—in 1932—the FBI obtained power to make arrests.

The Intelligence Bureaus had about $30,000 annually at their disposal. Hence all they could be were nuclei that might be expanded in time of war. Thirty thousand dollars was just about enough to pay a few officials, gather the information of the military attachés, and hope for the best.

Moreover—according to the opinions of American legal experts—the laws which could be interpreted as applying to espionage were altogether inadequate. It was also impossible to convict a man of espionage if the object of the espionage could not be proved. That an arrested man had in his pocket a secret document which he could not possibly have obtained except by illegal means was not sufficient evidence. In such a case he could be convicted of no more than theft.

This was the situation in 1933, and it changed little during the next few years. The United States had imperative need for a counterespionage organization of hundreds of men, even an organization which did nothing more than collect the information gathered by the various law-enforcement agencies, by local police forces, newspaper reporters, etc. For every day and every hour since Hitler had taken power, Nazi agents in the United States were plotting against America. During those years the United States was a paradise for spies. No wonder that Hitler and Goebbels often declared to their intimates that nothing would be easier than 'to produce unrest and revolution in the United States.'

When America gradually awoke, it was not because of the activities of German agents. The American public stared first eastward as though under a hypnotic spell—towards Japan.

In February 1936 Democratic Representative Sirovich at a session of the House Naval Committee openly accused Japan of military espionage. He spoke of the fishing boats which operated off the coast of Alaska and declared—quite correctly—that they were not fishing at all; they were taking photographs and soundings, and in case of war Japan would seize Alaska to provide bases for planes and submarines.

This was only the beginning. The safe of a U.S. battleship was opened; the vault in the Navy Department was tampered with. On 2 July 1936, Harry Thomas Thompson, former yeoman of the Navy, was tried on charges of selling U.S. naval information to Lieutenant Commander Toshio Miyazaki of the Imperial Japanese Navy. Miyazaki was also indicted, but before the trial he was recalled to Japan. Thompson was sentenced to fifteen years in the penitentiary.

Less than two weeks later, on 14 July 1936, Lieutenant Commander John Semer Farnsworth[3] was arrested on charges of selling a certain confidential United States naval book to the naval attachés of the Japanese Embassy in Washington, Yosiuki Itimiya and Okira Yamaki. The Japanese were again indicted and again recalled before the case came to trial. In February 1937, Farnsworth was sentenced to from four to twelve years in prison.

And all this time and during the years to follow, mysterious Japanese fishing boats sailed up and down the west coast of the American continent.

But there were other boats far more dangerous than these. The German passenger liners which made regular runs to New York (and to San Pedro and San Francisco) were far more important in the spy traffic. They were, so to speak, the underground railway which was used to smuggle material out of the country. The luxury liners of the North German Lloyd Line were the favourite boats of the German agents. They usually sailed from New York at midnight; there were always crowds at the pier; many passengers came from the theatre and night clubs at the last moment, accompanied by friends in evening dress and high spirits. It was impossible to keep a close check on these sailings, and it was ridiculously simple to get on board the

Europa and the *Bremen*, to present a bouquet which contained something besides flowers. Or there might be a few letters to relatives in the Fatherland which could be delivered at the ship post office.

It was child's play. And it was no problem for a German spy who was in danger to linger on one of these liners after the call, 'All visitors ashore!'

The German luxury liners were the most efficient transmission belt in the history of espionage. The FBI was soon to realize this.

Early in 1935 two men, William Lonkowski[4] and Werner George Gudenberg, were working in an aircraft factory in Buffalo, NY. Both were skilled workers, Later Gudenberg shifted to a job with Curtiss Wright, also in Buffalo. The Curtiss Wright plant was producing warplanes for the U.S. Government, then.

Had anyone trailed them at that time, he would have been surprised to discover that these two men, who before were total strangers to each other, met regularly in a small saloon on the outskirts of the city.

In September 1935 Lonkowski quit his job at the aircraft factory. He told acquaintances that he was going to New York. About a week later he turned up in New York. At 11 p.m. one night he came to the North German Lloyd Line pier and went up the gangplank of the *Bremen*,[5] which was to sail in an hour. He was carrying a violin case. But something seemed to have gone wrong, for shortly before the boat was to sail he went back to the pier, his violin case still under his arm.

This was a mistake. He had forgotten that the piers are watched by customs officials who have learned that smugglers bring contraband—particularly drugs—to shore a few minutes before a steamer sails. Two customs officers stopped Lonkowski.

He put up an argument, but when he saw that he would not be allowed to leave with his violin case, he shrugged and said he would come to the custom house for it in the morning.

The officers opened the violin case after Lonkowski left. They did not find drugs—in fact all they found was a cheap fiddle. Then they noticed an irregularity in the lining of the case and tore it open. Eight tiny photographic negatives were sewn into the lining. An hour later, after officers of the Naval Intelligence had been routed out of their beds and the negatives pieced together, it was discovered that the photos contained the plans for a new Curtiss bomber.

But by this time Lonkowski was on his way to Peekskill, NY. And a few hours later he sat in a plane that took him to Canada.

Without help his flight would never have succeeded. He was aided by a man whom he merely called 'Doctor.' The man actually was a doctor. But it was several months before the FBI succeeded in fitting together the parts of the puzzle, and got on the trail of Dr Ignaz Griebl.[6]

However, it would be bad history to begin a description of the Nazi underground organization in the United States with Dr Ignaz Griebl. We must begin at the beginning.

The real beginning was the foundation of the 'Teutonia' in Chicago in 1925. It was founded by a man named Ulrich Staack, and Messrs. Walter Kappe and Fritz Gissibl, were charter members.

In 1932 the North American *Landesgruppe* of the National Socialist Party was founded. Karl Manger of New York was appointed führer of this group. Whether they liked it or not, the members of the Teutonia Club found themselves taking orders from him. In October 1932 the first Nazi meeting was held in the Pfaelzer Hof in New York. At this meeting storm troopers appeared in uniform. All this was still months before Hitler became Chancellor. But this was to be only a prelude....

Early in 1933 the German Vice-Consul in New York, Dr Georg Gyssling,[7] had dissolved the Nazi Party: it had had too much unpleasant publicity. He established a club which he called the Friends of the Hitler Movement, a club which attracted a large membership, including many influential and financially powerful Americans. Gyssling did not have to wait long for his reward. In April 1933 he was appointed Consul in Los Angeles. Before he left New York, he renamed the club; it became the Friends of the New Germany.

Los Angeles.... Even during these first months of their work, the Nazis understood the tremendous importance of the West Coast as a field for espionage. During the next few years there grew up in and around Los Angeles what amounted to the central committee of German espionage. Here, too, there were ships for smuggling vital material and men into and out of the country. Here Count von Buelow appeared and rented himself a house at Point Loma in San Diego, overlooking the naval base. And here, there worked a young man with a Hitler moustache, who had acquired American citizenship—which he later forfeited when it was learned that he had acquired it under false pretenses. This man directed all German espionage in this part of the country. He spent most of his time in the German House at 634 West 15th Street, Los Angeles; but he occasionally took interesting trips to Mexico. His name was Hermann Schwinn.[8.]

Meanwhile the Friends of the New Germany prospered under the leadership of a photo-engraver from Detroit named Heinz Spanknöbel.[9] But Herr Spanknöbel was imprudent; he behaved somewhat too arrogantly; he tried gangster methods to persuade New York's population of German origin to obey his orders. Again there was unpleasant publicity, he was indicted by a grand jury for violation of the law covering the status of foreign agents, and had to flee precipitately to Germany—on one of those favourite German liners. It was in connection with this affair that Washington first became interested in Dr Ignaz Griebl.

Until now there had been no reason to pay any attention to him. He had fought in the German Army in the World War, and coming to America had settled down as a physician. He was a member of many German clubs, but until Hitler took power he kept clear of politics. After 1933 this attitude underwent a great change. He became a Jew-hater par excellence and a leader in the fight to Aryanize all German clubs. He also became—though this was not revealed until much later—Chairman of the Secret Execution Committee of the Friends of the New Germany—whatever that meant. When he was accused in court of having aided Spanknöbel's flight and of hiding him in his own home, he offered patriotism as his excuse....

The leadership of the Verein was taken over by Fritz Gissibl[10] until he also had to flee to Germany. For a time a certain Reinhold Walther took his place until Dr Hubert Schnuch came from Germany as an exchange student to take the Friends of the New Germany in hand. He, too, did not last long; there were quarrels and occasionally even open-street-brawls between the followers of Walter Kappe[11] and the followers of Schnuch, until finally, in 1935, Kappe sailed for Europe on a German liner. Sometime later, in March 1936, the Buffalo Convention of the Friends—renamed the 'Bund'—elected Fritz Kuhn as leader.

But the real leader of the Bund after 1936 was not Kuhn, any more than those other gentlemen had been the real leaders before 1936. The real führer, the power behind the throne and the man who was organizing Nazi espionage in the United States, was Walter H. Schellenberg.[12]

His career in Germany almost predestined him for the role that he was to play in the United States. During the World War he joined one of the bands of adventurers known as Free Corps which, under the pretence of fighting bolshevism in the Baltic states, sold their services to the highest bidder while becoming the terror of the native population with their looting, raping, burning, and murdering. Schellenberg belonged to the Free Corps von Brandis which 'liberated' Latvia. For his signal brutality he soon advanced to an officer's commission. By the end of 1919, Schellenberg's outfit had committed so many outrages that the Baltic states finally drove the 'liberators' back to their own Fatherland, where the German government disarmed them. Like all mercenaries, Schellenberg could not bring himself to find a regular job. To earn his livelihood by regular work was beneath his dignity. So he and a gang of his hoodlums hired out as guards on a large Prussian Junker estate. Schellenberg not only smashed the farmers' union which had been formed under the protection of the young German republic but started a cache of arms and ammunition on the estate of his employer Baron von Dangen-Steinkeller who was in full sympathy with the preparations for a *putsch* against the republican regime. However,

Schellenberg did not long enjoy the easy life on the estate because not even the tolerant German republic would stand for open murder. A poor farmhand had stumbled across one of the arms caches and was surprised by one of Schellenberg's men. He called his leader and Schellenberg beat out the farm worker's brains. The boy's brother openly cast suspicion of the murder upon the guards. When this came to Schellenberg's ears, he strode into the village inn two days later and pumped the nine slugs of his Parabellum pistol into the unlucky lad's head. The police simply had to intervene, but they contrived never to catch up with Schellenberg. A few months later Schellenberg joined, with the rank of First Lieutenant, the notorious Ehrhardt Brigade, a secret military organization sworn to overthrow the German Republic. In this capacity he participated in the Kapp *Putsch* in 1920, afterwards quickly changing back to civilian clothes when the government put down the insurrection. Schellenberg joined the Nazi Party and for the next few years his income came from various sources. As long as the party was legitimate he was a paid organizer of storm troops. As leader of one of the 'Rollkommandos'—special street-fighting detachments of the storm troops—his police dossier in the Prussian Ministry of the Interior, which already recorded two murder charges that were *never* prosecuted, was augmented by three more suspected murders, homicide, assault with deadly weapons, unlawful possession of firearms, and destruction of property. But like other storm-troop leaders he always got away with small fines. When the party was outlawed after Hitler's unsuccessful Beer-Hall *Putsch* Schellenberg had a tough time for a while living on whatever he could borrow. By 1925, when the Nazi Party came back stronger than ever, Schellenberg had a new racket. He was selling 'protection' to wealthy Jews in Berlin, Frankfurt, Munich, and Magdeburg. It was quite lucrative in two ways. Schellenberg promised to use his influence with the Party to tone down anti-Jewish agitation. His other and more profitable line was to promise that when the Party came to power he would personally see to it that his benefactors would be exempted from whatever anti-Jewish measures the Nazis would decree.

Shortly before Hitler came to power, Schellenberg came to New York. Without visible occupation or means of support, he began at once to organize Nazi intelligence activities. He organized a secret department of the German Consulate General in New York under Dr Walther Becker, at that time nominally German commercial attaché. This first work consisted of systematic espionage in the New York financial district. By October 1932, Schellenberg had people in the foreign departments of some banks who furnished information on transactions of German accounts or accounts suspected of evading the German foreign exchange restrictions. Several of these informers were subsequently found to be members of the German Nazi Party or the German-American Bund and its parent organizations. Schellenberg himself joined the staff of a small financial firm on lower Broadway, which turned out to be a cleverly disguised blind for Nazi financial transactions. Also in his new role as 'security salesman' and 'customer's man' Schellenberg was able to establish a plausible front. He nearly came to grief in 1934, when government agents heard that he had boasted of purchasing his American immigration visa in Berlin through a crooked American attorney. Questioned under oath, Schellenberg could not be prosecuted because it was impossible at that time to obtain the evidence from Berlin to convict him.

Shortly after Hitler came to power Schellenberg made a secret trip to Germany, despite the fact that he had taken out American citizenship papers and sworn his first oath of allegiance to the United States. American government authorities have in their possession a picture which appeared in the summer of 1933 in the official Nazi Party newspaper, *Voelkischer Beobachter*, of Schellenberg in full Nazi storm-trooper regalia. The caption on that picture reads: 'Party Comrade Walter H. Schellenberg, Special Assistant on the staff of Party Comrade E. W. Bohle, bidding goodbye to Party Comrade Colonel F. X. Hasenoehrl, who is on a special Party mission to the Far East.'

Shortly thereafter Schellenberg returned to the United States. Within a week Spanknoebl and all the other big shots of the American Nazi organization, the Friends of the New Germany, were living with Schellenberg at a hotel on Lexington Avenue. Schellenberg paid all the bills. For almost three months this was the nerve centre of the Nazi spy ring. In correspondence acquired later by private and government investigators, the espionage setup was referred to as the Cultural Division of the Friends of the New Germany. The inner circle consisted of Schellenberg, Spanknöbl, Dr Ignaz Griebl, Dr Gerhart Spanner, who was connected with Columbia University, Dr Otto Koischwitz, then at Hunter College and now with the Nazi Ministry of Propaganda in Berlin, Wendel de Monteroca of the intelligence section of the Nazi storm troops, and a Dr Schlink from Union City, New Jersey. At Schellenberg's behest Schlink took charge of the American branch of the Uschla (*Untersuchungs- and Schlichtungs Ausschuss—Investigation and Settlement Committee*) the dreaded secret Party tribunal with power over life and death. How many 'traitors' were kidnapped and dragged aboard German ships in New York harbour after being sentenced by the Uschla not even American government agents know.

When the McCormack Committee in 1934 seized the files of the Friends of the New Germany, reports to Germany of several possible kidnappings were found. It was also found that Schellenberg and Dr Albert Degener, secretary of the Board of Trade for German-American Commerce, were among the most generous financial contributors to the local Nazi organizations. For some mysterious reason this evidence was never made public.

Once public excitement over Spanknöbl's flight had died down, Schellenberg early in 1934 built the Cultural Division of the Friends of the New Germany into a most efficient espionage machine. Every member of the Friends was instructed, under threat of the punishment and disfavour of the Nazi Party in Germany, to make weekly reports on all his contacts, friends, and acquaintances, on what he had heard socially and during business hours. Schellenberg himself would instruct the *Kulturamtswalter* (Educational Directors) in the various Nazi units on the training of their people. Weekly, so-called *Schulungsabende* (educationals) were held in New York, Chicago, St Louis, Los Angeles, and the other eighty-odd American communities where the Nazis were organized. These reports were turned over to Schellenberg, who then would transmit pertinent data to the German Consulate General in New York. Schellenberg also worked with German naval intelligence agents who masqueraded as 'clerks' of the New York office of the North German Lloyd.

By 1936 Schellenberg's task had expanded to such an extent that when the Friends of the New Germany were reorganized into the German-American Bund and Fritz Kuhn[13] brought in as leader, Schellenberg set up an entirely new and separate organization for his purposes.

He adopted every possible precaution to remain in the background. He was never seen at Bund meetings or other Nazi gatherings except at the monthly secret meetings of German Nazi Party functionaries including all consuls. They were held behind strongly guarded doors at the Creole Room of the New York Turn Hall; he sometimes attended secret meetings, held up to 1939 at 5 East 66th Street in New York City. This was the building of the German Club, which since has been razed. But Schellenberg's importance is sharply illustrated by an incident which occurred on 2 October 1937, during a 'German Day' celebration at Madison Square Garden. The hall was jammed to its 22,000-seat capacity. In the front row were Fritz Kuhn in full storm-trooper regalia, Dr Kesseler, president of the pro-Nazi United German Societies, the Reverend Sigismund von Bosse, who was customarily speaker before the 'respectable' meetings of the Bund, and a son of one of the most notorious German agents in America during the First World War—and His Excellency, the German Ambassador, Dr Hans Heinrich Dieckhoff.[14] After the programme was under way, Schellenberg in immaculate morning coat and striped trousers strode down the aisle. Bund storm troopers, posted every ten feet, snapped to attention and saluted while Schellenberg gave them merely a condescending nod. When he reached the first row, Dr Wilhelm Tannenberg, First Secretary of the German Embassy, who sat next to the Ambassador, upon seeing Schellenberg, jumped to his feet like a recruit; his right arm shot up in the Hitler salute and he begged Schellenberg to accept his seat; he would find himself another. At that moment Mr Dieckhoff turned around and recognized Schellenberg. The ambassador of the German Reich greeted Schellenberg with respect and effusion which could not have been more elaborate for the Führer himself. Fritz Kuhn, not to be outdone, sent two uniformed orderlies to stand by Schellenberg's chair. Reporters standing nearby who understood German heard Kuhn order Rudolf Markmann, commander of Storm Troopers, '*So fort je einen Meldegänger and Ordonnanz für Parteigenossen Schellenberg abkommandieren*.' ('At once: detail an orderly and an adjutant for Party Comrade Schellenberg.')

So much fuss for an ordinary securities salesman?

SPLENDID ISOLATION OF THE I.S.

Baldwin was succeeded by Chamberlain. And German Ambassador Leopold von Hoesch,[15] a leftover from the Weimar Republic, died rather suddenly—many said he had taken his own life—and was succeeded by Joachim von Ribbentrop.[16]

Possibly English society and even British Government circles did not know exactly who this man Ribbentrop was. A few years before he had not even been a member of the Nazi Party, and now Hitler suddenly entrusted him with so important a Government post. But in the F.O.I.D.—and probably in the other intelligence departments as well—a great deal was known about Herr von Ribbentrop.

It was known that when the First World War broke out he had been in Canada, had escaped to the United States, and then gone to Europe on a Dutch boat. In 1915 he had been sent by submarine to New York to assist Herr von Papen in Washington. It was known, too, that he remained in Washington for several months after Papen left, continuing his work of sabotage. Later he had again collaborated with Papen in Turkey, where he saved the life of his superior and teacher when Papen got into difficulties— he had been preparing sabotage of the Suez Canal.

Perhaps the British intelligence departments wondered that a man with such a past could have climbed to the rank of German Ambassador to England, and perhaps they assumed that London society would snub a man with such a past. If they made any such assumption, they were mistaken.

In Government circles Ribbentrop was very much *persona grata*. Why not? In June 1935 he had helped negotiate the naval treaty between Great Britain and Germany—for two years London was proud of that treaty. And in society Ribbentrop had certain connections. He was the son-in-law of the great German champagne manufacturer, Henkel, who had many close friends in England. English society never imagined that Henkel's son-in-law would not be 'nice.' And, as a matter of fact, Ribbentrop was very nice. He was good-looking and well-mannered, he patronized the best tailors, and he gave grand receptions.

Perhaps it was not only the man who should be given credit for his social successes. Ruling circles in English society were becoming increasingly eager to come to an agreement with Hitler. It seemed to them the only way to save themselves from Communism, of which they were deathly afraid.

In addition, certain business—or, to use a less humble word, financial—interests played a part. Even during the Spanish war these financial interests had had a decisive influence. In vain Sir Robert Vansittart and many of his colleagues had warned that a Franco victory would leave France strategically in no enviable position. In vain they had pointed out the danger to Gibraltar. The interests of the City were on Franco's side. There was especially the *Societé Financière de Transports et d'Enterprises Industrielles*, a corporation controlled by the City, which had invested tremendous sums in Spain. If the Loyalists won, these investments would be lost.

It has never been thoroughly explained, and probably it never will be, how far his personal financial interests governed Chamberlain's policies. It has been proved that he had a financial stake in a certain German industry—but that is no proof that he allowed himself to be swayed by this alone. However, there is no question that he was influenced by certain people who, because they habitually spent the weekend at Cliveden, Lord Astor's country estate at Taplow, Buckinghamshire, were lumped together under the term, Cliveden set. Lady Astor's invitations gradually came into some notoriety after the autumn of 1937. It was at that time that Lady Astor invited the German Ambassador to tea; and it was at that time that Geoffrey Dawson, editor of *The Times*, started to urge the restoration of the German colonies.

There were other favourite guests at Lady Astor's teas besides the editor-in-chief of *The Times* and the German Ambassador. Lord Halifax was also a pet guest, and Lord Lothian, the relentless enemy of the Spanish Loyalists.

It is commonly held in Intelligence Service circles that Lady Astor's salons saw the first conversations which later led to Lord Halifax's visit to Berlin. This may or may not have been so. It is a matter of record, however, that Halifax's visit in November 1937 was undertaken over the head of Foreign Minister Anthony Eden. Not to speak of the Quai d'Orsay, which had hardly been informed. Hitler later declared that he had frankly told Halifax he intended to annex Austria, and the good Lord Halifax had not raised an objection....

Foreign Minister Eden was not alone in his dislike for the Cliveden set and the other circles which so strongly influenced Prime Minister Chamberlain. Winston Churchill, too, protested repeatedly; Duff Cooper and Hore-Belisha spoke pessimistically—in short, all those who had personal connections with the IS and knew what was going on in the world.

But Chamberlain closed his ears to them. He closed his ears to his own Foreign Minister.

It is still too early to determine why Chamberlain paid attention to certain persons and rejected the counsel of the very people who were there to keep him informed—in particular his Intelligence Service. Whatever the reasons, this was indubitably the case. Through the Cliveden set he absorbed indirectly the influence of Ribbentrop, while Sir Montagu Norman,[17] Governor of the Bank of England, exercised a direct and almost hypnotic influence upon him. Naturally, Ribbentrop did everything in his power to convince Chamberlain that Hitler's rearmament was nothing to worry about. It is, however, difficult to explain what motive Sir Montagu had in pooh-poohing as fairy tales the reports on German rearmament.

The situation in Berlin was little better. Chamberlain's Ambassador to Germany, Sir Nevile Henderson, was so enchanted with Göring's hunting and Goebbels' personality that he quite neglected the tips from the Foreign Office Intelligence Department.[18] And Sir Nevile was not the man to perceive the lay of the land for himself. A splendid huntsman, he had scanty understanding of people, and, quite innocent of any knowledge about gangster methods, he did not realize what it was all about until the very end.

At home, matters progressed from bad to worse. Sir Robert Vansittart had reliable information that Germany was building numerous submarines and in every way violating the naval treaty. He passed his information on to B4, and was invited to a conference. Here it was established that the Naval Intelligence Department, whose business it was to get such information and pass it on, had pigeonholed certain reports. When questioned, certain individuals in the Admiralty murmured that they had disregarded the reports because they thought them exaggerated. These gentlemen were of the mind that all the 'rumours' of German rearmament were exaggerated.

Evidently the fault was not always Chamberlain's that he was so poorly informed or completely uninformed. But in the main he was to blame. As time passed it became more and more obvious that he mistrusted the Foreign Office I.D.—so much so that he actually set up a kind of unofficial private intelligence service. The key man in this service was Sir Horace Wilson,[19] the pro-German and anti-French economist, a friend of Sir Montagu Norman's. Throughout 1938, Sir Horace made the work of the regular intelligence service almost futile. Under his coaxing, Chamberlain tossed their reports into the wastebasket and devoted his attention to the reports of special observers like Hoare and Simon. Chamberlain did not need much persuading. The latter reports were more encouraging than those of the Intelligence Service.

And then the storm broke.

In January 1938, Anthony Eden,[20] who was in Geneva, heard that Hitler intended to invade Austria within the next two months.

He received this information in a roundabout way. One of the chiefs of the *Deuxième Bureau* gave it to him. The man from the *Deuxième Bureau* did not bother to tell the British Foreign Minister that the information had come to him by way of the Foreign Office Intelligence Department in London.

Sir Robert Vansittart had taken this course as a last resort. He realized that if he delivered the report to Chamberlain in the ordinary fashion, it would lie unread on his desk until it was too late. As events soon proved, his guess was quite correct.

Eden immediately telephoned Chamberlain. With appalling serenity, Chamberlain promised to look into the matter. Then Chamberlain sent for Sir Robert. Naturally Chamberlain had not known that Eden had got his information from the French, and he reproached Vansittart for giving such important information to the Foreign Minister over his, Chamberlain's, head.

Vansittart might have said that Eden had not got the report from him. But he preferred to face the issue. The result was a heated quarrel, which ended in Chamberlain's promoting Vansittart. Vansittart's official position had been that of Permanent Under-Secretary of the Foreign Office. Chamberlain created a new post for him—Chief Foreign Adviser. While theoretically a promotion, it meant that Vansittart was excluded from the Intelligence Service. Vansittart's collaborator, Hankey, also was 'promoted.' Chamberlain made him a director of the Suez Canal Company.

Meanwhile Anthony Eden had returned. He was not interested in discussing the propriety of his receiving before Chamberlain the news that Hitler intended to annex Austria. He demanded that Chamberlain take an unambiguous stand on the question itself.

On 20 February 1938, Anthony Eden resigned and Lord Halifax became Foreign Minister.

In the case of Sir Robert Vansittart, the Intelligence Service for the first time put its foot down; this once it would not allow Chamberlain to go too far. When word got around that Vansittart was to be shelved, the Foreign Office

Intelligence Department conducted a kind of palace revolution. Within a few hours all the key men handed in their resignations. Chamberlain was compelled to keep Sir Robert as head of the IS.

When Schuschnigg[21] returned from his ill-fated visit to Berchtesgaden, Vansittart decided to swallow his personal pride. He knew that only immediate action on the part of England could stop Hitler. And he knew, too, that if Hitler were not stopped then, no one would be able to stop him for a long time to come.

His conference with the Prime Minister was brief. Chamberlain declared that the affair was between Hitler and Schuschnigg and no concern of England's.

And then everything took place as Ribbentrop had predicted. He had been a good prophet—or a good spy—when months before he assured Berlin that England would not lift a finger to help Austria. In this respect, at any rate, he knew better than the Intelligence Service.

Ironically enough, the man who at this time was operating in Vienna was Ribbentrop's former superior, the man for whose ability Colonel Nicolai had little regard: Herr Franz von Papen. This time none of his agents forgot their portfolios; this time he mislaid no secret codes. But the reason for his 'success' was that this time he had power behind him. He was no more clever than he had been twenty years before. For in those days before the fall of Austria anybody in Vienna could see what Papen was up to. Only this time Papen had behind him the menacing war machine of Adolf Hitler.

Operations proceeded according to schedule. Austria's Minister in London, Baron Frankenstein, made a last desperate effort. He asked Foreign Minister Halifax for an audience. But Halifax could not see him. He had a visitor. Herr von Ribbentrop stayed with him much longer than was customary, and when he took his leave of Lord Halifax, Hitler's columns were already on the march.

CHISMES AND CHISTES

They say that Mexico City is a town of about a million and a half inhabitants. And they say that it is the only cosmopolitan place between the Rio Grande and Rio de Janeiro. Then again D. H. Lawrence wrote of Mexico City: 'If you arrive unannounced and unexpected in the capital you are probably under an assumed name and have some dirty game up your sleeve.'

Perhaps that is so because everybody seems to know everybody else. That is so anyway, in political, artistic, and journalistic circles. When you belong, you know everybody at least by sight or by reputation—and the reputation is always bad.

You have so much time in Mexico City. You have all the time in the world for 'Chismes'—that is, spicy gossip inevitably of a political tone, since the sole source of big money is the patronage of bigger politicians and generals. And you have all the time in the world for 'Chistes'—that is, dirty cracks at persons of notoriety.

Chismes and Chistes: that is half your life in Mexico City. Now take for instance Sanborn's Coffee Shop, strategically placed at the corner of the narrow Avenida Madero, through which everybody passes at some time every day. You hear a lot of talk at Sanborn's. Frank Sanborn,[22] the old one, is no longer active but they still talk about him. The place is full of tourists sporting Mexican hats which no Mexican would put on his head. The coffee is very strong and little covered jars of hot water are provided. You can meet practically everybody at Sanborn's. From the Gestapo agent to the de Gaullist secret-service man, to the secretary of a president, to Miss Smith from Oklahoma City....

Oh, yes, old Frank Sanborn. Well, they say he ran oil for the German U-boats during the last war. Maybe it's true, maybe it is not. All you can say is they have a good memory down there in Mexico City....

They spin tales about German agents encamped there during the last world war. They still remember when Herr von Papen ran down to Mexico City from Washington to establish a kind of collaboration with President Venustiano Carranza, who was not on the best terms with Washington. It was an open secret in town then that the German minister, Herr Hintze, indulgent though he was with Herr von Papen, knew Mexico and realized all the time that it was no go. As it turned out, Hintze was right, and smart Herr von Papen could not do anything. Neither did his helper Captain von Boy-Ed succeed, or the German propagandists Mr Viereck or Herr Colin Ross, who drifted down at that time to see what could be done.

What did Berlin imagine could be done anyhow? There were lots of Chismes and Chistes around Mexico City at that time and there were some wild rumours. And you could not believe them then any more than you can believe them now. But it all seems to boil down to this:

The German agents were to keep an eye on the agents of other countries and their work in Mexico. They were to exploit the internal trouble so as to make it necessary for the United States Army to keep troops on the Southern border. They were to arrange hideouts for German agents who had to flee the United States, they were to smuggle agents who had landed in Mexican ports into the U.S., they were to supply fuel for U-boats and raiders, and collect provisions and all kinds of shipping information....

Well, after the war was over there were not so many German agents left in Mexico, but there was always a handful throughout the twenties, to keep the Commercial attaché at the German Legation informed of developments in the hills and the jungles and to lend a helping hand to German residents in acquiring monopolies in drugs, cameras, optical and surgical supplies, musical instruments, furniture, hardware, and electrical equipment....

The years rolled by and the year 1933 brought no visible changes, at least as far as the Germans in Mexico were concerned. And then, about six months after Hitler's seizure of power, a party of Germans crossed the United States border, came to Mexico and looked around. They were about to do some organizing—feel out the ground in Latin America. People who should know say that behind it was the old principle of weakening the United States by fomenting trouble in Mexico.

Bellinghausen's restaurant opposite the American Embassy seemed to be the headquarters of these tourists. Incidentally, it is still considered, so to speak, the antechamber of Nazi headquarters. Bellinghausen's had the look of a place where conspirators should meet. Well, anyhow, you could overhear plenty at Bellinghausen's in those days. You could catch some words to the effect that Mexico was a country made to be colonized and that Hitler would do the colonizing and buy the raw material. You heard that control of the Mexican Gulf Coast meant control of the Caribbean, that the Pacific Coast would be the perfect place for action against the California coast and that from there traffic between San Francisco and the Panama Canal could be practically cut off. And a whole lot of nonsense about how the United States could be invaded from Mexico. And, of course, you could hear a powerful lot of Chismes and Chistes.

But when Hermann Schwinn put in an appearance things began to look more serious in Mexico. Hermann Schwinn, you remember, came directly from the Deutsches Haus in Los Angeles. They say he came with a few interesting letters of introduction, from a certain Henry D. Allen, American citizen, sometimes known under other names. Herr Schwinn was energetic, enterprising, and no laggard. He did not sit around in Bellinghausen's shooting his mouth off. As a matter of fact, at first he did not go so far as Mexico City; he just went across the border, stopped in Mexicali, and got in touch with a few other late arrivals. It was then and there that the so-called Gold Shirts (Los Dorados—in imitation of the Villa Armies' name) were founded. The charter members had most divergent ideas as to the final goal. Nicolas Rodriguez,[23] who became the leader of the Gold Shirts, had ambitions to become the führer of Mexico. Most of his Mexican friends wanted to make some easy money. Herr Schwinn's purpose was to create trouble in Mexico and possibly set up a fascist state.

There was one man in Mexico City who was not consulted. This was Freiherr Ruedt von Collenberg, the German Minister, a diplomat of the old school, rather nice, harmless and dumb. If someone had tried to explain to him what it was all about he would never have understood.

Equally ignorant of what was going on in Mexico were the English and French Intelligence Services. They had no agents south of the Rio Grande at that time. They hadn't thought it necessary.

But almost everybody in Mexico City knew about Herr Schwinn and Rodriguez and the Gold Shirts, and that the Gold Shirts were becoming a sizeable organization. After all, Mexico City was full of people who had to keep their eyes open: hotel desk clerks, guides, taxi drivers, waiters, whores.... They all needed a licence from Gobernacion (the Ministry of Interior) and Gobernacion liked to get some monthly report in return for the licence. So, to keep alive, they had to keep their eyes open.

And so they promptly took notice of the arrival of Baron Ernst von Merck in Mexico City. Of course, they didn't know Baron von Merck had been a German spy in Brussels during the last world war. But even without such pertinent information they guessed that he had something up his sleeve.

Baron Ernst von Merck obtained a job as an agronomist in the Department of Agriculture. It was there that he got in touch with Saturnino Cedillo, who was a member of the Cardenas cabinet. He often visited Cedillo's ranch, Las Palomas, San Luis Potosi, for what were termed 'hunting parties.' A real friendship sprang up between the two men and grew even firmer when Cedillo fell out with Cardenas for having cut his profits in *ixtle* (a sort of sisal hemp) by breaking up his monopoly. It was about that time that Cedillo himself got in touch with Berlin. He was negotiating for planes. Maybe for a hunting party.

There was also the former President Calles, the 'strong man' of Mexico, a great admirer of Hitler's. He was pretty thick with some of the Nazis' agents and with the Chamber of Commerce and the Employers' Association, two institutions that did not hide their pro-fascist, anti-Cardenas and anti-Roosevelt feelings and intentions. To the great grief of all these friends of his, Calles was finally expelled from Mexico and was forced to do his conspiring from U.S. soil.

In June 1935 old Freiherr von Collenberg received a visit which upset him no end. His visitor was Brito Foucher, who headed a fascist organization backed by the Employers' Association and—without Collenberg's knowledge—by Nazi money. Foucher requested the minister to arrange for him to be sent to Berlin—for training. Foucher probably did not use the phrase 'fifth column'; the expression hadn't been coined, but that was the phrase for what he was trying to organize in Mexico.

Before the old minister could as much as formulate an answer, Brito Foucher became involved in a street battle in Villahermosa and had to flee the country. Shortly afterwards he was seen in Berlin.

Of course, there was nothing unusual in street brawls in Mexico City or anywhere in Mexico. Almost everybody carried a gun, preferably with a butt of filigree gold and mother-of-pearl.

Almost everybody who had to do with politics, hired a pistolero to watch that his master was not shot in the back. Of course, it was understood among those who had any manners at all that shooting in any night club or café just wasn't done. At the Waikiki, where some of the girls were Nazi spies, it was a rule of the house that guns were checked at the door and sometimes there were three or four armed policemen around who frisked you as you went in. In spite of this, shootings averaged three per week; they never looked for shoulder holsters.

It is a bad practice for everybody to be carrying arms all the time. Maybe that was why there was some shooting on 20 November 1935, in Mexico City.

No. The explanation is not that simple.

On 20 November 1935, Rodriguez and his Gold Shirts marched to the president's palace. Street fighting broke out; seventy persons were wounded; five Gold Shirts were killed; Rodriguez himself was stabbed and taken to a hospital. Later he was exiled and went to the United States to visit his friend Hermann Schwinn.

Doctor Heinrich Northe had arrived earlier, sometime in June 1935. He was the new 'Civilian attaché' to the German Legation. The old Minister had long since become accustomed to surprises.

Dr Heinrich Northe was quite a man. About thirty, elegant, clever, he became a man-about-town. His headquarters were the Bar of the Hotel Reforma, residence of big businessmen, film stars, and foreign nobles. You could see him there at all hours of the day. He never seemed to do any work.

Strangely enough, though Northe himself was quite poor and though his post was the lowest in the diplomatic service, he owned a pretty little private plane. He was fond of making trips in his plane. He would go over the weekend to Cuernavaca, which was frequented by Mexican society, and where he would meet a number of German barons, gentlemen such as: Baron von Imhoff, Baron Hermann von Richter. To Acapulco, which was not only an elegant resort but also an interesting harbour; to Tampico and to Vera Cruz. And sometimes he even went as far as the Panama Canal.

Northe did not stay alone very long. Soon the Baron Hans Heinrich von Holleuffer, alias Hans Helbing, was seen regularly in his company. Herr von Holleuffer had embezzled some money in pre-Hitler Germany and had gone to Mexico in 1926. And then, when threatened with extradition, he fled to Guatemala. On his return to Mexico in 1931 he had made a living swindling the German colony by selling bogus stocks. After Hitler came to power he was better off; he did not have to fear extradition because it so happened that the police president of Berlin, Herr von Helldorf, was his brother-in-law. And it so happened that he began getting a regular salary from Berlin which relieved him of the tiresome necessity of swindling the German colony in Mexico.

Herr von Holleuffer worked together with one Paul Garbinski. Garbinski's speciality had been to forge Mexican birth certificates, which brought in no more than a paltry living. He was therefore only too glad to work with von Holleuffer for the Gestapo.

That was not Chismes and that was not Chistes; that was the plain truth.

There were then, in the middle of 1936, three distinct Nazi-inspired movements in Mexico: the first was a kind of fifth-column movement, the kind which Brito Foucher had attempted. It was sponsored by the pro-fascist Chamber of Commerce and the Employers' Association, and provided with Nazi money via the Legation. On 19 June 1936, the Federation of the Middle Class was founded to do the job the Gold Shirts and Foucher's organization had failed to do—including terrorism.

Then there was the Northe-Holleuffer-Garbinski combination which started espionage proper, organized the German residents and the German Mexicans.

And then there was Baron von Merck, whose friendship with Cedillo waxed stronger as the moment neared when he would start an uprising. This faction represented the attempt at absolute control.

Unfortunately for the Federation of Middle Class, the secret police discovered its intentions too soon. The homes of Dr Carmen Calero, an elderly woman physician and of Ovidio Pedrero Valenzuela, president of a fascist organization, were raided. Dynamite and papers implicating Axis diplomats were found. An international scandal threatened. However, at the time Cardenas did not feel secure enough to face such a scandal, and therefore ordered the release of the arrested persons.

During the following years more and more so-called Nazi cultural attachés came to Mexico. They were supposed to aid and supervise Herr von Northe's work of reviving the patriotism of the Germans in Mexico. Even old Collenberg had to lend a hand. All the Germans were forced to give money for the Winterhilfe (German Winter Relief). Levies were made on German firms and the funds sent to the Reich. The Hitler salute was introduced into the German school in Mexico City. Beick, Felix, the biggest German drugstore in Mexico City and Guadalajara, began wrapping parcels in propaganda leaflets. Clerks in many companies were compelled to make the firms' books available to Nazi agents. Worse still, many Germans in Mexico who had no desire to support the Nazi cause were forced to display

Nazi insignia in front of their stores or on their automobiles, thereby compromising themselves.

So the Germans were finally organized. They were not particularly enthusiastic about Hitler but there was not much else they could do. Mexico was full of Nazi agents and more arrived daily.

LORD RUNCIMAN GOES TO PRAGUE

The men of B4, particularly those with long memories, had some odd experiences. Sometimes it seemed to them they were reliving times long past. Only now everything was reversed, topsy-turvy.

They saw that the Germans were imitating the methods the English had applied so well during the First World War. But the Germans were spreading their web of espionage far wider than the British had ever done.

The men of B4 saw German Consulates springing up like mushrooms in all countries, particularly in the small, traditionally neutral countries around Germany. They were not stupid; they knew what that meant. For they had once done the same thing themselves. In Norway, for example, before 1914 the British had stationed their Minister and one consul. But almost immediately after the outbreak of the war, every little Norwegian port had a British consul. Before long there were thirty-three consuls and twenty-five vice-consuls in the country. And each of these consuls and vice-consuls kept an enormous staff.

And now the Germans were doing the same thing, in peacetime. And they were doing it not only in a few neutral countries, but throughout the world. Where the British had had a few hundred men abroad, the Germans had one or two thousand.

During the First World War the British had established commercial firms in various neutral towns to act as a front for the secret service. Shipping lines proved to be the best sort of front. Now the men of B4 saw to their astonishment and dismay that branches of German shipping companies, offices of German railways, and above all, travel bureaus, were springing up all over the world. Travel bureaus were opened even in countries to which no one would care to travel and whose populations were far too poor to take vacation trips to Germany.

B4 knew what was brewing.

There was, however, one consolation. In England itself German espionage had made little real progress. Scotland Yard saw to that; it was a splendid machine and functioned as efficiently as ever. Not that German agents had not attempted to establish themselves in England. One trick, for example, was to work their way into the merchant marine. But every such attempt had been foiled.

The Nazis tried to coerce former Germans who had long been living in England into acting as spies. They concentrated especially on women who had become naturalized through marriage. But Scotland Yard kept close watch, and almost all this blackmail was in vain.

Naturally some agents did get in; that could not be avoided. Most of them appeared under the guise of small merchants, newspaper and tobacco dealers. But their results were pitiful. They were watched too closely.

More serious was the problem of German servant girls. Scotland Yard quickly realized that not all the girls who suddenly began streaming into England from Germany were actually servant girls. Of course, some of them had come to England for honest jobs at better wages. But these were only a small minority of the horde. What disturbed Scotland Yard most was that most of these German servant girls tried to get situations in small ports or in coastal towns near important naval bases, or in towns near aircraft or munitions factories. They observed that these girls preferred situations in the homes of managers of such factories, or naval officers—even at lower pay.

Scotland Yard soon found out that all these servant girls were under the strict supervision of the Nazi Party. They had to pay regular visits to some Party headquarters, where presumably they made reports.

Perhaps the Nazi organizations in England had grown too sure of themselves and therefore became incautious. This appears to be the only explanation of their rash mistake in April 1938, when they issued an appeal to German servant girls to go aboard the ship *William Gustloff*, which was lying in the port of Tilbury, and vote on the annexation of Austria. It was a handsome opportunity for the British to make a census of the Nazi agents posing as servants. The number was more than 14,000....

However, Scotland Yard had already taken active measures. Fräulein Ilse Wolf, the president of the 'Woman's League' (Frauenschaft) in England— that is the head of the entire espionage organization of the servant girls— had been deported.

Another worry of Scotland Yard's was the German commercial planes which regularly landed at Croydon. They could not help observing that these planes came in all kinds of weather, even when they carried only one or two passengers—under circumstances in which other lines would have cancelled the flight to save expense. The British noticed that often the planes arrived by two's or three's rather than singly; sometimes they were filled with men who had alleged business in England, but whose status seemed at best dubious to Scotland Yard. Moreover, these planes took the strangest roundabout routes to arrive at Croydon, flying over parts of England that were nowhere near their destination. But reports on such matters always lay untouched on Chamberlain's desk. Scotland Yard strenuously protested to Chamberlain and finally moved him to speak with the German Ambassador. Lufthansa—the German airline—was reproved and it promised that it would not happen again. But it did happen again and again. Scotland Yard sent in more reports, but Chamberlain took no further action.

Then, in June 1938 came the great blow.

In the Naval Intelligence Department—the Department which had considered the reports of Germany's rearmament so exaggerated—there were many distraught faces. Vital plans had been stolen. Just what plans these were has never been revealed. But it was whispered that they were plans for a new antisubmarine device.

The theft had been committed on board the HMS *Osprey*, which was used by the Admiralty as an antisubmarine training ship. The documents had vanished from the ship's safe. There was a zealous investigation and even a number of arrests, but the arrested persons were innocent and were soon released. And then, suddenly, the plans reappeared, mailed from Edinburgh in an ordinary envelope to the Chief of the Naval Intelligence Department.

About this time the IS suffered a second shock. Once more the sorely tried Foreign Office Intelligence Department was faced with an inexplicable *fait accompli*. This had to do with Lord Runciman's trip to Czechoslovakia.

This trip had been arranged by Chamberlain and a few of his intimate co-workers, and discussed with no one—except, of course, some members of the Cliveden set. During July Captain Fritz Wiedemann, an obscure personage—obscure at least to the Intelligence Service—had called on Chamberlain and proposed the trip. Not even the British Government's ally, France, was informed. Even Sir Robert Vansittart learned of the plan only a few days before Lord Runciman's departure.

Such a trip was a complete reversal of the Eden-Vansittart position; moreover, it was the kind of foreign policy which the reports of the Foreign Office Intelligence Department had exposed as criminally unrealistic.

Vansittart knew very well that Runciman's mission was to persuade the Czechs to surrender. The moment he heard of the projected trip he realized that Czechoslovakia was doomed. But he also realized that the terms of the surrender would depend on Berlin's conception of how far England was willing to go. Obviously, Berlin must not know that Lord Runciman was prepared to give way on every point. His mission had to be made as mysterious as possible, and no hint of his real intention must get out. Hence Sir Robert suggested to Chamberlain that a large number of intelligence men accompany Lord Runciman.

Chamberlain asked Vansittart for a list of the men he would like to have accompany Runciman, and cut it by half. He told the horrified Vansittart that the Germans might take it amiss if Lord Runciman brought in a troop of British agents.

As Vansittart's few agents in Prague soon found out, the Germans had no such qualms of tact. Prague was swarming with German agents. Some of them had arrived in Prague long before Vansittart had heard of the projected journey. Among these German agents were two specialists in the installation of microphones for radio and telephone transmission. One of these two men, a Dr K., who travelled on a British passport and passed himself off as a tourist, took a suite of rooms in the Hotel Alcorn, where Runciman was to stay. The hotel management was more than helpful because—ironically enough—it assumed that he was an agent of the British Intelligence Service. It was only by chance that Vansittart's agents spotted Dr K. and removed the microphones he had installed in Lord Runciman's suite before they could do any damage.

But the British Intelligence men failed completely in one respect. They could not keep Lord Runciman from talking. Berlin really need not have sent any agents to Prague. It was quite superfluous to have installed microphones and placed spies among the hotel personnel. Lord Runciman had no secrets. On his weekend visits to Slovak industrialists and Czech magnates whom the Germans had bought, Runciman took none of Vansittart's agents along. And he spoke quite freely to his hosts. Indirectly, Berlin learned from Runciman himself that Chamberlain was ready to sacrifice Czechoslovakia.

Vansittart's agents returned to London knowing they had been defeated. What made the defeat all the more bitter to them and to the whole Intelligence Service was the fact that they had been beaten not by an enemy espionage organization, but by their own government.

THE CASE OF THE GERMAN TANKS

On 17 September 1938, Colonel Gauché and his officers of the *Deuxième Bureau* had the shock of their lives; that was three days after Adolf Hitler's celebrated Nüremberg speech demanding the right of self-determination for the Sudeten Germans.

On this very day a former high officer of the German Army had sent information to Paris that the German Army was concentrating troops near the Czech frontier. Twenty-four hours later the *Deuxième Bureau's* agents in Czechoslovakia confirmed the report.

Still the War Ministry was unconcerned. The general staff also felt that Hitler was merely bluffing. He would not risk a war then. After all, his tanks were poor; they had it on the authority of Saverne's reports, those reports which had furnished the *Deuxième Bureau* with such excellent information on German tanks.

And then things began to happen. There was the ultimatum of Henlein, the leader of the Sudeten Germans, to the government in Prague; there was Chamberlain's flight to Berchtesgaden, and his conference with Hitler on 17 September.

And then there were some new reports from Saverne....

On Saturday, 12 March 1938, two men had succeeded in evading arrest, slipping through the fingers of the uprising Austrian Nazis and the already invading German troops; they escaped over the Austrian border into Switzerland. Half an hour later they would have been lost. They left their office on a moment's notice, nor did they go to their homes where the secret police were already waiting for them. In a car belonging to one of them they drove out of Vienna, then they took a bus, exchanged it for a train, changed trains twice, found themselves at one time in a train trapped at a railway station on account of the innumerable troop transports moving in from Germany. While the train was being searched by the Gestapo, they made their getaway across the tracks. The last eight miles to the Swiss frontier they had to walk, or rather run, through woods and fields.

One of them was Waldemar Pabst,[24] the other Werner Grund. Pabst was a native German; Grund was Austrian. And both were violent anti-Nazis. Pabst, about fifty years old, had been a member of the Free Corps and connected with the reactionary German Nationalist Party before he came to Vienna. Here he became an officer of the Heimwehr, the private army of Prince Starhemberg. Grund, seven years younger, had been private secretary to Baron Stuckly, publicity director of the Heimwehr; besides, he was manager of the first and only Austrian gas mask factory.

Among those who, like Pabst and Grund, preferred to skip the country while Hitler marched into Vienna, was not included the Freiherr von Ketteler.[25] Why should he run away? He was an attaché to the German Legation in Vienna. He was one of the closest friends of the German Minister, Franz von Papen. It would have caused some remark if he disappeared at the dawn of the great German victory.

Still, it might have been healthy for him. He was last seen on Monday, 14 March. He left the Legation at 6:30 p.m. He never arrived at his home. Three weeks later his body was fished out of the Danube. His death was considered a great mystery. Some people thought it an act of revenge by Austrian patriots. Strangely enough, however, the German authorities never played up von Ketteler's death and let it be forgotten.

They had good reason for this. Because they themselves had murdered von Ketteler. Or perhaps, one should say, executed. Spies in the service of foreign powers are executed by the Nazis even in peacetime.

Neither Pabst nor Grund had heard of von Ketteler, or of his activities. Upon their arrival on Swiss soil, they proceeded to Basle. That same evening they were visited by a man who was the owner of a fur business which had dealings all over the Continent. They had a long talk with the furrier. Pabst said that he still maintained close relations with Army comrades in Germany who were now in high positions. Grund had equally good connections.

A few hours after this conversation the furrier sent a long letter to a business friend in Paris. He wrote elaborately about furs, new prices, and new fashions.

This letter was delivered an hour after its arrival in Paris to the *Deuxième Bureau*. It was decided to take Pabst and Grund on for a trial period.

If Pabst and Grund had known the true activities of Freiherr von Ketteler and his sudden death, they might have been more chary of offering their services. Because Freiherr von Ketteler, intimate friend and collaborator of the German Minister in Vienna, for some time had been an agent of the *Deuxième Bureau*.

With an agent right in the German Legation, the *Deuxième Bureau* should not have been surprised when Hitler marched into Austria. It did not come as a bolt from the blue. As early as two months before, on 8 January, Ketteler had informed Paris that Hitler would march. One day later the same tip came from the Foreign Office Intelligence Department in London. During the following weeks other agents had sent in alarming reports. On 12 February, the day Schuschnigg went to Berchtesgaden, Ketteler warned again. On the night of 9 March, an agent in Munich reported to the branch office of Muehlhausen (near Basle) that Hitler was planning to strike before Schuschnigg could go through with his plebiscite—then three days away. Two days later, at noon on 11 March, Paris again was informed via Muehlhausen that motorized German troops stationed in Bavaria had left for the Austrian frontier.

The *Deuxième Bureau*, then, was very well informed. The government, however, and especially Premier Chautemps, chose to dismiss the information. He preferred to trust the reports of his Minister, Puaux, in Vienna, who retained his naive optimism up to the day before the Germans marched. It was only then that he scented something in the air. He then wired: '*C'est le coup du 7 Mars qui recommence.*' On 7 March 1936, Hitler had marched into the Rhineland. What the French diplomat meant was that he had at last discovered that Hitler was marching again. But then it was too late. Even if something could still have been done, it could not have been done by the French government, for the simple reason that there was no French government.

After many days of deliberation, on Thursday, 10 March, Chautemps had decided to resign. This was just twenty-four hours before Puaux's wire, and the very time that the press chief of the Czech government arrived in Paris to discuss emergency measures. There was nobody for him to talk to.

The whole world looked on in horror at what was happening in Austria. But Paris had been absorbed in its own government crisis. Aside from that, there were lots of other things to interest and amuse the Parisians. There were the Moscow trials. On the Champs Élysées the latest Garbo picture, *Maria Walewska*, was opening before a packed house. In the Salle Pleyel, the Wiener Sängerknaben were giving a concert. When in the midst of it came news that Hitler had marched into Austria, the choir boys, with tears in their eyes, began to sing the Marseillaise.

There were a few incidents in the following days. Some young men drove out to the grave of Aristide Briand, the great French liberal who had tried so zealously to collaborate with the democratic German Republic. On the tomb they placed a wreath with the swastika and an ironic inscription. It read: 'To Aristide Briand—from a grateful Adolf Hitler.'

They were arrested.

Marcel Saverne was providing the *Deuxième Bureau* with interesting material.

Marcel Saverne—that was Werner Grund, who lived under this name and possessed a French passport. He sent in his and his friend's reports.

The material dealt with the progress of German rearmament. During the first few weeks the *Deuxième Bureau* followed its usual course with new agents: it checked up, comparing their information with that sent in by other agents. It was soon found out that Saverne was extremely reliable and was working faster than other agents. Most important, the difficulties were mounting; the old agents could hardly get any kind of line on the German rearmament programme, and, one after another, hunted down by the Gestapo and cut off from their channels of news, they ceased to be heard from. But Saverne kept on sending in material. Pabst and Grund had not lied when they assured the *Deuxième Bureau* that they had very good connections.

There was still another reason which made their material so pleasing to the General Staff and the War Ministry. It was consoling. Highly placed French officers allowed themselves to smile when Göring and Goebbels made big speeches about the invincible German rearmament. They knew better. They knew it was just bluff.

'We must not let ourselves be hypnotized by Hitler,' someone in the French War Ministry remarked. This sentence was repeated over and over again in the *Deuxième Bureau*.

Saverne sent marvellous material about the poor quality of German tanks. During July 1938 he forwarded long reports about war manoeuvres that had taken place in the Black Forest. He stated that the German military experts themselves were appalled at the inferior quality of their tanks. Saverne even sent photographs that he had got from one of his old army friends. They showed tanks sunk into mud and evidently unable to get out.

The whole War Ministry was delighted with these pictures. 'The Nazis won't be able to start a war with tanks like that,' they said. There had been, of course, other information along such lines. There had been the experience of the Spanish Civil War. In Spain the Germans had used mostly six-ton tanks with a two-man crew, armoured with .3 to .6 inch plate, and with two machine guns mounted in turrets. Such armour plate was, of course, no match for the French standard 25 mm anti-tank gun. Such tanks, despite their speed of thirty miles an hour, could not possibly harm the mighty Maginot Line. There were ample reports, too, of the many accidents that had overtaken German tanks when they rolled through Austria. The main roads had been blocked for hours. The *Deuxième Bureau* had received detailed reports from many agents on this point. Oddly enough, the agents needn't have bothered ferreting and spying; only two days after their reports came in, the newspapers of the world reported the same disasters and breakdowns. Two or three men in the *Deuxième Bureau* wondered that the Nazis let such an incriminating story get out. But it was too pretty a story to spoil with worrying.

It was admitted in Paris that the Germans had excellent anti-aircraft guns and fighter planes, but no bombers and no tanks to speak of. 'In a way, all they'll be able to do is defend themselves,' it was said. 'They'll have to use their tanks for scrap iron. They'll have to build fifteen hundred or two thousand new tanks. That should take eighteen months. Who knows if Hitler will still be in power then?'

To understand the great joy of the highly placed officers at the inferiority of the German tanks, it must be remembered that the tank question had been a sore point with French army officers for a long time. And this is where Charles de Gaulle comes in.[26]

He had fought in the First World War as a lieutenant; he had been wounded three times; as prisoner of war he made many daring attempts to escape. Later on, his rise in the army was rapid. He was the right-hand man of General Pétain, the Commander-in-Chief of the French Army until his retirement in 1927. Later he entered the General Staff. Even at that time his unorthodox ideas about modern warfare created resentment among his colleagues. And after he had published a book, in 1934, *Vers l'Armée de Metier* ('Towards a Professional Army') General Weygand, Pétain's successor, was so disgusted with De Gaulle's views that he delegated a certain officer to rebuke him openly in a military magazine. In this book, De Gaulle wrote:

Tomorrow an army of professionals will advance on wheels. Not a single man, gun, shell, or loaf of bread will be carried by a man on foot.... A great unit will break camp at sunrise, to encamp in the evening a hundred and fifty miles away....

Only a few hundred experts read the book. One of them was a young member of the Chamber of Deputies, Paul Reynaud, who used it as the basis for a bill he proposed in May 1938 to establish motorized divisions. The bill was defeated. De Gaulle defended his views. He gave a lecture at the Sorbonne in 1937, which provoked a general riot at the university. For this he was removed from the General Staff, demoted, and sent to Metz.

Early in the summer of 1938 the *Deuxième Bureau* received another offer from the furrier in Basle. It concerned a former German officer, of a famous noble family. This former officer was on extremely good terms with Göring, was supposed to be one of his intimate friends. Adolf Hitler, too, seemed to be well disposed toward him; according to the furrier, what the Nazis didn't know was that the former officer was a monarchist at heart and a foe of the Nazi regime, especially since Hitler had assassinated General von Schleicher during the blood purge of June 1934. The man in Basle had reason to believe that this man would be inclined to play ball with the French.

Colonel Gauché had his doubts at first, but he thought it a shame to surrender such a chance. Of course, certain details would have to be cleared up. Exactly what position within the Nazi regime did the former officer hold? How far did his influence reach? How much was he in the know?

After some communication back and forth, the former officer was given a test to prove whether he really commanded the influence he boasted of. The name of a prominent German democratic politician who was being held at the concentration camp of Dachau was given him, and he was asked to arrange for the man's release. Twenty-four hours later the man was free to leave Germany.

From August 1938 on, this ex-officer sent in regular reports. These, too, were not frightening, their burden being that the old guard of the army wasn't happy about all the developments under Hitler. They complained there were not enough good officers to train a large army based on compulsory military service.

And then came the shock of 17 September.

Since 10 September, the reports of the former high officer, Göring's bosom friend, had suddenly taken an alarming turn. Now he spoke of huge concentrations near the Czech frontier. And then there came the strange visit of a high French officer to the private office of Colonel Gauché.

Later it was said that this officer was Charles de Gaulle. It is true that de Gaulle happened to be in Paris on this very day. However, he was far too retiring and devoid of personal ambition to come to the *Deuxième Bureau* without having been summoned. The man who did come was, however, one of his close friends and followers. He said he wanted some information on German tanks.

Gauché showed him some of the Saverne reports and as a climax the pictures of the tanks stuck in the mud. The officer looked at them and frowned. 'I think these pictures are fake,' he said. He took a photo showing a tank, surrounded by soldiers struggling to get it out of the mud. The background of the picture showed not a house nor a tree nor a stone. 'I wonder where the mud came from,' the officer said. And then he added:

> I know something about photography. Do you see these little irregularities here? I think that mud was drawn in by a retoucher's air-brush. And look at the faces of the soldiers. For men supposed to be straining every muscle, they look strangely relaxed.

He put the photo aside. 'But suppose, gentlemen, these photos are not faked. Suppose this tank did get stuck. Suppose dozens of German tanks get stuck. What does it prove? It doesn't prove that tanks are useless.'

The point was driven home. Colonel Gauché and his colleagues were properly impressed with what they learned. For on that very 17 September, report after report came in, each more alarming than the last. Göring's 'friend' transmitted the information that there was not the slightest doubt that Hitler would march. And Saverne, the same. His reports sounded more panicky, if possible.

Chamberlain flew back to London. Terrifying and nervous dispatches poured hourly into the *Deuxième Bureau*. On 18 September, at eleven in the morning, the German officer sent in a message reproducing a marching order for 1 October, signed by Hitler. Saverne spoke of mobilization. The *Deuxième Bureau* no longer had the slightest doubt that Hitler would march.

In the War Ministry they still didn't grasp the gravity of the situation. So Colonel Gauché went to the War Ministry and had a long talk with Daladier. No one else was present.

And then, the next day, Daladier and Bonnet flew to London. And some days later, on 29 September, Paris read in its afternoon newspapers: 'At 4:30 p.m. there will be a conference between Hitler and Mussolini, Daladier and Chamberlain in Munich.'

It was cold and rainy that day in Paris. Everybody was nervous. Most people didn't even know what the Sudetenland was. Newspapers were torn out of the hands of the newsboys.

PEACE, the newspapers cried, in the biggest block letters in their fonts. Paris was crazy with joy. Daladier's return was like the triumphal parade of a general who had won a war. Hundreds of thousands were out in the streets embracing total strangers.

It was only late in November that the reports of one of the London War Office Intelligence Department operatives arrived, a man who had through desperate feats succeeded in getting into the Siegfried Line, the same Siegfried Line which had had such a decisive influence on the Munich conversations.

The report created a sensation in the venerable quarters of the SIS as well as in the offices of B4, near the Admiralty Arch. Had it been published then it might even have aroused a revolution. However, it was not read by more than a dozen people. To this day not more than a hundred people know of it.

The report indicated that the Siegfried Line had basic weaknesses which would make it not too difficult to break through; also it had been flooded in many parts, and a great many of the underground fortresses had had to be abandoned for good even after the water was pumped out. There were long descriptions of the faulty construction of the underground hangars. As to the fortified mountains—the Siegfried Line was intended as fortified landscape rather than a line—they were hardly adequate and the Germans were already rushing guns from the Czech border defences into the Hundsrueck Mountains. Finally there was a whole list of sabotage acts including such items as the use of faulty cement which would have to come out, at a great loss of time to the Germans.

So much for the Siegfried Line.

Three days before Christmas, in 1938, one of the most valuable agents of the *Deuxième Bureau* was arrested in Berlin. This arrest utterly confounded the *Deuxième Bureau*. How was it possible? The man, a Greek, had never done any work in Germany. As a matter of fact, he had been away from Europe for a long time; his field, since 1928, had been South America. This man would never have made a mistake. He was an old hand at the game. Moreover, he had not associated with any of the other agents. He had been in Berlin for only three days.

The *Deuxième Bureau* checked and rechecked. But nothing could be found out. Then there was another arrest which, though not as sensational, was annoying. The man in question was the owner of a little shop in a small town near the Franco-German border. He made good money through his partnership with a gang of professional smugglers who worked this part of the frontier. And that in turn had made him an extremely valuable courier for the *Deuxième Bureau*. In fact he was so valuable, dependable, and prompt that he was used only in cases of extreme urgency or importance. Very few agents had ever had his address.

Again the *Deuxième Bureau* checked. Yes, the Greek from South America had sent his reports through this man. Who else? There were four agents who had been allowed to work through the channel, and one of them was now in Africa, the second one in Argentina. The third was the Greek and the fourth was the former German officer who had been the source of so much valuable information. He was now watched carefully for some time. And then the case broke surprisingly fast. Yes, he was indeed an intimate friend of Göring's and many other high Nazis. In fact, he was working for the German Secret Service. He was none other than a Nazi who had been planted with great skill in the *Deuxième Bureau*.

The case of Messrs Pabst and Grund was slightly different. They, too, had been tools of the German Secret Service, but they had not known it. They believed until shortly before the war that they were working against the Nazis, while they were working for the Nazis all the time.

To arrange this had been easy enough. Berlin knew that the *Deuxième Bureau* tried out its new agents before taking them on permanently. In the case of the two men from Vienna, as indeed in many other cases, Berlin did not interfere for a long time with their work. For some months they were allowed to find out whatever they could. Then, after the *Deuxième Bureau* was quite certain of their integrity, Berlin started feeding them precisely the information that the *Deuxième Bureau* was supposed to get.

The most important item they were supposed to report, and which they did report faithfully, was the inferior quality of the German tanks.

What was grotesque about the whole situation was not so much that the Nazis had deceived the *Deuxième Bureau*. But that the *Deuxième Bureau* could have got enough and to spare of information had it read—the German military press.

Early in January 1936, *Deutsche Wehr*, a German military publication, had spoken of an army with a wartime strength of 300 divisions. Taking into account the consumption of fuel, it was possible to maintain for such an army 10,000 tanks and an equal number of warplanes. Other German military publications listed all the types of German planes and their characteristics, including those models not yet in mass production. Germany's military literature frankly discussed all problems of strategy and tactics ... the use of tanks and the *Luftwaffe*, offensive and defensive operations, staff work, military organization of various arms. No military literature had ever described a future war with such thoroughness as did the German magazines between 1932 and 1939. Military literature therefore became an essential source of military information.

The Allies could have learned anything they pleased about German armament. Available in the German military publications was the whole system of German total warfare and accurate statistics on German war strength. The only types of weapon which were not described were the medium and heavy tanks. But there was no doubt that the Third. Reich could and would build them, for the military press constantly emphasized their importance and predicted that they would be used.

The military press even described the general plan of the German offensive. The Chief of Staff of the German Armoured Corps wrote in the organ of the German General Staff, *Militaerwissenschaftliche Rundschau* (*Military Science Review*) an analysis of the coming German invasion which was an exact prediction of what took place in the Battle of Flanders. The Anglo-French Intelligence Service in Germany need only have collected additional information to fill in certain gaps.

But no one cared to look. No responsible authority in England or France paid any attention to the Germans' own account of German rearmament. Perhaps the German figures were considered unreliable; for this so-called reason the whole mine of precious material went unworked.

You might call it conservatism in thinking. There are other names for it, too.

PART III
Peace in Our Time

HESS, THE ORGANIZER

After Hitler's seizure of power, Rudolf Hess had returned to obscurity. Once more he was the man in the shadow, the man with no actual position or function. So it seemed, at least, to outsiders. He was not even a member of the Government. Not until 1934 was he granted the position of Minister without Portfolio. A minor post compared to those which Göring, Goebbels, Himmler, Ley, and others occupied....

It is strange that no one was struck by the insignificance of Nazi Number 2. His role was almost ostentatiously modest. Had anyone taken pains to investigate, he might have found a clue to the true situation. This clue was a circular letter which early in 1934 was sent out to all groups, branches, and strategic points of the Party located outside Germany.

This circular mentioned 'the solemn swearing in of all political leaders of the NSDAP (National Socialist Party) by the Deputy of the Führer, Rudolf Hess....'

Had one followed Rudolf Hess's activities during the first few months of the Hitler regime, one would have seen him sitting at many interesting conferences with Goebbels, Himmler, Schacht, General von Epp, and others. Some of these meetings were mentioned in the Party press, but their purpose was carefully concealed.

At that time Hess was organizing a body which by the end of 1934 had become enormously important to the Third Reich. This body was the 'Liaison Staff' (*Verbindungsstab*).

Hess also had many conversations with people from abroad, some from South and North America, some from Australia and Japan. And then all was in readiness. Now there existed the framework for the gigantic organization Hess intended to erect. It was the kind of organization which Colonel Nicolai in his most ambitious moments might have dreamed of, but without illusions that it would ever come true. Here was the organization which could undertake espionage on a monumental scale. This organization, whose head was the Liaison Staff, had three basic principles:

Everyone can spy.
Everyone must spy.
Everything can be found out.
Total espionage was ready to begin functioning.

Total espionage—it had been thought out and organized by that colourless, insignificant young man who was so much in the background. Organized by this same Rudolf Hess who had been around a good deal, who had done much to bring the Party to the seat of power, and who during all the years of struggle for power in Germany was thinking not of Germany but of the whole world.

This man in the shadow was greater than those who scrambled to get into the spotlight. Compared to his concept of conspiracy, the intrigues of Dr Goebbels seem silly games. Compared to his concept of world conquest, the soldier of the Third Reich, Hermann Göring, seems like a noisy subaltern. Hess was the romantic of the movement, the visionary. He was the only really great adventurer of the Nazi Party.

It is no matter of chance that he concentrated on espionage. With the profound instinct of a certain type of genius, he recognized—probably without ever being conscious of it—that the truest expression of this movement of racketeers, gangsters, criminals, and degenerates lay in the realm of espionage. In espionage so complete, so total, that the inhabitants of this globe would have no secrets from it; espionage that would tear away the last veils from all private life.

The plans and victories of Rudolf Hess cannot be understood without knowing something of his teacher, adviser, and friend: Karl Haushofer,[1] born in Munich in 1869, became a professional army officer. During the First World War he was promoted to the rank of general.

Even before 1914 he had undertaken some scientific studies, and later he lectured at the Munich University. He was one of the founders of the 'Geo-political School'—a school of German political economists and geographers who before the First World War had come to the conclusion that geography had a decisive influence upon politics, that a country's development depended on landscape, climate, etc. These political theorists maintained that the development of a country was not so much the result of accidental political factors as of the natural resources, raw materials, opportunities for expansion. Foreign policy did not determine the history of a country, but the land itself determined the foreign policy and hence the history.

Ludendorff was one of the first to take notice of Haushofer and his theories. And when, in 1918, General Haushofer retired to devote himself entirely to scientific matters, the *Reichswehr* remained in close touch with him. Every so often the scholar sent *Reichswehr* leaders 'confidential reports on the world situation.' In addition Haushofer wrote a *Guide to Geo-political Instruction for General Staff Officers.*

In 1925, Rudolf Hess came to the Geo-political Institute with a letter of recommendation. He came because he needed some kind of job to earn his bread. But before long the ageing professor and the young man became close friends, and this friendship was to prove fateful for both of them.

Hess was so overwhelmed by Haushofer's ideas that he introduced the professor to Hitler at the first opportunity. Hitler was also impressed, but not so Haushofer. Haushofer could not bring himself to take this so-called Führer seriously. In his book, *The National Socialist Idea in the World* the only Nazi he mentions by name is Rudolf Hess. This book, incidentally, came close to being banned by the Party because it maintained that National Socialism must be spread over the entire world.

Rudolf Hess worked in the Geo-political Institute for several years. The Professor assigned him Japan as a field of study, and Hess plunged into the work with great eagerness. Haushofer had always been especially interested in Japan and East Asia. Before the First World War he had travelled a great deal in those regions. He was among the large number of Pan-Germans who had always clamoured for an alliance with Japan. He believed that by the nature of its geo-political situation Japan must expand, and that it would eventually control all East Asia. It was painfully disappointing to him when Japan joined the Allies during the First World War.

Perhaps Haushofer was surprised when Hess limited his general subject, 'Japan,' to 'Japan and Espionage.' But if he knew his pupil, he was not surprised.

Rudolf Hess's paper on Japanese espionage was written over a period of two years, from 1927 to 1929. During this period he put in more than ten months of actual work on the paper. There were 132 typewritten pages, or about 40,000 words of manuscript. As late as 1934 people who had some connections in the Geopolitical Institute were permitted to look through the work. By the autumn of 1936 this was no longer possible.

The paper was divided into three sections: (1) History of Japanese Espionage, (2) Espionage on a Mass Basis, (3) The Objectives of Japanese Espionage.

If in 1935 or 1936 Hess's paper had come to the attention of Sir Robert Vansittart or of some other of the more alert members of the British Intelligence Service, many events might have turned out differently. Those who have glanced through the Hess paper are convinced that Hess was decisively influenced by what he had studied of Japanese espionage.

According to Hess, Japanese espionage had its origins about eighty years ago.

Perry had forced the Japanese to open their ports to foreign trade, and Japan opened its mind to Western civilization; the Nipponese Government then sent countless diplomatic, trade, and naval missions to Europe. For half a century these missions gathered precious information in Europe, and in America as well. The Japanese also sent engineers, trained men who pretended to come in search of training and who were, therefore, let into the great engineering works and arsenals of the Old and New Worlds. Manufacturers paid a price for trading with Japan; they had to agree to hire a few Japanese engineers or workers.

Economic and industrial espionage was practised by delegations, tourists, and students.

Japanese naval and military espionage did not begin along systematic lines until the end of the last century. At that time it concentrated chiefly on China and Russia, and paid only slight attention to Canada and the United States. Japanese imperialism developed soon after the modernization of Japan and inspired the Russo-Japanese War, the occupation of Korea, the Twenty-one Demands on China during the World War, the Shantung affair, and the Japanese invasion of Eastern Siberia during and after 1918. During the past ten years it has followed in Manchuria and China the course laid down in the notorious Tanaka Memorial of 1927. (This paper, which takes its name from the former Japanese Premier, Baron Tanaka, envisaged the conquest by Japan of the Siberian Maritime Provinces, Manchuria, China, and all the areas bordering on the Pacific Ocean, and ultimately Japanese domination of India, the rest of Asia, and Europe.) This document was worked out by the army, the navy, and the Foreign Office, and was presented to the Emperor, who gave it his seal of approval. Agents of the Russian Intelligence Service obtained a copy, which they had published in the United States, rather than in Russia, to throw the Japanese off the track.

As to the objects of Japanese espionage, Rudolf Hess presented the following general picture:

The Japanese, he said, pried not only into secrets of military value, but into industrial, economic, political, and cultural affairs of foreign nations. Much of the information the Japanese espionage services collected was not espionage in the strictest sense.

Japanese military espionage, he wrote, was interested in anything directly or indirectly relating to disposition, equipment, training, and organization of the armed forces of all countries that border on the Pacific and Indian oceans. Blueprints, descriptions of ships and aircrafts, gas masks and naval bases, battleships and bombsights—all were grist to their mill. They sought information on the location of factories and on the technique of production of military equipment.

They studied the development of coastal defences in all Pacific regions, and try to learn the location of air and naval bases, particularly American bases.

According to Hess, the Japanese were always on the alert for information about military and naval conferences or plans and manoeuvres. Movements of ships in the Pacific area—in fact, of any naval vessels, belonging to the United States, England, or Russia—were followed.

Hess summarized: Any military and naval information such as the number, disposition, training, experience, and leadership of men, or the existence of bases, strategic roads, and airports, was the object of Japanese military espionage. Moreover, it studied personal habits and weaknesses of responsible officers in the armed forces or important persons in the industrial defence effort. Japanese spies drew up maps of communications; they would study the output and supply of an aircraft plant, for example, and would seek to determine what plants supply this aircraft plant with parts, over what routes these parts are shipped, and whether there are alternate routes. Such data were necessary if they were to know where a bomb would be most effective.

The heavy industry of the United States and of Russia was of special interest to Japanese espionage, since the waging of war depended on its industrial base. Japanese agents had worked out charts of the entire organization of heavy industry, indicating on these charts present or future expansion.

In the diplomatic field, the Japanese were always looking for secret agreements and confidential consular reports. They had long suspected that the United States and Great Britain had secret agreements regarding the use of bases in the Far East against Japan.

Hess goes on to make a point which had far-reaching results for the German espionage service:

Social and political discontent produces individuals who can be bribed to act against the interests of their own country. Such discontent was very strong in Asiatic nations under white domination, and the Japanese had long utilized such disaffection for their own purposes.

Japan was at this time (Russia was still building up her Far Eastern Army) more interested in Russia's defences in the Far East than she was in the United States. This was because Eastern Siberia is part of her *lebensraum*; moreover, the Russian forces there constituted a definite threat to the security of Japan. However, it was much more difficult for the Japanese to secure information about Siberia than about the United States.

Most interesting of all, however, was what Hess had to say about espionage on a mass basis:

Espionage was almost second nature to the Japanese. For generations they had had an internal system of mass espionage; they spied on each other and neighbour reported neighbour to the police. The Japanese system compared favourably with the efficiency of the Cheka system in internal Russian affairs. The Japanese governments had always treated their people like children, and since the days of the Shogunate had used plain-clothes detectives and voluntary or impressed informers to keep watch over the people. By now, spying was so ingrained into the Japanese that they pursued it whenever the opportunity offered, particularly when travelling abroad. The Japanese were intensely patriotic and were eager for opportunities to serve their country. One of their favourite contributions to their country was the espionage work they did while abroad, whether as travellers or permanent residents.

That is, he continued, not every Japanese abroad was a trained spy, or an agent of the Japanese Intelligence Service; nor did every Japanese travel abroad in order to spy. But whenever a Japanese did have the chance to do a little spying, he did it, and passed his information on to a Japanese consul or to the home police on his return. The Japanese tourist was seldom without his camera, and if there was an opportunity to photograph a warship, a naval base, or anything else he thought the Japanese Intelligence Service might admire, he would take the picture, often quite publicly. Such pictures could not be taken in Japan, of course, and he generally thought the foreign authorities very stupid for giving him so many chances.

Japanese travellers were keen observers, but they suffered from a deplorable lack of judgment. As a result they collected a great deal of information, and much misinformation which—usually carefully noted down in travel diaries—eventually found its way into the files of the Intelligence Services.

Probably the most efficient amateur spies were the Japanese residents abroad. Whatever valuable information they laid their hands on was promptly reported to the Japanese Consulate. In order to get information, many of them would speak ill of their native land and pretend to agree with a foreigner's unfavourable opinion of Japan. However, Japanese who really did not think well of the country of their birth were extremely rare.

By long tradition, a spy who is caught is denounced by the country that employs him. Japanese diplomatic and consular representatives, however, attempted to protect their agents. They would make indignant protests and put up bail for their spies, although this was tantamount to an admission of complicity in espionage.

The reports of Japanese agents, amateur and professional, were sent to Japan in a number of ways: (1) through consulates, thence by courier to the embassies, and thence to Japan, (2) through secret emissaries on 'inspection trips' from Japan, (3) through the captains of Japanese ships.

Because of the extreme difficulty of the Japanese language, Japanese agents enjoy a considerable measure of protection against eavesdroppers. In keeping notes they are quite safe, for Japanese script is a kind of national code.

The Intelligence Service of the army and navy and the Information Bureau of the Foreign Office in Tokyo collected all this information, studied, classified, and cross-indexed it, and submitted it to staff officers. These staff officers also sent out instructions to the agents abroad. Foreigners in the employ of Japanese agents had no direct contact with Tokyo.

The consulates and embassies also sent in a vast amount of information collected from Japanese firms abroad and from foreign agents. Whenever a Japanese citizen returned from abroad, he paid a 'courtesy call' at the Foreign Office. Here he was given plenty of time to discuss his impressions and any special information he might have or think he had.

Such were the findings of Rudolf Hess.

This was espionage on a mass basis.

Shortly after Hitler came to power he gave Haushofer unlimited funds to expand his Institute—probably at the instigation of Hess. The expansion was very rapid, and before long Haushofer had more than a thousand research workers in Germany and abroad—students, historians, economic statisticians. Significant material covering the political, financial, and economic structure of foreign countries was systematically collected abroad and sent to the Institute. Haushofer and his associates sifted, collated, and interpreted. When they were finished, they had a series of X-ray pictures of all the countries in the world.

Professor Haushofer's Institute became a laboratory for the science of conquest. The professor kept a strict check on his 'spies' abroad, and he worked them hard. They were supposed to be objective observers, simply studying conditions. They were given strict instructions to avoid passing themselves off either as anti-Nazis or pro-Nazis; and they were forbidden to carry on any sort of propaganda.

Professor Haushofer's analyses of individual countries were complete to the minutest detail. For example, a geo-political study of a country devoted a great deal of space to the question of minorities; how the attacker might utilize the discontent of such minorities. Not only the geographical vulnerability of a country was discussed. Haushofer and his men examined what kind of people, what professions, and what economic and social classes would be most likely to betray their country for mercenary or other reasons.

During the following years Hess and Haushofer remained in close touch. All of Haushofer's final reports were transmitted to Hess before they reached Hitler or the General Staff. There is no doubt that almost the whole pattern of Hitler's expansionist policy had been blueprinted by Haushofer and Hess long before the opportunity came to act upon it.

Haushofer's conversations with his former student were no more nor less than war games in peacetime. In the peace in our time.

They established the scientific bases for total espionage.

The set-up of total espionage, which began to function toward the latter part of 1934 and which reached its top efficiency by the middle of 1937, was as follows:

1. The Intelligence Service of the War Ministry, unofficially and later officially directed by Colonel Nicolai.
2. The Organization of Germans Living Abroad, directed by Ernst Wilhelm Bohle.
3. The Foreign Department of the Gestapo under Heinrich Himmler and Reinhard Heydrich.
4. The Foreign Political Office, headed by Alfred Rosenberg.
5. The Special Service of the Foreign Office, which did not begin to function properly until Ribbentrop replaced the too-conservative Neurath. Lieutenant Captain Canaris was Ribbentrop's right-hand man.
6. The Foreign Department of the Propaganda Ministry, under Joseph Goebbels and Hermann Esser.
7. The Foreign Department of the Ministry of Economics and Finance, which continued to be headed by Hjalmar Schacht even after his official retirement.
8. The Reich Colonial Office, directed by General von Epp.

All these authorities were subordinate to the Liaison Staff. Three representatives of the War Ministry were always included in the Liaison Staff, with authority to examine all material that might have military value. Two of these officers were changed annually; the third was Nicolai himself.

Aside from these three, the Liaison Staff also comprised: Goebbels, Ribbentrop (since 1936), Alfred Rosenberg, Ernst Wilhelm Bohle (since late 1935), Hanns Oberlindober, Otto Abetz, Robert Ley, Philip Bouhler, and Martin Ludwig Bormann. Hess, the founder of the Liaison Staff, was Chairman.

The Liaison Staff was the nerve centre of the whole espionage system, its brain-trust. It issued all general directives; all the foreign organizations of the Party and of the separate ministries were subordinate to it. This was true, in fact, of the whole administrative machine, within Germany as well.

The only exception was the War Ministry, which to some extent enjoyed freedom of action. It was, however, charged with keeping the Liaison Staff informed, and the Liaison Staff in turn had to keep the War Ministry informed. All the confidential reports of the Liaison Staff were turned over to Professor Haushofer for examination and analysis.

The Liaison Staff was more than a brains-trust. It also operated as a kind of mediation board for eliminating friction and settling differences between the various authorities, especially those with foreign departments. There were frequent disagreements and much jealousy, particularly between Himmler and Goebbels. Each was contemptuous of the foreign activities (i.e., espionage) of the other, and each man tried to snatch missions and triumphs away from the other's organization.

Himmler was in a particularly difficult situation because his Gestapo abroad was charged not only with certain special tasks, but with the supervision of all who worked for the other foreign departments.

Finally, there were frequent disputes between Rosenberg and Bohle. Ribbentrop supported Bohle, for Rosenberg had always been an uncomfortable rival.

But these were petty hitches which occur in any great machine. And the machine Rudolf Hess had created was really great: the greatest espionage organization that had ever existed.

THE DUAL FOREIGN POLITICS

Hermann Rauschning declares Hitler once told him the Nazi Party needed two movements abroad: one loyal and legal and one revolutionary. Hitler said: 'Do you think that is so difficult? We have proved we can do it: otherwise we would not now be here.'

This utterance is significant because it shows Hitler's intention to conquer other countries with the same means he used to conquer Germany.

Two movements.... The idea of two movements formed the leitmotiv of German foreign policy from the very beginning. Just as there were to be, and actually were, two movements in every country, so there were also two foreign policies: one loyal and one revolutionary; one official and one underground.

The official policy was pursued first by von Neurath, but during the time of its sternest trials, by von Ribbentrop. The unofficial foreign policy, which was disowned by Hitler as often as the revolutionary Nazi movements abroad were disowned, was directed by Alfred Rosenberg.

Naturally, some clashes between these two foreign policies were inevitable, and there were some bitter disputes between the men in charge of them. Rosenberg had the quite normal ambition for some position of prominence. It seemed to be his opportunity when the German Ambassador in London, von Hoesch, died in 1936. Rosenberg went to London—and everyone thought he would remain. After all, during the years Hitler had been struggling for power, Rosenberg had been the faithful 'foreign minister' of the Nazi Party.

Rosenberg soon made himself unpopular in London. He was utterly lacking in tact. Typically, he created something of a scandal when he laid a swastika wreath on the Tomb of the Unknown Soldier. London made it clear to the Nazis that Herr Rosenberg was not wanted; he soon departed.

Herr von Ribbentrop, who was given the post of Ambassador, was much more adroit. He was tactful—at least in the beginning; and before long he was a popular figure in London society. Indeed, to have failed to become that would have been a breach of his mission. He was duty-bound to cultivate English society, for this kind of contact had two functions. It permitted him, through the Cliveden set, to exert considerable influence upon British political life; and it was fruitful for espionage.

The idea of putting social life to such advantage was not Ribbentrop's; it had been conceived by Putzi Hanfstaengel,[2] the bizarre aesthete who had been one of Hitler's first backers. Hanfstaengel, who came from the best Munich society, had early recognized—or perhaps had always known—that with the right forms and the proper introduction it was very simple to gain entrance into society. And he knew also that highly placed persons who were entirely discreet in their own offices would freely unbend to discuss matters of a confidential nature in a salon or at a party—with people they met on a social plane.

Naturally, the German Ambassador in London was not given an assignment to ferret out military secrets. There were other secrets, equally valuable to Germany, which clever espionage in high society could uncover. Ribbentrop was clever. To be sure, he had the advice and aid of one of the cleverest women in Europe, a woman who, as it was reported in the European press, worked directly or indirectly for Hitler in many countries. It was Princess Stefanie von Hohenlohe who prepared the ground for Ribbentrop in London.

What made the situation the more fantastic was that Ribbentrop had been a strong Anglophobe all his life. Some wits in the Third Reich said that the only reason he went to England was to snatch the post of Ambassador from any other comer who might be less anti-English. At the time he took the post he was already the unofficial German Foreign Minister and had far more influence with Hitler than his superior, Herr von Neurath.

This man whom English society embraced with open arms was England's mortal foe. There was nothing about England he liked. He found that the labour problem was handled sloppily, the colonial question attacked improperly; he was bitter about the far-flung trade relations of the British Empire and predicted they would soon collapse. It would seem that the British society circles who were so charmed by him did not have very good instincts.

When Rosenberg returned from London he seemed like a political has-been. For some time after Hitler took power, it had looked this way, analogous to the case of Hess, one of the leading Nazis who had received no government position. Many thought that Hitler had dropped Rosenberg because he had compromised himself too badly in his struggle with the Church. But Rosenberg and his associates were probably well content to be out of the public eye. For his assigned tasks were of a confidential nature. The underground Foreign Minister worked better in obscurity.

Wilhelmstrasse 70a, where he had his offices, was a small unimpressive building. And his work was by no means so strictly defined, so meticulously organized, or his power so limited as that of other ministries. He had his fingers in many pies, his agents in many places which were the proper domain of agents of other departments. For Rosenberg had grown up with the Party; he had at one time or another ably taken on many different functions, and he was loath to abandon entirely the powerful organizations he had built up.

Wilhelmstrasse 70a was the Foreign Office of the Nazi Party. The organization was divided into various departments, a department for each country; for example, Department for France, Department for the United States, etc. Then there were a number of more inclusive departments, such as the Department for Foreign Trade, the Youth Section, etc. There was a large personnel and a multitude of agents streaming in and out of the building. They were an odd conglomeration. There were Germans from abroad, Hungarians, Latvians, Lithuanians and Estonians, White Russians, international adventurers and swindlers. The whole building had something of the atmosphere of a large café; there was a great deal of chaotic activity, much smoking and loud talk, cigarette butts lying about everywhere. It was very different from the offices of Goebbels, Göring, Himmler.

Here, at Wilhelmstrasse 70a, many diversified strands were woven together. It was here that relations were maintained with the Russian emigrés, with Hungary, Italy, and England, with dozens of anti-Bolshevist organizations, with anti-Semitic and anti-Freemason organizations. Here was located the central office of a giant conspiracy against many states and forms of government throughout the world.

There was, thus, an essential difference between the work of the Reich Foreign Ministry (for a long time unofficially and later officially headed by Ribbentrop) and that of Rosenberg's Party Foreign Office. While the official Foreign Ministry dealt with governments and, over the heads of the governments, with the ruling circles (as in England, for example), Rosenberg kept in touch with the circles which opposed these governments and were working for their overthrow. One could never know. The Nazis themselves had come to power as an opposition party, not through an armed uprising but simply through the growth of their political apparatus. Rosenberg tried to engineer a similar development in other countries. He worked for an internal political revolution, to be followed, of course, by close co-operation or even union with Germany.

Rosenberg dispatched his own agents, and these in turn hired sub-agents. He also made use of clubs and associations founded in Germany which were linked with a particular nation or a particular section.

Their name was legion. There were, for example: the Nordic Society, which formed a link to Danish, Swedish, Norwegian, and Finnish artists, educators, and industrialists; the Baltic Legion, which maintained contact with Lithuanians, Latvians, and Estonians; The German Colonial Society, which kept in touch with sympathetic aliens in former German colonies; the Aryan Christian Alliance, which organized all anti-Semites of importance, particularly in Central Europe, the Balkans, and South America. Rosenberg also took over the Ibero-American Institute, which was ideologically strongly influenced by Haushofer; this institute concentrated on Central and South America. The Kyffhaeuserbund, which until 1933 was more nationalistic than Nazi, was a club of very reactionary veterans. Rosenberg permitted this club to go unaltered outwardly, the better for Nazi purposes. Further there was the Eastern European Institute, located in Königsberg. The main duty of this organization—in which it conspicuously failed— was to carry on espionage in Soviet Russia. Finally, there was the German Students' Exchange.

The Fichtebund, too, was eventually subordinated to Rosenberg's spy organization. During the First World War the Fichtebund had been founded by Pan-Germans as a propaganda bureau. In the postwar period it barely managed to keep alive, but after the seizure of power Rosenberg revived it and fed it with large subsidies. The central bureau of the Fichtebund was in Hamburg. The membership of the executive committee became a close secret immediately after 1933; but it is known to have included a number of Haushofer's disciples, and some army officers. Rosenberg, of course, was the real director.

The task of the Fichtebund was to flood foreign countries with letters and other propaganda; to win friends abroad, particularly among the students; and to gain admittance into cultured circles. The organization had secret offices in every country of importance throughout the world.

The Fichtebund worked together with all German firms which had business connections abroad. These firms were supplied with propaganda material which they had to enclose in their business letters; the firms also had to deliver to the Fichtebund copies of their mailing lists.

All Party members travelling abroad, especially students, members of the Hitler Youth and of the women's organizations, were required to take with them leaflets of the Fichtebund for distribution abroad. They were instructed either to turn the material over to friends or sympathizers, or to leave it lying about, preferably in trains, ships, aircrafts, restaurants, and hotel rooms. Rosenberg himself had drawn up the general instructions.

In its annual report for 1935 the Fichtebund proudly announced that it had distributed five million leaflets and ten thousand pounds of books and pamphlets in sixty-four foreign languages. There are no official German figures for the following years; but an estimate based on analogous expansion gives us a figure approximately ten times as great for 1938.

Also subordinate to Rosenberg and his Foreign Office was the so-called World Service in Erfurt, an anti-Semitic news agency which flooded France, Switzerland, and South-eastern Europe with its propaganda, and also sent agents abroad. In this latter activity it co-operated with the Anti-Jewish League and the World League of Anti-Semites—both organizations also under Rosenberg's control.

Over all these leagues, associations, and what not, stood a kind of central organization: the Anti-Komintern. This was founded in Switzerland in 1934 with the ostensible purpose of combatting communism everywhere in the world and with the real aim of fighting for fascism and undermining all non-fascist states. There are a number of opinions as to Rudolf Hess's being the actual founder of the Anti-Komintern. However that may be, there is no doubt that it was founded on his initiative. He worked with Rosenberg, but Rosenberg always took orders from Hess. Hess laid down the general principles of operation for the various organizations that worked under Rosenberg. In Spain the Loyalists discovered many written orders to espionage groups which were signed with Hess's initials.

Although Herr von Ribbentrop represented the official foreign policy of the Third Reich, he did not feel himself excluded from underground work, from intrigue, sabotage, and murder. The type of men he chose for assistants in the Foreign Office clearly indicates this.

For example, in 1938 he sent a man named Nolda to Le Havre as consul. Nolda had formerly been a naval officer. It was quite natural that a professional naval man should be placed in Le Havre; for in case of war it would serve as the port of debarkation for English troops. Herr Nolda, of course, immediately went to work weaving a spy network in Le Havre, where his organization functioned splendidly during the war.

Shortly after Nolda arrived in Le Havre, the French liner *Paris* burned in the harbour. From the beginning the French authorities recognized that the fire was caused by sabotage; and before long they realized that Nolda was behind the affair. A day after the fire on the *Paris* the Paris-Lille express train caught fire. Herr Nolda was a passenger on this train. That he was nevertheless permitted to remain in Le Havre until the outbreak of the war, is one of the many mysteries of the French Intelligence Service—to which we shall return later....

One of Ribbentrop's foremost assistants in the line of direct espionage was Dr Eberhard von Stohrer, former German Minister to Egypt. In the summer of 1937 von Stohrer became Ambassador to Spain when the former Ambassador, General Faupel, resigned 'for reasons of health.' Von Stohrer had been in Madrid before; during the First World War he had been Secretary of the German Embassy in Madrid. The files of secret services throughout Europe held lengthy records of his activities during that period—as organizer of German espionage in Spain.

The purposes of his spying in Spain during the First World War were manifold. Germany was bent on maintaining Spanish neutrality by whatever means were at her disposal, by blackmail and intrigue. Furthermore, Spain was the ideal country from which agents could be sent into France, for the Pyrenees border was extremely difficult to patrol. Then there was much espionage work in connection with the submarine blockade. From Spain, the Western Mediterranean, the Azores, and French North Africa could be watched. It was during this period that Stohrer wrote a paper in which he pointed out the great strategic value of Dakar and advocated the occupation of Dakar in a future war....

Stohrer used mainly submarines to place his agents. In this way in 1917 he planted Harry Wood, an alleged American sailor whose real name was Karl Fricke, in Cartagena. Fricke was supposed to go to Argentina to undertake sabotage of Allied shipping. But the British Intelligence Service got on his trail; Fricke was put in prison and Herr von Stohrer was expelled from Spain.

Fricke spent two years in prison, stayed on in Cartagena after the war, and married the daughter of a rich Spanish mill owner. In 1924 he was appointed German Consul in Cartagena. At the beginning of the Civil War in Spain he was extremely active in procuring German soldiers and officers for Franco. The commercial firm of which he was head was one of the greatest Nationalist munitions centres during the Civil War. Today Fricke is one of Franco's closest advisers....

Soon after he came to Madrid in 1937, Herr von Stohrer proved that he had not lost his touch; he was as ever full of daring and enterprise. He was still a man with foresight, as he had been twenty years before. He began to make preparations for a European war which would be on a far greater scale than the Spanish Civil War. He created the nucleus of German espionage in the Second World War: the great spy centre of Portugal.

However, he did not neglect Spain. At first he concentrated on the Spanish port of Vigo, situated about 250 miles from Lisbon and 125 miles from Porto on the Spanish-Portuguese frontier. Vigo was an important port, particularly for Spanish ships on the South American run. Moreover, Vigo had direct cable connections to England, Germany, and South America.

Herr von Stohrer first sent a number of German technicians to Vigo. At the outbreak of the Spanish Civil War, the German colony in Vigo comprised some few hundred persons. By the early part of 1938 there were some thousands of Germans. Even during the war, German engineers were building a large and completely modern airport. In the neighbourhood of Vigo there sprang up workshops which supplied spare parts for German planes.

Stohrer's agents did not confine themselves to Vigo. They explored the coast in the neighbourhood of Vigo and Coruna and found a number of places which might be used for refuelling submarines. At Corcubion Ria, near Cape Finisterre, a regular submarine base was built.

But all these activities were negligible compared to the organization Stohrer was constructing in Portugal.

Stohrer seems to have foreseen as early as 1937 that in the coming war Lisbon would be the logical espionage centre, rather than, as in the last war, Berne, Zurich, and Amsterdam. Probably with the assent of Ribbentrop and Hess, Stohrer elected Lisbon as the espionage headquarters of the Second World War from the very beginning.

Toward the latter part of 1937 he sent a certain Herr Biefurn to Lisbon. For the next few months Herr Biefurn travelled back and forth between Portugal and Spain. But he spent a good part of his time in Lisbon.

During these months he established relations with the Arcadia Night Club and arranged a contract for a number of German dancers to perform on each programme—the programmes were changed once a month. The girls who danced in the Arcadia never appeared as Germans, of course; they all had passports from Rumania, Yugoslavia, or some other country.

A short distance from the Arcadia was a similar night club, the Olympia. Here the whole atmosphere, including the show was Spanish. In this club Herr Biefurn placed a number of dancers and singers who were in constant touch with Madrid.

Then there was the Hotel Metropole, in the Plaza Rossio, the Broadway of Lisbon; opposite it was the Hotel Frankfurt, and a few blocks away the Hotel de Francfort. The lobby of the Hotel Metropole became the meeting place of Herr Biefurn's agents. The two last-named hotels were ideal for espionage, since they were characterized by negligence and considerable confusion. For example, when the mail arrived, it was not placed in pigeonholes by the desk clerks, but left lying on the desk, so that anyone pretending to look for a letter could glance through the whole lot.

Another interesting feature in Lisbon life was the International Police. It is not known for certain whether Herr von Stohrer used Biefurn to establish relationships with this police. However, by the time the war broke out, the Secret State Police was working hand in hand with the Germans. It had a rule ideal for any spy with whom it co-operated; it took charge of the passports of all foreigners entering Portugal who remained over forty-eight hours—including diplomats.

And the wife of Police Chief Cumano was a German.

Even more important than Herr von Stohrer in Ribbentrop's organization was a man who had been Stohrer's military attaché in Spain during the First World War, Lieutenant Captain Canaris. Canaris was a daring, reckless, soldier-of-fortune type, full of wild and grandiose ideas, ruthless, unscrupulous, and foolhardy.

During the First World War he had worked with Mata Hari in Spain, and it was he who, intentionally or by mistake (the case has never been quite clarified) delivered her over to the French.

After the Armistice Canaris immediately joined up with the nationalistic officers and participated actively in the Kapp Putsch; but after the suppression of this putsch he remained one of the leading members of the War Ministry. He had a small office which was innocently called 'Department for Naval Transport.' Here he reorganized naval espionage and was the liaison man with heavy industry, which was financing the Black Reichswehr. He had enormous secret sums at his disposal; but since these sums were insufficient, he speculated on the stock market with them.

This led to a great scandal during the twenties. When the Phoebus Motion Picture Studios in Berlin collapsed, it was revealed that Canaris had invested millions in the firm. It also developed that Canaris had invested more millions in a number of very questionable foreign enterprises. The German public demanded to know where he had got the money; but in court he simply declared that the Army High Command had imposed silence upon him.

Naturally the War Minister had to wash his hands of Canaris—in public. He was officially removed from the payroll and went right on working in his own home, assisted by Lieutenant Captain Steffan (also a former associate of Stohrer and Nicolai), on plans for a future expansion of the military intelligence. (Steffan later, under Hitler, became military attaché in Stockholm, Copenhagen, Oslo, and Helsingfors and was put in charge of military espionage in the Northern countries.)

Canaris was given a place in the Foreign Office as soon as Hitler came to power, and worked with Ribbentrop before the latter had officially entered the Department of Foreign Affairs.

It was Canaris who organized a new department within the bounds of the special Ribbentrop Bureau which Ribbentrop had established mainly because of his rivalry with Rosenberg. Called Personnel Department B, it was under Canaris's personal direction and was involved with the Ministry of Justice. Occasionally it drafted specialists for particular territories, like Otto Abetz for France, Konrad Henlein and his adjutant, Frank, for Czechoslovakia, or General von Tippelskirch, the head of the military Intelligence Service in the Balkans, for Balkan problems. Final decisions were passed by a committee of three consisting of Canaris, Ribbentrop, and Hess.

The purpose of Personnel Department B was to search out men abroad who possessed wide influence or held important positions and who could be persuaded to work for Germany, whether directly or indirectly. In a word, it was the task of this bureau to comb the world for potential 'Quislings.'

The inspiration of Personnel Department B derived partly from the Haushofer Institute and partly from Dr Goebbels' collection of dossiers. It has already been pointed out that the Haushofer Institute analysed what classes and groups in foreign countries were discontented and hence fertile breeding grounds for traitors.

Goebbels' material was of a far more specific nature. Since 1931 Goebbels, first as head of the Propaganda Department of the Nazi Party and after 1933 as Minister of Propaganda, had been gathering every available bit of information on foreign notables. His fat dossiers contained the answers to all pertinent questions: Was this statesman mercenary? Was that industrialist vain? Was a certain minister fond of women? Could such-and-such a senator be bought? Had this or that business leader a dubious past? And so on.

Rosenberg tried to create entire revolutionary movements abroad. Personnel Department B looked after the individual traitors.

Such traitors were won over in three ways. They were converted by means of propaganda and became real National Socialists; or, frightened by stories of an invincible Germany, they were persuaded they would be better off in coming to an agreement with the Nazis; or they were promised important positions after the Nazi conquest of their country.

Naturally, Personnel Department B would have been unnecessary had Rosenberg's revolutionary organizations given promise of immediate success. But Ribbentrop and Canaris quickly decided that treason was a surer method. It was simpler to buy members of a government than to force the government to take members of the opposition into the cabinet.

Austria affords a good example. The Nazis had forced Schuschnigg to take Arthur Seyss-Inquart,[3] the Nazi leader, into the Ministry of the Interior; but to assure the success of the coup, it had also been necessary to buy off Foreign Minister Guido Schmidt, who betrayed Schuschnigg at the very end.

Czechoslovakia could not have been conquered by Henlein and his clique alone; but Personnel Department B negotiated with individual members of the reactionary Agrarian Party, and also bribed General Sirovy, he who for a long time called for resistance and at the psychological moment suddenly advocated capitulation, to the thorough demoralization of the Army.

The story of the assistance given to the German invasion of Norway by a group of officers under the leadership of Major Vidkun Quisling and Major Spender, who betrayed the plans of the Norwegian Coastal defences, is too celebrated to need recounting.

In Poland the Nazis not only had Senator Wiesner, the leader of the German minority, but also Foreign Minister Colonel Beck, whom Canaris personally had won over to the German camp.

In Belgium, Rosenberg had done poorly, for the Degrelle movement which he financed lost ground steadily after 1937. But Personnel Department B acquired the services of a former socialist, Henri de Man, who had a great deal of influence with Leopold and the whole royal family. Lieutenant Dombret, a member of the Belgian General Staff, sold the Germans all the secret plans of defence long before the war broke out. General van Overstraaten, the military adviser to the King, while not in the pay of the Germans, was completely under German influence.

Canaris spent no time nor labour in Rumania because he thought he could depend on the Rosenberg-supported Iron Guard of Codreanu; as events proved, this was an error in judgment. In Bulgaria ex-Premier Cankoff was bought—it is said, for a disgracefully low price. After 1938, Cankoff became personal adviser to King Boris, and this bribe proved an excellent investment.

Finally, in Yugoslavia Canaris had an exceptionally good man in General Kosić.[4] In 1940, Kosić became Chief of the Yugoslavian General Staff—probably at the instigation of Berlin and despite the energetic opposition of War Minister General Milan Nedić.[5] Kosić was entrusted with the task of removing all higher officers of anti-Hitler sentiments. He was so successful that in the end he forced out Nedić himself. Seventy-year-old General Pešić,[6] who succeeded to Nedić's place, was, of course, Kosić's straw man.

Personnel Department B kept no regular staff of agents. It borrowed the services of ambassadors and consuls, occasionally the employees of other ministries or organizations. There were a few rare cases of men working for

Personnel Department B who apparently had no connection with any other organizations in the Reich. It has been impossible to learn whether they were paid directly or indirectly for their services.

The man of outstanding success in this field was Otto Abetz,[7] whose activities in France will be discussed later. Captain Wiedemann, later Consul Wiedemann, also worked for Personnel Department B. Another was Herr von Papen, who won a number of personal triumphs in Austria and Turkey.

One can hardly speak of Wiedemann without mentioning a woman who has been linked with him in all the important newspapers in the world: Princess Stefanie von Hohenlohe.[8]

Princess Stefanie Hohenlohe Waldenburg Schillingsfuerst was not born a princess. When, in 1915, Prince Friedrich Franz Augustin Hohenlohe Waldenburg Schillingsfuerst fell in love with the beautiful red-haired girl, his family—we shall call them the Hohenlohes for short—were scandalized. Stefanie according to the European press placated them somewhat by undergoing baptism. Six years after their marriage she was divorced and from then on she was seen frequently in aristocratic circles in Vienna, Berlin, Budapest, London, and Paris. In the mid-twenties she became a close friend of Lord Rothermere's, whom she could wind around her little finger; during that period he entertained some dashing plans for restoring the Hungarian Monarchy. When Hitler came to power, the Princess operated in London and Paris as a link between the Führer and international society. Lord Rothermere later admitted under oath that for a time he had been extremely pro-Hitler—and there is little doubt that this was in large part due to the influence of Princess Stefanie. It was the princess who introduced Ward Price, the notorious pro-Hitler *Daily Mail* correspondent to Hitler. During the first Salzburg Festival after the Anschluss she lived in the castle that had been taken from Max Reinhardt[9] and attempted—in vain—to entice international society to the castle. She assisted Otto Abetz' work in France and above all Ribbentrop's conspiracies in London. Later, before an English court, she admitted modestly that it was she who made Munich possible.

Shortly before he took power, Hitler declared to friends:

When I wage war, on some calm day, in the midst of peace, my troops shall appear in the streets of Paris; they will march in broad daylight .... they will occupy the ministries, the parliament ... in a few minutes, France, Poland, Czechoslovakia will be deprived of their leaders; there will be incredible confusion .... The greatest improbability is the most certain.

The greatest improbability is the most certain. This would be the best imaginable motto for the work of Personnel Department B.

In England its work failed, in spite of Ribbentrop. The attempt to build up Sir Oswald Mosley[10] and his Fascist Party was unsuccessful. The activities of the Governor of the Bank of England, Sir Montagu Norman, were in the end as ineffectual as those of Horace Wilson, Chamberlain's personal adviser, or of Geoffrey Dawson,[11] editor-in-chief of *The Times*, who for a time, used to obtain Ribbentrop's O.K. before the publication of any article concerning Germany. (All these Englishmen were, of course, not bought. They were not, in the strict sense of the word, German agents, but in actuality they were; that is, their actions benefited Germany.)

In France the idea thrived better. The systematic creation of fifth columns began there in 1936. The appropriate men were already available from among pro-Mussolini and pro-Franco circles. Otto Abetz and his agents had no more to do than organize these anti-democratic groups under one head and give direction to their energies.

The Germans were not particularly interested in finding single agents of the old type within the French officers corps. They wanted to disrupt the entire corps, to infect it with defeatism, and for this they needed a multitude of allies in its midst. This was accomplished by various means. The *Cagoulard* organization, for example, was unquestionably built up with German money and on a German plan. The organizer of the *Cagoulards*, Eugène Deloncle, a wealthy industrialist, had long been a hundred per cent German agent. The owners of the Michelin works in Clermont-Ferrand, greatest rubber tyre factory in France, had also worked hand in hand with Germany for a long time, and contributed a great deal of money to the *Cagoulard* movement. This family had many connections in the French army, in particular General Michelin, chief of the fifth French Defence Area, who was in turn a close friend of General Gourand, Commander of the City of Paris, and of Marshal Pétain.... All this was common knowledge long before the war. When the *Cagoulard* Affair first broke, *Le Populaire*, the organ of Minister of the Interior Marx Dormoy wrote: 'The real leadership of Eugène Deloncle's whole secret organization, may be found in Germany.' At the time Pétain and company thought it wiser to raise no charges of libel. But in July 1941, Marx Dormoy was assassinated....

From the very beginning Berlin tried to influence the top men in the French Army—either directly or through Abetz. Naturally, men like Weygand and Pétain could not be bribed. But it sufficed to establish connections with them and try to impress them with a favourable attitude toward the Third Reich. It helped considerably that both men were anti-democratic. The political circle close to Weygand, including Maurras and Laval, had for years played with the idea that a lost war or an understanding with Germany would have the positive result of 'liquidating' democracy. The Germans had only to make this emphatic to the two army men. Pétain figured as the principal pawn in German plans from 1939 on. On 22 December 1939, Henri de Kerillis wrote in the rightist newspaper, *l'Epoque*:

> It was a matter of convincing Marshal Pétain that he must resign himself to accept leadership of a cabinet of national union that included the most notorious defeatists and Seyss-Inquarts! The plotters would like the aged Marshal to play unwittingly the role analogous to that of Hindenburg, opening the door to a Hitler in a moment of despondency. Clearly this idea could not have been born in French minds.

It was not. When in May 1940 Reynaud appointed Weygand Commander-in-Chief and Pétain Vice-Premier, he created the very situation the Germans had hoped for; for Weygand and Pétain were tools of a clique of politicians who wittingly or unwittingly were carrying out Berlin's orders.

Above all, there was the group surrounding Laval, who remained in the background for the while, although by 1936 he had advanced from his pro-Mussolini attitude to a pro-Hitler position. Then there was Doriot, who under the guidance of Laval had been converted from communism to fascism. Then there was a certain group within the Radical Party; a group around the newspaper *La République,* who were paid by Germany. At the beginning of 1938 these groups, which from 1936 on had more-or-less worked together, were joined by Flandin and Bonnet. After Munich almost all the rightist parties swung over to this group.

It would be incorrect to picture all these politicians as bribed and bought. There were many motives driving them into the German camp: ambition, a benighted sort of pacifism, the desire for peace and quiet, fear of losing property—and all these motives were used by the German agents to cement a strong pro-Hitler front. Canaris and Abetz had a great talent for using men without their realizing they were being used.

The number of French statesmen who were directly paid by Germany was not very large. But there were a great many unpaid and in part involuntary agents. Unquestionably, Laval was not paid; Flandin very probably was. But both used their power in parliament, in the press, and in business circles to further a policy useful to Hitler. Charles Maurras[12] certainly did not want to be a German agent and would have resented it had someone called him one. But he was so passionate a supporter of Mussolini that the objective results of his activities conspired in Hitler's favour. Old Joseph Caillaux undoubtedly did not even have personal connections with the Third Reich; but he was close to Emile Roche, who was at best an unwitting German agent, and Deputy Montigny, who was unquestionably a conscious German agent. Caillaux was swayed by these men; and he was, after all, the chairman of the Senate Finance Committee.

All this prepared the collapse. But it did more; it provided another advantage of tremendous importance to Germany. There were no longer any secrets from Germany; the Germans knew all that went on in the French State. There were too many men in key positions who consciously or unconsciously, paid or unpaid, directly or indirectly, were spying for Hitler.

Obviously Personnel Department B had an easy job in France. But it did that job well.

How contemptuous the Germans were of these Quislings whom they bought or won over; how little they took them seriously, is indicated by a story that went the rounds of the *Deuxième Bureau* in January 1940.

At this time a Spanish officer who was working for the *Deuxième Bureau* came to Commandant Gauché. The man was angry. 'You French have committed an unpardonable error. After the Hitler-Stalin pact, all Spain was indignant with Germany. It would have been the easiest thing for France to get Spain on her side. But somehow Madrid never felt that France was seriously at war with Germany.'

'Why?' Gauché asked.

'It's your Ambassador. He seems to be on the best of terms with the German Ambassador. He shows it publicly. If, for instance, he meets Herr von Stohrer in General Franco's anteroom, he talks to him at great length.... Once I asked a German attaché why Stohrer was so friendly to your Ambassador. The German laughed. 'We do that on purpose to compromise the old fool,' he said.

The French Ambassador in Madrid was Henri Philippe Pétain.[13]

HERR BOHLE COVERS THE GLOBE

In the spring of 1934 delegates of Germans living abroad came to a congress in Berlin. The Führer addressed them. He said:

> You are listening posts. Far from the front, you must prepare certain undertakings. You must prepare our own groundwork for the attack. Consider yourselves under orders; military law applies to you.

In May 1933, a year before this congress, Ernst Wilhelm Bohle[14] was appointed chief of the AO—*Auslands-Organization* (League of Germans Abroad).

There are many Germans and people of German descent scattered throughout the world. According to German statistics there are about thirty millions. Most of them long ago adopted citizenship in the countries of their residence.

But that did not concern the Nazis. Fritz Kuhn, the führer of the German American Bund, once expressed the Nazi point of view when he said:

The citizenship papers in our pockets have not made us into another type of people. We have remained what we were, German men and women in America.

Or, to give the official version, Bohle himself declared:

We recognize only one idea: a German always and everywhere remains German and nothing but German and thereby a National Socialist.

It was Bohle who was chosen to execute Hess's idea that everyone could and must spy. In fact, he extended this principle. 'Spying can be done *everywhere*.' he once wrote to an agent in a South American Republic.

Everywhere. It was a grandiose idea, and very simple. Everywhere in the world, in every city, every village, every street, and every house spies were at work and nothing could remain secret. And this globe-embracing espionage was organized by Bohle.

When he took over the direction of the AO, Ernst Wilhelm Bohle was just thirty years old, and a personable young man. He was one of the few intimate friends of Rudolf Hess, who placed him in the AO.

Like Hess, Bohle was born abroad—in Bradford, England. His father, a naturalized Englishman, was for a long time professor at the University in Cape Town. Bohle himself studied first in Cape Town, later in Cologne and Berlin. He then entered the import-export trade, joined the Nazis, and quickly rose in the party. This swift rise was—strangely enough—largely due to his excellent command of English, which deeply impressed Hitler.

The AO was, of course, neither his invention nor an invention of the Nazis. The original AO had been founded in 1881 under the name of the *Verein fuer Deutschtum im Ausland* (Association for Teutons Abroad). The German School Club, which had branches all over the world, merged with this organization. Before the Nazis came to power it had approximately 2,000 district groups and more than 1,000 school branches. Even the German Institute for Foreign Countries (*Auslandsinstitut*) in Stuttgart, which later became the main Nazi propaganda centre, had been founded back in 1917. In addition, shortly after the end of the First World War, was founded the German Protective League for Germans in Frontier Regions and Abroad, which propagandised mainly in Austria, Czechoslovakia, and Poland. And dozens of special associations were established in regions which had been taken from Germany by the Versailles Treaty. Thus there were Leagues of Baltic Germans, Alsatians, Sudeten Germans, etc.

All these Leagues were reactionary and nationalistic; they did not recognize the black-red-gold flag of the Weimar Republic and supported the theory that Germany had not been legitimately conquered in the World War, but betrayed from within. There were good sound economic reasons for such a stand. The Germans in the surrendered provinces had lost most of their former property, the Germans living overseas had lost a great deal of prestige. These factors helped create a situation which made it comparatively easy for the Nazis to take over all these various organizations.

The Nazis for their part, had taken an interest in Germans living abroad since 1930; and at a Party session in Hamburg it was decided to set up Nazi cells within all organizations of Germans abroad. In 1931 a special Foreign Department of the Reich Chief of the National Socialist Party was set up, with Rudolf Hess at the head. This Foreign Department filled out a special filing card for every Party member who lived abroad or travelled abroad. This became the basis of a gigantic file which the Nazis were later to use to control almost all Germans living abroad.

In 1935 the AO removed from Hamburg to Berlin and set up one of the biggest offices in the city. By 1937 it had more than seven hundred employees; according to conservative estimates, this number has by now been doubled.

In 1937—the last year for which we possess official figures—the AO numbered among its members some three million so-called Germans abroad, and between seventy and one hundred thousand sailors on German ships. Organizationally the AO was divided into Territorial Bureaus (*Laenderaemter*). There were eight of these:

Northern and Eastern Europe
Western Europe
South-east Europe
Italy, Switzerland, Hungary
Africa
North America
South America
Far East, Australia, England, Ireland

The Sailor's Bureau, which kept a check on German sailors, was a special department. It had branches in Bremen, Hamburg, Kiel, and Stettin. (Since the war it has opened branches in all the European ports occupied by the Nazis.)

Then there were a large number of sub-departments called special bureaus (*Sachaemter*), the number of which gives some idea of the variety of matters with which the AO dealt:

Foreign Trade Bureau
Inspection Bureau
Cultural Bureau
Press Bureau
District Court
Bureau of Justice
Speakers Bureau
Repatriation Bureau
Education Bureau
Bureau for Technical Affairs

Moreover, many AO organizations within the Reich were directly connected with and worked with Germans abroad through the AO. The most important of these were:

The German Labor Front
The Bureau for Officials
Bureau for Educators and Teachers
Bureau for Teaching Fellows
Bureau for Students
National Socialist Cultural Association
National Socialist League for Justice (*Rechtswahrerbund*)
German Woman's Labor Association
Youth Bureau.

Until 1937 the AO was principally a Nazi Party agency. Then it became an affair of the German Government, and therefore of German policy.

At Hess's suggestion, Hitler placed Bohle in the Foreign Ministry. At Wilhelmstrasse 74-76, he became the second most important man after Ribbentrop. The appointment of Bohle to the Foreign Office was accompanied by a decree of the Führer which gave official sanction to the longstanding co-operation of the Foreign Office with the AO. An AO was created within the Foreign Office, naturally headed by Bohle. From then on Bohle was permitted to attend all Cabinet meetings, although he was not a Minister. Hitler's decree helped considerably to unify German foreign policy—a necessary step if the great mass of Germans living abroad was to be utilized for purposes of propaganda and espionage, for it would not do for the Nazi diplomats in various countries to be in ignorance of what the German patriots around them were up to.

From 1937 on there was no such misunderstanding. On the contrary. From then on the consuls and the ambassador more or less directed the activities of the masses of Germans abroad.

What activities? The so-called Foreign Identification Pass given all members of the AO contained the ten commandments for the expatriate German. The Catechism began innocently enough, the first commandment reading: 'Obey the laws of the country whose guest you are.' The second read: 'Permit the inhabitants to make the laws of the country where you are a guest.'

But the seventh commandment orders: 'You cannot remain merely a member ... but you must actually stand in the front line....' A fighter—for what? And the eighth commandment read: 'Recruit every honest German into the ranks. Convince him of the necessity of our victory that Germany may live.'

The necessity of their victory. That is, from the very beginning they were preparing for struggle and victory throughout the world. And in this struggle the millions of Germans abroad, no matter what nationality they had meanwhile adopted, were to lend their aid. How could they aid? Were they to buy machine guns and march against their own governments?

What was demanded of them was far more modest. All they were asked to do was answer a few questions. Questions like:

What is exported? Where is it exported, by what means, and by what route? In what quantities and at what prices?

From what countries do imports come? What things are imported? Who does the importing? At what prices?

List factories and small businesses that employ more than ten workers. What is manufactured there? Where do the raw materials or the parts come from? Who is the manager? What nationality are the technical and commercial directors? Who is the owner?

And hundreds of other questions. Hundreds? Thousands, tens of thousands.

Bohle had said, 'Spying can be done everywhere.' Everywhere. The idea was simple and grandiose.

It was not merely industrial espionage. Spying on foreign markets and single manufacturing processes was important both for commercial purposes and from a military point of view. Knowing how a factory worked, where it got its material, how it could be switched over to war production, was valuable in the preparation of military operations—from submarine warfare to bombing.

The engineer would be the man ideally equipped to answer these questions. Throughout these years the AO made strenuous efforts to place reliable Party comrades in engineering positions abroad. It established a special magazine for this purpose, *The Engineer Abroad*. The AO saw to it that whenever foreign countries purchased machinery, heavy industry sent with the machinery a number of engineers to set it up or start it going. When such opportunities did not exist, they were fabricated. Great German factories like Siemens, for example, had to offer machinery at ridiculously low prices to customers abroad about which the AO needed information. And those customers were only too glad to accept the offers, and perfectly agreeable to the condition that for the first year a German engineer must be hired 'because the apparatus is somewhat difficult to handle at first.'

In this manner some 2,500 German engineers were placed abroad within a few years. Since it was quite impossible for an outsider—that is, someone who was not working for the AO—to leave Germany, it is manifest that these engineers were all spies. Chemists were sent out in similar fashion, but their task was infinitely harder, since the chemical industry throughout the world was full of suspicion toward the Nazis and their intentions.

The engineers and chemists comprised only two of the hundreds of professions and fields represented in the AO whose members sent information from abroad. The extraordinary number of special bureaus within the AO makes it abundantly clear that the organization did not limit itself to collecting passively the information that was sent in. Rather, from time to time the representatives of hundreds of different professions were given very definite assignments as to what they must find out.

The Sailors' Bureau was, of course, in a splendid position to carry on espionage. Goods that were shipped on German freighters were carefully examined and their origin, quality, quantity, and destination determined. If there were no other way, German freight lines which were government-subsidized underbid other lines in order to obtain shipments that seemed valuable to them as objects of industrial espionage. German seamen had to try to get work aboard foreign ships, that they might report on their routes and the shipments they carried.

A subdivision of the Sailors' Bureau was the Port Service Bureau, which had a number of special branches under the direction of one of Bohle's deputies, Kurt Wermke.[15] Subsidiary to the Port Service Bureau in turn were the Port Bureaus (*Hafenaemter*) which had been opened in every port in the world, even in the tiniest. These Port Bureaus were often headed by gangster brutes who would cheerfully carry out a murder or two on orders of the Gestapo. This gave rise to the incorrect impression that they had always been a branch organization of the Gestapo.

By this means Bohle's simple and grandiose idea had jurisdiction even over the high seas. The ocean itself, was, so to speak, under constant supervision. The sum of reports from German seamen on German and foreign ships and from the port officials kept Berlin informed on the situation on every ocean, in every port, every day, and every hour.

Besides the sea lanes, the railways were naturally of enormous importance for industrial espionage. Here it was far more difficult for the AO to penetrate into foreign organizations. The German Railroads Central succeeded in only a few countries (mainly Spain and the Balkans), where by dint of incredible underbidding they obtained some of the freight transport business. In such instances a number of offices were set up at the great freight terminals from which agents could observe what was being loaded and unloaded.

The AO was insatiable in its urge to learn. And so it did not limit itself to Germans, but sought to enlist a number of foreign assistants, most of them involuntary helpers. The prestige of German techniques and German science was abused to persuade young men—especially from the smaller countries—to visit Germany for purposes of study. Special emphasis was placed upon engineers, chemists, and technicians already active in their professions. These young men were told to look around in Germany and enjoy their vacations—all at practically no cost.

Thereby, contacts were established which were later to prove extremely useful.

These invitations were not extended higgledy-piggledy. Bohle had special files of thousands of foreign specialists in the most diverse fields, who would have important information to give Germany. Naturally, only an infinitesimal percentage of those invited actually proved useful later on. But Bohle did not expect more. The League for the Cultivation of Personal Friendships with Foreigners looked after these foreigners who were to be transformed into involuntary spies. This League, conceived by Goebbels, put into effect and incorporated into the AO by Bohle, compelled its members—who were members more or less under compulsion—to write regularly to their friends abroad and so establish a kind of sentimental bond with Germany. It is amazing how effective these letters 'for the cultivation of personal friendships' were in the long run.

Naturally, not all the millions of Germans abroad wrote weekly reports to Herr Bohle. The AO had a very tight organization in every country. Each country was divided into 'Strategic Points,' 'Local Groups,' and 'Districts.'

The Strategic Point (*Stuetzpunkt*) was the smallest unit and consisted of single cells, the membership of which ranged from ten to one hundred and fifty. Each Strategic Point had its own leader. If there were a number of Strategic Points in a given locality, they comprised a Local Group, with a Local Group Leader. Several Local Groups formed a District, whose leader was called the District Leader. Above the various districts of a country stood the Territorial District Leader, who in turn was subordinate to the Territorial Group Leader. The latter often controlled several countries. Only the Territorial Group Leader and his office had any direct tie with the embassy or the legation and the consuls, and with the central office of the AO in Berlin.

In this manner the enormous quantity of material that poured in every week was sifted at each level. Thousands or tens of thousands of Strategic Point leaders received tons of material. The Territorial Group Leader received only what was of the utmost importance; the enormous quantity was eventually refined into quality.

Territorial Bureau 6 (North America) was established in the spring of 1932. Since then the Bureau has grown to many times its original size. It is not surprising. The Territorial Group Leader for the United States did splendid work. This Leader was not, as the American public assumed for a long time, Carl C. Orgell, a naturalized American who registered with the State Department as a German agent. Orgell was never anything more than a straw man. The real Territorial Group Leader was Walter H. Schellenberg, whom we have had occasion to mention before.

Let us see how his espionage organization worked.

Before the United States started paying attention to foreign agents, there were fifty thousand individuals in the country who in one way or another, voluntarily, semi-voluntarily, or by compulsion contributed to the stream of information whose end was in the Nazi espionage centres in Berlin and Hamburg. Housemaids, grocery clerks, beauty parlour operators, nurses, chauffeurs, opera singers, bookkeepers—they all handed in their weekly reports. Much of this information—in accordance with the strict instructions to report everything—consisted obviously of material irrelevant to the Nazi intelligence system. Much was gossip, much meaningless information overheard by agents during their daily routine in their places of employment. Yet some little chance remarks might contain a valuable lead to an American business deal, to morale in certain sections of the population, to shipping movements, etc. The Nazis had an elaborate system for sifting these reports. The system which finally was adopted had been tested in the German American Bund. The new Bund espionage organization which Schellenberg organized in 1936 became known as the *Bundesnachrichtenstelle* or Bunaste; it was the centre for 91 *Ortsgruppennachrichtenstellen* or Ogrunaste in 91 communities throughout the United States. The latter had to read and clip every newspaper, weekly, trade paper, magazine, everything that was printed within their district and forward three clippings to Ogrunaste in New York.

One can see what a formidable task this was in itself. Twenty per cent of the material reaching New York headquarters was sent on to Schellenberg, and half of what he received went to Germany. But if by 1936, the printed matter gathered weekly by the *Bundesnachrichtenstelle* was voluminous enough to fill an automobile, the volume of individual reports had become truly amazing, and continued undiminished up to late in 1939. The system involving so many people and such a volume of reports would seem to the average American fantastic and unbelievable. Had it not been for some clever sleuthing and the fortunate connections of a well-known American newspaperman in Berlin the full scope might never have become known. To get an idea of the total spying system set up by Schellenberg, let us look into a portion of a confidential factual report made by this journalist when after two decades there, he returned from Berlin:

> The amount of money spent by the Nazi regime for propaganda and espionage abroad is the second largest item in the secret national budget. The amount spent in the United States for the year 1939 was slightly over seventy-three million dollars!... It is amazing to see how much information of real military value of tremendous importance to Axis war efforts is culled in Berlin from the reports of thousands and thousands of amateur agents in the United States. The intelligence officers have not much use for these people as individuals, small fry at whom they sneer contemptuously, but in the same breath they grudgingly must admit that the Nazi party has done a magnificent job in whipping them into line for their comparatively humble task.

If only 10 per cent of the printed material gathered by the huge army of Nazi agents in this country ever went to Germany, only about 1 per cent of the individual non-professional reports ever crossed the ocean. By the time they reached Schellenberg at least half had been weeded out. Schellenberg did some more sifting, condensing and editing, while the final process of whittling down was done in the German consulates in the United States and at the German Embassy in Washington. It can now be revealed that this activity was one of the main reasons for the American government's closing down the German consulates here. Perhaps some day after the war is over the full story can be told and the full report of the American foreign correspondent, who rendered his country an enormous service, can be revealed to the American people.[16]

THE SPECIAL ENVOYS OF DR GOEBBELS

Those chosen beings whom Propaganda Minister Joseph Goebbels has received in his private office come away with their respect for Hollywood much diminished. Hollywood, they say, is completely outclassed. They never tire of describing the room which during the last five years has been headquarters for the greatest propaganda campaign the world has ever seen. There is an enormous desk with half a dozen telephones. The principal apparatus in the room is a little miracle that the telephone company constructed especially for Goebbels. It is a switchboard by means of which Dr Goebbels can plug into any line and listen to any conversation anywhere in the building—and not only in the building.

But this kind of espionage does not interest us here. We are not concerned with six of the seven departments Goebbels heads, which give him power over propaganda, radio, the press, the movies, and the theatre. Our attention turns to just one department, the Counter-Action (*Abwehr*) Department.

Here the separate threats of propaganda and espionage are knit together. This department—by far the largest within the Propaganda Ministry— consists of no fewer than twelve sections. It was allegedly founded to combat the so-called atrocity propaganda abroad. Today it works in closest co-operation with the Liaison Staff on the one hand, and with Rosenberg, Bohle, Himmler, and especially Nicolai on the other hand. Fifteen officers of the War Ministry Intelligence Service are permanent members of the Department. Probably this number has been considerably increased since the outbreak of the war.

The department collects all news reports from abroad. All-important newspapers, magazines, and books are sent to it. They are not sent directly, but are transmitted by way of agents abroad to a false address, or via book dealers in Germany. Today they are probably transmitted via Swedish or Swiss book dealers.

The Counter-Action Department also contains the personnel file of which we had occasion to speak in connection with Personnel Department B (of the Ribbentrop Bureau). It is said to be the largest personnel file in the world, overtopping by far that of Scotland Yard. We have already shown how the information available in this file could be used for purposes of espionage.

Goebbels lives in the Propaganda Ministry with his wife Magda and his children. It is, of course, an open secret that since 1934, relations between them have not been too smooth. There have been some unpleasant scenes in public, and once the Führer himself had to intervene. It is said that Goebbels took up bachelor quarters in the Rankestrasse on Berlin's West Side in order to get away from his wife. Certainly this is one reason. Everyone in Berlin knows that he uses this bachelor apartment to receive whatever actress or movie star happens to be in his favour at the moment.

But the apartment in the Rankestrasse has still other functions.

Here Goebbels can receive associates whom he could not receive in the Propaganda Ministry. Here, for example, he sees Herr Winkler.

Probably not fifty people in Berlin know who Herr Winkler is. He was once the mayor of some two-penny German town. Around 1925 he came to Berlin and entered the Foreign Office. When Hitler came to power he was ostentatiously thrown out. But this dismissal was a gesture for the public eye. He continued to work, with his apartment in the Altonaerstrasse as his office.

Winkler's activities might be called propaganda; they might also be called bribery. His task was to finance foreign newspapers. (He must not be confused with Dr Karl Boemer, the man who was in charge of the foreign press in the Propaganda Ministry until August 1941, when he went on vacation; some say he was sent to a concentration camp because he had tipped off foreign newspaper men before the beginning of the Russian War.) At first Winkler concentrated on German-language newspapers in non-German-speaking countries. By 1937 Goebbels controlled, through Winkler, some 330 German newspapers in non-German-speaking countries. This figure did not include the large number of newspapers in Switzerland, Alsace, and Czechoslovakia, nor the newspapers in other languages in which Winkler invested money. Figures for these are not available, and probably there are few living persons aside from Goebbels and Hitler who have even approximate information.

To outward appearances, Winkler's activities are propaganda. But as Goebbels had said to Colonel Nicolai, where does propaganda stop and espionage begin? There is no question but that Goebbels perceived how friendly contacts with the foreign press could be used for purposes other than those of propaganda. The object of a newspaper is not only to express an opinion and convince its readers of the justice of that opinion. A newspaper also must print news. A newspaper receives hundreds of news reports, many of which cannot be printed for lack of space and for other reasons. A newspaper has reporters who see and hear a great deal that they exclude from their stories because the public would not be interested. Fraternizing with these reporters, lingering about a newspaper office, can yield a rich harvest of profitable information. Nor are the offices of great metropolitan newspapers necessarily the best hunting grounds. It is the small newspapers, the provincial press, which are full of little personal items; and the wastebaskets at the editorial desk and the reporters in neighbourhood bars reveal many more such small items. Items on accidents in factories, employment, visits from Washington, London, and Paris— there is something of interest every day for a man with good eyes and ears and the right connections.

Bohle and his AO were primarily concerned with Germans who lived abroad permanently, or with sailors who did not stay in their home ports. It was Goebbels' task within the framework of total espionage to look after those who took only occasional trips abroad, or to arrange that on given occasions certain people would go travelling.

Bohle's principal activity was to gather the information sent in by the millions who worked for him. (Only in exceptional cases, as we have pointed out, were tasks actually assigned.)

But Goebbels was not content with information that simply fell into his lap; it was not in his character. Goebbels had always been a systematic person. He became a first-rate propagandist because he studied and understood propaganda; because he realized that the best way to sway millions was by working through the few. You had to choose the proper channels of public opinion.

Goebbels' theory of espionage was fundamentally the opposite of Bohle's (and to an extent of Hess's). This theory was formulated most clearly in his written instructions on the organization of foreign broadcasting issued in the autumn of 1936. Goebbels maintained that two agents strategically placed could accomplish more than Herr Bohle's millions. He believed that espionage as well as propaganda, required 'key men' and 'channels.'

System was a fetish with Goebbels. For instance, included in the Counter-Action Department was a special section, whose task was to determine what guises, masks, and disguises were most appropriate for espionage in various countries.

This was by no means a duplication of the work of the Psychological Laboratory. The Laboratory studied the psychological prerequisites of a spy, whereas this section determined the technical equipment for successful espionage work.

The difference between this and previous individualistic espionage (particularly that of the romantic era) is that now the agents were robbed of all initiative. They had to portray faithfully the role in which they were cast by this section of Propaganda Ministry—the role that was the best for a given purpose in a given country under given circumstances,

Many of the agents who were sent out were auto mechanics. There were, indeed, a great many representatives of German automobile factories who fairly swamped countries like Poland and Czechoslovakia, and set up branches everywhere, even in small towns where for months on end they did not sell one car.

Then there were the movie companies that travelled about either to make documentary films in foreign countries or 'colossal' dramas requiring months of travelling and shooting. There was, for example, the company which was to do *Robinson Crusoe* and which spent months on an island off the coast of Chile. By chance, this island of wonderful scenery also had considerable strategic importance. The movie, which in view of the long voyage of a whole company and the weeks spent on the island must have been very expensive, was never released.

Another film which never saw the light of day was a documentary one which the UFA corporation (the great German motion picture company) was to make of Poland in 1938. The company sent out crews that travelled through Poland for months. However, another movie on Poland was released. This one was directed by G. W. Pabst,[17] who for years posed in Hollywood and Paris as an opponent of Hitler's. The picture was called *Campaign in Poland* and was presented by Goebbels in Scandinavia, Belgium, and Holland to frighten the governments and populace into submission.

Then there were artists, from the great Wagnerian soprano who sang in the greatest opera houses until a few months ago (whose espionage activities will be made known to the public shortly),[18] to the little cabaret singers in second-rate night clubs.

There was, for instance, the manager of the Berlin Scala, Herr Duisberg. The Scala was a vaudeville house of enormous proportions, something like the late New York Hippodrome. The vaudeville business can, of course, be conducted only along international lines. It was therefore not at all surprising that between 1933 and 1939 Herr Duisberg came regularly to Paris to see and engage new artists. Incidentally, Herr Duisberg was courageous. His Paris representative was a Russian Jew and he declined to dismiss him, even after the powerful weekly of the SS, *Das Schwarze Korps*, attacked him for doing business with a Jew. He was quite fond of showing the clipping around when he came to Paris. Late, much too late, only shortly before the war broke out, it was discovered that this press attack had been nothing but a very clever alibi for Mr Duisberg.

Or there was the director of the Gärtnerplatz Theater, in Munich, Herr Fischer.[19] His establishment, devoted to musical comedy, became famous during the season of 1938-39, when the *Merry Widow* was revived and the American dancers, Marion Daniels and Miriam Verne, made a triumphant appearance. When Hitler himself was introduced to Miss Daniels, Herr Goebbels discreetly let it be known that there was a romance in the air.

Director Fischer's repeated visits to Paris were rather strange, since his theatre had long runs and there was no reason at all for him to scout for new talent or material. In fact he never engaged anybody or acquired any new plays in Paris. He spent most of his time in night clubs where he used to tell his theatrical friends many Hitler stories. It was plain that Fischer was fundamentally a vigorous anti-Nazi. Only later, much too late, was it found out that Fischer had had substantial business to attend to in Paris—in these night clubs, in those whose proprietors, managers, headwaiters or hat check girls were mostly white Russians and in close touch with white Russians in Berlin, who in turn were in close contact with the Nazi authorities. In a word, Herr Fischer, as well as Herr Duisberg, as well as many others connected with the German amusement industry, were nothing but couriers whose task it was to get out of France valuable information assembled by German agents and to give their accomplices new instructions.

Then there was the story of the three German cabaret singers who were arrested in Antwerp four days before Hitler invaded Belgium. These beautiful young women who spoke many languages fluently had been employed for some months past in one of the most distinguished night clubs in the city. Although the police had kept a close watch on them, nothing suspicious had been noted. But when they were arrested 'just in case,' they became panic-stricken and admitted that for months they had been transmitting to Germany reports on the movements of shipping in the Albert Canal.

Usually such cabaret girls were not even German. Dr Goebbels preferred Russians, Hungarians, and Yugoslavs. It made collaboration with the Germans harder to prove.

Then there were the circuses. The smuggling in of agents under the guise of circus performers and workers was particularly effective in Poland and Czechoslovakia. It is, after all, natural that circuses should travel from place to place, and the police usually leave them in peace....

Waiters ... exchange professors ... language teachers ... domestic servants....

It was Dr Goebbels who sent the young servant girls who were to spy for Germany to England and Holland. Between 1933 and 1939 more than 20,000 domestic servants arrived in Holland and some 14,000 in England. While the British soon grew suspicious, the Dutch cherished no doubts as to the honesty of German domestic servants. The somewhat prudish Dutch were pleased that these servant girls did not run around, but spent their off evenings in such centres as the meeting place of the 'Women's League' in Utrecht. There they danced, read newspapers, and saw amateur theatrical performances. How could the Dutch suspect that this meeting place was an espionage headquarters?

Finally, there were the German newspaper correspondents abroad, who were, as journalists, naturally under the orders of the Propaganda Minister. Goebbels did not try to send out agents who would act as journalists. Instead he sent out real journalists whose avocation was to spy.

For example, there was the trip of the editor-in-chief of the *Angriff* (Goebbels' newspaper), Hans Schwarz von Berg, who travelled to Australia with a group of specialists in 1938, journeyed through the entire country, set up espionage headquarters, established contact with Japanese organizations, and returning to Berlin delivered a detailed report to the Liaison Staff.

There was Colin Ross, whose career had begun in the Jewish Ullstein Publishing Company. Shortly before the outbreak of the war he travelled through the United States, took pictures of factories and fortifications, to vanish when Washington agents got on his trail.

In 1937 there were more than a hundred German journalists in London alone, many of whom Scotland Yard expelled from the country. A year before the outbreak of the war there were nine German journalists in Denmark (there were one French and two English correspondents and no American representatives at all), who watched the movements of ships, set up secret radio transmitters, and at night signalled from the roof of a house with lamps to German ships in the vicinity.

And then the tourists....

The tourists were a department in themselves. They formed, of course, a section of the Propaganda Ministry, subordinate to Dr Goebbels; but they took their orders directly from a man who was a close friend of the Führer: Hermann Esser.[20]

This special section originated at the time of the Spanish Civil War. Hitler never had any intention of abiding by the non-intervention agreement; of course he proposed to send officers, troops, fliers, and technicians to Spain. The question was: How? How could it be done without openly violating the agreement? At the time this dilemma was being discussed, Hitler's old friend, Hermann Esser, happened to turn up in Berlin. He was asked for suggestions. He suggested that the troops be sent to Spain as tourists. Perhaps he had meant it as a joke, but Hitler immediately realized that there was no reason against it. And so the German tourists descended on Spain and contributed materially to Franco's victory.

Esser had been one of the earliest members of the Party. He was one of the first editors of the *Voelkischer Beobachter*; but he had so compromised himself by his dissolute private life, countless scandals with women, drunkenness, and fraudulent operations that more than once he would have been expelled from the Party had Hitler himself not intervened. Now Hitler saw another chance to do something for this old comrade. He appointed Esser to head the newly founded Tourist Department.

And Esser proved that in this respect at least, Hitler had not misplaced his confidence. He built up the Tourist Department into a great organization. From 1936 on, thousands and tens of thousands of German tourists began to overrun all Germany's neighbour countries. These countries were delighted at the amount of money this tourist traffic brought—all the more so because the great hotels and tourist enterprises had been in a bad fix due to the decline of travel. Now hordes of tourists came—many of them travelling with the expeditions of the 'Strength through Joy' organization, and some of them even stayed on. This was the more magnificent because those who stayed always had enough money to pay their hotel bills and to tip generously.

During all these years there was no suspicion abroad, except for a minor scandal in the spring of 1940 when the Yugoslav Government refused to grant visas to some 15,000 German tourists. Herr Esser flew to Belgrade in an army plane, and the Yugoslavs were finally prevailed upon to lift the ban.

Who were these tourists? The countries through which they travelled always found out too late. They were soldiers, engineers, technicians, and spies. They carried in their knapsacks or their suitcases complicated photographic apparatus, surveying instruments, radio transmitters. They went to Austria and Czechoslovakia, to Poland and Scandinavia. They went to the Balkans and to Greece. In the spring of 1940 the number of railway porters in Athens had to be doubled—so many tourists had suddenly appeared.

They travelled from one country to another—true cosmopolitans. Some remained, and the native population rejoiced at the opportunity to earn a little money catering to them. And the rest reappeared. And the population no longer rejoiced.

Then there was the radio. Radio naturally fell under the authority of the Propaganda Ministry. But Dr Goebbels, who at first had devoted a great deal of his attention to this department, gradually turned it over to his young friend, Eugen Hadamovsky,[21] who under the Republic had held an insignificant position in German radio. Since 1934, Hadamovsky had been chief of radio propaganda for the interior and abroad, He was particularly concerned with the value of radio for espionage. Every year he spent many weeks travelling outside of Germany. He always travelled under an assumed name.

Hadamovsky soon realized that radio could play a major part in espionage only if Germany could command enough trained radio technicians. Therefore, as early as 1934 it was decreed that every young Party member who went abroad or who was sent abroad should have a certain amount of technical radio training. In Göttingen the Radio School of the Hitler Youth was established. Here courses were given on radio methods in other countries. A special Radio Bureau of the Hitler Youth was also organized.

However, the really decisive step was taken by Nazis worming their way into foreign radio stations. That was easy enough in countries whose industrial plants were not sufficiently developed for them to build their own transmitters. Here the German *Telefunken*—subsidized by the Government—moved in to build transmitters at unbelievably low prices. These transmitters were then run by German engineers. In 1936 alone, *Telefunken* built fourteen transmitting stations in Greece, Bulgaria, the Belgian Congo, Argentina, Afghanistan, Siam, China, etc. They were all run by German crews.

For the espionage organization that meant a complete net of radio stations throughout the world. It was simple for the German engineers at these stations to send messages that would be picked up in Germany. On the other hand information or instructions to agents could easily be incorporated in disguised form in some of the hundreds of overseas broadcasts emanating from Germany.

It was merely a question of a clever code. Indeed, radio affords extraordinary opportunities to espionage. Formerly, agents and espionage headquarters communicated through advertisements in newspapers. It is even simpler to effect such communication through radio commercials or through the repetition or succession of certain words in a given broadcast. Radio solved the problem of communication. The German spies needed only to tune in on certain broadcasts to receive their instructions. And they could broadcast their reports according to a prearranged code.

We have no proof that German agents used the radio in this manner, but everything points to it. It is a fact that Hadamovsky had thousands of small transmitters made, many of which were sent abroad. During the battles in Poland, Norway, Holland, and France it was repeatedly discovered that German agents were equipped with such transmitters. In Poland the Nazis had even built some big transmitters, and broadcast on the wave length of the Warsaw Radio contradictory reports which confused the populace and the army. In England two spies were recently discovered in possession of a small transmitter. There is little doubt that German espionage has made use of radio for many years.

Dr Goebbels has an inventive mind and—alas—a very ingenious one. His latest idea is quite obvious, but strangely enough no secret service of any country had ever thought of it.

Dr Goebbels found out that the work of many good agents went for naught because they used tricks that had been used before and consequently were known to the enemy secret service. He therefore had blacklists drawn up of these outmoded tricks, which were sent to the various bureaus and departments.

A very simple idea, indeed. But—someone had to have it.

SCHOOLS FOR SPIES

Heinrich Himmler's headquarters are on Prinz Albrecht Strasse and Wilhelmstrasse 77, Berlin. Located here are the various subsections of the Foreign Supervisory Bureau—UAI. These subsections are called territorial bureaus. Until 1937 there were eight such territorial bureaus; by the early part of 1939 there were twelve:

1. Scandinavia (including Finland and the Baltic States)
2. France
3. Italy
4. The Balkans and Turkey
5. Switzerland, Hungary, Czechoslovakia, and Austria (It is interesting that the two last-named countries, which at that time were already occupied, are nevertheless considered foreign countries and their territorial bureau continues to function.)
6. Belgium and Holland
7. Spain and Portugal
8. United States
9. Central America to the Panama Canal
10. South America
11. Great Britain (the whole Empire)
12. Far East

These territorial bureaus were subdivided into units of which there were more than 800 early in 1939. (No reliable figures are available for later dates.)

For many reasons, above all from fear of counterespionage, Himmler and his closest associate, Reinhard Heydrich, felt it inadvisable to let too many at the Berlin headquarters know too much. The Gestapo therefore began more and more to decentralize its espionage activities. After 1935, offices were dispersed throughout the Reich at which agents from abroad could be received and from which they could be sent out. There were such offices in Cologne, Hamburg, Magdeburg, Dresden, Munich, Baden-Baden, and so on.

These Gestapo offices, which were set up in ordinary private dwelling houses, were all very much alike. To the innocent visitor they might appear to be internal revenue offices. The rooms were not large and had an air of military austerity. In each room sat two officials. One of them did most of the work; the other was apt to be a heavy strong-bodied man who worked little. His principal function was that of bodyguard, but he also would use his strength to extract information from visitors who were unwilling to give it. The rest of the building was filled with files and documents, especially the cellar, where they were piled high. All the windows were barred.

The existence of these offices in the town might have remained secret if the Gestapo had not made the mistake of bringing to them citizens of the town who had committed some offence against the regime, or who had Jewish grandmothers. Many of those who entered the buildings were not seen again. That soon got around and thus the whole purpose of these secret, camouflaged offices was set at naught.

Finally, the Gestapo maintained offices outside Germany. They all hid behind some front, and in no case was the front organization at all suggestive of Germany or German institutions. Never, for example, did the Gestapo work behind the front of the German Railways Information bureaus—as has often been asserted—or within any of the foreign branches of German business houses. Rather, some small private enterprise was chosen, whose owner was a citizen of the country in question. The Gestapo preferred small saloons and bars, tailor shops, grocery stores, and small neighbourhood movies—in short, places where, without exciting remark, people might enter and leave all day long and sometimes late into the night.... There were such Gestapo branch offices in Prague, Innsbruck, Lyons, Roubaix, Mexico City, Tokyo, Rotterdam, and many other cities.

But—this must be emphasized—nowhere did the Gestapo function abroad on the grand scale that the so-called experts have imputed to it. For years every German agent was assumed to be a Gestapo official. This is quite wrong. Numerically, Himmler had far less men abroad than, say, Goebbels—let alone Rosenberg or Bohle. The error probably arises from the fact that within Germany Himmler did have a great many agents. But we must remember that these were used primarily for police purposes and for counterespionage. And even within the German police force the numbers of the Gestapo were relatively small.

According to the best estimate (still on the basis of the latest dependable figures—beginning of 1939) Himmler had no more than 4,000 men and women working for him outside of Germany. Since 1938 has been shown as the year of greatest espionage activity, today this number can hardly be much greater.

Nor is such a number inadequate in view of the real task of the Himmler machine. Himmler's men were not supposed to practice the general, undifferentiated espionage of Bohle's men—but were assigned to specific missions. They generally did work for the military intelligence service and the Foreign Ministry, in particular for Ribbentrop and Canaris. They were specialized spies who often kept a whole staff of agents (selected from envoys of Dr Goebbels or Bohle's masses of Germans abroad, for instance). In fact, they rather approximated the role of the old-fashioned spy of the romantic era.

The majority of these men came from the SD—the Security Division of the SS, a kind of intelligence service which had been founded a year before Hitler's accession to power. Its purpose at that time was principally to keep watch on Party members and see to it that nothing was done or said in the Party without Hitler's knowledge. Later a large portion of these SD men transferred to the Gestapo and then were detailed to the Foreign Department when they were needed.

But most of the new men had to undergo long, hard training before they were sent out of the Reich. They had to pass through what are popularly known as the spy schools.

During the past few years much has been written about these schools of espionage, and most of it is false and nonsensical. According to most descriptions, the spy schools are astounding and highly romantic institutions. There has been much talk about classes of only five students, who all wear masks so that later on should they meet they will not recognize each other; of oaths of secrecy; of other oaths of obedience even to the point of murdering a member of one's immediate family; of courses in opening complicated locks, using cameras the size of pins, etc. Had such methods been the rule, German espionage would not have got very far.

The true picture is more sober, but more correct. Some of the future members of the German espionage system, others besides Himmler's agents, are given training. The number is comparatively small; they are those who are destined for a leading position that calls for initiative. Not only Germans, but some foreigners are trained. Most of these foreigners, however, are used only by Himmler and the Military Intelligence Service. That young foreigners are admitted to the training courses was due to Himmler; he realized that Germans are no good at understanding the psychology of other peoples, while Romanians and Bulgars, for instance, very quickly adjust to a new environment and can enter into the frame of mind of other nationalities. Finally, the spy schools are by no means devoted exclusively to the education of spies. As we shall see, these schools, with one exception, have other educational aims.

Espionage schools are no new development. In the First World War there were many of them, French and English as well as German.

The new German spy school (for the sake of simplicity this popular term will be employed) represented a synthesis of the tested principles of the old spy schools and the newest Nazi methods. As has been shown, earlier espionage was concentrated in the secret services of the General Staffs and the military and naval attachés. Their methods, however, were no longer sufficient for total warfare, and the new spy schools had to teach modern subjects. Formerly agents were trained for the purloining of secret plans; now they must be taught how to handle men and how to influence them.

The general basis for these training centres was laid long before Hitler came to power. But it was not until 1934 that the first institutions which can be called spy schools were established. The administration of the schools was given into the hands of Colonel Hans von Voss,[22] retired, who was also head of the Psychological Laboratory of the War Ministry.

These new spy schools had one principle in common, a principle which had been laid down by Professor Haushofer.

The idea was not to give spies general training, but to train them to cope with a specific enemy whose weaknesses and strong points were known.

The selection of students was based upon the aptitude tests which had been developed by the Psychological Laboratory. Those Germans who passed these tests were first sent to the Secondary School for Politics (*Hochschule fuer Politik*). (They were recommended for the aptitude tests by the Hitler Youth, the SA, the SS, or certain student organizations.) In this school they were given courses on foreign countries. The instructors came from the Haushofer Institute and from Rosenberg's organization. There were also some former officers who taught *Wehrwissenschaft*—Science of War.

Those who passed some final tests were then sent to leadership schools, called *Ordensburgen*. While training in these *Ordensburgen* was not solely for espionage, about one quarter of the four to five thousand students were later given espionage assignments. Rudolf Hess and his Liaison Staff were the highest supervisory authorities of these *Ordensburgen*. The further education of the students was decided by Hess and his staff on the basis of the reports sent in to him. Students had to attend the *Ordensburgen* for four years, but those whom the Liaison Staff singled out for espionage work were released sooner. They were then sent to the so-called High School (*Hohe Schule*) at Chiemsee in Bavaria. This school was a great research institution on foreign countries, and possessed an enormous library. It was attended only by future spies. They took courses in race biology, languages, character and customs of various nations, and geo-politics. The language teachers were all foreigners. They not only gave language lessons, but also retailed much valuable information about their home countries.

Then the students were sent to a foreign university for a short time. While there they had to send in monthly reports and prove their talents for observation and gaining important connections.

And the foreigners?

Since early 1934 many camps have been established in Germany which were not labour camps, but vacation camps. To these came Russians, Sudeten Germans, Ukrainians, Austrians, and men from the Baltic States— all pro-Nazis who hoped some day to become *führers*. These camps were administered by Rosenberg.

Here, too, came not only prospective *führers*, but prospective spies as well. The courses in these camps were more or less general in character.

Then there were the congresses of Bohle's AO, which were held every year in Stuttgart just before the Nuremberg Party Congress. At these congresses there were a number of public lectures and debates on cultural matters; but at the same time there was a special course for a few picked men which dealt mainly with the problems of espionage. These few picked men remained long after the congress had adjourned. Most of them were sent to the camps, where they met other aspirant spies. At the camps they attended specialized courses, their instructors being officers from the War Ministry, Haushofer's professors, members of the Psychological Laboratory. At the end of the courses they had to take examinations. While these examinations were in progress, a few observers from the *Reichswehr* generally visited the camp.

Those who distinguished themselves in the examinations were sent to Altona (near Hamburg), where in 1935 a veritable university of espionage had been set up. Here specialized training was given; for example, spies learned code telegraphy, deciphering, signalling. Memory exercise was one of the subjects.

When their education was complete, the students were distributed. That is, various organizations chose individual students whose particular talents seemed best suited to their purposes. With very few exceptions, only Germans were eligible for the organizations of Bohle, Goebbels, Rosenberg, and Ribbentrop. And the studies they had undertaken were sufficient for the tasks that would be set them.

The War Ministry and the Gestapo employed both Germans and foreigners. Foreigners had to become naturalized Germans—so that, if the worst should happen, the Nazis would have some hold over them; and this requirement was never waived. But the naturalization was not made public, so that many agents who had been born abroad could continue to use their own foreign passports.

The War Ministry (Nicolai) and the Gestapo then sent their men to specialist schools. These schools, which taught military espionage, were, with two exceptions, located in the vicinity of Berlin. The syllabus of the schools was approximately the same as that of the lower espionage schools, except that the length of the course was only six months—extraordinarily short. The students had already had considerable schooling.

The Gestapo schools were mainly located in the Rhineland and in the northernmost sections of Germany. The final courses at these schools lasted nine months, but were frequently abridged if it became necessary to send out certain of the students. Nothing definite is known about the syllabus itself. However, we may assume that the students here received a final technical polish.

There was still another Department in Himmler's machine. This was Experimental Department D. Nothing has ever been written about this department. Few of the Nazi leaders have even heard of its existence. It is headed by Theodor Habicht,[23] who works with a small staff of a dozen or so agents. His offices arc in the Turmstrasse, in the North of Berlin.

In 1933 Hitler sent Habicht to Austria to prepare the 'conquest from within.' With the defeat of the early Nazi attempts, Habicht was expelled from Austria, though the German Government tried to keep him there by appointing him press attaché. He then set up his headquarters in Munich and organized arms smuggling and terrorist activities in Austria. He also compiled lists of Austrian anti-Nazis which later proved of value. Gradually he disappeared from the public eye, and it was assumed that he had fallen into Hitler's disfavour for his failure in bringing about a revolution in Austria. But as so often happens with the bigwigs of the Nazi organization, Habicht had been allowed to retire into obscurity in order to build up a new organization. Obviously someone—either Hitler himself or Hess, or Himmler—was convinced that Habicht had done good work in Austria and that his talents for terrorism ought not to lie fallow. He was assigned to head Experimental Department D and was responsible only to Himmler. Here, on the basis of his experience in Austria, he worked out the principles for the use of terrorism in espionage and in the undermining of a country.

It could not be determined whether Habicht still heads this department since the outbreak of the war, or whether he has been transferred. In any case, he was still in his office in the Turmstrasse shortly before the outbreak of the war.

MOBILIZATION IN OUR TIME

When in the autumn of 1937 Hitler informed his General Staff that he intended to invade Austria and force the *Anschluss*, he met with considerable opposition from leading officers—which led to a big shake-up early in 1938. But more than that, Hitler's decision surprised the Intelligence Service and somewhat embarrassed Colonel Nicolai and his associates. For at this time Colonel Nicolai made slower progress than others of the total espionage system. At least the work proceeded more slowly in Austria. Strangely enough, German military espionage had met with particularly strong resistance there. As it later developed, Austria's resistance was stronger than any other country's besides England. The Austrian counterespionage system was on its toes. There was, for example, the Debrunner case.

Ministerial Councillor Debrunner was the chief of the decoding division of the Austrian Foreign Ministry. The most confidential documents and correspondence passed through his hands, particularly Mussolini's letters to Dollfuss and later to Schuschnigg. Debrunner was no longer a young man; he had proved his talents during the First World War. During the putsch of July 25, 1934, which resulted in the death of Dollfuss,[24] he too was imprisoned by the rebellious Nazis. But in the face of all the threats against his life, he refused to decipher the telegrams that poured into the Austrian Capital. After the putsch had been put down, Debrunner was hailed as one of the few reliable officials and given great authority.

Nevertheless, his behaviour must somehow have awakened suspicion. General Ronge,[25] the Chief of Counterespionage, who had distinguished himself in the First World War and who was credited among other feats with the unmasking and arrest of the famed Colonel Redl,[26] personally kept watch on Debrunner. Before long Ronge had evidence that Debrunner each week delivered several important state secrets to the Nazis. This trusted patriot communicated with the German Intelligence Service by means of letters apparently addressed to his married daughter, who lived in Munich. Ronge proved that long before the assassination of Dollfuss, Debrunner had been a henchman of the Germans, and that his refusal to help the Nazis at the time of the putsch had been no more than a cleverly trumped-up gesture.

Debrunner was arrested and one of Nicolai's most important contacts was lost.

Austrian counterespionage was so competent that many other contacts were also lost. Towards the latter part of 1937 Nicolai resolved to take the whole military espionage organization in Austria under his personal direction. He sent a number of his best agents there to establish relations with 'dissatisfied' officers, and during this period a great many German officers began to visit garrison and frontier towns. Nicolai and his agents, to their great relief, discovered that the Austrian Army was neither technically nor morally prepared to offer serious resistance. In the end, it did not matter. One cannot say that the invasion of Austria would have been forestalled had her military situation been better. The invasion of Austria was never a military problem.

By this time Nicolai had accomplished the thorough reorganization of military espionage. The basic idea of his espionage system was that minor matters (like deployment plans, blue prints, etc.) counted for little besides the establishing of fundamental relationships. His was, above all, a statistical and scientific investigation. The state of the opponents' armaments— particularly those of the Western Powers—was studied attentively in Berlin. All the flaws in this armament, as well as in the opponents' military training, were carefully indexed. Perhaps the most important task of this scientific espionage was the construction of the probable strategic plans of the enemies ... the scientific prediction of the way the Allies would conduct the coming war.

As early as 1 October 1936, the leading German military publication, the *Handbuch der Neuzeitlichen Kriegswissenschaft* (Handbook of Modern Military Science), had recommended the literature of other countries as

a first-rate source of military information to agents busy with 'research.'
Now, two books—one published in France, the other in England—were a
great help to the German General Staff. One of these was by the French
General Chauvineau: *L'Invasion est-elle encore possible?* ('Is Invasion Still
Possible?'); it was published in 1938 with a foreword by Marshal Pétain.
From this book the German Staff officers could deduce that the French
would wage a defensive war because they believed their fortifications to
be invulnerable. From Pétain's foreword it was clear to the Germans that
the French Army leaders had no conception of modern breakthrough
operations; that they totally underestimated the effect of modern weapons
and had optimistic illusions about the resistance fortifications could offer.
Marshal Pétain gave vent to the fantastic assertion that barbed wire and
machine guns were sufficient to prevent the break-through of modern
armies. He wrote: 'If the entire theatre of operations is obstructed, there is
no means on earth that can break the insurmountable barrier formed on
the ground by automatic arms associated with barbed wire entanglements.'
And General Chauvineau declared:

> By placing two million men with the proper number of machine guns and
> pill boxes along the 250-mile stretch through which the German armies
> must pass to enter France, we shall be able to hold them up for three years.

The German General Staff could wish no more in the way of a complete
exposition of the French war plan. Knowing that plan, they would prepare
their own strategy for the breakthrough.

Another book which offered just as important—or, if you will,
disastrous—information was that of the well-known English military writer,
Liddell Hart. His *The Defence of Britain* was published shortly before the
outbreak of the Second World War.

Mr Liddell Hart was an adviser to the British War Ministry, and in his
book he published the memoranda on British strategy which he had written
for the War Ministry. These memoranda revealed that the British land army
would be kept small; that Great Britain intended to participate in combat
on the Continent only in a very limited way. It is significant that Liddell
Hart's book was the subject of a discussion among Hitler, Hess, Nicolai,
and a number of leading officers of the General Staff. This discussion took
place on 25 July 1939, and lasted for several hours. According to very
trustworthy sources, the Germans drew the following conclusions from the
book:

1. For the present the Allies would not attempt any offensive war against
   Germany.

2. Neither the English nor the French had recognized the possibility of operating with flying corps and mechanized units.
3. The French and British had not recognized the value of aircraft reconnaissance, and it would take a long time before they made the necessary shift.

It must be admitted that the Germans drew correct conclusions from these two books. And it is easy to understand why at the close of the conference, Hess said, 'Liddell Hart's book has been of incalculable value for the German estimate of the situation, and has important practical applications....'

Strange as it sounds, Austria was the toughest nut the Military Intelligence Service had to crack. In other countries everything was much easier. By January 1938 the War Ministry had established a definite programme of action. After Austria was to come Czechoslovakia, then Poland; then the Germans would go into the Balkans, down to Greece and into Turkey. These military actions were already being anticipated on the espionage front.

The next target of the espionage machine was therefore Czechoslovakia. Here Nicolai had been at work for a long time, and if we are to believe his statement of December 1938, for a long time Czechoslovakia had held no military secrets that he did not know. His agents had operated with a number of ends in view. They had tried, with a certain amount of success, to undermine the morale of the army by playing off against each other the Slovaks, Magyars, Poles, and Ruthenians. Furthermore, they had won over two instructors at the military academy. Practically all the secrets of the fortifications, particularly of Theresienstadt, between Prague and the German border, were in Nazi hands (we are quoting Nicolai himself on these points). The locks and barriers which were to block any passage of the Elbe—a device that was the most zealously guarded of Czech secrets—were known to the Germans. More than a year before Munich, Nicolai had donated money to the Sudeten German peasants that they might build new barns. These barns were used as munitions dumps. Nicolai declared that if the Munich conference had not yielded an agreement, and if Czechoslovakia had gone to war, the Czech Army would have broken up in the first few days....

A great deal of espionage was undertaken in Poland, where this had proceeded according to plan since 1933, despite the treaty of amity between Germany and Poland. In 1936, Nicolai established Camp Rummelsburg in Pomerania, where he trained between two and four thousand prospective spies and terrorists for work in Poland. After completing the course, the students were sent directly into Poland.

In Warsaw itself Nicolai had a number of agents who watched the Polish War Ministry and reported everything of importance that happened there.

Nicolai even succeeded in smuggling some of his men into the Polish General Staff. He was clever enough not to use these men until the outbreak of the war, so that they were never tainted with the slightest suspicion. In the war itself they were invaluable, for they kept Nicolai informed of every move of the Polish General Staff.

The direction of military espionage in Poland was placed—many years before the war—in the hands of Colonel Gerstenberg,[27] the military attaché to the German Embassy in Warsaw. Under him worked two other attachés: Dr Evald Kruemmer and Dr G. Strube. The success of the Nazis was not altogether complete. Occasionally the Polish counterespionage got wind of a German device. For instance, the Poles caught up with a spy named Baldyga, who had once fled Poland to escape a prison term. His arrest led to the arrest of an official of the Polish Military Geographical Institute named Reszka.

It is amazing how much the Poles did discover. They found many ammunition dumps which the Germans had established in churches; they found espionage headquarters in the branches of great industrial plants, like I. G. Farbenindustrie and Siemens-Schuckert.

To be sure, much that they found out was discovered hopelessly late. For example, Nicolai had contrived an excellent system by which German spies could signal to German fliers during war. A system of signals was set up which could be recognized from the air, the signals formed by the disposition of hay and corn sticks, by scything grain according to the designs shown in the accompanying diagrams, by painting the roofs, by light signals.

The badges by which the advancing troops could recognize German agents were:

1. Red cloth with a large yellow spot in the centre.
2. A light blue armband with a yellow dot in the centre.
3. A light-brown and grey overall with a yellow grenade on the collar and left sleeve.

The password had cost Nicolai much thought, for it had to be a word which is pronounced the same in a number of languages. Echo is pronounced the same in German, Polish, Ukrainian, Russian, and Czech.

Other campaigns, in fact all preliminary work for the coming war, were prepared down to the last detail on the espionage front. In this connection it is amusing to recall that at the outbreak of the war a German decree was published to the effect that German citizens living abroad in neutral countries could not be called up for military service, and even volunteers

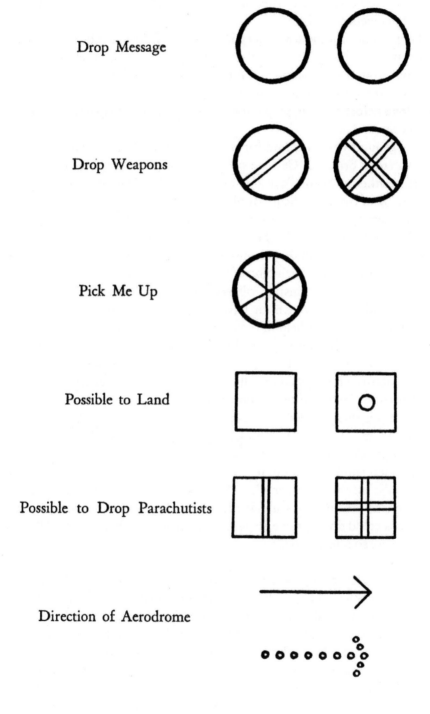

Drop Message

Drop Weapons

Pick Me Up

Possible to Land

Possible to Drop Parachutists

Direction of Aerodrome

were not to be accepted. After all, the Nazis did not want to disrupt their own Intelligence Service.

Preparations for the sea raiders' manoeuvres were made by the espionage organization only at great cost and under the severest difficulties. It was obvious from the beginning that the creation of refuelling stations for ships like the *Graf Spee* and the *Bismarck* could only be undertaken under cover. Yet, long before the war, preparations were complete in Spain, Mexico, and on the South American Coast.

The groundwork was laid for the invasion of Holland. The capture of the Moerdyk Bridge by German soldiers in Dutch uniforms must have been an idea either of Nicolai's or one of his disciples. The same applies to the smuggling of troops in the holds of Rhine barges....

A modern type of reconnaissance which the Germans rehearsed for years was air reconnaissance. To the amazement of the Germans, the Allies had no conception of it, but they themselves had it so thoroughly organized and tested that right at the beginning of the war every inch of French militarized territory was under constant observation by German flyers. Centres of the war industries, French air bases, railway lines, troop movements—everything of the sort behind the enemy lines was immediately wirelessed to headquarters by German air observers. The German General Staff had an exact picture of the French theatre of war over an area of hundreds of kilometres. How systematically and accurately the Germans worked is evidenced by the tripartite organization of air espionage.

There was the so-called operative air reconnaissance, which had the task of observing the industrial and transportation centres of the enemy and his military organization. Then there was the practical air reconnaissance, which determined the deployment of the enemy. Finally there was reconnaissance of the enemy's military position in the battle zone, and these observers had to locate artillery placements and fortifications. The Germans could do extensive air research, particularly because the Allied air forces were so inferior to theirs.

We see the cleverness and foresight of the German Military Intelligence Service as it emerged from a little misadventure that its rival—the *Deuxième Bureau*—experienced in the first few days of the war. Many serious observers believe that but for this incident, the war might have taken a considerably different turn. But there is little point in discussing such an outcome now.

When the war started—or to be exact—on the night of 1–2 September 1939, the *Deuxième Bureau* arrested one hundred and ninety-eight persons suspected of being in the employ of the German secret service. Had it arrested two thousand persons, it would have come closer to achieving its purpose.

On that night, needless to say, there was furious activity in the War Ministry. There were lights in all the windows. Hundreds of conferences were going on. The most important took place, of course, in the private offices of the Premier and War Minister, Édouard Daladier. He was closeted for hours with General Gamelin and members of the General Staff, with Georges Bonnet, his Foreign Minister, and other ministers.

Now something may be revealed about this conference which, though rumoured for some time, has always been denied by French authorities. The Commander-in-Chief, Gamelin, made known his intention to invade Italy without a declaration of war. The plan, of course, had been worked out years before by the General Staff, as every General Staff in the world works out every conceivable plan. But it was only now that Gamelin espoused this particular plan. Georges Bonnet protested vehemently. But Gamelin had better arguments. He said that with the Siegfried Line mounted with Czech guns, a march through Italy was the only way to attack Germany while Hitler was still busy in Poland. Gamelin had nothing but contempt for the Italian military apparatus. He said in so many words that he would be sure to smash Italy within a few weeks and to open a front at the Brenner pass. Nor had he any qualms about attacking Mussolini, for he was of the opinion that sooner or later Mussolini would make common cause with Hitler.

It was then that Colonel Gauché, the head of the *Deuxième Bureau* appeared upon the scene. Or, to be exact, he appeared in the anteroom and insisted upon M. Daladier's being called out. He explained that he had received exceedingly important information. He handed Premier Daladier a bundle of telegrams.

Daladier read them. He then looked with utter amazement at the Colonel. 'It is absolutely reliable?' he asked.

The Colonel said, 'It comes from a very reliable source.'

The telegrams were copies of telegrams which Mussolini personally was supposed to have sent to his ambassadors in London and Paris. They were exceedingly confidential messages which said in so many words that Mussolini was not in accord with the foreign policy of his son-in-law, Count Ciano, and that he did not want to be mixed up in a war—which at the writing of the telegram was still in the offing. Reading between the lines, one could assume that Mussolini's intention was to persuade Hitler that he would go into the war with him, but that he would actually bow himself out at the last moment.

Daladier returned to the conference. Perhaps up to now he had not cast his die for or against Gamelin's plan. Now he told the commander that he did not approve. Perhaps Gamelin has never learned why Daladier so definitely vetoed his project. In any case, there is no use in reflecting upon the turn the war might have taken had Gamelin gone into Italy.

Four weeks later, after the first rush was over, Daladier began to have some doubts. One day while receiving the Italian Ambassador, he suddenly asked him a question connected with the secret telegrams of Mussolini. The Ambassador looked blank. Either he is an extremely good actor, or such telegrams had never been sent, Daladier thought. And the Ambassador was not a very good actor, he decided.

There was some commotion at the *Deuxième Bureau* when Daladier informed Gauché that he thought the telegrams were fake. Gauché immediately started an investigation.

It appeared that the source was not quite as reliable as Colonel Gauché had thought, that two French agents had acquired the telegrams by a very roundabout route from an employee of the German Legation in Switzerland who had managed to convince them that the messages came straight from Mussolini's private secretary. Finally, after retracing, it was discovered that this employee was Fritz Weinmann—who was no stranger to the *Deuxième Bureau*. Years ago Fritz Weinmann had left Germany, ostensibly as a refugee unwilling to live under Hitler's regime, had joined the French Foreign Legion, and had later been hired by an agent of the *Deuxième Bureau* and sent to Switzerland. But before very long the *Deuxième Bureau* learned that Fritz Weinmann was not working for them, but for Germany, and they got rid of him before—so they thought—he had done any serious damage.

But the damage was bad enough. Fritz Weinmann had been industrious; he had made sufficient connections, obtained addresses of enough agents, to swing this coup with the Mussolini telegrams.

Incidentally, the reaction of the Italian Ambassador proved that the Italian Government knew nothing of the whole affair. The Nazi agents just went ahead and forged the telegrams without even bothering to inform those who were soon after to become their allies.

But such adventurous and theatrical stunts were the exception. The really important acts of espionage were characterized by their simplicity. In January 1940 a German plane landed on Belgian soil. The pilot declared he had lost his way in the fog. He had with him important documents, which he tried to burn, but which were seized from him. The documents indicated that a German invasion of Belgium was in preparation. Naturally the Anglo-French Command was warned and measures long since prearranged were put into effect. Then nothing happened, nothing at all. The following weeks saw no sign of invasion.

The press and the public began to wonder what it was all about. Wasn't it strange that a German pilot carrying such important documents should get lost so easily? The obvious answer seemed to be that it was all part of the war of nerves. The forced landing had been a fake; the Germans had put the documents into the hands of the Allies merely to create unrest.[28]

As events showed, that was not the case. Rather, the forced landing was a trick of the German Intelligence Service, a trick which was to have terrible consequences for the Allies. The Nazis had hoped that the Allies would be alarmed by the documents. They realized that when the warning came the British and French troops on the Belgian border in the North would take up the battle positions prescribed by Allied plan of operations in the event of a German invasion of Belgium. All the Germans did was use their observation planes to take pictures of the troop movements and the positions, so that the German High Command would have a complete picture of how the Allied troops would be disposed for a real German invasion of Belgium.

From these photographs the Germans learned that the main weight of the Anglo-French troops was thrown in the North, along the coast. It was therefore clear that the Allies were planning to carry out their counter-manoeuvre from Northern France to Northern Belgium. In the course of this operation, the French central sector, between the Maginot line and the coast—that is, the Sedan sector—was only lightly held.

The Germans therefore started their offensive of 10 May 1940 with a feint to convince the Allies that the main blow would come in northern Belgium. The Allies then followed their plan—as the Germans had intended—and disposed their main force in the north. In the Sedan sector they were relatively weak, and three days later the Germans broke through there. A large part of the Allied armies fell into a trap; the Allied front was divided and the armies of the north were encircled.

It had taken an entirely new manoeuvre in espionage to make this triumph possible. It was a manoeuvre in which the enemy was provoked into laying his cards on the table; and the latest type of air reconnaissance was used to get a good look at those cards. An entirely new type of espionage. New, perhaps, in its simplicity.

INTERMEZZO: CLOUDS OF SPIES

Step right in, ladies and gentlemen! Here you will see the greatest show on earth, 'Peace in Our Time.' Here is a world without secrets. You see it all. A world invaded by armies of spies. A sky darkened with clouds of spies. Step right in.

Spies.... Spies....

Are there figures? Plenty of them. Some people say thousands, some say hundreds of thousands of spies. Long before the German Army struck, long before the tanks lumbered over the roads in the lands of innocent peoples, long before the Stukas shattered their houses into dust and ashes. The clouds of spies are forming above our heads. But it's still peace. Peace in our time.

Step right in, ladies and gentlemen. Here they are, right before you. The armies of Colonel Nicolai, the armies of Herr von Ribbentrop and Alfred Rosenberg, the armies of Joseph Goebbels and Heinrich Himmler....

Step right in, ladies and gentlemen. Here you can see Dr Froelichtstal, the trusted private secretary of Chancellor Schuschnigg who planted microphones in his private office so that the Germans would hear what Dr Schuschnigg was planning.

Here you can see Hildegard Heinrich from Czechoslovakia, who went to South America and sent monthly lists to Germany of men who had to be disposed of.

Here you can see Sean Russell,[29] head of the Irish Republican Army, who went to Hamburg for money and bombs, so that he could stir up a little trouble for England.

Here you can see Herr Greindl, who set up a scenic railway in the Vienna Prater—which ran through a tunnel where Nazi leaflets were printed calling for an armed uprising against the Austrian Government.

Here you can see Mattieu Antoine, the chief of the espionage organization of Eupen and Malmedy, and his friend Buhrke, the man who organized the Flemings.

Here is the private secretary of Dr Zernatto, the Austrian Minister, who sent all important official secrets to Berlin. Here is Dr Viktor Steyskal, who had a sanatorium in Steiermark and a short-wave set in his X-ray room so that he could send reports directly to Berlin.

Here you can see a Swiss who worked in the Avenida Palace in Lisbon and kept the Germans informed about arrivals and departures. Here you can see Baron de Potters, citizen of many nations, who had passports under the names of Farmer and Meyhert; the man who supplied the *Cagoulards* with money and who worked for the *Deuxième Bureau* and for Berlin at the same time.

Here you can see Mr and Mrs Luis Barcata, Austrian intellectuals who came to Athens, tried to make contacts with the French and English, and gave out that they were anti-Nazi—two of Herr Bohle's best agents.

Step right in, ladies and gentlemen! We have a cast of hundreds, thousands, hundreds of thousands. Just glance at one or the other as they pass by. That's quite enough. It would take years, ladies and gentlemen, if you tried to study them all closely.

Come in and admire our beautiful costumes, ladies and gentlemen. We've spared no cost, no effort. We've supplied our actors with the most magnificent disguises you will ever see. See this young girl, here? She is the governess of the son of one of America's greatest woman journalists. See that man there? He is a waiter in the best hotel in Paris. Those young fellows back there are workers in an aircraft factory on the Pacific Coast.

The old gentleman standing near them is a language teacher. Oh, we have many language teachers. We have servant girls, theatre owners, and whole film companies—yes, we even have whole circuses included in our unique, colossal, greatest circus of all time.

Step right in, ladies and gentlemen. Here you will see miracles: people who are here one moment and gone the next. Where are they? Perhaps at the other end of the world. Certainly halfway across Europe.

We are going to let you in on a little secret, ladies and gentlemen. There's no black magic about it, everything is very, very simple. Did you ever hear of international express trains? There's the Arlberg-Orient Express, for instance. Starts out from Calais, stops in Paris, Basle, Zurich, Innsbruck, Vienna, Budapest, Belgrade, and Athens. Or there's the Nordexpress. Leaves Ostend and stops in Brussels, Liège, Cologne, Berlin, Breslau, Kattowitz, Krakow, and Bucharest. Or there is the Orient express: Calais, Paris, Munich, Belgrade, Sofia, Istanbul.... Nothing easier than changing trains. Europe is small if you know the train connections, and it isn't necessary to use the airlines which are watched by every secret service in Europe.

For instance, there's the London-Paris-Prague express and a section of the Orient Express, and both pass through Nüremberg. Just a short stop, and there's nothing to changing trains. In fact, many international trains pass each other in Nüremberg, and in Cologne and Leipzig. And the operatives of the *Deuxième Bureau* or the British Intelligence Service who have a tip and are waiting for some man in Paris or London, don't find him. And they have no way of knowing that another man who came on the train has exchanged roles with the man they expect and is just as dangerous. ... Step right in, ladies and gentlemen....

You want to know what these men and women filing past you are murmuring? Just step up closer. Do you hear them? *Telephone and telegraph trunk lines ... civilian morale ... shipments to military centres ... reservoirs ... supplies of material ... air-force concentrations ... canals and locks ... fortifications ... photos ... dry docks ... destruction of communication facilities ... munition plants ... navy yards ... blueprints....*

What's that, ladies and gentlemen? You're not going? Why, the performance has just started! Don't you hear these marvellous explosions? In London, Birmingham, Liverpool? Bombing outrages of the IRA.[30] Don't you hear the shots? That's the Rumanian Iron Guard liquidating their opponents. All with the help of the Germans, all the work of the great army of spies.

Just look around you. See the slaughtered students in Prague, the weeping children in Belgium and Holland, the starving people of France. See the ...

It's the greatest show you've ever seen, isn't it, ladies and gentlemen? It's the most tremendous espionage machine that has ever existed. It's the

... What's that? You don't want to see and hear any more? You live in an age like this and you don't want to see its most magnificent show? You want to go home? You want to hide away within your own four walls? You say that doesn't matter to you? You want to isolate yourselves? Ladies and gentlemen, you can't do it. The parade here is going on. Ladies and gentlemen, these armies don't stand still.

PART IV
The Debacle

THE FRIENDS OF MONSIEUR BONNET

On 28 June 1939, Premier Daladier made a highly sensational speech in the Chamber of Deputies, all the more sensational because not even his colleagues in the Cabinet had had any inkling of what he was going to say:

> We are witnessing in our midst, a singular act of propaganda, and it is now in my opinion established beyond doubt that it emanates from abroad. The goal of these activities is to destroy the unity of France, to drive a wedge into the block of French energy in order to facilitate all kinds of sinister intrigues and manoeuvres....
>
> We have been able to start certain investigations. We have been able to follow up certain trails. And we are absolutely convinced that an attempt is being made to imprison France within a net of intrigue and espionage....
>
> I don't want to exaggerate. But I will not try either to conceal the gravity of the situation, for I think it is better to tell the straight truth to the country.

He then proceeded to explain that several arrests had been made a few hours before he had begun to speak. He declared that the apparatus of German espionage within France was much more powerful than he had thought, but that the strictest measures would now be taken—especially since it had been found that not only foreigners but French citizens were involved.

A few hours after this speech a breathless public learned the names of the Frenchmen involved. They were Alois Aubin, associate editor of *Le Temps*; Julien Poirier, director of the *Figaro*; Gaston Amourelle, official stenographic clerk of the Senate. The tip-off as to who and what were behind these arrests was that the apprehended men were not taken into the prison of the Prefecture (Police Department), nor into the Santé, the jail under the administration of the Ministry of the Interior. They were transferred to the military prison in the Rue du Cherche Midi; they were therefore under the jurisdiction of the Ministry of War, or, to be exact, of the *Deuxième Bureau.*

The *Deuxième Bureau,* for once, had taken the initiative.

Twenty-four hours before Daladier made his speech, Colonel Gauché and his two *sous-chefs,* Commandants Perrier and Novarre, had visited the Premier. The Colonel in an ominous voice asked to be received immediately. The Premier, who was not very fond of the Colonel, stared rather dismally at the fat portfolios the officers had brought along, and said nervously that he had no time to look over documents just then. The Colonel then put his foot down:

> The matter is urgent, it is urgent and something must be done about it immediately. It is my duty, Monsieur le Premier, to inform you that if you do not promptly take action on what I am going to tell you, I will resign immediately. So will these gentlemen. The security of our country is at stake.

The Premier paled and the deprecating smile froze on his lips. He had not asked the gentlemen to sit down, but the Colonel took a chair and opened the first portfolio. And now a strange story was revealed to the dismayed Premier. It was the story of the activities of the Baroness von Einem, the charming, beautiful, and wealthy German spy. It was a story of her accomplices, of the gentlemen of *Le Temps* and the *Figaro,* and of a banker, Hirsch, who had been the paymaster for a whole network of spies—through whose hands within the last five months ten million marks ($4,000,000) had passed.

The story started with Ferdinand de Brinon; of course, Daladier knew who Ferdinand de Brinon was. M. de Brinon was a journalist who had often gone to Berlin, and who finally became Berlin correspondent of the French newspaper, *L'information,* which served the interests of and was financed by the big steel and coal industries. He had become one of the most important French promoters of the Franco-German Committee—first dissolved then revived by Hitler—which was to bring about a better understanding between the two peoples. His name as a journalist had become well known since 1933, because he was the first Frenchman to interview Chancellor Hitler.

These were known facts. But it was not generally known—there were many facts quite unknown and even the *Deuxième Bureau* did not find out until late in 1938—that de Brinon had received enormous amounts of money from Doctor Goebbels. Millions of francs, that were distributed by him to French journalists or newspaper owners—in order to bring about a greater understanding of Hitler and his quest for *Lebensraum*. But by the end of 1938 it was late, much too late, to do anything about that.

Then there was Herr Otto Abetz.[1] Abetz was the German leader of the Franco-German Committee, and therefore it was only logical that he and de Brinon should meet from time to time.

Otto Abetz was much younger than de Brinon. He had lost his father in the war, had had a very hard life in his youth, and finally became drawing teacher in a provincial high school. His real interest, however, had always been France—French literature and French culture. And he dreamed of a close Franco-German collaboration, and, unlike de Brinon, of close collaboration between the two democracies.

He came rather late and reluctantly into the Nazi camp. Only in 1937 did he become a member of the Party. And then, suddenly, he was no longer a poor drawing teacher. He now lived in an elegant Berlin apartment; he had money, a car; and he had connections. He still was interested in Franco-German collaboration—but from the point of view and for the ends of the Nazis.

He didn't exactly say so when, in 1935, he came to live in Paris. He frequented elegant circles, he met many writers and moving-picture people. And he had lots of money to spend. It seemed to be easy for him to arrange for the works of famous French authors to be translated into German, to arrange for French businessmen to make profitable connections in Germany, to get French journalists interesting interviews with the chiefs of the Third Reich.

It was during one of his stays in Berlin that de Brinon met Baroness von Einem, a beautiful, elegant young woman with platinum blond hair and great charm. The Baroness soon went to Paris to stay. She took an apartment at the fashionable Hotel d'Jena. She spoke beautiful French, and it was not long before she was well entrenched in certain salons. These were, curiously enough, the salons of moving-picture people. She met Otto Abetz frequently—she became friendly with him, which, after all, was only natural, since both were Germans. As for M. de Brinon, she only met him again in June 1937 at a party. Both must have forgotten completely that they had met before, for neither seemed to recognize the other when they were formally introduced.

Then, however, a beautiful friendship developed. De Brinon saw the Baroness often. And since he was a journalist, it was only natural that she met other journalists through him. One of them was Alois Aubin, an associate editor of *Le Temps*, the semi-official French newspaper that was always in the know about what went on behind the scenes. Another was one of the directors of *Le Figaro*, Julien Poirier.

Since the Baroness had so many friends in moving pictures, it was only logical that she took a real interest in this exciting industry. And since she had ample funds, she had the idea of buying moving-picture theatres. But she wanted to remain in the background. So it was M. Aubin who did the actual buying. Just a few theatres; just about three hundred. M. Poirier, on the other hand, suddenly had plenty of money, enough to establish a new moving-picture company. This company was to produce films that would educate for a better understanding between Germany and France. He also let it be known that he wouldn't mind investing money in small radio stations.

Perhaps the most interesting acquaintance the Baroness made was Gaston Amourelle,[2] an official stenographer of the Senate. He was indeed interesting, since he was, for instance, one of the few men who could get hold of the minutes of the secret sessions of the Senate Arms Committee. Somehow, they got into the hands of the Baroness, too. Of course there were some expenses. M. Amourelle received 400,000 francs for procuring them. Nobody suspected anything for a long time. After all, the Baroness was such a charming young woman, and really not interested in anything but the movies. Maybe she wanted to become a star herself.

Daladier was told by Colonel Gauché of the close co-operation between Messrs Aubin and Poirier and the German Chamber of Commerce in Paris; only two weeks before, they had supplied the Chamber of Commerce with a long list of what they termed 'dependable Frenchmen,' mostly from the frontier districts—that is, Frenchmen who could be depended upon to work in the interests of Hitler when and if the time came. Daladier could hardly believe his ears. He learned that Gaston Amourelle had been delivering the minutes of the secret sessions of the Senate military committee for a long time. 'The damage done,' Colonel Gauché ended his report, 'is incalculable. We can be sure that Berlin today is in possession of most important figures concerning our artillery, our anti-tank guns, our aviation bases. We'll have to change everything. But the question is: Do we have time?'

The Colonel concluded by again threatening to resign unless Daladier acted immediately. Daladier acted.

The Baroness von Einem was not arrested.[3] She was able to escape to Germany. Whether this escape was lucky for her is not certain. The *Deuxième Bureau* later on got information which suggests that she was executed. Perhaps Berlin thought she was to be blamed for the discovery of the plot.[4]

How could she have escaped? The Bureau was assured by the Premier that he would not tell anyone, not even his most intimate colleagues in the Cabinet, about the planned arrests. And Daladier did not tell anybody. But perhaps his whole conversation with the Colonel was overheard and reported immediately to one member of the Cabinet, M. Georges Bonnet, Minister of Foreign Affairs. This, at least, is what the *Deuxième Bureau* believes. It had, of course, followed the Baroness von Einem for days.

The Baroness, only a few hours after the Colonel's interview with the Premier, hastily left her hotel. She took a taxi to the Hotel Scribe and entered the bar. She met a woman there. The woman was Madame Georges Bonnet, with whom she was on friendly terms. The two ladies each had a cocktail and then parted. The Baroness took a taxi again and went out to Le Bourget airport. There she kept her private plane, which was guarded by police. It had been guarded for many months. But not, as one might suppose, to forestall an escape. It had been guarded on the orders of Minister Bonnet to assure the safety of the plane. The private plane of the Baroness was soon ready, and she took off, never to return.

Another lady left Paris about the same time. Her original name was Elisabeth Büttner. Years before she had been the private secretary of Julius Streicher, the notorious Nüremberg anti-Semite. For the past sixteen months she had been in Paris, working for the Gestapo. Like the Baroness, she was beautiful and charming and of considerable wealth. Of such wealth, in fact, that she could marry an impoverished French nobleman, thereby acquiring French citizenship, which, of course, made it much easier for her to operate.

She, too, seemed to be on intimate terms with Madame Bonnet. But while the Minister's wife really liked the Baroness, she continued relations with Elisabeth Büttner rather against her will. It seemed—and many people had this impression—that the Gestapo agent had some kind of hold over her.

Anyhow, the *Deuxième Bureau*, which had had Elisabeth Büttner watched also, knew that she had seen the Minister's wife almost immediately after Daladier's conversation with Colonel Gauché. The visit was short. It was only after this visit that Madame Bonnet went to see and perhaps warn the Baroness von Einem.

As for Elisabeth Büttner, the agents of the *Deuxième Bureau* lost trace of her after she entered Bonnet's home. Maybe she left through a side entrance. Anyway, she disappeared into thin air. To abet the escape of a foreign spy, or for that matter, of two foreign spies, is a serious charge to make against a Minister of Foreign Affairs.

It was not the first time that M. Bonnet had gone out of his way to serve German interests. And while this collaboration with the Baroness von Einem and Elisabeth Büttner was and still is known only to a few, other of his services to Hitler have been public property for a long time. As a matter of fact, a joke made the rounds in Paris which went, 'Do you know that our Minister of Foreign Affairs is also paid by France?'[5]

By the middle of 1939, it was pretty generally known that he, more than anyone else, had been responsible for what six months before was hailed as the guarantee of peace in our time and what now was plainly recognized as the fatal betrayal of the Czechoslovakian people. It was he who had forced Prague to accept the Anglo-French proposal to surrender the Sudetenland and the country's defence. It was he alone—for in the critical hours he suppressed all urgent communiqués from Prague and did not consult his colleagues. And when some of his dissenting colleagues, especially Paul Reynaud, protested, Bonnet did not shrink from pretending that it was Prague itself that had asked to have its hand forced in order to save its prestige before the Czech people.

It was he who, shortly after Munich, arranged for the Ten Years Peace and Friendship treaty with Germany. And when, hardly a month afterward, President Herriot of the Chamber made a speech criticizing certain activities of Hitler, Bonnet telephoned the German Ambassador in Paris and told him not to mind this particular speech; that it was only for home consumption and that the collaboration of Germany and France would continue along the lines he and Herr von Ribbentrop had laid down.

When he was attacked for such behaviour as unbecoming in a Minister of Foreign Affairs, he used to smile suavely and say that his first concern was peace. But what did peace have to do with his visit to the Brown House in Paris, where he accompanied Herr von Ribbentrop during the latter's stay in Paris? He knew that the Brown House was nothing but the centre of German espionage in France, thinly disguised as a centre of propaganda for co-operation, where excursions, lectures, and sports events were arranged. He knew because the *Deuxième Bureau* had long ago given him and all the other ministers the necessary information.

He knew, too, the real identity of Ferdinand de Brinon, the so-called French journalist, who for years had practised German espionage. He knew, if not before, at least from October 1938, when the *Deuxième Bureau* had presented to all the members of the Cabinet a dossier containing the most precise charges against de Brinon. Still, in the Spring of 1939 he sent this very Ferdinand de Brinon to Berlin to have a talk with Göring, and to assure the worthy Field Marshal that the days of democracy in France were numbered; that he and Daladier would see to it that a totalitarian regime was established, that the freedom of the press and the influence of Parliament would be abrogated—all this in order to assure closer co-operation with Nazi Germany. All this became known very soon because the French Ambassador in Berlin, M. Coulondre, felt slighted—not about what de Brinon said, but because Bonnet had sent a special envoy instead of entrusting him with the mission to Göring.

The French Minister of Foreign Affairs acted as though he were the German Minister of Foreign Affairs. And there was good reason for this behaviour.

Many former friends of Bonnet's—among them important statesmen and intellectuals, men who were beyond suspicion and who now live as refugees in the United States—have again and again declared that they cannot believe Bonnet was a traitor; some of them admit that he acted short-sightedly, stupidly even, but assert that he wanted what was best for France—peace. They have again and again stressed that there have never been any proofs of a betrayal on the part of the Minister of Foreign Affairs.

Such proofs exist. But they came into the hands of the *Deuxième Bureau* only by the end of 1939.

This takes us back to the famous Stavisky affair in 1934. After the alleged suicide of the crooked financier, Stavisky—which was perhaps no suicide at all—there was quite a scandal when it was discovered how many highly placed people had received money to 'arrange' various matters. There had even been a small revolution, with street battles and uprisings, in Paris. Then everything was hushed up. And though it was rumoured for a while that many more people were involved in the affair, and many more in even higher places, the matter was never taken up again.

Many more and higher-placed people had received money. And one of them was Georges Bonnet. He received a rather large cheque. Now, the history of French scandals shows that French cheques have a disturbing habit of turning up years after they are cashed. Anyway M. Bonnet's cheque—and similar ones to other prominent people—came into the possession of M. Albert Dubarry, publisher of the newspaper *Volonté*, who in the twenties had been in the pay of the Germans. He had sold them to Berlin for a considerable sum of money. They were now in the hands of Goebbels, and therefore certain Frenchmen were in the hands of Hitler.

It was Elisabeth Büttner who first came to Paris with photostats of some of the stubs. Armed with such telling arguments, she had no difficulty in obtaining the collaboration of M. and Mme. Georges Bonnet. It was outright blackmail all the time, up to the hurried departure of Baroness von Einem and Elisabeth Büttner. And, even afterward, Georges Bonnet had to do what he was told when Berlin gave orders. This was why he objected violently to Daladier's proposal to expel Otto Abetz, whom the *Deuxième Bureau* had established beyond doubt as the head of German espionage in France, but who, having the status of a diplomat, could not be arrested. It was only when the courageous journalist and politician, Henri de Kerillis, attacked Abetz openly and at the same time delivered his material—which was extremely revealing—to the government, that Bonnet's hand was forced.

It was said that Otto Abetz was expelled. He never was. M. Bonnet had a talk with the German Ambassador and merely asked whether it was true that Herr Abetz was leaving Paris for a short time. He even went so far as to arrange for some very intimate friends of his to give a farewell dinner to the man who at this time had been proved a German spy. One of those present at the dinner was Gaston Henri-Haye, then Mayor of Versailles, today French Ambassador in Washington.

Bonnet never stopped working for Berlin even during the war. It was he who gave Ferdinand de Brinon the tip to disappear from France shortly before the outbreak of the war and go to Brussels. It was he who later tipped de Brinon off that it was safe to return to Paris. It now was easy for him to give such tips, because shortly after the outbreak of the war, in the middle of September 1939, he had been transferred from the Ministry of Foreign Affairs to the Ministry of Justice. And in his new capacity he could demand all the reports on compromised people, under the pretext of preparing a trial against them. He did get hold of lots of material. As a matter of fact, when he left the Quai d'Orsay for the Ministry of Justice, he took with him many files. Since that day, files on Abetz, de Brinon, the Baroness von Einem, and many others have never been found.

It was only at the end of 1939 that the *Deuxième Bureau* found out what hold Hitler had over Bonnet. One of the French agents in Berlin was told about the cheque stubs in the possession of the Nazis. At that time many people in Berlin heard the story—the Nazis didn't bother to protect Bonnet any more since he had outlived his usefulness to them.

Why didn't Premier Daladier act immediately upon being informed by the *Deuxième Bureau* of Bonnet's true colours? He probably felt that a country at war could not afford so ugly a scandal: to see its Minister of Justice arrested and tried as an accessory to enemy espionage.

PARIS: SPY CENTRE

Shortly before the outbreak of the war, the *Deuxième Bureau* was finally able to lay its hands on Councillor Roos of Alsace. He was arrested, sentenced as a German spy, and executed in January 1940. Roos had worked for the German secret service for many years. The *Deuxième Bureau* had suspected him for a long time, but had been unable to get conclusive evidence. It was only in 1939 that it succeeded in planting two of its agents in Roos's own office. It was too late then, for Roos had been informing the Germans for years about the secrets of the Maginot Line, and especially about the new construction in Alsace undertaken in the last years before the war.

The arrest of Councillor Roos led to other interesting disclosures. Among Roos's papers were found papers that led to the search of the premises of the Abbé Brauner, Municipal Librarian and Keeper of the Archives of the city of Strasbourg. During the search the Abbé stood by looking hurt and shocked. Finally he asked if he might leave the room for a moment. He was given permission, but a detective who followed him, retrieved in time certain papers which the Abbé had tried to destroy. They proved that the Abbé himself and several others, among them the Abbé Emile Scherer-Trautmann, had large bank accounts in Switzerland.

The accounts were traced, and it was found that certain people had received large sums regularly from these accounts.

One of them was Victor Antoni of Lorraine, who was known as a violent separatist. Antoni published a newspaper, *Jung-Lothringen* (Young Lorraine) which could not possibly have yielded him a very large income. Still, for years he had lived luxuriously; he had built himself a mansion and never seemed in need of money. When he was questioned, he admitted cynically that he had received German money, but asserted that he was not the only one who had done so.

He was indeed not the only one. Another was Marcel Stuermel. Before the First World War he had been a German petty official who had hoped for a career and who was sadly disappointed when, after the war, Alsace-Lorraine was returned to France. However, he made something of a career anyhow. He became a member of the Chamber of Deputies and acquired a great deal of money. What were the sources of his fortune? Surely not his small newspaper, *Die Heimat*, which for years was almost openly anti-French.

Both Antoni's and Stuermel's newspapers were printed in the great printing plant of Joseph Rosse. Rosse, by far one of the most important men in Alsace-Lorraine, was chief of the *Union Populaire Republicain d'Alsace*, which under cover of defence of clerical interests was the most rabid separatist party in Alsace-Lorraine. He had created the *Chemises Grises* (The Grey Shirts)—a youth organization patterned after the SA, with a membership of more than twenty-five thousand. He owned and directed the newspaper trust, *L'Alsatia*, a group of dailies that appeared in morning and evening editions all over the frontier section. He held interests in several banks. He had large real estate holdings. He owned a number of villas in which he lived. And he was, of course, a member of the Chamber of Deputies.

His salary certainly could not account for his riches. Where, then, did he get his money? The pro-French democratic press of Alsace-Lorraine had asked this question for years, had attacked him, attacked Antoni and Stuermel. But these attacks achieved little. There was one tip-off. Shortly after Hitler's accession to power, almost all the German-language newspapers appearing outside of Germany were banned in the Reich: certainly all the papers in Alsace-Lorraine, except the papers of Rosse and those of Antoni and Stuermel.

When questioned about the money which came to them via the Swiss bank accounts of Abbé Brauner and Abbé Scherer-Trautmann, Stuermel and Antoni claimed this money belonged to German Catholics and had been brought out of the Reich to safeguard it. Such an explanation did not hold water because, while the French Catholic Press, the logical repository for such money, never received a cent from these accounts, the newspapers of Antoni, Stuermel, and Rosse never were interested at all in the fate of the Catholics.

Anyhow, the *Deuxième Bureau* knew better.

In the first place, they knew who Abbé Scherer-Trautmann was. He had left France and gone to Berlin eighteen months before the outbreak of the war, where he conferred with Minister Goebbels. He then left for Poland, where he had tried in vain to convince the Polish clergy that they must co-operate with Hitler. When the Nazis attacked Poland, he had already left. He was on his way to Brazil on another of Dr Goebbels' assignments.

The *Deuxième Bureau* knew more. In 1938 the Swiss police had arrested a lawyer named Wildi and the Gestapo agent Bongartz, when the two met at a railway station in Basle. Strangely enough, Rosse was in Basle at the same time. But since he was a French Deputy, the police did not dare arrest him. And shortly afterwards they released Wildi and Bongartz, since it could not be established that they had conspired against the security of the Swiss nation. The *Deuxième Bureau*, however, easily established that in the following months there were many conferences in Basle between Wildi and Scherer-Trautmann and Bongartz—conferences at which Dr Robert Ernst presided. Ernst was the chief organizer of Nazi propaganda in Alsace-Lorraine—or, to put it plainly, the chief of the secret service operating in that border region. At these conferences Bongartz distributed large sums of money. There could never be the slightest doubt about where this money came from, because Bongartz carried a permit to export unlimited amounts of money from Germany. Such permits were very rare. They were given only to persons on government business.

Messrs Rosse, Antoni, and Stuermel were arrested by the *Deuxième Bureau*. But it was not often that the French secret service could lay its hands on very important Nazi agents. Only a small percentage of those who were scheduled to be arrested the day war broke out could be apprehended. There were, as has already been mentioned, some one hundred and ninety-eight arrests. But only the small fry were caught. And these arrests did not lead to the higher-ups. The Nazis had introduced an interesting method of frustrating this. Very few of the minor agents knew the whereabouts of their superiors. All they knew was that they received telephone calls and were ordered to go to some café or bar.

The *Deuxième Bureau* let one of the men arrested in Paris go free and watched his house and tapped his telephone. Sure enough, there came a telephone call ordering him to go to a café near the Opera. A few agents of the *Deuxième Bureau* went there. But neither the minor agent or his superior ever showed up. The agent was apprehended when, hours later, he returned to his apartment. Under grilling he said that while he was walking toward the café a taxi had overtaken him, his superior hailed him and drove him away. Apparently the German agent had been very well informed about the interest of the *Deuxième Bureau*.

Incidentally, from the beginning of the war the *Deuxième Bureau* no longer held important sessions within its own building. It moved to a different place every day. Once it was in the War Ministry, the next day in the Hôtel des Invalides, the next day somewhere else. The official explanation was that since certain men, especially Daladier, had so little time, the *Deuxième Bureau* just had to follow them around. But there was another, less comic explanation which was, of course, not revealed.

Three days before the outbreak of the war, a M. Guerin was leaving his apartment on the Boulevard Saint Germain, just across the street from the headquarters of the *Deuxième Bureau*. He was leaving for a short journey. For a short trip he took along an enormous amount of baggage. The taxi driver who took him to the station dropped one of the heavy bags on the street. It opened and a quantity of photographic plates and cameras fell out. M. Guerin blew up and said he would hold the driver responsible if there were any damage. It was really his shouting more than the contents of his suitcase that attracted the attention of passers-by, and finally of a policeman. The policeman looked at the expensive apparatus and at some of the plates. He seemed doubtful and ordered the man to return to his apartment.

Here, M. Guerin gave a rather puzzling account of himself. Yes, the policeman had seen rightly, those were cameras with telescopic lenses. And the pictures were indeed photographs of the entrance to the *Deuxième Bureau*, showing whoever entered or left. But the policeman might as well know that he, Guerin, worked for the *Deuxième Bureau*, and was doing this on orders. Would the policeman mind phoning over to the Bureau to find out. The policeman thought this was a good idea. He went to the telephone, took the receiver off the hook. The next thing he knew was when he awoke in a near-by hospital with a terrific headache.

M. Guerin, who had left by then, did not come back after a few days. And the material he left behind convinced the *Deuxième Bureau* that for years everybody who had entered its building had been photographed for the German secret service.

There was a tremendous amount of work during the first few weeks of the war. There were, as in all wars, thousands of denunciations to be followed up. It seemed that every second Frenchman had run across a spy in a café or in the apartment next door to him. Most of these spies turned out to be perfectly honest people who, in turn, had run across spies. But to find this out, valuable time was consumed.

Of course, the *Deuxième Bureau* was enormously expanded. More than two hundred additional men were put to work. But the work was much more complicated than before. Each army division now had its own intelligence service, constantly in correspondence with the Bureau regarding the movements of the enemy.

On the other hand, communication with the agents within the enemy country was difficult. Of course, every secret service is prepared for war. All agents of the *Deuxième Bureau* operating in Germany had to leave for a neutral country at least forty-eight hours before general mobilization. Each one knew exactly which frontier to make for. And into Germany moved an army of new spies from various neutral countries, spies not yet known to the German counterespionage, or so the French hoped. This was all pure routine. But it did take time and work.

Worse than all this, was the fact that the Nazi secret service never ceased operating from Paris during the whole war. As a matter of fact, its headquarters had never left the city limits. In January 1940 it struck for the first time.

An engineer of Yugoslavian nationality appeared at the War Ministry to offer what he termed a sensational new invention. He explained that he had invented a process which would simplify the running of field kitchens. His idea seemed new and of some value. An investigation carried out by the *Deuxième Bureau* revealed that he had lived in Paris for ten years and was apparently all right. Then he was given permission to construct one field kitchen for experimental purposes. Of all places, the Parc De Vincennes was selected as the site for the kitchen—and in a near-by armoury a number of regiments were stationed.

The inventor experimented for weeks. He was given a pass by the authorities which entitled him not only to enter the Parc, but the armoury as well. He could look at the newest machine guns and all other armaments; he could make drawings which were sent via Brussels to Berlin.

He would probably never have been apprehended had there not been a woman involved in the case. The inventor was married, but had left his wife, a native Yugoslavian, too—only a few months before. He intended to divorce her. By chance, the deserted wife, who knew that he had been working for the Nazis for years, learned about his so-called experiments. But it was only when she found out that he was living with another woman that she denounced him.

That was not very easy. She went to the police and told a detective what she knew about her husband. The detective should have turned the whole matter right over to the *Deuxième Bureau*. Instead, he was curious as to why the wife was denouncing her husband. And when she told him about the other woman, he laughed. 'It's just a matter of jealousy,' he said, and decided to forget about it.

But the woman grew angrier and told her story to everyone who would listen. Finally the concierge of the house where she lived got in touch with the *Deuxième Bureau*. The inventor was investigated again, this time more carefully. And now something unbelievable was discovered. The so-called invention was nothing new. It had been used by the German Army for some time. Moreover, the French army knew all about it but had rejected it for reasons of their own.

It was clear that the man had been instructed in this 'invention' by the Germans, so that he might get into an armoury. He was arrested—but, of course, the harm was already done.

About a month later a tax inspector appeared in one of the most important aircraft factories in France, situated outside Paris. He arrived early in the morning and explained that he was to examine the books to find out whether all the workmen were on the social security lists. The management opened the books and the man sat down with them, to count the workers, working hours, etc.

Then he said he would like to take a look around the plant and question some of the workers. He was shown around by an engineer who was polite enough to explain every detail to him. He inspected the whole plant, thanked the engineer, and left.

After he departed it was discovered that he had forgotten his briefcase. The tax inspector's office was called. There, nobody knew anything about the self-styled inspector. The briefcase was opened. It contained nothing but blank paper.

The *Deuxième Bureau* was called in. But no trace of the man was found.

These two cases show clearly with what daring and imagination German espionage worked in the very heart of France.

At about the same time the editor of *Paris-Soir*, Pierre Lazareff, had sent a photographer to take pictures of the deserted German Embassy in the Rue de Lisle. While preparing his apparatus, the man discovered to his surprise that the German Embassy was not deserted at all.

The blinds were drawn and two French soldiers were standing guard. But suddenly the door opened, a middle-aged man appeared, locked the door behind him, and walked away, ignoring the two soldiers. The photographer followed the man to the Swedish Embassy on the Avenue Marceau. An hour later he emerged, returned to the German Embassy, unlocked the door, and entered.

The mystified photographer came back the next day, and several days thereafter. He took pictures of the man and brought them to his editor, who called up the *Deuxième Bureau*. The Bureau seemed strangely unperturbed and declined to give any explanation. Thereupon, the editor got in touch with Premier Daladier.

At first Daladier had nothing to say. But a few days later he sent one of his assistants to the editor. The assistant explained that there had been an arrangement between the German and the French governments. Both Embassies had been allowed to leave their librarians behind in order to look after the papers and documents. The librarians lived in the Embassies. If the German librarian chose to visit the Swedish Embassy, the French Government could see no harm in that. After all, the Swedish Embassy had taken over German interests in France for the duration of the war.

That was all Daladier was willing to say, although there was more to the story. The *Deuxième Bureau* had informed him that the German librarian was in touch with men like Doriot, Bergery, Deat, men who more or less openly were working for Hitler. Evidently, Daladier did not think it advisable to make this public.

But there was one thing about the German librarian that not even Daladier nor the French secret service knew.

During a debate in the Senate, shortly before the war, a Socialist senator had asserted that there were more than two thousand unlicensed private radio transmitters in France. Most of them, he said, probably belonged to amateurs who meant no harm. But the very existence of unregistered transmitters was a danger, he declared. And it seemed suspicious that there were so many transmitters in Alsace-Lorraine and in the North of France, near the Belgian frontier.

Nothing came of the debate. But later on, in May 1940, it was established that many of the secret transmitters were working for the enemy. Some broadcast on the same wave lengths as the big French government stations, and aroused panic in the populace of Northern France. Arras and Amiens, for instance, were evacuated because of fraudulent radio alarms, and the roads were blocked with refugees, hampering troop movements in the crucial hours.

The *Deuxième Bureau* was gravely concerned about the secret broadcasters. But it could do nothing itself. Its radio facilities were too limited. Therefore one of its officers was sent to the PTT building (*Postes, Telegraphes, Telephones*) to discuss the problem with the Minister of Communications. That was in December 1940.

PTT was a very large, brand-new building. Typically enough, it was not quite finished when the war began, though construction had been started more than two years before and it had really been built with an eye to the war; because from this building France was supposed to direct its radio war. From here, broadcasts in more than twenty languages were to be sent around the world. Therefore it was a legitimate military objective, and protected accordingly. The broadcasting apparatus was buried under concrete three stories below the surface, and was reached by going through corridors with massive steel doors. On the sixth floor were the editorial offices, where all the broadcasts were prepared. All about, there were signs: '*Silence! L'ennemi guette vos confidences.*' ('The enemy is watching you.')

The enemy had good reason to watch the PTT building with particular care. To the sixth floor came all the news obtained by the various information services of the French. In these editorial rooms the censors sifted the material that could be broadcast or published from that which must be suppressed. In these editorial rooms information was available that could be found nowhere else. Furthermore, here, and only here, the identity of many of the announcers could be learned.

This was, of course, immaterial so far as the French announcers were concerned. But it was of utmost importance to conceal the identity of the German, Austrian, Czech, and Polish announcers. All these men had families and friends in their native lands upon whom the Nazis would have taken immediate revenge.

Anyone who had access to the editorial rooms, could also sound out the whole tenor of future French propaganda, so that its effects could have been counteracted in advance. It was therefore only logical that the PTT building was strongly guarded. It was also logical that the men who worked in the building, especially the foreign announcers, were investigated with the utmost care. They all received identification cards without which they could not enter the building.

But the officer from the *Deuxième Bureau* discovered to his dismay that in spite of all these precautions it was not particularly hard to get in. For the identification cards were practically the same as those issued by many ministries. They were the same colour, and were distinguished only by different stamps. Nothing in the world was easier than to procure a red card from some other ministry or government office.

The French agent explained his fears to the Minister of Communications. And they laid a net for the false fish. And one evening the whole building was surrounded by soldiers and closed off, and everyone in it was asked to present his identification card. Eleven men had identification cards that had been given out by other ministries, or cards that were obvious forgeries. Eleven in one evening. These men were arrested.

But the Arab was caught only by accident. In February 1940 a search was on for an Arabian to broadcast in his language. There came to the

PTT building a young Arab with excellent recommendations. It was the *Deuxième Bureau* that had furnished them to him; in fact, the man had given the French secret service valuable information about the activities of the Nazis in Morocco.

He was hired and spoke night after night to his people back home. His work seemed satisfactory. It is probable that the man would have gone on entering and leaving the PTT building up to the final debacle if his true identity had not been exposed.

It was really nothing but coincidence. One evening in April 1940 the Brigade Mondaine (the vice squad) raided the Hôtel des Élysées des Beaux Arts on Montmartre, a known hideout of drug addicts. A notorious redhead, Jeannine, was wanted. Upon forcing her door, the police found two men with her. One was Italian, one Arabian. They were both taken to police headquarters. There it was discovered that the Arabian had a red card admitting him to the PTT building. In vain he protested that the card was valid. The police did not believe him.

When they investigated they found that the card was indeed valid. But they also found that the bearer of the card was a long-sought murderer.

His Italian friend had not known that. Frightened that the police might think him a murderer, too, he broke down completely and confessed his real crime. He had been working with the Arab for some time, transmitting all the information the latter gathered in the PTT building to a man who 'paid very well for it.'

The man, who according to the Italian was French, could not be found, in spite of all the efforts of the *Deuxième Bureau*. If those efforts had succeeded, they might have found out what a few men learned after the Germans took Paris: that all the Arab's PTT information was delivered, through many different channels and in oblique ways, into the hands of the librarian of the German Embassy.

And if the *Deuxième Bureau* had then made a visit to the German Embassy, it would have discovered that the librarian was in constant contact with all the German agents in France; that from here—in the German Embassy, of all places—the German espionage was directed. And finally, they would have found out that the Librarian had a secret transmitter built into the legs of a table in the dining room from which he sent daily broadcasts to the German secret service.

But even without knowing all this, and without knowing many other things of equal importance, the *Deuxième Bureau* was sensitive enough to feel the ground quaking under it. Long before the Nazis took Paris, the officers of the *Bureau* knew that they were already encircled and that the enemy was in their midst.

Not a day passed without their finding out that the Nazi secret service knew things they were sure were secret. It was the affair with the photographer Guerin that had led the *Deuxième Bureau* to adopt the system of moving every day. But there were many proofs that the Germans always knew where they were located. They knew all the places where the various officers met their agents. They knew their favourite bistros and cafés. They knew about the corner table in the bar at the Grand Hotel, and the nook in the Café Madrid on the Boulevard Montmartre. In the homes of two officers microphones were discovered—but too late to capture those who had installed them.

B4 HAS AN IDEA

On 8 November 1939, in the *Buergerbraeukeller* in Munich a bomb exploded at the speaker's desk. It came a few minutes too late. Adolf Hitler, who had just made a speech from this spot, had left the beer cellar a few minutes before.

When the first reports of the attempted assassination came over the wires, most of the world thought it was a plant, framed by the Nazis themselves to inflame the German people with indignation and fill the broad masses with renewed love for their Führer. World scepticism did not diminish when the Gestapo arrested a man named George Elser, who promptly confessed that he had been hired by British agents. Some said that Elser was another van der Lubbe, who was probably doped and unconscious of what he was confessing. Some said that he was the former commandant of the concentration camp of Sachsenhausen, that he was merely playing a part written by the Gestapo. On 9 November two Gestapo agents in Dutch uniforms crossed the German-Dutch border near Venlo, killed a Dutch Army officer, Lieutenant Klop, and forced two British agents, Captain Richard H. Steven and Major Siegismund P. Best to accompany them back over the German border. As a result, the chief of the Dutch Intelligence Service, Major General J. W. van Oorschot, handed in his resignation in disgust.

No one in the British Intelligence Service resigned. But there was, to put it mildly, great excitement in London. Never before in the history of the British Intelligence Service had the enemy kidnapped two agents of the Intelligence Service.

What made the wound smart more sorely was the fact that the two kidnapped agents were two of the best men in the IS. Two out of the few men who still had connections in Hitler's Germany and who could transmit valuable information to London.

These were fateful hours for the IS—more grave even than the officials suspected at the time. Nevertheless, they realized that they must take steps. There was little point in talking with Chamberlain. Old Chamberlain was conducting a war in the most peaceful fashion. The men who had been educated in the tradition of the IS knew that war was war.

Moreover, they saw no point in discussing with Chamberlain the intimate connection between Munich and the kidnapping in Holland. Nor would he have understood why at this time the men of the IS had but one thought in their minds. Captain Steven and Major Best must be brought back—at any cost. Could they perhaps effect an exchange? The exchange of important agents was nothing new; it had been done more than once in the last war.

When the archives at last are opened and historians write about what went on behind the scenes in the Second World War, someone will remark the change that came over the men of the B4, over the entire secret service, at this time. They were filled with a new spirit, which was in reality their old spirit. They were determined not to take the kind of beating they had been taking during the last few years. They were once more aggressive; they had recaptured something of the spirit of the great Lawrence.

This new era was born with the question: How shall we recover our agents?

Exchange.... But whom could they barter for two of their most capable men? Whom did they have in their power? Well, at the beginning of the war Scotland Yard had arrested a great many people. The British had four hundred Nazi spies in their hands, most of them non-Germans.

Ironically, one of the arrested men was Herr Franz von Rintelen, the man who had spied against the Allies in the First World War, whom the British had taken off a ship on the high seas and imprisoned. The same Herr von Rintelen who had preferred to live in England instead of under the Nazis. He had already been released once and then arrested again....

No, Herr von Rintelen would not do. The Nazis did not value him so highly. And the rest of the four hundred imprisoned spies were only small fry.

But other people had been arrested. To be sure, they were not spies, but perhaps the Germans were interested in them. And then there were still others who had not been arrested, but who, all unaware, were being watched constantly.

B4 considered a number of members from the Link, an organization composed partly of Nazi followers, partly of misguided pacifists who wanted to collaborate with Germany. Naturally, the Link had been dissolved when the war broke out, but its membership had then entered Norman Hay's Information and Public Policy Group, which was pro-Mosley, pro-Hitler, anti-British, and anti-Semitic.

There was Captain A. M. Ramsay. There was Sir Oswald Mosley. There was an official in the Ministry of Health, a vice-chairman of a provincial Chamber of Commerce, the brother of Lord Haw-Haw, and a hundred others.

B4 had an idea, one of the best ideas the British IS had had in a long time. But it was some time before they could do anything with their idea.

Late in March 1940 a woman agent of the Foreign Office Intelligence Department arrived in Lisbon by Clipper. She intended to stay in Lisbon no more than a week and then fly to England. In accordance with Portuguese regulations, she delivered her passport to the International Police. A few hours later she heard that the conference for which she had come to Lisbon would not take place. She therefore immediately went to the headquarters of the International Police to retrieve her passport and take the plane to England that same day.

She was about to enter the building when she saw someone who interested her more than her passport. He was a young man, about twenty-eight years old, of medium height, slim, with blonde, thinning hair. There was nothing particularly outstanding about him. But she had seen this man often—in Brussels, Madrid, Zurich and Vienna. She stepped to one side; undoubtedly he would have recognized her and she preferred not to be seen. The man, who worked under many names in many European cities, was now using the name of Werner Schmidt.

Cautiously the British agent followed Herr Schmidt, who soon entered the Café Chiado in the Rua Garetta, the rendezvous of Germans in Lisbon. Here sat technicians and engineers who had worked in Lisbon for many years—and new ones were always coming. Here sat employees of the Hamburg-American Line. The Englishwoman informed a number of her friends, who were interested enough to take up the trail of Herr Schmidt. They found out that he was a 'machinery inspector' and that he frequented the neighbourhood of the dockyards. Whenever a ship came in, he was always at the pier speaking with people who afterward approached the sailors from the boat, chatted, and inquired, 'Were you stopped by the English? When? Where?'

The woman agent's friends were also able to tell her why Herr Schmidt paid such frequent visits to the headquarters of the International Police.

She reported to London what she had seen and what she suspected, and a few days later some more of her friends arrived in Lisbon—by now there were a good many of them—and all of these friends were extremely inquisitive.

They found out that Herr Schmidt and others were getting supplies to Germany by a roundabout route. The British had permitted certain goods to come from Portuguese colonies, since they were allegedly destined only for Portugal. With the collusion of Portuguese merchants these goods had been transported to small Portuguese villages. Here they were stored, quite as though they would remain in Portugal. But after a few weeks they were taken out of storage, repacked, and sent in small packages across Spain to Germany. The method was expensive and complicated—but the Germans had no choice.

The British agents learned that the saloons and cafés of the dockyard district were swarming with Herr Schmidt's men. One of their jobs was to persuade sailors on shore leave, particularly Danes and Norwegians, not to return to their ships. The guileless sailors were offered inducements of all sorts, were promised everything imaginable when they returned to their homes. Girls played their familiar part in such persuasion. Sometimes the Nazis were successful—and then at the last moment, the captain would have to postpone his departure. The result was inconvenience and difficulty, and goods which were expected in England would not arrive.

But they were not always successful....

The British agents learned to their considerable amazement that Herr Schmidt and his friends openly visited the palatial German Legation. And they learned to their even greater surprise that while the British Embassy had a staff of less than two dozen, more than 200 Germans were employed in Baron von Honagger's Legation and in the Consulate General. This in a country of seven million inhabitants, of whom perhaps forty thousand are Germans.

Herr Schmidt had an unpleasant shock. He was arrested. Perhaps the police who arrested him had followed him for a few days and discovered that he liked to go out on fishing boats, where he made friends with the Portuguese, and drew from them whatever they knew about the movements of British patrol ships—which was often a good deal. They could not have arrested him for that; fishing parties are not illegal. But the police who arrested him made no mention of such matters. They said he had stolen a watch. And although Schmidt protested vehemently, they searched him and found the watch.

That evening one of the British agent's friends received a visit from one of Schmidt's friends. They had a few drinks and chatted a while.

Just about this time letters began arriving in Lisbon from former members of the Link movement. They came to the Park Hotel in Estoril and the somewhat less elegant Sitmar Travel Bureau in Lisbon itself. There were many letters. They spoke of the foolishness of the war between Britain and Germany. They hinted at the possibility of a Scottish Independence Movement. Among these letters were some from people who claimed membership in the Link, although their names had never been carried in its membership lists. One of the letters was signed by Ivone Augustine Kirkpatrick, who held a rather important post in the Ministry of Information.

The letters from England, which at first were answered curtly or not at all, began to have more and more effect. Naturally those who wrote them could not know that some seven months after the first letter had been sent, the Nazis would be very eager to make peace with England.

The heads of B4 wanted nothing more than to save their two agents.

In the autumn of 1940 the scene changed from Lisbon, which is unbearably hot in the summer, to the hotels and Casino of Estoril, the little Riviera of Portugal.

That summer and autumn of 1940, Estoril was the Riviera plus Biarritz plus Deauville. It was the rendezvous of the aristocratic and fashionable world which had had to flee from Hitler. In the Park Hotel a dozen languages were spoken. In the lobby of the Palace Hotel the latest gossip was exchanged. Curiously enough, in Estoril people knew the current events a few hours before the rest of the world. It was here that Paderewski stopped before he came to America. Here was Camille Chautemps, the none-too-trustworthy politician of the Third Republic, who was now beginning on his job for Vichy; the former Premiers of Belgium and Luxemburg; Louis Weiller, the French aircraft manufacturer, whom Pétain lured back to France with false promises and then promptly arrested. Here, the rich men of the Old World waited for passage on the Clipper flying to the New World; here British and American diplomats came for a few days' rest....

And then Herr Friedrich Sieburg appeared. Herr Sieburg was a journalist by profession, for years Paris correspondent of a leading German newspaper, and incidentally—or perhaps principally—the right-hand man of Otto Abetz.

Herr Sieburg had been in Lisbon often recently. When he stayed in Estoril, he lived at the Park Hotel, where he always had a suite reserved for him, although the hotel was sold out for weeks in advance. Sometimes he came there to work on a book; sometimes to make a speech.... But Herr Biefurn was always with him—the same Herr Biefurn whom Herr von Stohrer had sent from Madrid to Lisbon in 1937.

When in September 1940, Herr Sieburg once more appeared at the Park Hotel—and those who had narrowly escaped from Hitler were not overjoyed, for they now had reason to believe that Hitler himself would soon appear—he had a long conversation with Biefurn and a friend of the English woman agent. Sieburg seemed greatly interested and said he would see, and it was quite possible that something could be done....

It was after Sieburg's return to Berlin that the letters from Berlin to London began to show increasing signs of interest. It was then that the letters from England to Berlin began to be more direct. The definite opinion was expressed that if Germany should wage war against Russia, public opinion in England would immediately switch in favour of Germany. Churchill would probably make difficulties, but difficulties existed to be overcome. Anyhow, the dissatisfaction with Churchill was constantly increasing.

But it was some time before any proposals for concrete action was contained in these letters.

CURTAIN FOR FRANCE

Today the world knows all about German tanks. But even when they raced across Poland, the French secret service didn't know very much. At that time, in the *Deuxième Bureau* they were rather optimistic. All the reports from the Polish front spoke of medium tanks from thirty to forty tons. The Bureau knew these tanks very well. They had been manufactured by Krupp, and it had been proved beyond any doubt that the French standard 25 mm anti-tank gun could easily pierce their armour. These tanks were nothing to worry about, they felt.

Even Charles de Gaulle thought this. In a memorandum he sent on 26 January 1940, to several highly-placed people—Daladier, Reynaud, Gamelin, and Weygand, for instance—he said of the Germans:

> Their tanks are too light to break French resistance supported by the Maginot Line. There is reason to believe that Hitler's government now bitterly regrets that they did not transform the German Army even more thoroughly. No one can reasonably doubt that if on 1 September of last year Germany had had double her aviation, a thousand hundred-ton tanks, three thousand fifty- or thirty-ton tanks, and six thousand twenty- or ten-ton tanks, she could have crushed France.

On the other hand, General de Gaulle was not optimistic. His memorandum read, in fact, like the last cry of a drowning man.

> How many wars have started by surprise for at least one of the combatants! Actually, if the enemy has not yet created a sufficient mechanized force to break our line of defence, everything makes us think that he is working hard at it.... Now we have to realize that the Maginot Line, however reinforced ... can be crossed. That is, in the long run, the fate of all fortifications.

Left: Franz Joseph Hermann Michael Maria von Papen, (1879–1969). Von Papen listening to a Violin Recital, Berlin. *See* Part I note 2. *Courtesy President and Fellows of Harvard College*

Right: Hitler, Franz von Papen and Werner von Blomberg outside Berlin's Staatsoper for *Volkstrauertag* (Remembrance Day of the Dead), 12 March 1933.

Horst von der Goltz, (b. 1884), standing second from left. Von der Goltz (real name Wachendorf) was a counterintelligence agent during the First World War. His autobiography, *My Adventures as a German Secret Service Agent*, was published in 1918. There is a theory that Wachendorf was in fact a double agent working for British naval intelligence.

Above left: Captain Franz Dagobert Johannes von Rintelen, (1878 –1949). Rintelen was a German spy master during the First World War, location unknown.

Above right: Captain Rintelen arriving in New York. *See* Part I note 4.

Kurt Ferdinand Friedrich Hermann von Schleicher, (1882–1934), photographed in 1932. *See* Part I note 5.

Ernst Julius Guenther Röhm, (1887-1934).
Röhm meeting Adolf Hitler during the planning
for merging the Army with the SA, 1933.

Kurt Daluege, Heinrich Himmler and Ernst
Röhm, August 1933. *See* Part I note 7.

Joseph Goebbels, (1897–1945). *See* Part I note 9.

Left: Heinrich Luitpold Himmler, (1900–1945). *See* Part I note 9.

Right: Rudolf Hess, (1894-1987), photographed in 1937.

Karl Ernst Haushofer, (1869–1946). Haushofer with Rudolf Hess, 1920. *See* Part I notes 10 and 11.

Hermann Göring, (1893-1946), photographed in 1939.

Left: Eugen Ott, (1889–1977). Ott was adjutant to General Kurt von Schleicher and later ambassador to Tokyo. *See* Part I note 13.

Right: Richard Sorge, (1895-1944). Sorge had been working for Ott in Japan as an agent for the *Abwehr*. He was unmasked as a double-agent spy for the Soviet Union in Japan in late 1941. Sorge did a great service to the Soviet Union, his intelligence that Japan did not pose a threat enabled Stalin to move vital armed divisions to the west—a depth and breadth of reserves that stunned the Germans and halted their progress in 1941 leading eventually to the ultimate German defeat.

Left: Wilhelm Franz Canaris with the insignia of *Korvettenkapitän* (Commander), *c.* 1931-32.

Right: Canaris with Reinhard Heydrich. *See* Part I note 14.

Rudolf Hess with *Reichskriegsopferfuehrer* Hanns Oberlindober and Captain Hawes, a veteran British officer at a reception in the garden of the *Neue Reichskanzlei* in Berlin, 15 July 1935. A photograph by Heinrich Hoffmann, Hitler's favourite photographer. *See* Part I note 15.

An Enigma machine with spare naval wheel in its wooden box to the left of the wireless operator on U124, 1 March 1941. *See* Part I note 16. *Bundesarchiv*

Left: Alfred Duff Cooper, (1890–1954). *See* Part I note 17. In this photograph, 3 October, 1938, Duff Cooper is arriving at the Admiralty to hand in his resignation, accompanied by Lady Diana Duff Cooper.

Right: Leslie Hore-Belisha, (1893–1957). *See* Part I note 18.

Left: Robert Gilbert Vansittart, (1881–1957). *See* Part I note 19.

Right: A rare photograph of Colonel Maurice-Henri Gauché attending a ball given at the U.S. Embassy, 1 February 1939. No head of any security bureau likes to be photographed. *Kitrosser, Life Picture Collection*

The *Cagoulards* were a French ultra-right-wing underground movement. As a suspected leader, Jean Dominique de la Meuse was arrested for interrogation.

Top: A *Cagoulards* arms cache is discovered.

Middle: Cagoulards arrested for interrogation. After the occupation of France in 1940, many *Cagoulards* became active collaborationists and supporters of the Vichy regime.

Right: John Semer Farnsworth, (1893–1952). Farnsworth was a former United States Navy officer who was convicted of spying for Japan during the 1930s. He was identified as Agent K in radio messages intercepted by the Office of Naval Intelligence (ONI). *See* Part II note 3.

American Storm Troopers in Chicago. The German Bunds were all too real. Many of the Bunds were based in German-American population centres in New York, New Jersey and the Upper Middle West.

Left: Georg Gyssling, (1893–1965). Gyssling was German consul to the United States from 1927 until 1941; from 1933 in Los Angeles. Gyssling is photographed here with Nazi film maker Leni Riefenstahl. *See* Part II note 7.

Above: Hermann Max Schwinn, (b. 1905). *See* Part II note 8.

Above: On 12 August 1938 Peter P. Gissibl testified before the Special House Committee investigating un-American activities. The German-born ex-führer of the Chicago Post of the bund, told why he resigned in May after a disagreement with Fritz Kuhn, over the organization's policies. 'I didn't want to be so radical on some points', Gissbl said. 'For instance, the Jewish question, and working with German-American organizations.' *See* Part II note 10.

Walter Kappe, (1904–1944). *See* Part II note 11.

Portraits of Walter Kappe and Joseph Schmidt.

Fritz Julius Kuhn, (1896–1951).

Fritz Julius Kuhn. *See* Part II note 13.

On 1 March 1938, the Nazi government decreed that no national *Reichsdeutsche* could be a member of the Bund, and that no Nazi emblems were to be used by the organization. Undaunted, on 20 February 1939 Kuhn held a large and highly publicized rally at Madison Square Garden in New York City.

Hans-Heinrich Dieckhoff, (1884–1952), *right*, with Hugo Eckner. Dieckhoff was ambassador to the United States from 1937 to November 1938. He was recalled in direct tit-for-tat response to the American recall of its ambassador in protest over *Kristallnacht*. Dr Hugo Eckener, (1868–1954) was the manager of the *Luftschiffbau Zeppelin* during the inter-war years, and also the commander of the famous *Graf Zeppelin* for most of its record-setting flights. He was an anti-Nazi who was invited to campaign as a moderate in the German presidential elections. He was blacklisted by the Nazis and eventually side-lined.

Left: Leopold von Hoesch, (1881–1936). Von Hoesch was a career diplomat who was appointed to France in 1923. In 1932 Hoesch was transferred to London, where he remained until his death.

Right: Ulrich Friedrich Wilhelm Joachim von Ribbentrop, (1893–1946). Joachim von Ribbentrop (*left of* centre) and Hans Heinrich Dieckhoff (*left*) leaving the Carlton Hotel in London 1936. *See* Part II note 16.

Montagu Collet Norman, (1871–1950), Governor of the Bank of England from 1920 to 1944. *See* Part II note 16. Norman, pictured here on the right with a beard is with German Central Bank President, Hjalmar Schacht *c.* 1935.

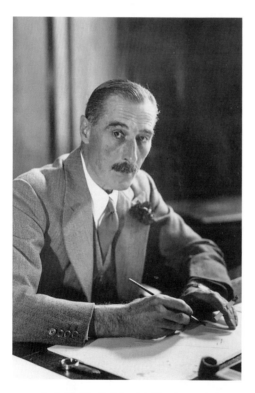

Left: Sir Nevile Meyrick Henderson KCMG, (1882–1942). Henderson was Ambassador of the United Kingdom to Nazi Germany from 1937 to 1939. *See* Part II note 17. *Bundesarchiv*

Right: Sir Nevile Henderson accompanied by Sir Horace John Wilson, (1882–1972). Wilson was a British Government official who had a key role in the appeasement-oriented ministry of Neville Chamberlain. He was present at the Munich conference of September 1938. *Bundesarchiv*

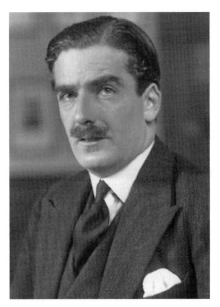

Left: Ambassador Nevile Henderson and Horace Wilson on the stairs of the Hotel Dreesen, Bad Godesberg, in preparation for the Munich conference, 23 September 1938. To Henderson's left is an unknown German Foreign Officer minder. Behind Wilson is Alexander von Dörnberg, head of protocol of the German Foreign Office. They are all flanked by SS guards. *Bundesarchiv*

Right: Robert Anthony Eden, (1897–1977). Eden was Secretary of State for Foreign Affairs 22 December 1935—20 February 1938, 22 December 1940—26 July 1945 and 28 October 1951— 7 April 1955. He was Prime Minister 6 April 1955—10 January 1957. His resignation in February 1938 was largely attributed to growing dissatisfaction with Chamberlain's policy of appeasement.

Kurt Schuschnigg, (1897–1977). Schuschnigg was Chancellor of the Federal State of Austria, following the assassination of his predecessor, Engelbert Dollfuss, in July 1934 until Hitler's annexation of Austria in March 1938.

Left: Waldemar Pabst, (1880–1970). *See* Part II note 24.

Right: Wilhelm Emanuel Freiherr von Ketteler, (1906–1938). Freiherr von Ketteler was a German diplomat, mainly known as one of the young conservative opponents of Nazism in 'Edgar Jung-circle' and close associate of Hitler's Vice-Chancellor and Ambassador to Vienna, Franz von Papen.

Wilhelm Freiherr von Ketteler (*left*) on 21 February 1938 three weeks before his assassination. The picture shows him together with Franz von Papen (*centre*) and Hans Graf von Kageneck (*right*) in the Wiener Westbahnhof, *en route* to a meeting with Hitler in Berchtesgaden. He disappeared on 14 March 1938 and his disfigured body was discovered several weeks later in the Danube near Hainburg.

From top to bottom:

Charles André Joseph Marie de Gaulle, (1890–1970). *See* Part II note 26.

From left to right: Rudolf Hess' adjutant Alfred Leitgen; Professor Karl Haushofer; Reich Doctor's Leader Dr Gerhard Wagner, (1888–1939; Rudolf Hess and the German envoy in Sweden, Prince of Wied; 13 May 1935. Gerhard Wagner was jointly responsible for euthanasia and sterilization carried out against Jews and the handicapped, and showed himself at the Nuremberg Party Congress in 1935 to be a staunch proponent of the Nuremberg Laws, and thereby also of Nazi Germany's race legislation and racial politics. Under Wagner's leadership, the Nazi killing institution at Hadamar was established. Alfred Leitgen was a journalist and an acquaintance of Otto Dietrich, Hitler's press secretary. *See* Part III note 1.

Ernst 'Putzi' Hanfstaengl, (1887–1976). Ernst Hanfstaengl with Hitler and Göring, 1932. *See* Part III note 2.

Arthur Seyss-Inquart, (1892– 1946).
See Part III note 3.

Arthur Seyss-Inquart with Adolf Hitler in Vienna,
16 March 1938. Also in the photograph: Heinrich
Himmler, Reinhard Heydrich and Wilhelm Keitel.

Heinrich Otto Abetz, (1903–1958). *See* Part III
note 7.

Heinrich Otto Abetz (*centre*) with Marshal Philippe Pétain (*left*) and Pierre Laval, (1883–1945). Laval was Prime Minister of France from 27 January 1931 to 20 February 1932, and also headed another government from 7 June 1935 to 24 January 1936. He served in a prominent role under Philippe Pétain as the vice-president of Vichy's Council of Ministers from 11 July 1940 to 13 December 1940, and later as the head of government from 18 April 1942 to 20 August 1944. After the liberation Laval was arrested by the new French government tried for high treason and executed by firing squad.

Above: Heinrich Otto Abetz with his French wife, Susanne de Bruyker, whom he married in 1932.

Right: Stephanie Julianne von Hohenlohe, (1891–1972). *See* Part III note 8.

Sir Oswald Mosley, (1896–1980). *See* Part III note 10.

Above: George Geoffrey Dawson, (1874–1944).
Dawson was editor of *The Times* from 1912 to
1919 and again from 1923 until 1941. *See* Part III
note 11.

Right: Charles-Marie-Photius Maurras, (1868–
1952). *See* Part III note 12.

Henri Philippe Joseph Pétain, (1856–1951), with Adolf Hitler and Hitler's interpreter, Paul Schmidt at Montoire; with Foreign Minister Ribbentrop at the side, 24 October 1940. *See* Part III note 13.

Left: Ernst Wilhelm Bohle, (1903–1960). Bohle was the leader of the Foreign Organization of the NSDAP from 1933 until 1945. *See* Part III note 14.

Right: Ernst Bohle with Winston Churchill, 2 October 1937.

A still from a film by Georg Wilhelm 'G. W.' Pabst, (1885–1967). Pabst was an Austrian theatre and film director. In 1910, Pabst travelled to the United States where he worked as an actor and director at the German Theatre in New York. Pabst abandoned his Hollywood career to return to Austria in 1938 to take care of 'family business', he said later, but other pressures may have been applied. In 1955 he directed the first post-war German full-length film to feature the character of Adolf Hitler; *Der letzte Akt* (in the English version) *The Last 10 Days*, with Albin Skoda as Adolf Hitler and Lotte Tobisch as Eva Braun.

Left: Kirsten Malfrid Flagstad, (1895–1962). Flagstad was a Norwegian opera singer and a highly regarded Wagnerian soprano. *See* Part III note 18.

Right: Herman Esser, (1900–1981). Esser entered the Nazi party with Hitler in 1920 and became the editor of the Nazi paper *Völkischer Beobachter* and a Nazi member of the Reichstag. *See* Part III note 18.

Left: Eugen Hadamovsky, (1904–1945); third from the right in this photograph with Goebbels, 28 January 1941. *See* Part III note 21. *Bundesarchiv*

Right: Theodor Habicht, (1898–1944). *See* Part III note 23.

Engelbert Dollfuss, (1892–1934). Dollfuss rose from the position of Minister for Forests and Agriculture to Federal Chancellor in 1932 in the midst of an Austrian political crisis. In early 1933 he forced the closure of the parliament, banned the Austrian Nazi party and assuming dictatorial powers. Dollfuss was assassinated as part of a failed coup attempt by Nazi agents in 1934. *From left to right:* Galeazzo Ciano, Benito Mussolini's son-in-law and Foreign Minister of Italy; Engelbert Dollfuss, Chancellor of Austria; Benito Mussolini, Duce of Italy; photographed during a visit by Dollfuss to Italy.

Above: Alfred Gerstenberg, (1893–1959). *See* Part III note 27. This photograph is of a military mission to Bucharest, 1 May 1943: *From left to right:* Admiral Tilesen, Luftwaffe General Kammhuber, Luftwaffe General Alfred Gerstenberg and General von Man.

Below left: Georges-Étienne Bonnet, (1889–1973). Bonnet was a leading figure in the Radical Party. In April 1938, following the fall of the second Blum government, Bonnet was appointed Foreign Minister under Daladier as Premier. He was a staunch supporter of the Munich Agreement in 1938 and was firmly opposed to taking military action against German expansion. *See* Part IV note 5.

Above right: Georges Mandel, (1885–1944). Mandel helped Clemenceau control the press and the trade union movement during the First World War. He served as Minister of Posts and Telecommunications from 1934 to 1936) and Minister of Colonies from 1938 to 18 May 1940 when Premier Paul Reynaud appointed him Minister of the Interior. He opposed the Armistice and on 16 June 1940 in Bordeaux he was arrested but released shortly afterwards. He was offered the chance to leave together with Charles de Gaulle on a British aircraft but he declined, saying: 'It would look as though I was afraid—as if I was running away.' *See* Part IV note 6. Photograph: Georges Mandel (*left*) in March 1935, on an official visit to one of his departments when he was minister of the PTT. The other person is Ernest Chamon, Directeur Général of the Compagnie des Compteurs à Montrouge.

Left: Hjalmar Horace Greeley Schacht, (1877–1970). Schacht was an economist, banker and politician. In 1934 Hitler appointed him as Minister of Economics and Schacht supported public works programmes, most notably the construction of autobahns to alleviate unemployment. *See* Part V note 1.

Right: Baldur Benedikt von Schirach, (1907-1974). *See* Part V note 4.

Baldur Benedikt von Schirach addresses a crowd in 1940.

Fritz Konrad Ferdinand Grobba, (1886–1973). Grobba was appointed as the German Ambassador to Iraq in October 1932 and was sent to Baghdad. He was able to speak both Turkish and Arabic. He frequently spoke of Arab nationalism and of ousting the British from the Middle East. In this 1935 photograph German ambassador Fritz Grobba is to the right, standing behind King Ghazi. *See* Part V note 5.

George Sylvester Viereck, (1884–1962). *See* Part VI note 3.

Colin Ross, (1885–1945). Ross was born in Vienna, Austria and was a traveller and writer of Scottish descent. *See* Part VI note 4.

Fritz Wiedemann, (1891–1970). Wiedemann was for a time the personal adjutant to Adolf Hitler, having served with him in the First World War. *See* Part VI note 5.

Left: Manfred Freiherr von Killinger, (1886–1944). Killinger was a veteran of the First World War and took part in the military intervention against the Bavarian Soviet Republic. *See* Part VI note 6. *Bundesarchiv*

Right: Nikolaus Adolph Fritz Ritter was head of Abt. I Luft of the Abwehrstelle X Hamburg. He went to the United States in January 1924 and except for a couple of visits home to Germany lived there in the New York area until 1937. He had previously attended the Prussian Military Academy before leaving Germany and about that time received training as a textiles engineer at the Prussian Technical School for Textiles in Sorau. He was recruited for the *Abwehr* in 1937 and he returned to Germany on a promise of employment. He lived there with his first wife and two children but travelled extensively, living in Bremen, Hamburg, and Budapest while working as a spymaster for operations in England, the United States and Egypt. Ritter was an *Abwehr* agent in Great Britain under the name 'Dr Rantzau'.

From left to right: Horst Böhme, (1909–1945); Reinhard Heydrich, (1904–1942) and Karl Hermann Frank, (1898–1946); in Prague, September 1941. Böhme was a German SS-*Oberführer* and a leading perpetrator of the Holocaust. Heydrich was a high-ranking Nazi and commencing with the Wannsee Conference held on 20 January 1942, one of the main architects of the Holocaust. Frank was a prominent Sudeten Nazi official in Czechoslovakia prior to and during the War. He was executed by hanging after the War for his role in organizing the massacres of the people of the Czech villages of Lidice and Ležáky. *Bundesarchiv*

Heydrich in Prague giving a Nazi salute. He was attacked while being driven from his country villa at Panenské Břežany to his office at Prague Castle on 27 May 1942 by a British-trained team of Czech soldiers who had been sent by the government-in-exile to kill him in *Operation Anthropoid*. He died from his injuries a week later.

Adolf Hitler with Heydrich's two sons at his state funeral in Prague, 7 June 1942. Heinrich Himmler is to the right, also visible are Robert Ley and Joseph Goebbels.

Above: The Lidice Massacre. The inhabitants of the village of Lidice, about 500 in number, were falsely accused of having harboured Heydrich's attackers. During the night of 10 June 1942 SS units surrounded the village. All men over age 15 were shot, and the women and children were sent to concentration camps. The village was then burnt to the ground.

Right: Lidice, Czechoslovakia, Corpses of a Czech family after they were murdered.

Below: Camille Chautemps, (1885–1963). *See* Part VI note 10.

A still from the film
Confessions of a Nazi Spy
(1939) with Edward G.
Robinson and Wolfgang
Zilzer. In 1938, several
members of Friends of
the New Germany, a Nazi
front group presenting itself
as a Germany-American
bund, were put on trial for
espionage. Warner Brothers
sent writer Milton Krims to
cover the story and create
a script. The script was
culled together from Krims'
reporting and from articles by
the FBI agent Leon G. Turrou.

A still from *Confessions of
a Nazi Spy* with Frederick
Vogeding and Hans Heinrich
von Twardowski. *Confessions*
was the first overtly anti-
Nazi film from one of the
major Hollywood studios.
Germany tried to put pressure
on the Production Code
Administration (PCA) to stop
the film, but failed. Warner
Brothers faced down fierce
opposition to the making of
the film from both German
officials and German-
American groups allied with
the Nazis at the time before
the U.S. formally entered the
Second World War.

Franz Schlager in *Confessions
of a Nazi Spy*. As a group,
the studios had agreed to
lay off direct attacks on
Adolf Hitler because several
companies were still doing
business with Nazi Germany
and German diplomats were
regularly threatening to ban
all American films. Warner
Brother were the first to pull
out of Germany but studios
including MGM, Paramount
and 20th Century Fox failed
to stand up to Hitler.

Left: Frederick Joubert Duquesne, (1877–1956). *See* Part VI note 13.

Right: FBI agent William Sebold with his wife Ellen. The Duquesne Spy Ring, as it was known, was brought down by William Sebold, the FBI's first double agent. *See* Part VI note 12.

Members of the Duquesne spy ring.

Left: Reichswerke Hermann Göring was the simplistic umbrella name for the group of companies Göring built with stolen, sequestered and 'gifted' assets. Next to the IG Farben and Vereinigte Stahlwerke AG, it was the largest company in the Nazi Germany. In preparation for war a policy was introduced to reduce the dependence on foreign raw materials to a minimum. U.S. citizen Herman Alexander Brassert assisted Göring in building up the steel industry. Here Hermann Göring visits construction site of the *Reichswerke* in Linz. *See* Part VI note 12.

Right: Herman Alexander Brassert, (1875–1961). *See* Part VI note 13.

Operation Claymore took place in March 1941, by No. 3 and No. 4 Commandos. This was the first large scale raid from the United Kingdom during the War. Their objective was the undefended Norwegian Lofoten Islands. They successfully destroyed the fish-oil factories, petrol dumps, and 11 ships, capturing 216 Germans, encryption equipment and codebooks. Here troops, including men from No. 4 Commando are returning from shore in landing craft after the raid.

He was a precise prophet. And it does not detract from his intelligence that he didn't know then that the Germans had already built the supertanks of eighty and a hundred tons. It was again the fault of the French secret service, which had no knowledge at all of the mass production of these tanks. And it speaks once more for Hitler's great talent for deception that he did not use his supertank in the Polish campaign, where he could do with much smaller tanks.

So, when the new tanks appeared in Flanders and in France, nobody was prepared to meet them. Their armour was much too thick to be pierced by the 25 mm standard anti-tank guns of the French infantry. And the German tanks just went on and on. There was no stopping them.

Finally the French started bringing forward their famous 75 mm field guns, leftovers from the last war. Where they arrived at the front, they could and did stop the German tanks. But very few of them arrived in time.

And how was it possible that Hitler could build so many heavy tanks without the *Deuxième Bureau*'s finding out? It was simple enough. After Hitler took Austria, he immediately moved the greater part of the German aviation and tank production into Austria. In Vienna-Neustadt the factories worked day and night. In Vienna, the French secret service had never thought of organizing a service specializing in spying on armament production. They now tried, after Hitler was in, but then, of course, it was much too late. They never even got started.

The same thing happened all over again after Munich. This time the scene was Czechoslovakia. This time Hitler moved most of his tank production into the Skoda works. Again the *Deuxième Bureau* was powerless. Czechoslovakia had always been an ally of France; the French intelligence service, therefore, had never built an organization there. It had worked hand in glove with the Czech secret service. And then, when Hitler was in, again it was too late to do what had not been done before. The numerous Frenchmen who were working at the Skoda works either left Czechoslovakia of their own accord, or they were forced to leave.

And it was only then, only in the spring of 1939, that the Germans started building the supertanks at the Skoda works. But they were in time.

On 18 May 1940, the battle of France was on and the news from the front was gravely disquieting. The *Deuxième Bureau* had some news which did not concern the war directly. It really concerned only the *Bureau*; but it was disturbing enough.

In the French secret service offices six cryptographs were in use. These machines were little miracles. They served to transcribe messages into code, or to decode messages in code. The number of interchangeable codes was infinite, and a new code could be established just by making a slight adjustment.

The secret services, the foreign offices, and the embassies of practically all countries, were equipped with cryptographs. They made everything so much easier. And the infinite variations made it impossible for any possessor of such a machine to decode messages of another country if he didn't know the code.

This admirable machine had been invented by a Swedish engineer. He had founded his own company, the Aktiebolaget Cryptograph Co., and sold his machines all over the world. They were expensive, too. There was only one disadvantage: certain parts had to be renewed frequently. And you could obtain the spare parts only in Stockholm.

In January 1940 the *Deuxième Bureau* urgently needed some spare parts for one of its cryptographs. A telegram was sent to Stockholm. Weeks passed and the parts did not arrive. The French became very concerned, since a second machine had stopped working. Again they telegraphed; again no response from Stockholm. One of the Swedish agents of the Bureau went to the factory himself. He was first told that there were difficulties with transportation. Finally, the manager admitted that there was a shortage of material and the customer in Paris would have to be patient for a while.

The *Deuxième Bureau* became desperate. By the end of April only two of the six cryptographs were working. And they worked much too slowly. Messages which should have been transmitted in a few hours, took days. Again the Stockholm agent received a telegram. This time he did not go to the factory; he made some investigations on his own. And, sure enough, he found out that shortly before the outbreak of the war, the controlling interest in the Aktiebolaget had been acquired by a German bank.[6] Now, of course, it was perfectly clear why all the orders were being systematically sabotaged.

This the French secret service learned on 18 May. It was a bad omen.

Five days later Reynaud appeared before the Senate and made an impassioned speech which ended with the words, 'If tomorrow someone should tell me that a miracle is necessary to save France, I should tell him: "I believe in a miracle because I believe in France."'

The word 'tomorrow' alarmed the Senate. When the speech appeared in the newspapers a few hours later, this one word had been eliminated.

A miracle was indeed necessary to save France. Only thirteen days before, a period had ended which in France had been dubbed '*une drôle de guerre,*' and in the United States 'a phony war.' On 10 May Hitler invaded Holland, Belgium, Luxembourg.... 11 May, France and England promised help to the invaded countries.... 18 May, the enemy had already broken into French territory. Gamelin proclaimed his famous order of the day: 'Win or die!' Premier Reynaud asked Marshal Pétain to come back from Madrid and join the Cabinet.... 20 May, Gamelin was removed, Weygand was made Commander-in-Chief.... 21 May, Marshal Pétain went to the front.... 22 May, Weygand told Reynaud that he was confident he could hold the front.... But not twenty-four hours later, he sent a courier to Paris, warning the government that he could no longer guarantee Paris, since it was possible that isolated armoured columns would get through to the Capital.

It was on this evening that Reynaud made his speech.

It was on this evening that the *Deuxième Bureau* started packing.

There was something pathetic about the *Bureau*'s preparations to leave Paris. It was as though a very old and dignified business firm had suddenly to quit the premises where it had been established for many prosperous years, in fact, for many generations. It was pathetic because once the packing started, it was evident that the *Bureau* had never foreseen the possibility of having to move. Everything in the big, old building had been ordained for permanency.

To say that the *Deuxième Bureau* was about to move means, of course, that it was about to move its files. Those files were arranged in enormously large, heavy steel cabinets which ranged the walls of endless corridors on the third floor of the building on Boulevard Saint Germain. Each cabinet had its own lock. It could only be opened with the right combination, which was changed at least once a month. And in addition, two keys were necessary. One of them was in the hands of the section chief who was concerned with the papers in a particular cabinet. The other key was held either by Colonel Gauché or one of his *sous-chefs*.

Therefore, it took almost eighteen hours to open all the files and put their contents into packing cases. Then when everything was done, the *Deuxième Bureau* got instructions from Reynaud that it was to remain in Paris. The cases were unpacked. The reason for this change of plan was that the Germans seemed to be driving toward the Channel instead of to Paris. However, the daily work became more complicated. The General Staff, which had been quartered in Chantilly, only a few miles from Paris, was now—by the end of May—secretly transferred to an old château in Coulomniers, some thirty miles from Paris. Since there had to be close contact between the *Deuxième Bureau* and the General Staff, some of the officers of the Bureau were forever racing between Coulomniers and Paris.

On 19May, Marshal Henri Pétain entered the Cabinet as Vice-Premier. And Georges Mandel became Minister of the Interior. The tragedy was that this man had not been given control of counterespionage long before. Had it happened earlier, perhaps a few years or even only a few months earlier, the worst might have been averted. France might have been saved from betrayal.

Georges Mandel went to work immediately. Within two hours after his appointment he had dismissed the Chief of the *Sureté*, the treacherous M. Boussière, who under Mandel's predecessor, Sarraut, had so ably defended the interests of Hitler. M. Boussière was told to leave the premises of the *Sureté* without even being allowed to return to his private office. His successor was already installed there. It was M. Winter who had been made Chief of the *Sureté*.

Three hours after Georges Mandel's arrival at the Ministry of the Interior—that was already late at night—the *Deuxième Bureau* received a phone call. The Minister wanted one of the officers to come to see him immediately and to serve as a contact man. An officer was assigned. He was astonished at Georges Mandel's sudden desire to co-operate so closely with the *Deuxième Bureau*. For it was known everywhere that he had often bitingly criticized the organization. He had declared publicly that he considered it a club of inane officers who were dead and didn't know it. Naturally, such remarks had not endeared him to the *Bureau*.

It didn't take the officer long to develop a high opinion of Georges Mandel.[7]

Mandel was not yet old. However, he had never been young. He was pale, always seemed to feel cold. He wore black suits and an extremely high collar with an old fashioned four-in-hand.

His old chief, Clemenceau, was known to have required the utmost of the men who worked for him. But the young Georges Mandel had satisfied even the Old Tiger. When the master fell, Mandel had to go, too. But though the politicians had exiled him from public office, he did not stop working for the good of France. He was isolated, but he continued to work. He lived at 40 Avenue Victor Hugo, a fashionable quarter. The apartment was really an office. There was no woman around and no feminine touch. The only person in whom Mandel had complete confidence was a manservant, a silent old man.

Mandel seemed to work all the time. He was often at his desk until four in the morning, and he was back at it at seven. Sometimes he was offered money in one guise or another; big trusts approached him. He always refused. He could not be bought. Nor could he be swayed by flattery.

Strangely enough, he was working on his files. He had started them on Clemenceau's orders in 1916, when he began to gather information about important politicians, officers, and other personalities in public life. And he never stopped revising and augmenting these files. For, like Clemenceau, he had felt since the end of the last war that France must look sharp lest she fall victim to another war of revenge by Germany. And like his master, he was sure that some of the danger originated from within. It was necessary, then, to unmask the enemies within. Toward that goal Mandel had been working since the end of the last war. They called him—rightly—'*La Tête Dure*'—the Mule.

In the early thirties he was offered the post of Minister of Communications. This particular Ministry had been run with scandalous inefficiency. In no time, Mandel built it up; reorganized the mail, the telegraph, and the radio. But he did more than this. He took advantage of the position to improve his files—commonly known in Paris as Mandel's '*Cabinet Noir*' (Black Cabinet). He had great ability in selecting efficient men to fill key posts, men he could depend upon. They were given a free hand to tap telephone wires, whereby they heard interesting things, and let him know. Of course, that was not strictly legal. And some of his enemies later said he had established a French Gestapo. Mandel just shrugged.

He didn't keep his post long, because governments in France were juggled frequently. But even when he was out, he still received lots of material from his old employees.

Later in the thirties he became Minister of Colonies. Again he did a superb job of reorganizing a corrupt Ministry. And again he used his position to gather more material, more information. Politically, he was a nonentity. He was a member of the Chamber of Deputies and he was the leader of a small group of rightists—his Independent Republicans had twelve seats.

But his indirect power was much greater. His power resided in his information. He knew everything. He knew everything about the private life of every politician; everything about his financial standing, his obligations, his connections. He knew every conceivable detail about many thousands of people. He was the best-informed man in France. He had become a national symbol—for those who were not content with developments in the country. They could easily enough get in touch with him; he was the only public personage whose telephone number and address were listed in the telephone book. He answered every telephone call, every letter. He was always willing to listen.

Many men came to him or wrote him. Some whom he had never met before, who had only heard of him, volunteered their services. There was a small army around him, an army of dependable men. They sat in every ministry in Paris. They sat in French Embassies, Legations, and Consulates all over the world. They even sat within the *Sureté* and within the *Deuxième Bureau*; within newspaper offices and the directorates of banks. It was an army of men who felt that France was heading for disaster. Mandel had a good nose for seemingly insignificant news that invariably proved to be important. He got a lot of information from minor agents of the *Deuxième Bureau* stationed in Paris or near frontiers, agents who were disgusted because their reports were treated flippantly by their own superiors.

Mandel had a good memory. He never forgot anything he once heard. In the Chamber it used to be said of him, 'He knows France like the inside of his own pocket.'

When on 19 May he entered the Ministry of the Interior, he was greeted by a group of reporters. He said, as always, that he had no time for interviews. 'Where are your files?' the reporters asked him.

'Here,' Georges Mandel said, pointing to his forehead. And he shut the door.

How was it that this man was made Minister of the Interior so late, too late, in fact?

Because most politicians were afraid of him. If a man, while more or less a private citizen, could get so much dangerous information, what would he not do with a whole police force at his disposal? Men like Daladier, Bonnet, Laval, could only shudder at the thought. And far from calming their fears, Georges Mandel had a nasty habit of mentioning his files and saying how many politicians he could expose. For most of his colleagues, he had open contempt. After Munich, he did not even greet Daladier any more, though he was a member of his Cabinet. Later, when Paul Reynaud became Premier, he first refused to become Minister of the Interior, though Reynaud was really his best and only friend, for the reason that Daladier was to continue as War Minister. Only when Daladier was on his way out, did he consent to take over. It was late, but he didn't realize how late it was.

The one condition he stipulated before becoming Minister of the Interior was that no one should interfere with him. And since nobody did, he accomplished an enormous amount of work.

Everyone who worked with him in the following three weeks was amazed at Mandel's speed and efficiency. Within these few weeks, the last weeks of the French Republic, Mandel and Winter dismissed almost half the agents of the *Sureté Nationale*. They arrested whole groups of German spies who were working under the guidance of the traitor, Fabre-Luce. They arrested Charles Lesca, editor of the weekly *Je Suis Partout* ('I am Everywhere'), which was financed by the Nazis and worked for the Nazi cause. They finally caught Count Serpeille de Gobineau, who had served as a courier between the Paris fifth columnists and the German espionage headquarters in Brussels.

The *Deuxième Bureau* was delighted. For it had told the *Sureté Nationale* repeatedly that these men were traitors and spies, only to be laughed at by Messrs. Dubois and Sarraut. Now, finally something was being done.

More was done. Within three weeks, over a hundred of the highest police officials throughout France were dismissed without warning. It was the one occasion during the past ten years when some appreciable step was taken against espionage. Georges Mandel wanted to do more, much more. 'I need only three months,' he said, 'and we will have no more traitors in our ranks.'

Even while he was supervising the moving of the Ministry of the Interior, Georges Mandel did not lose his optimism. 'I need only three months,' he repeated. He thought he would have three months and many more. 'This war will be won, as all wars are won, by those with the better information,' he said. He was, of course, referring to himself as the best-informed man in France. Strangely enough, it did not occur to him that the war, or at least that chapter of the war, was about to be won by those with the better information—the Nazis.

In those last hours, he spoke freely to the officer of the *Deuxième Bureau* who was working with him. He told him that France never would have got herself into such a predicament had it not been for the outdated ideas of her military leaders. He went on to point out the failure of the Intelligence Services—the *Sureté* and the *Deuxième Bureau* sharing the honours. He lashed at their petty jealousies, their stupidity, their red tape, their inability to modernize their apparatus, their hundred little slips and oversights committed at moments when an error was a crime.

Mandel said:

worst of all, you didn't understand the one phenomenon you had to understand in order to save our country. You didn't understand Hitler. You didn't understand that he was planning a total war. Everybody had been talking about total war for so long, but you never stopped to consider that total war is—total. That it really includes everything. You didn't see what was coming closer and closer. And we who did see were called hysterical.

Later in Bordeaux, Mandel, fighting to the last, tried to convince old Marshal Pétain—tried to convince everybody—that the war should be continued from Africa, from the end of the world if necessary. Then he understood that it was all in vain.

He looked very old that day. 'Perhaps I won't have my three months after all,' he said softly to one of his friends. 'However, the truth will all come out some day.'

One of the last acts of Minister Mandel had been to send his most important documents out of the country. They were safe in England now.

On 9 June, Premier Reynaud notified the *Deuxième Bureau* that it would have to leave Paris and that it would have to pass the Porte d'Orleans not later than Monday, 10 June at 1:00 p.m. The German armies came nearer and nearer. On 29 May Leopold of Belgium had capitulated.... On 3 June, Paris had been bombed for the first time and there had been more than two hundred deaths. Three days later General de Gaulle had finally become Undersecretary of War. Late, much too late.

Again the *Deuxième Bureau* packed. But this time there were only a few hours in which to get ready. It was not enough time. The situation became more and more complicated, since certain section chiefs were not to be found—certain files could not be opened. Couriers raced to Coulomniers to get the officers, or at least their keys. Two of the officers never showed up; it was later found out that they had been sent to Tours. Some cabinets could therefore not be opened. As a result, they had to be brought down to the street as they were. They couldn't be moved around one corner of a stairway landing between the third and second floors. Firemen were called to get them through the windows. That night Paris was at a high pitch of nervousness, and through a misunderstanding the fire department thought that the whole *Deuxième Bureau*, or perhaps even the adjoining War Ministry, was in flames. An army of firemen arrived, causing tremendous excitement all over Paris. The wildest rumours spread.

All during the night, the officers of the *Bureau* worked like madmen. They didn't talk much. Their sweat ran freely, they breathed heavily, sometimes they cursed. There was a constant din of packing cases falling down the stairs. Colonel Gauché began burning correspondence in his fireplace. At this, somebody called the fire department again. They worked all through the night. By ten o'clock the next day the cases were all on the street. It had already become very hot. Only shortly after noon did the trucks begin to appear. They were medium-sized, dirty-brown trucks with the tricolour in a circle on both sides. There were more than a hundred of them. It took all afternoon and all evening to load them. The first ones started leaving the Boulevard Saint Germain around 9:00 p.m.—the last after 2:00 a.m. the following morning. Hundreds of Parisians had gathered to watch. They didn't say anything. They looked pale in the dimmed lights of the cars. They just stood there until the last truck rolled away. That was the exodus of the *Deuxième Bureau* from Paris. They went to Tours.

When they arrived there, they were told not to unload, but to proceed to Bordeaux. They went to Bordeaux.

The government, which had established itself in Tours on 11 June, soon followed. It was no longer a retreat, it was a flight. On 13 June, Reynaud made his last desperate plea to President Roosevelt. He wanted aircrafts, 'clouds of aircrafts.'

The *Deuxième Bureau* unloaded in Bordeaux. The files were put into a warehouse. Two days later the officers were told to load them back into the trucks and leave Bordeaux as soon as possible. They scarcely could find men enough to help them with the tremendous job. Some of their drivers had somehow got lost in Bordeaux and never turned up. A number of the officers took over the wheels themselves.

They left Bordeaux.

The roads were now blocked by thousands of cars, bicycles, and pedestrians. It was very hot. The sky was cloudless. The automobiles drove in four lanes; most of the time they could not move at all. Every hour or so they advanced a few yards and then stopped again. The drivers never took their hands from the horn.

Pedestrians could move much faster. But most of them were exhausted. They collapsed on the side of the roads. Women and children wept.

At night it was better because the road was clear. The pedestrians had gone into the fields to sleep. But with the first sign of dawn, they filled the road again. By six o'clock the cars could no longer move. The people walking along the roads were unshaven, their clothes were crushed and soiled, their eyes were red from lack of sleep. The transformation of solid citizens into wretched refugees had begun.

One of the trucks could go no farther. Something was wrong with a valve. The driver said it would take hours to repair. The others felt they could not wait. They went on.

They passed through villages that were utterly deserted. They passed through a little town that had been bombed. Bodies of dogs were on the streets, their bellies ripped open. Corpses were lying about, covered with sheets. Hundreds were supposed to have died or have been injured.

They went on. And they had no difficulty getting fuel, since it was the government's prerogative to be served first. Since the main highways were too crowded, they took to smaller roads. Some drivers collapsed from lack of sleep. Others lost their way. Now there were only some seventy trucks left out of a hundred and two. And the group became fewer and fewer. Again and again someone lost his way. Which way? Where were they heading? They didn't know themselves. They only knew that they had to get away from the Germans, somewhere where the Germans couldn't find them.

Every so often they tried to get in touch with the War Ministry to get directions. Was there a War Ministry? And where? Was there a government?

They slept in barns, the deep sleep of the exhausted.

They went on. Somewhere—anywhere. Everywhere they came they heard, 'You must go on. The Germans will be here any moment.'

And they went on. At twilight, one car raced down a slope into a river. The driver jumped to safety. His leg was broken. They took him along.

They found a small hotel in a little town. All the rooms were occupied by refugees. Anyway, they would not have dared to go into rooms. They slept on chairs in the lobby, their revolvers in their hands.

In the morning they learned that an armistice had been signed. Once more they returned to Bordeaux. There were fifty-nine trucks now. 'Get away as fast as you can,' they were told, 'the Germans are coming any minute.'

They drove away immediately. They drove into the night. Inside the trucks there were many documents, documents with damning evidence against men who were now the victors. On Otto Abetz, who was to become German Ambassador in Paris a few days later. On Ferdinand de Brinon, who was to make a triumphant appearance in Vichy at the end of that week. On Pétain, who was now the Chief of what was left of France. On Bonnet, who was to be the power behind the scenes.

They had won, these men whose treacherous pasts were in documents now being sped through the night. They had won—but for how long? They had won, but a document can outlast many a passing victory.

These documents fled into the night. And then they disappeared. Perhaps they were taken to private homes of trustworthy Frenchmen; perhaps they were buried in lonely spots. The trucks disappeared too, one by one. Some were driven over cliffs and plunged into the sea; some were soaked with gasoline and burned like torches.

Where are the documents? Maybe a small boat by night took what was left of them to Africa. Perhaps some of them were carried over high mountain passes into Spanish territory. Perhaps British planes landed at deserted spots and picked up some of them.

If anyone knows, nobody will tell. Only one thing is certain; not one scrap of paper from the files of the *Deuxième Bureau* ever fell into the hands of the Nazis. The officers—perhaps they had acted short-sightedly, stupidly, perhaps they had made horrible mistakes—but they were loyal to the last. They defended these sheets of paper whose secrets would have meant certain death to thousands of persons, defended them with their lives.

Where are those men? They, too, have disappeared. They shook hands, saluted, and separated. Maybe they do not intend to lose track of each other; maybe they are going on with some kind of work for their country, to whose defeat they will never submit.

If anyone knows, nobody will tell. For us, for the outside world, they have vanished. Vanished from the limelight into the fog, into the night, where many things may be waiting for the morning.[8]

PART V
Tomorrow—The World

HJALMAR SCHACHT DOES HIS BIT

Hjalmar Schacht,[1] the financial wizard of the Third Reich, who was made President of the Reichsbank in March 1933 and Minister of Economics in January 1935, resigned his Ministerial post in November 1937 and the presidency of the Reichsbank in January 1939.

Informed circles in Berlin declared at the time that the resignation of Herr Schacht was due mainly to disputes with Herr Bohle. Schacht was said to have protested against the enormous expenditures of the AO.

Herr Schacht's relation to Herr Bohle and to espionage in general was primarily a financial one. Someone had to raise the money, and Herr Schacht soon learned to his dismay that total espionage involved no little hard cash. What does espionage cost? The question is certainly as old as espionage itself. It is one which has been discussed a great deal, but little definite information has been available. In general we may say that whatever the published espionage budgets, real expenditures far exceeded these budgets and were paid out of so-called secret funds.

When Hitler came to power, all the sources became invisible. One of Hitler's first governmental strokes was to abolish the fiscal report—under the Constitution the Government had to make an accounting to the people or their representatives of all expenditures. This eliminated all chance of checking espionage expenditures.

The difficulty of arriving at any sort of estimate is enhanced because in many cases the machinery of espionage is also applied to other purposes—particularly for propaganda. One can best get a conception of the costs of espionage in the Third Reich by examining the expenditures of the Propaganda Ministry.

In 1934 the official budget of the Propaganda Ministry was approximately 28,000,000 marks. In addition there were some 40,000,000 marks revenue from advertising taxes; 36,000,000 marks revenue from licence fees and the monthly payments by owners of radio sets. Then the Propaganda Ministry received some 40,000, 000 marks for its news service, 9,000,000 marks from the Foreign Political Office of the Party, 7,000,000 marks from Rudolf Hess's special fund. Altogether the Propaganda Ministry in the year 1934 had at its disposal more than 190,000,000 marks. In 1935 the total sums received by the Propaganda Ministry amounted to 260,000,000 marks.

In 1937, 360,000,000 marks.

But that was only part of it. In addition, there were since 1935 enormous sums which the German Labour Front (the compulsory organization of German workers) had to contribute; further, contributions from the Winter Relief, the Fichtebund, AO members abroad, etc. All in all, Dr Goebbels had in 1937 about 500,000,000 marks for 'propaganda abroad.' What part of this enormous sum is really used for propaganda; what part is used directly or indirectly for espionage? There can be no exact answer to this question, but some experts believe that approximately one third is set aside for espionage. According to other estimates, the AO alone in 1937 spent more than one hundred million dollars. All this, of course, does not include the costs of military espionage and the costs of the Gestapo's espionage—which are probably not large.

It is therefore scarcely an exaggeration to say that the costs of total espionage during recent years were over one hundred million dollars a year.

After Hjalmar Schacht resigned as Minister of Economics, he remained in the Government as Minister without Portfolio. And in German espionage he continued to play an important part, although now he was mostly off stage—his successor, Herr Funk, having undertaken to finance the espionage system. Schacht's importance consisted, as it always had, in his contacts with financial circles abroad.

To make this clear, it is necessary to go back several years.

There are two versions of the story of Hitler's and Hjalmar Schacht's alliance. The first is that the Führer welcomed the great financier into his organization because of Schacht's close contacts with the world of finance and industry. Aside from his personal abilities, which Hitler undoubtedly appreciated, a man with such connections was bound to be enormously useful. During the struggle for power Hitler realized that he could maintain his Party only with the financial support of German heavy industry. It is more than likely that he dreamed of an alliance with the financial and industrial powers of the whole world.

The other version puts it just the other way around. According to this story, Schacht as the representative of industry and finance made the first overtures toward Hitler. Just as Thyssen and his friends supported Hitler within Germany in order to avert the danger of Communism, so international finance wished to strengthen Hitler's power in order to eliminate the danger of Soviet Russia. One fact that gives credence to this version is the material assistance that Sir Henry Deterding (Shell Oil) gave to the new Hitler regime.

But whichever version we accept—whether world capital hired Hitler or Hitler tried to interest world capital—Schacht's function in the Third Reich was essentially the same. It was his business to conclude economic alliances, develop a certain intimacy between the representatives of German finance and industry and those of other countries. He established economic alliances which, as we have often seen, particularly in the case of Rumania, were but preludes to actual conquest.

This matter of friendship with key men in the business world somewhat resembled Putzi Hanfstaengel's idea of society espionage—the kind of espionage Ribbentrop had carried out so brilliantly in London. It is not a matter of chance that one of Schacht's principal envoys was Duke Adolf Friedrich zu Mecklenburg, who from 1934 on was constantly travelling abroad for his 'private observation of economic affairs.' It was all very impressive and in grand style. And from the point of view of espionage, why should not contact with business leaders be as instructive as contact with the leaders of society who incidentally were also politicians?

Hjalmar Schacht had a special organization exclusively for this sort of work. He did not, as might have been expected, use the foreign offices of the Reich Ministry of Economics and Finance, but he had office space at Taubenstrasse 37—the headquarters of the Council for Propaganda for German Economic Affairs. Here he worked hand in hand with the Foreign Office, the Propaganda Ministry and Rosenberg's Foreign Political Office. The main task was to use the opportunity afforded by the conclusion of trade agreements, by negotiations on loans and, in fact, by all sorts of international conferences, to establish contacts with influential foreign business circles.

This activity was frankly admitted. Of course the official reasons for such contacts were given as: 1. Propaganda for the Third Reich among influential foreign personages. 2. Penetration into foreign economy.

Naturally, nothing was said of economic espionage. It was not mentioned that the Nazis could obtain favourable trade agreements if they had full knowledge of foreign economic conditions. It was not mentioned that the leaders of the Third Reich regarded such trade agreements as an amicable preliminary to *Anschluss*.

It is understandable that in this game, oil played a significant part.

In 1913 the United States Ambassador to England, Page, exclaimed, 'What the devil does Mexican oil amount to, in comparison with the close friendship between the United States and Great Britain?' By this he meant that the conflicts of American and British oil firms should not influence the politics of the two countries. But just at this time Sir William Tyrell, on behalf of the London Foreign Office, accused Secretary of State Bryan of 'talking like a Standard Oil man,' while President Woodrow Wilson was furious at the suspected collusion between British Minister Sir Lionel Carden and Lord Cowdray, who then held 85 per cent of Mexico's oil.

This situation, in which the governments of two nations followed the foreign policy of their big industries, rather than their own government's foreign policy, was an ever-recurrent one. In the field of oil it came up whenever there was an oil boom—as, for example, in 1921 and particularly in 1927, when the struggle between Standard Oil and Shell reached its bitterest point.

Such situations were just what Schacht needed. Skilful envoys who knew how to handle such things could reap great rewards. They could find out a great deal which they could never have found out when peace prevailed among the great industries.

The situation was especially propitious for Schacht in 1938. President Cardenas of Mexico had nationalised oil and expropriated foreign oil wells. The repercussions were tremendous. Secretary of State Hull sent indignant notes, Washington stopped buying Mexican silver. The great oil companies declared they would not recognize the decision of the Mexican Supreme Court, which had not yet passed on the question. Oil companies in the United States, England, France, Belgium, and Holland started a boycott against Mexican oil.

President Cardenas, a man whom no one can accuse of harbouring sympathy for fascism, tried in vain to sell his oil to South America. When this failed, there was nothing left for him to do but accept the Axis bids for it. He bartered oil for German machines, Italian tankers, and Japanese soy beans.

And Schacht sent his envoys. Not only to arrange the oil deals, but to keep their ears open and draw conclusions from what they heard....

Schacht's right-hand man in all oil affairs is Helmuth Wohlthat.[2] Helmuth Wohlthat is Ministerial Director in the Finance Ministry. His name is seldom mentioned in public. He first appeared in the world press in 1938, when he concluded the important German-Rumanian trade agreement—an agreement which marked the first step in Germany's peaceful conquest of Rumania. Recently it was rumoured that he was in Japan. Probably he was trying to secure for Germany a larger share of the United States oil deliveries to Japan.

Wohlthat, of lower middle-class parentage, entered the Army when quite young and became an officer. During the First World War he was for a time adjutant to von Blomberg, who was to become Nazi War Minister. It was then that he lived for a time near Bucharest in the villa of a Rumanian oil magnate and made his first entry into oil circles. After the war, when his military career seemed crushed, he went to the United States and tried to get into the oil industry. He failed in this, and for many years he had to live on the money sent him by a former schoolmate, a Jewish banker in Berlin.

Finally he did manage to work his way into the petroleum industry. Just what he did has never been clear. He frequently changed jobs, and from 1927 on he regularly made annual trips to Mexico and Central America. Slowly he amassed a considerable fortune. Then he divorced his first wife and married a Philadelphia school teacher of German descent; this second wife was, incidentally, a cousin of Hjalmar Schacht's wife. At this time—under the Weimar Republic—Schacht was democratic President of the Reichsbank.

When Hitler came to power von Blomberg wrote to Wohlthat asking him to come to Berlin at once—he was needed. Wohlthat returned. For a time he worked in the War Ministry, then became a kind of liaison officer between the War Ministry and Schacht. Soon he became Chief of the Foreign Exchange office. Among his duties was that of supervising the distribution of foreign exchange funds which were to be used for the purchase of raw materials imported from abroad.

His position was so important that he was a privileged character; his failure to join the Nazi Party and his continued association with old Jewish friends within and outside of Germany were countenanced. In fact, they were not only countenanced but desired, for it helped business if the world could be convinced that many of the stories about Germany were merely the exaggerations of anti-Hitler groups. During all these years, Wohlthat concentrated on business concerning petroleum.

Late in 1938, Wohlthat was to come to the United States. He had just been appointed Commissar of Jewish Affairs, and the Nazis hoped that with his excellent connections he would be able to raise sufficient funds for a wholesale emigration of the German Jews—the victims of the November pogroms. But shortly before he was to depart, the whole plan was dropped. Apparently Washington had suggested to Berlin that Wohlthat should stay at home. He, therefore, remained in Berlin and took over the Office of Trade Agreements, which negotiated and arranged oil shipments. An Oil Purchasing Company was formed, with offices in Berlin and Hamburg. With the help of this company and hundreds of agents, Wohlthat succeeded in maintaining or renewing his contacts with oil circles in the United States and Mexico. Since then he has become the foremost oil specialist of the Nazi Government and German industry. Any matter even remotely pertaining to oil passes through his hands. It is impossible to make any kind of oil deal with the Third Reich without negotiating with Wohlthat or his agents.

There is, therefore, no question that Wohlthat also had his finger in the oil deals which W. R. Davis arranged with the Third Reich, although there is no proof of a direct link between Davis and Wohlthat. There is no question that the man who came to Mexico to buy oil for Germany was an envoy of Wohlthat's and one of his closest associates.

Dr Joachim H. Herstlett appeared in Mexico in 1938—at the time of the United States-Mexican crisis—together with Herr Briscke of the Reich Economic Ministry. Because Standard and Shell had been boycotting Mexico since March, the situation was particularly favourable for him and the Mexicans were willing to listen to barter propositions. This boycott was a severe blow to Mexican economy, since it was not restricted to oil but extended to a number of other commodities.

President Cardenas was in a ticklish situation. He would have preferred to sell oil to the democracies, but he 'could not pay too high a price for doing it.'

In July 1938, Davis was shipping some 60 per cent of all Mexican oil exports to Hamburg, where it was refined. Cardenas became worried, knowing that increased trade would mean increased German political influence in Mexico.

The Mexican labour unions also became worried, especially after they discovered that certain 'experts' whom Dr Herstlett had given Davis as assistants were—certainly without Davis' knowledge—also experts at spying. Without creating any sort of incident, many of these 'experts' were simply put on board the ships and sent to Hamburg along with the oil. Many others, however, had gone off mysteriously—up the jungle-fringed banks of the Panuco River in the interior.

But Dr Herstlett's programme of work was by no means done. He had not come only as an economic expert. Before very long he got in touch with the agents of Nicolas Rodriguez, the exiled leader of the Gold Shirts. Possibly this contact was established through Hermann Schwinn of Los Angeles, who had been the first to negotiate with Rodriguez and who had made possible the establishment of the Gold Shirts. And there were conferences with Humberto Tirado. Tirado turned to the American and British oil companies and offered to return the expropriated oil fields if they would finance a Nazi-inspired Gold Shirt Revolution. The oil companies refused.

Herr Briscke of the Economic Ministry left Mexico at the end of 1939. Herstlett remained behind. It was his task during the following months to transfer German funds from the United States to South America to avoid freezing. He worked hand in hand with associates of Montes de Oca, who remained head of the Bank of Mexico, although he had been treasurer of the Almazan campaign.

In the case of Herstlett it became obvious that economic tasks were but a small portion of the mission of Herr Wohlthat's envoy. In many other cases that was not so obvious. The most prominent case of this kind is that of Dr Gerhard Alois Westrick, who came to the United States via the Orient in March 1940 and registered in Washington as commercial attaché to the German Embassy. Then he began a series of negotiations which apparently aimed at establishing trade relations between Germany and the United States, once the Second World War was over.

But Dr Westrick surrounded himself with mystery. He lived in a spacious mansion in Scarsdale, New York; he employed only Irish servants; he received a number of strange visitors; and none of his neighbours, not even the man who had rented the house to him, suspected that he was attached to the German Embassy. Besides his mansion, he also had an apartment in the Hotel Carlyle and another apartment in the Waldorf-Astoria in New York—although he almost never lived in these apartments. He was very friendly with the head of Texaco, Mr T. Rieber, who however insisted later that his association with Westrick was on a purely social basis.

When a reporter on the *New York Herald Tribune* revealed the whole mysterious manner of Dr Westrick's life and questions began to be asked, Westrick without more ado packed his bags and left the United States.

The mission of Schacht's next envoy, Dr Kurt Heinrich Rieth, did not end quite as pleasantly.

Herr Rieth had a remarkable past. Born in Belgium of German parents— there are many instances of prominent Nazis of other than German birth— in the First World War he fled through the Belgian lines and joined the German Army. After the war he entered the diplomatic service and, in a manner which has never been explained, became suddenly very wealthy. In 1934 he became German Minister in Vienna, and unquestionably he was involved somehow with the assassination of Dollfuss. Indeed, after the putsch failed he was so bold as to try to get safe conduct to Germany for the Austrian Nazis who were Dollfuss' murderers. Hitler was compelled to disavow him temporarily and have him recalled.

Now Rieth came to the United States—via South America. He appeared in Rio de Janeiro on 8 March 1941, travelling under the title of Special Reich Ambassador 'on a mission to Latin America.' Ten days after his arrival, four German diplomats held a conference in Santiago, Chile. They were Baron Edmund von Thermann, Germany's Ambassador to Argentina; Wilhelm von Schoen, Ambassador to Chile; Willy Noebel, Minister to Peru and Ernst Windler, Minister to Bolivia. Dr Rieth was also present at this conference, which lasted several days. The subject of the conference was never announced. In fact, the German diplomats said they had met by chance, all of them having taken a brief vacation in Santiago.

However, after this conference the Popular Socialist Vanguard, Chile's Nazi Party, received German money and its activity revived. On 16 May the party stormed the headquarters of an opposing faction. At the end of the fracas there were several wounded and one dead.

On 21 March Dr Rieth entered the United States from Mexico. He explained to the immigration authorities that he was a good friend of Walter C. Teagle, Chairman of the Board of the Standard Oil Company of New Jersey. Teagle afterwards denied that he knew Rieth at all. Rieth also declared that he had come to the United States to take care of certain private financial affairs.

In reality, he began negotiations with the owners of rich oil properties in South-eastern Europe. Would they sell these properties to Germany? He offered quite a reasonable price.

But before these negotiations could come to anything, Washington intervened. Dr Rieth was arrested for entering the United States under false pretences, was taken to Ellis Island, and later deported. In all three cases, Herstlett, Westrick, Rieth, the principal aim was the establishment of personal connections. Through such connections information could be gleaned. Through such information, the Nazis could work themselves into a stronger position.

Hjalmar Schacht tried his best to do his duty to the German espionage machine. It is not his fault that he failed. Indeed, he did not fail completely. He recruited a number of allies for German espionage from financial and industrial circles. Voluntary and involuntary allies.

But these were not the only allies of German espionage.

ESPIONAGE IN THE *LEBENSRAUM*

Shortly after Hitler seized power, a number of unusual visitors invaded Geneva. At first no one thought it odd; later—it was too late.

From his first public speech in 1921, Hitler had never ceased to inveigh against the League of Nations. It was therefore strange that the number of Germans attending League sessions in Geneva should have increased by leaps and bounds as soon as he became Chancellor. In fact, when Germany formally quit the League in the fall of 1933, the number was still growing. Above all, journalists from all parts of Germany came to Geneva.

And not only journalists. There were a number of very young men and women who introduced themselves as 'students of politics.' At first no one thought it important enough to write about. Even when General von Epp appeared in Geneva—both before and after Germany's withdrawal from the League—no comment was evoked. But General von Epp came only a few times. Something must have gone wrong. Perhaps he was too well known; the political world knew that he was one of Hitler's closest friends and earliest supporters.

In the General's place came a certain Ernst Haack, who settled down in Geneva. He was a former naval officer, and his credentials stated that he was a special correspondent of DNB (the official German news agency).

And here was food for thought: This man, who held one of the most important journalistic positions in the Reich, openly declared that he was anti-Nazi and that Hitler would soon be through. He spent much breath making such declarations to his French, English, and Czech colleagues, and there is no denying that they believed him and that he had no difficulty in making friends with them.

All went well until in March 1935 an attractive young woman named Lydia Oswald was arrested as a German spy in Brest. The whole affair was romantic, to say the least. Lydia Oswald admitted that she had come to Brest as a German agent to get information on French warships. She had begun to work on Lieutenant Jean de Forceville, but then had fallen in love with him and decided to forego her mission and marry Forceville, who had fallen in love also with this 'girl with the green eyes.'

In the course of the investigation it came out that the man who had given Lydia Oswald her orders was Herr Ernst Haack of Geneva. This created something of a stir in League circles, and the Secretariat of the League decided to deprive Haack of his press card and strike him off the list of officially admitted journalists.

Herr Haack, however, took no notice of this action and appeared at the next sessions of the League of Nations. However, now he no longer sat in the press box, but on the diplomatic tribunal. The Secretariat of the League heard that Herr Haack had meanwhile been appointed press attaché of the German legation in Berne.

Much later it was found out that the journalists who had come to Geneva since Hitler and especially the 'students of politics' were German agents. League circles wondered why Hitler had sent so many agents to Geneva, of all places. They should have realized how astute a policy it was. In Geneva, statesmen of all countries came together. Here, in an unobtrusive fashion, connections could be established, particularly with statesmen and diplomats from Africa, Asia Minor, Iran, etc. In their home countries one could hardly approach these people without the knowledge of the British Intelligence Service. But in the little town of Geneva with its innumerable bistros, spacious hotel lobbies, and many picnic grounds around Lake Geneva and in the Alps, it was easy to arrange meetings and develop friendships—away from the stern and chilling gaze of an interested third party.

In the hotel rooms and conference halls of Geneva many conferences were held without the precautions which were routine in London or Paris.

A few words picked up here and there might be pieced together into a valuable bit of information. It is no wonder that those little microphones of the Nazis were first tried out in Geneva. Although the Nazis have used them far more sparingly than the latest espionage literature would have us believe, still they were used. In Geneva, incidentally, the Nazis had bad luck with them. By pure chance one of these microphones was discovered in the Hotel des Anglais in 1934, and from then on every diplomat was microphone-conscious and looked under his bed in his hotel room before he breathed a word. However, for a time the Nazis were quite successful in eavesdropping on Geneva long-distance telephone conversations.

Ernst Haack's chief assistant was Baron Kurt Hahn, a good-looking man of rather gloomy countenance. He came from one of the Baltic States, had been a Russian officer of the guard and was very close to Rosenberg. Now he was a 'journalist' and played the part of an impassioned pacifist and a member of the Oxford Group.

Later he went to Vienna. As a journalist, of course.

Even after he left Geneva, General von Epp remained the head of the organization there. It is ironical that the man who as head of the Bavarian *Reichswehr* had given Hitler his first job as informer, was now heading a branch of the espionage organization of his former protégé. Naturally, this was but a part of his work. Officially he was Chief of the Reich Colonial Department.

The job of this department was to arouse unrest in the former German colonies and organize them, along Nazi lines—in brief, prepare them for their eventual restoration to the Reich.

The General was not the man who had begun this work. The groundwork was laid by Professor Hermann Bohle—the father of the great Bohle—who lived in Cape Town and was a British subject. As early as 1932, Professor Bohle founded the first Nazi 'cell' in South Africa, which was later to become the centre of disruptive—and espionage—work. In 1933 he was made Territorial Group Leader.

Professor Bohle had certain ideas about methods of procedure. They were by no means impracticable. Thus on 10 March 1934, he wrote to Major Weigel, the leader of the National Socialist Party, who lived in Windhoek:

> ... I have had fairly lengthy discussions with Von Neurath about South West and the Union, but cannot say in a letter what transpired. I have always been of the opinion that the colonial problem will ultimately be decided in Europe and not in the various Mandated Territories. I, therefore, consider it wrong to broadcast that South West must return to Germany. After all, ten years ago, the people in South West spoke to the

contrary.... There is mostly too much talk among the Germans and they give themselves away. Therein lies the grave danger, and the task of the Government of the New Germany is thereby not made easier. The present government leaves none of its people in the lurch but it would do no harm if the people of South West were to take a broader view of matters.... Even among our Party members discipline is lacking very much. It will be my first duty to put the Party in order in this respect and to teach Party members to keep quiet....

Perhaps discipline was too much to expect of the Party members. Perhaps, too, the leaders in Berlin did not agree that everything must be 'decided in Europe.'

In any case, Professor Bohle soon vanished into obscurity.

But General von Epp also could not fail to recognize that the work must be done cautiously, although his reasons for favouring caution were different from those of Professor Bohle. 'The position taken by the Chancellor toward the colonial problem is at present a very circumspect one, particularly as the influence of the Party over the Foreign Office is not very strong,' one of his associates had written to the above-mentioned Major Weigel as early as 1933. 'An endeavour is, however, being made to give colonial thought an unofficial impetus that is purely from the Party,' the letter continued.

It was quite true that at that time General von Epp had little enough influence in the Foreign Office, nor did the Party itself have very much. But influence or no influence, there was need for caution. They were, after all, conspiring with British subjects—almost all the inhabitants of the former German colonies were naturalized—and if a conspiracy were uncovered which had the sanction or the co-operation of the German Government, there would have been serious complications with England.

Epp and his Colonial Department therefore worked more for the Party than the Government in these early days. The whole affair was really a tight-rope walk. Some difficulties, for instance, cropped up when Epp demanded that all sympathizers in the former colonies should take an oath of allegiance to Adolf Hitler. Dr Schwietering, the leader of the Deutscher Bund, feared with good cause that such a solemn oath of allegiance would encounter serious opposition. 'The person of Adolf Hitler can today no longer be separated from the German Reich and it is difficult to make the British subjects in a Mandated Territory swear an oath of allegiance to the German Chancellor,' he declared in a discussion with Major Weigel.

General von Epp swiftly expanded his Colonial Department. He worked closely with Nicolai and the War Ministry, Canaris, and the Foreign Office, and with the Foreign Office and, of course, the AO. As an espionage organization, the Reich Colonial Department was an independent unit. Headquarters was in Munich and there were branches in Berlin, Hamburg, and Bremen. Its activities centred mainly around the former German colonies in Africa. Its tasks were to create dissension among the Boers and South Africans, to control the existing German business enterprises in the former colonies and develop them into espionage agencies. The most important of these was Woermann, Brock and Company, which had been in existence for fifty years and had agents in Cape Town, Windhoek, Swakopmund, and Angola (Portugal). A good portion of this company's employees were agents of the Colonial Department who were assigned to organizing the Germans in the colonies and enlisting them in espionage work. Here, the fact that most of the Germans in the colonies were British subjects was a great help, since they could move about as they pleased without exciting suspicion.

As the influence of von Neurath declined and the power of Canaris and Ribbentrop mounted (this was before the latter was officially appointed Foreign Minister), Epp was able to act with more and more freedom in Africa. Thanks to the Locarno Treaty of 1925, he could settle Germans in the former colonies, and he made good use of this generous Anglo-French concession. The idea was to build up a German majority. The German settlers were supplied with sufficient means to buy land, which was all the easier because the native farmers were over their heads in debt. 'The possibility exists ... of acquiring through cleverly concealed manipulation comparatively cheap farms for German settlement purposes. This situation, which will in fact be aggravated, should in my opinion be turned to our advantage,' wrote Major Weigel, who meanwhile had taken Bohle's place.

Moreover, the Colonial Department had ties with the Grey Shirt Movement, which for a time enjoyed a certain popularity among the discontented, impoverished farmers. To a certain extent this movement was financed by Germany, though the Nazi contributions were rather modest. All this, however, went on behind the scenes; official Germany pretended to have nothing to do with it.

Late in 1934 Epp and the Foreign Office sent 'merchants' and 'technicians' to settle in Spanish Morocco and Tangiers. The Franco revolt was casting its shadow before....

Not until after Ribbentrop had taken over the Foreign Office was there full co-ordination of the work of Epp and Lieutenant-Captain Canaris. Canaris began setting up consulates throughout the former German colonies, and also in the French possessions in Africa. The number of scientists and businessmen who poured into Africa swelled steadily. Morocco, Tunis, Algiers became the domains of Colonel Nicolai. Here the same method was applied that had been used before the First World War, when spies were sent into the Foreign Legion.

In South Africa conditions got steadily worse. In April 1939, General Smuts, Minister of Justice of the Union of South Africa, revealed that hundreds of young Germans were being sent to Germany every year from South Africa to receive training as specialists. It takes little reading between the lines to know that by specialists General Smuts meant spies.

It was as though in answer to this that in the same month a new German Consul General to South Africa was appointed. This was Dr Liebau, who had formerly been Consul General in Reichenberg, Sudetenland, where he had organized the espionage for the Henlein movement.

In spite of these manifold activities, the Reich Colonial Department and the Foreign Office soon came to share the view of Professor Bohle. Africa must wait until the decision had been made in Europe. All this work was therefore merely provisional sketch-work for future expansion.

This was true also of German espionage in Asia Minor and Asia—that is, outside of the former colonies. Before the outbreak of the war the work, wherever it was undertaken, was no more than provisional—and it was undertaken only sporadically. In no country did it attain anything like the intensity of espionage in Mexico and South America. In the main, German espionage in Asia was limited to keeping watch on the British Secret Service and obstructing its work wherever possible.

Delegations of merchants and scientists were sent to Iran relatively early. Among these were agents who stayed on in the country after the departure of the delegations, and who later, after years of underground work, would be appointed consuls and vice-consuls.

These operations were directed by Herr Max von Oppenheim, a well-known archaeologist who became the chief of the Near East Division under Canaris and co-operated with General von Epp. He made many journeys, partly with real scientific interest. As a spy he remained in the background for a long time, restricting himself to directing the organization. But after the armistice between France and Germany, he came to Beirut, ostensibly to supervise the execution of the armistice conditions and actually to make contact with certain Arab tribes and induce them to revolt.

The Epp-Canaris-Oppenheim combination were prompt to pay special attention to Palestine, and the German colony in Jerusalem was tightly organized. The head of German espionage here was the German Consul in Haifa, Max Ringelmann.[3] In 1937 Baldur von Schirach,[4] the youth leader of Germany, took a group of Hitler Youth group leaders and SS men to Jerusalem and filled in the gaps in the existing spy organization. Close links were drawn among the German consuls and ministers in the various Arab states—the purpose of this collaboration being the delivery of arms to the Arabs. This was undertaken in co-operation with Krupp, who by the latter part of 1935 had agents scattered everywhere in the Near East.

The procedure was unvarying. An Arab prince who had shown himself amenable to anti-British plans was first presented with an aircraft and a few machine guns. Later he was given arms in greater quantities, either for nothing or for trifling prices. In these activities the Nazis frequently had the assistance of French officials of the Colonial Ministry, which was a centre of anti-English sentiment.

Germany's best agent in this work was Dr Fritz Grobba.[5]

Grobba had been with the German-Turkish Army in Western Asia during the First World War. Even at that time he had been interested in the Arab problem, and at the end of the war began to study the problem seriously. He stayed in Munich, where he met Ludendorff and later Hitler. Ludendorff recommended him to the War Ministry, which thought he might be a good liaison man in the Foreign Office. Then he was sent to Afghanistan, where he so distinguished himself that he was soon appointed German Minister. Next he went to Saudi Arabia, where, by gifts of German planes and machine guns, he won over Ibn Saud. Grobba—his real name is Arthur Borg—was the first to propose the short-wave broadcasts in Arabic which were later regularly sent by the Zeesen radio station.

Later Dr Grobba became Minister to Iraq. He and his agents, who came to the country as scientists, were entrusted with the task of carrying on anti-British propaganda. He persuaded young Arabs to travel to Germany, where they studied at the expense of the German Government and were crammed full of Nazi propaganda. Of course, all these young Arabs were not students; there were also officers of the Iraq army among them. Perhaps that had something to do with the arrival in 1938 of a number of *Reichswehr* officers, ostensibly to observe manoeuvres. When the manoeuvres were over, only a few of them departed; most remained in Iraq.

Perhaps that also had something to do with the fires that broke out on the principal pipeline during October of that year. The incendiaries were bands of Arabs. A few months later the Ghazi died in a car accident near Baghdad.[6] Grobba's agents asserted that the English had killed him.

Although Dr Grobba had been appointed Minister to Saudi Arabia, he continued also as Minister to Iraq. Thus, until the outbreak of the war he was able to remain in Baghdad and some of his agents remained even after the war had begun. They stayed in the Italian Legation and kept in touch with Grobba, who was making many secret trips back and forth between Saudi Arabia, Syria, and Iran.

The Iraqi uprising of 1941, which led to war between England and Iraq, was in part his personal achievement. However, he had able assistants. In Ankara there was Herr von Papen, through whom Goebbels had long financed a number of Iraqi newspapers. In January 1941, an Iraq army delegation came to Turkey on a secret mission to Herr von Papen. When they left him they had a signed agreement pledging the creation of an Arab State. At that time also a number of Iraq generals in Baghdad attempted a *coup d'état* which came within a hair's breadth of success.

Another of Herr Grobba's assistants was Otto von Hentig.[7] Hentig appeared in Syria shortly after the Franco-German Armistice, ostensibly on a commercial mission; in reality to stir the pot of unrest and to organize spy headquarters in Beirut and Damascus. His agents were Arabs who were equipped with arms and dispatched to Iraq. He threatened the rich Syrians with concentration camps if they did not support Germany, and incited the poor Arabs with the propaganda that England intended to divide Syria between Palestine and Turkey. His espionage headquarters organized a number of sabotage and assassination gangs.

When the French finally, in an impulse of energy, protested against the presence of Herr von Hentig, Berlin recalled him.

But he did not return to Berlin immediately; instead he entered Iraq illegally and worked there with Grobba. Later he actually boasted in Ankara of this neat piece of trickery.

Herr von Roser, former German consul in Beirut, also did his bit in preparing the uprising in Iraq. Early in 1941 he came to Syria and organized groups of Arabs independently of Herr von Hentig. He was abetted in his work by Sheik Arslan of the Libanese Druses, who had been a paid German agent for a long time. When the Iraq revolt began, he secured permission from the French authorities to solicit volunteers among the Arabs of Syria. He paid ten pounds to each man he enlisted. His contact man with the French authorities was General Fougère. The honorable general tried to enlist French officers in Herr von Roser's cause, but failed. When the Iraq uprising collapsed as a result of the prompt British military action, Dr Fritz Grobba fled with Prime Minister Reshid Ali. But this is probably not the last we will hear of Dr Grobba.

EUGEN OTT GOES TO JAPAN

In the autumn of 1933, Colonel Eugen Ott, one of Colonel Nicolai's closest associates and favourite disciples during the First World War, journeyed to Tokyo.

It was not surprising that the Third Reich should be so prompt in establishing contact with Japan. The governing ideology of both countries was the same. Both were authoritarian regimes—Germany completely so; Japan still evolving toward that end. Both countries were essentially imperialistic. More than twenty years ago Professor Haushofer had advocated co-operation with Japan, and on the basis of his geo-political studies had predicted that Japan would someday rule the Orient.

Rosenberg, too, had interests in Japan. In August 1933 he had welcomed in Berlin delegates of the Japanese Fascist National Youth Movement. In October, Prince Tolugawa, one of the most important of the men behind the scenes in Japan, had visited him. Almost at the same time the Chinese General, Chang-Hsueh-ling, had visited Göring.

But the impelling force behind Ott's trip to Japan was his old teacher, Colonel Nicolai. Since 1932, Nicolai had been in touch with Sazo Nakamo, who had made a fairly forthright suggestion that German and Japanese civil and military intelligence should co-operate on a world scale. The idea was that Japan should reinforce Germany's espionage net in the Far East and in Russia, while the Germans should extend their admirable apparatus to fields in which they were only indirectly interested, but which concerned Japan very much. Japan needed Germany's help in countries where her own spies were overwhelmingly handicapped by their racial characteristics.

Eugen Ott went to Japan in the capacity of military observer. He was to study conditions there and hand in a report by the spring of 1934.

He arrived at the German Embassy, 141 Chome Nagatocho Kokimachi-ku. The German Ambassador, Dr von Dierksen, was none too pleased to be saddled with this military observer. Herr von Dierksen was a diplomat of the old school who had not bothered to join the Nazi Party.

The first weeks passed swiftly for Eugen Ott. The Western diplomats invited one another to parties almost every evening. A few weeks after his arrival Ott entered the Japanese Army—as an observer, of course. The Japanese officers, too, did their best to make things pleasant for him.

Before long, at a luncheon in the grill of the Hotel Imperial, he met some officers of the Kem Pei Tai, the military intelligence.

And some time later, in the Grand Hotel in Yokohama, he met Admiral Nobumasa Suetsugu. With a frankness unusual in a Japanese, the Admiral straightway professed that Ott could count on him in every respect; that he was thoroughly in sympathy with Hitler's ideas.

Still later, a number of younger officers from the War Ministry gave him a party in a tea house. That evening the geisha girls who danced and sang were outstandingly beautiful. A great deal of *sake* (rice wine) was drunk. At first Ott was worried because he thought they were trying to make him drunk; but then he saw to his surprise that his Japanese friends were themselves getting drunk very swiftly.

That evening he met Major General Kenji Doihara.

Ott knew very well who Doihara was. You couldn't be in the intelligence service without knowing. Doihara was the chief of the so-called Continental Service, that is, the espionage machine which embraced all China. General Koiso, the Chief of the General Staff of the Kwangtung Army, had once said that he would not let one single soldier march before Doihara had prepared the way. He was credited with the actual responsibility for the conquest of Manchuria. Although outwardly he was only the head of the Continental Service, he in reality controlled the entire military espionage system of Japan, with its innumerable branch organizations and unlimited funds.

Doihara did not look the part of so formidable a man. He was small, inclined to corpulence, and wore a tiny Charlie Chaplin moustache. But marvellous stories were told about him. It was said he was able to lose or gain twenty pounds in a very short time, and to disguise himself so well that not even his closest associates could recognize him. His gift for languages was astounding. Besides a number of Asiatic tongues and dialects, he also spoke eight European languages. Eugen Ott in his report emphasized that he spoke only German with Doihara....

For some time afterward Ott was very thick with Doihara, who permitted Ott to accompany him on his journeys. Ott learned that the idea of co-operation between German and Japanese espionage had originated with Doihara. He made the acquaintance of one of Doihara's best assistants—a young girl with bobbed hair, who dressed in men's clothes. Her name was Yoshima Kawashima. She was the tenth daughter of Prince Su of the Manchu Dynasty—so went the tale, at any rate. She was supposed to have a strange and romantic past, and in espionage circles she was called Japan's Mata Hari....

During his stay Ott became a frequent visitor to the tea houses of Tokyo. He spent a great deal of his time with the younger set of officers of the War Ministry. Since Doihara had more or less officially vouched for Ott the officers were very open with him. They were bitter foes of their conservative Japanese government and boldly declared that the ministers ought to be killed off as fast as possible. Indeed, more than one minister had been murdered in the recent past. (Affair of 15 May 1932, and the Brocade Flag Incident of 1932.)

One of this clique of ardently chauvinist and imperialist officers was Hiroshi Oshima, with whom Ott became very friendly. Oshima, who at the time was still a colonel, worked closely with Doihara, and it was at Doihara's request that he began to explain the machinery of Japanese military espionage to Ott. What Ott saw and learned during the following months formed the basis of the report he transmitted to Berlin in January 1934.

Ambassador von Dierksen, who had only the vaguest notion of what Ott was doing or was supposed to do, did not learn of this report until much later.

A short time after Ott sent his report to Germany, he himself returned. He had a number of conferences with Nicolai and possibly with Hess. His superiors praised his report and decided to take up Japan's suggestion of large-scale collaboration in espionage work. That same year—1934—Ott returned to Tokyo. This time he was military attaché.

Not long after—at the close of 1934 or early in 1935—Hiroshi Oshima was sent to the Japanese Embassy in Berlin as military attaché. The Japanese Ambassador then was Admiral Shigenori Togo.

The roles were now assigned; the play could begin.

Ott's report, however, omitted certain aspects of Japanese espionage simply because at the time Ott himself was not acquainted with these aspects. He later spoke of this and complained of the lack of trust the Japanese manifested, despite all their apparent candidness. He was later to complain of this more frequently....

Early in 1935 Nicolai's star pupil began to study on his own initiative those aspects of Japanese espionage which had not been explained to him. This was none too easy, but since Ott by this time had many connections, and a number of the young officers were very friendly with him, it was not entirely impossible. The *sake* helped considerably....

What Ott wanted to find out—and in time did find out—was the function of the so-called secret societies within the Japanese system of espionage and sabotage.

The most notorious of them, and the most powerful and active in this field was the Black Dragon Society headed by Mitsuru Toyama. This society was formed at the end of the last century and named after the Amur River (called 'Black Dragon River' by the Chinese and Japanese) which flows between Manchuria and Soviet Siberia; for the Society's original aim was conquest of Eastern Siberia and Manchuria. These arrogantly jingoistic, often terroristic secret societies were one of the mainsprings of Japanese aggressiveness; their influence on the course of the Japanese ship of state in international waters was at least equal to that of the politicians and officials who ostensibly ran the Japanese Government. These secret societies, which incidentally were also responsible for the numerous political assassinations in Japan, were imperialistic, with an irrational and fanatic belief in Japan's divine mission to rule the world; they were prepared to do everything to further Japanese conquest, and in their eyes the end justified any means, however unfair and brutal.

In the field of secret service the Black Dragon Society had been operating, since the turn of the century, on a vast scale in Manchuria and China, these being their first objectives. It had hundreds of 'wave-men'—named after the samurai, who had no lord to serve and who were called '*ronin*' or wave-men—engaged on the mainland in spying and in provoking incidents.

These wave-men collaborated fairly closely with the Army Intelligence Service, and at least part of their expenses were defrayed from Army

Intelligence funds. Many Army officers, particularly the extremist younger officer clique, belonged to one or another of these secret societies, and the avowed aims of the younger Army elements somewhat coincided with those of these societies. On the other hand, there was no evidence of co-operation between the secret societies and Naval Intelligence; the Navy seemed to be very cool both to the extremist Army clique and the hooligan secret societies. The secret societies' agents operating on the Asiatic mainland were surely the lowest scum imaginable. They were strong-arm thugs, hired murderers, ruthless adventurers, blackmailers, who had never done a day's decent work in Japan; who lived on the wages of blackmail, or compulsory 'patriotic' contributions, on 'fees' for strong-arm jobs, whence indeed came most of the funds of the secret societies. However, these thugs were imbued with a devout jingoism, and while they had absolutely no consideration for human beings as individuals, for human decencies, they risked their lives in the cause of the great Japanese nation.

Since the beginning of the century many of these ruffians roamed all over Manchuria and China, disguised as peddlers of medicines and opiums and sundry goods; as small shopkeepers, as mendicant monks wearing hoods over their heads, completely hiding their faces; as pilgrims, even as Buddhist priests, as journalists, photographers, and what not. The more sordid professions, such as those of the brothel keeper and slave trader, concocter of opium compounds and distributor of opium, particularly appealed to this class. Conceited, physically courageous, brazen-faced, they were always able to create adverse incidents, brawls, street fights which the representatives of any other country would have been most anxious to hush up, but which Japan seized upon, to make demands, to claim apologies, to make of a molehill a mountain, to store up a pretext for future hostilities.

It speaks well for the extraordinary capabilities of the military attaché that he was able to secure such precise information. Other envoys of the German espionage machine were less fortunate. For example, there was Richard Zeisig, the Territorial Group Leader of the AO in Japan. Zeisig wanted to co-operate with the Japanese authorities. But for some reason difficulties always cropped up. Not only would the Japanese not co-operate, but they made his work, that is, the work of the whole German organization, almost impossible. The police were constantly (and literally) at his heels. They believed he wanted to spy—which was exactly what he did want to do. For weeks after his arrival, when he went around on his business, he noticed that he was invariably followed by a little Japanese in plain clothes. Trotting a short distance behind him, riding at the other end of the tram car, camping outside customers' doors and in the hotel lobby, he shadowed him faithfully. The poor detective even had to trail the German, who was an athletic, fast walker, on Sunday hiking trips. After a few weeks the two got rather friendly, and the poor Jap plainclothes man, who had been walked off his feet for many days, used to ask his 'prey' where his weekend's outing would be; then the Jap instead of scurrying after him, could take a bus or the train to the destination of the excursion, and wait there for the German to arrive. The detective also requested the Nazi to take tramways rather than taxis when going around to visit customers; for his (the detective's) superiors were grumbling about his high expense accounts, a result of his numerous taxi fares.

This amusing game continued for about four months till Ott intervened and straightened matters out for Dr Zeisig.

Dr Walter Donath had an even tougher time. He was the chief of the German Cultural Institute, one of Rosenberg's organizations. This institute existed to familiarize Japanese students with German conditions. This, at least, was the ostensible purpose. But behind this official front, they tried to win the students over to spying against their own country. The distrust which was later to permeate Japanese-German relationships took root early.

It was just as strong on the Japanese side.

In 1938, Herr Donath took a two-day trip from Kobe to Shikoku, an island about 60 miles from Kobe. As this was a 'business' trip, he had a Japanese student with him.

After an overnight boat trip he got into Takamatsu, in Shikoku, at about six o'clock in the morning. A policeman detained his companion briefly on the pier and questioned the Nazi about his business and his plans for the day. Shortly afterwards, while they were breakfasting at a Japanese hotel, a 'visitor' was announced. Without further introduction he sat down and started to question Dr Donath at great length about his antecedents, his occupation, his feelings and opinions, about the Japanese people, about the war, about chances of a Japanese war with America, etc. etc. Then Donath had to give him his itinerary for the day.

When, later in the day, he left by train for another town on the island, another plainclothes man awaited him at the station and 'escorted' him to his destination.

Early next morning he had another 'visitor' at the Japanese inn. Same questions, same rambling talk for over an hour, with attempts to trip him up. He had to give his itinerary for that day.

Sometime later, while he was sitting in the reception room of a factory outside this town, the police called him on the telephone. The talker was the early morning visitor, who warned him that on his way back to Kobe that day, according to his itinerary, he would pass through one of Japan's numerous fortified zones—which Donath knew very well—and that he would be arrested if he took photographs there. Earlier, Donath had told the man that he carried no camera, which indeed was no news since the luggage had been thoroughly searched at the hotel.

On his way back to the hotel, he was stopped on a street corner by another detective who directed his Japanese companion as to which bus they should take; in fact gave him instructions which would make it more convenient for the gendarmes to watch them. For about two hours, on an omnibus to the embarkation point, on the motor boat across a narrow strait, and again on a bus across an island, Donath enjoyed the constant company of a plainclothes man, whom, of course, he was not supposed to recognize. The little man dutifully watched until the steamer pulled out for Kobe.

On the crowded pier at Kobe, that evening, another dark-clothed, stupid-looking person tapped Donath on the shoulder and told him to open his valise. It was put down on the pier, in the midst of a milling, grinning crowd revelling in this 'arrest' of a foreigner. The man proceeded to pull out and throw on the dirty pavement pyjamas, toilet articles, and notebook—every page of which he scanned. At last he came to a couple of topical Japanese books about the war in Manchuria. The detective scowled even more, while the highly embarrassed Japanese student expostulated that a foreigner who went to all the trouble of learning to read Japanese must surely feel sympathetic to Japan; to this the detective replied that on the contrary it made him more suspect. At the end, having found nothing incriminating, he left abruptly, growling, leaving the things strewn all over the pavement, much to the enjoyment of the Japanese crowd.

Messrs Zeisig and Donath were not the only Germans to suffer from Japanese counterespionage. Most Germans were under constant supervision, not only by the police but by their own servants. They were occasionally arrested on suspicion of espionage; but nothing was ever proved against them. This, however, did not disconcert the Japanese police. As a matter of fact, the Japanese distrust of all foreigners—not Germans alone—became almost a mania from 1938 on. The authorities arranged anti-espionage exhibitions displaying what the Japanese imagined were the devious and criminal ways of foreign spies. They designed hundreds of anti-espionage posters; they instituted anti-spy weeks and anti-spy days; anti-spy pictures and slogans were printed on match boxes, exhibited in shop windows. All of these invariably pictured the spy as a white man. Through the newspapers, the radio, and speeches, the Japanese populace were constantly exhorted to be on the watch for and report these foreign spies who were plotting incalculable harm to their fair country. By branding every foreigner in Japan a probable spy, the authorities succeeded in whipping up an unprecedented hatred of foreigners, including the Germans.

In November 1936 the Anti-Comintern Pact was concluded between Japan and Germany. At the time diplomats said that it was in the main the work of Ott and Oshima, who was soon thereafter promoted to the rank of Lieutenant General. Besides the official version, this pact also included a number of secret clauses which had reference to co-operation in the realms of military activity and espionage.

Probably as a reward for the arranging of this pact, Eugen Ott was appointed Ambassador to Tokyo in 1938; Herr von Dierksen was transferred to London. A short time afterwards Hiroshi Oshima became Japanese Ambassador in Berlin.

SPY AXIS

Germany was not exactly blessed by the gods in her co-operation with her allies in the field of espionage.

German army circles had never cherished any illusions about their Italian partner. It is said that even in the twenties the leading officers of the German General Staff—which by the Treaty of Versailles had no official existence—declared, 'The next war will be lost by the country which takes Italy for an ally.' A joke, of course, but it reflects the attitude of Germany's leading military men. Their attitude was no different where espionage was concerned.

Colonel Nicolai early made it clear that he had no intention of working with the Italian Intelligence Service. He told everyone who wanted to know that he considered the Italian Intelligence Departments of both the army and the navy the worst in the world. They were headed by imbeciles, he declared, ably assisted by a few blind and deaf men.

He had good reason for such violent criticism. He knew that countless spies of foreign powers, particularly of France and Yugoslavia, roamed freely through Italy and took photographs of all important plans. In one case they even secured the plans for a battleship whose keel had not yet been laid. Nicolai—and the intelligence departments of the rest of Europe—knew all about such matters. Only the Italians themselves seemed in blissful ignorance. Occasionally an arrest was made in Italy. When that happened, the results of the secret trials were always alarming to the Italians, indicating as they did how long the spies had been active before they were caught.

There was one rumour current in the intelligence departments of Europe which offered some explanation of the freedom of foreign spies within Italy. According to this rumour, Mussolini's hands were tied. At the time of the assassination at Sarajevo, when Italy was still officially allied with Germany and Austria-Hungary, Mussolini had worked as an agent for the *Deuxième*

Bureau. The *Deuxième Bureau* was supposed to have a dossier on him—a good bargaining point when the agents of the *Deuxième Bureau* got into difficulties in Italy. A copy of this dossier was supposed to have been in the Roman Questura—but Il Duce had seen to it that it disappeared.

Besides the Army and Navy Intelligence, there was, of course, another Italian espionage machine. This was in the hands of the Ovra.

When Mussolini came to power he boasted—at least at first—that he had no need of a Cheka. But he soon saw that a secret police was indispensable, and so he created the *Opera Voluntaria Repressione Anti-Fascista*, called Ovra for short. It was headed by Arturo Bocchini, one of Mussolini's closest associates. The Ovra purported to have only police functions: its duties were supposed to be the capture and prosecution of criminals. How this aim was borne out in actuality is indicated by the results of an investigation conducted in 1928. This investigation produced the truly unique revelation that 35 per cent of the Ovra officials had criminal records.

The Ovra never attained anything like the efficiency of the Cheka, let alone the Gestapo. However, it could scarcely be outdone by these two organizations in brutality of methods. During the early years of the Fascist regime it was used to put down opposition inside Italy. Its major weapon was the well-known castor oil; that the use of castor oil often had fatal consequences is not so well known. Abroad, where the Ovra could not very well apply such brutal methods, it had much less 'success.' It devoted most of its time to pursuing the Italian socialist and democratic refugees. For years Paris was its main sphere of activity. But the conduct of the Ovra was patterned after comic opera. Those it pursued were well aware that they were being pursued, and they had little trouble shaking off the lazy and unintelligent Ovra agents. Occasionally the Ovra concocted elaborate frame-ups, planting dynamite in the homes of anti-Fascists living in France. But these attempts always failed because the French police were not as stupid as the Ovra agents believed.

The Ovra had more luck when it hired French gangsters to assassinate political opponents. The Roselli brothers, Carlo and Nello, were the victims of such a murder. It is a public secret in Italy that the Ovra was also responsible for the deaths of the great Italo Balbo and the popular flyer, Umberto Maddalena.

It surprised no one that an espionage organization with such poor leadership failed completely. In vain did the Ovra persistently send its agents to strategic points in France, in Germany, during the early days of the Hitler regime, and later in Yugoslavia. The agents accomplished little or nothing. For a time the work of one agent was crowned with some success: Commendatore Boccalaro, the nominal head of the Government Arsenal in Genoa and in reality a liaison man between Army Intelligence and the Ovra. Since 1928 he had the task of smuggling arms and munitions from Italy to the Balkans to aid fascist groups in their projected uprisings. It was Boccalaro who supplied the French *Cagoulards* with most of their arms during 1936. But his work was essentially so sloppy that with the first overt acts of the *Cagoulards*, the whole thing was up; the French authorities were immediately able to determine the source of the arms. Incidentally, no sooner were Boccalaro's agents arrested by the French *Sureté Générale* than they talked and revealed all the secrets they knew.

This dilettante machine of the Ovra cost a fortune. The agents were underpaid, but they were all so inefficient that a great number had to be engaged. In numbers alone, the Ovra outstripped both the Gestapo and the OGPU.

The Ovra failed miserably in Tunis. It failed in Palestine, where—on the basis of a tip from the Germans—it had an opportunity to incite the Arabs to revolt. (This work was later done more efficiently by the Gestapo.) The Ovra failed in Addis Ababa, where it had followed the army. It killed and tortured many of the inhabitants, but secured no information of any value whatsoever.

But the Ovra's prize debacle was in Greece. It had more than two years in which to prepare by espionage the Greek campaign. Mussolini had insisted on Bocchini's doing this work himself. He worked there somewhat as the Germans had worked in Austria, Czechoslovakia, and France. The Italians believed that the officers' corps was rife with dissension, that some of the officers had been bought, that the Ovra had the deployment plans of the Greeks and knew all strategic points, knew the location of the munitions factories, and had many sympathizers among the Greek populace.

When the war began, it turned out that none of the Ovra's machinations had worked out. There was no Greek fifth column of any proportions; there were no sympathetic and bribed generals; there was nothing but a Greek resistance so stanch that the Italians were completely befuddled.

Finally the Germans had to intervene in the Greek affair. Not only on the military front, but, beforehand, in espionage work. This, as a matter of fact, was not the first time the Germans had collaborated with Italian espionage.

As early as 1935, Rudolf Hess considered co-operation with the Ovra. Colonel Nicolai warned him that it was folly. Hess was apparently impressed by this warning; but two years later he nevertheless made a trip to Rome to speak with Signor Bocchini. Very likely he was disappointed by what he saw, but he did not risk injuring the sensitive feelings of the Italians by criticism. In any case, a certain amount of co-operation between the Gestapo and the Ovra did come about. What happened was that the

Gestapo gave occasional tips to the Ovra and the Ovra then proceeded to waste the tips by their blundering. Himmler did not protest, probably out of respect for Hess. Whatever the reason, the Germans did nothing to show Mussolini the faults of his secret police.

When the war broke out, the Germans realized that something must be done for their ally's secret service. Reinhard Heydrich, Himmler's right-hand man, was sent to Italy early in 1940 to investigate. He returned to Berlin with the word that the situation was impossible. Three-quarters of a year later, after Italy had joined the war, the Gestapo began to take over the Italian apparatus. The Gestapo worked as it had worked in Germany during 1934 and repaired the gaps left by the Ovra. Within a few weeks there were Gestapo agents in all important Italian bureaus, in the key posts of the police, and in control of communications. In short, Himmler's men began to close off the country and make it safe against outside espionage.

Signor Bocchini did not survive the humiliation. He died—officially of influenza. It was rumoured that he took his own life. His successor was Signor Senise, who was merely a front for the real man in power, Heydrich (who twenty-one months later was to receive world publicity when he was appointed as Protector of Bohemia and Moravia—that is, as hangman of the rebelling Czechs).

The foreign apparatus of the Ovra was also subordinated to the Germans. This was done hurriedly but thoroughly in North and South America. The personnel of the embassy and consulates in the United States really had to get on the job, in German fashion; they had to get information from the Italian population, the various clubs, the Black Shirts. The information was then sifted and passed on to their German masters. This procedure yielded little fruit in the United States. And even in the spring of 1941 there were ugly scenes between German consuls and their Italian subordinates, for the Nazis simply could not believe in the existence of so much inefficiency, and put it down to sabotage.

The Ovra agents in Central and South America were incomparably better than their colleagues in the United States. One of the best men in the Ovra was General Camorita, who was posted in Lima and in command of the Peruvian police. Nearly his equal was Giuseppe Sotanis, living at the Grand Hotel in San José, Costa Rica, who was an ardent philatelist and an equally ardent collector of arms and munitions for President Jorge Ubico.

Then there was Pablo Massoni, an ex-officer, who came to Mexico in the early Thirties. In 1937 he operated on the far southern peninsula of Yucatan, where he was in touch with Sotanis. Massoni became a trusted member of the Federation of the Middle Class, which has already been mentioned in connection with the Nazis in Mexico. He was also in touch with Baron von Merck, the old Brussels spy who was on such intimate terms with General Cedillo....

German espionage in Central and South America co-operated by preference with the third partner of the Axis. The Japanese had a great many agents in the regions that particularly interested them: China, Russia, and the South Seas (by which the Japanese mean all the islands and the countries bordering on the South China Sea and the adjacent regions). There were the celebrated Japanese barbers in Panama who almost never give haircuts and who apparently live by taking photographs and holding secret meetings. There were the fishermen and their luxurious fishing boats with expensive radio apparatus which could both send and receive, high-powered engines, and sounding lines to determine how deep fish can swim without getting hurt by rocks. *Minato Maru*, *Minova Maru*, and *Saru Maru* were the three biggest and most modern of these boats. There were fishing companies whose fish trading was nowhere to be seen and whose shares were owned by the Japanese Government. There were the Japanese who bought land in Costa Rica for cotton plantations which unfortunately produced no crops; undoubtedly it was purely by chance that the land was situated only 250 miles from the Panama Canal. Business firms backed by the Japanese Government bought or rented many other pieces of real estate, ostensibly for economic exploitation, which were by chance always situated at strategic points.

There were Japan's best agents, J. Yamashito and Y. Matsui, who came to Mexico on fishing boats in 1936 and worked in the vicinity of Guaymas.

For their part, the Nazis had been giving information to their Japanese friends for many years—for years before the Anti-Comintern Pact with its secret clauses. In particular they had given the Japanese much information on Russia, where on account of their appearance the Japanese could get no foothold. To mention but one example, from 1934 on the Japanese Consul in Los Angeles was repeatedly invited to confer with the captains of German ships, and supplied with the latest information.

But the willingness to exchange information was one-sided. When, for example, German agents on the Pacific coast of the Americas or in the Canal Zone went aboard Japanese ships, they learned exactly nothing. Had this happened once or twice, it might have been forgiven as oversight; but it happened so often that the Germans realized there was malice behind it.

In Mexico especially some subordinate German agents protested vigorously. The Japanese were always polite, but they merely shrugged and did nothing. The Germans saw that they would have to wring from their allies the information that was rightfully theirs under the terms of their agreement.

They embarked upon the necessary steps.

On 5 October 1937, there was a conference in Mexico City between the German Minister, Ruedt von Collenberg, and his Italian and Japanese colleagues. To avoid attracting attention, they followed the suggestion of the Japanese Minister, Saechiro Koshda, and came to the meeting place in taxis instead of their private cars. They met in the offices of the Italian Union in the Ribera de San Cosme. The conference lasted two and a half hours.

At this conference Ruedt von Collenberg, a diplomat of the old school who did not know quite what it was all about but obeyed the instructions of his civilian attaché, Dr Heinrich Northe, complained that the Japanese espionage (he probably minced the word) was not co-operating.

His arguments must have carried weight, for from then on the Japanese collaborated to the full. This collaboration was especially fruitful in Costa Rica, between Takahiro Wakawayashi, Sotanis, and the German agent, Gerhard Henschke. The Japanese had picked out a flat field suitable for an airport, and Sotanis had secured Wakawayashi a concession for a cotton plantation. The Japanese imported twenty-one labourers from Chimbota, the big Japanese colony in Peru. They stayed in first-class hotels and bought one bag of cotton seed which never left the hotel room.

Shortly after the diplomat's conference, the fisherman-owner of the biggest fishing boat in the world, the *Amano Maru*, Yoshitaro Amano, put in an appearance and tried to get in touch with Wakawayashi's cotton experimental station. He was immediately arrested. The Germans came to the aid once more. Henschke got in touch with Sotanis, who used his influence with the President. The first case of real Axis collaboration had curiously enough again concluded to the advantage of the Japanese.

Ruedt von Collenberg's reproaches were not the prime subject of discussion at the conference of 5 October. More important were the plans for intensified espionage and conspiratorial work in Mexico. The Axis diplomats had received an offer from the Federation of the Middle Class. The Federation was willing to undertake certain underground work if they would supply the funds. The offer was sealed, but as has been described, the police were able to arrest Dr Carmen Calero and the other conspirators and to confiscate their dynamite before they could do any damage.

This was a serious blow to the Axis diplomats. They became somewhat nervous, especially old Ruedt von Collenberg. But that did not discourage the German espionage machine in Mexico.

CASA CHICA

You have so much time in Mexico City. You have all the time in the world for 'Chismes' and 'Chistes.' You talk about everybody, and usually you do not say nice things about them.

No, there is for instance the *Secreta*—the Mexican *Sureté* in the *Secretaria de Gobernacion*. There were always a lot of dirty cracks about this police department. They said that you could arrange anything with the officials, and if you did not like some files they kept, there was always a way to make them disappear.

Maybe the *Policia Secreta* did not mind such Chismes and Chistes. Because work was so much easier as long as people did not take you seriously. But those people were mistaken, because the *Policia Secreta* had done a lot of quiet reorganizing around 1936 and 1937, and many of the files which were said to have been lost were not lost at all. And many things which those concerned thought were a dead secret were no secret at all to the *Policia Secreta*.

Especially about those German tourists who kept pouring into the country in the late Thirties. The *Policia Secreta* knew a lot about them though it kept what it knew pretty close. There were the waiters and desk clerks and taxi drivers, all reporting to the *Gobernacion*, when they thought they had anything of value.

Of course, by that time the Germans had become rather wary and did not talk so loudly at Bellinghausen's and other public places. They tried their best to be inconspicuous and to live like Mexicans. And the more important of them, of course, had their Casa Chica. Casa Chica, that is the extra house any man of means in Mexico has—not his own house where his wife and his family live. A Casa Chica is a little house where he keeps a woman of some brains who can entertain him and his friends, who arranges for drinking parties.... Most of the important talks in Mexico go on in Casas Chicas.... Anyway, many of the Germans who came to live in Mexico had their Casa Chica and were able to get a whole lot of their information there.

But how were they to know that some of those 'women with brains' were friendly with the *Policia Secreta*? How were they to know that the *Policia Secreta* was fast becoming an extremely modern Police Department, checking very carefully on foreigners, installing modern radio apparatus, arranging for collaboration with Washington?

All this was necessary because lots of foreigners came into Mexico, without being checked up when they entered. United States citizens could enter on ordinary tourist cards. It was strange how many of those United States citizens spoke fluent German.

That, at least, is what the waiters of the Hotel Maria Christina said. That was a favourite residence of the German tourists.

Those tourists were not fifth columnists in the real sense of the word. Most of them were actually American citizens, of German birth. But there were so many of them that a real agent could enter without being conspicuous. They were sent to give a push to the somewhat reluctant, old, established

German colony, to act as mongers of rumour and Nazi goodwill, to keep their eyes open, and to convert promising young officers and policemen.

Then there were others who looked dangerous and probably were. You could generally find them in some sinister dive. Their favourite hangout was the Green Lantern, where bad nude shows are staged, and in whose back room you might buy marihuana and smoke it right there. Sometimes a few of the customers had a serious talk together, and went out somewhere in the middle of the night. And the next day you would hear of an accidental death.

Chismes and Chistes....

You still remember General Saturnino Cedillo, who was on such intimate terms with Baron Ernst von Merck, who had been a German spy in Brussels during the last world war, and who was still one of the favourite sons of Colonel Nicolai. Von Merck still did a lot of travelling in 1937 and 1938. Sometimes he was on Cedillo's ranch at San Luis Potosi and then again he was at Tampico, where a freighter would arrive, bringing some mysterious cargo for which he would sign a receipt. And these mysterious packing cases—containing rifles, cartridges, pistols, machine guns—would someday appear in San Luis Potosi.

Strangely enough, the Baron was still employed as an agronomist in the Department of Agriculture, but he could not have been very busy there, because he had so many other things to do. He was also in touch with our Italian friend, Pablo Massoni (even before the three diplomats had met to arrange for more collaboration), and also with the nice, elderly woman physician Dr Carmen Calero, who was so fond of dynamite. After the conference of the diplomats, von Merck was formally assigned the job of co-ordinating Axis espionage behind Cedillo. He, therefore, was also in close touch with the Japanese agent Chito. Yes, the Baron was quite a busy man....

Old Cedillo, in the meantime, was getting more and more aloof. You could not visit him on his ranch any more. There were armed guards who saw to that. You had to have very good recommendations to get into the place. And when you waited outside the fence, you pondered why so many 'tractors' were arriving—imported from Italy, as you could read on the big boxes—and why so many of the German tourists appeared there to instruct Mr Cedillo's men in the use of such tractors....

And then, in May 1938 there was the uprising headed by old General Cedillo. It was a flop. Cedillo was killed. Maybe Baron von Merck wouldn't have taken the death of his good friend so hard, and maybe the Federation of the Middle Class, which was involved too, wouldn't have minded it either if, nevertheless, this thing had developed into a full-grown revolution and a general civil war. However, it didn't. It was later said that it was all a question of money. And that if Freiherr Ruedt von Collenberg had come through with certain 'expenses,' the revolution would have been a success. However, the Freiherr, still old-fashioned, thought that the expenses involved were 'outrageous.'

So it was all over, scarcely after it had started. And Baron von Merck departed for the United States, and shortly after he was seen in Berlin in the company of his old boss, Colonel Nicolai.

It was the Calero fiasco and the increasing vigilance of the *Policia Secreta*—effectively aided by the labour unions—and the increasing collaboration between the *Policia Secreta* and the United States authorities, which decided the Axis espionage chief to use the Spanish Falange as a front.

The Falange had established their foreign bureau at first in Milan, then had transferred it in September 1938 to Salamanca. It went under the title of *Departamento Nacional del Servicio Extranjero de la Falange Espanola Tradicionalista*. Dependable sources declare that there was a pact between Hitler and Franco, permitting German control of Spanish foreign activities. In any case, late in 1938 money was poured into the Mexican Falange, and by the beginning of 1939 most German propaganda was distributed by the Falange. The Foreign Department of the Falange was later merged into the *Consejo de Hispanidad* which was formed in the winter of 1940 in Salamanca, in the presence of Heinrich Himmler and—interestingly enough—Lieutenant-captain Canaris. Its avowed aims were the spreading of Falange doctrines in Latin America and the preaching of Axis collaboration everywhere. It constituted a second league between the Falange and Axis espionage, this time evidently via the Gestapo and the Ribbentrop Bureau. *Consejo* agents took precedence over Falange chiefs, and Nazi methods for extorting funds and services from the large Spanish colony in Mexico were introduced. Attempts were made to install Falange agents as consuls everywhere—not always with success.

The German espionage system used the Falange as its pay-clerk, especially to finance the so-called Sinarquista movement.

This was revival of the former Cristero movement, which in 1926-1927 had specialized in blowing up trains and other useful work. Its name, incidentally, was a puzzle to those interested in getting their facts straight. Even the Sinarquists themselves did not know. Some said it meant that they were for the introduction of order and discipline; some said it meant that they recognized no earthly rulers, for the state should be ruled by God alone.

Question of name aside, the Sinarquists were a large murder gang, in West and Central Mexico, who waged guerrilla warfare against labour unions (which they denounced as Communistic) and against peasants to whom President Cardenas had given land. They were organized after the *führer* system, of course. For a time, Manuel Zermeno was *führer*. He was succeeded by Salvador Abascal, a friend of Brito Foucher's, who had to flee to Berlin after his plot failed. Abascal gets plenty of money from somewhere, controls ten thousand armed men, and has the Sinarquists organized on a military basis with an Intelligence Service, hideouts, and arms caches. The Sinarquists must be considered today the most dangerous fascist movement in Latin America....

Shortly after the Nazis' Falange arrangement got under way, their old protégé, Leon Osorio, the Cuban adventurer whose group they had patiently financed and nursed, tried his hand at a little riot around Christmas, 1938. It was staged as a 'spontaneous anti-Semitic' demonstration, but it was actually against the entry of International Brigade refugees. The riot was a fizzle into the bargain (the Nazis did not have much luck in those days). Baron Hans Heinrich von Holleuffer, alias Hans Helbing, the man who before Hitler had lived by defrauding and swindling, and who lately had worked under Dr Heinrich Northe to keep the German colony in Mexico in line, started a Mexican National Socialist Party in February 1939. The authorities didn't take to the idea, and he had to leave the country within a fortnight.

Then there was his friend, Paul Garbinski, whose speciality before he worked for the Gestapo, which paid better, had been to forge Mexican birth certificates. He had to get out of the country rather fast.

Slowly the Mexican presidential elections were approaching. It was in view of this crucial event that the Nazis created still another popular movement which they could control for their own purposes. They organized an auxiliary to the Gold Shirts—once established with the help of the. German agent, Hermann Schwinn—a Party called PRAC (Revolutionary Anti-Communist Party) whose candidate was the extreme rightist and military adventurer, General Joaquin Amaro. PRAC was a purely terrorist party. The Nazis had a twofold purpose for this machine: (1) to disorganize the campaigns of the two other candidates and to create violence, (2) to influence local authorities to help them get control of strategic points on the coast and in the hills; this in case civil war broke out, when the Nazis could intervene. Groups of armed horsemen were stationed near those strategic points, and they communicated through a number of secret radio transmitters. Peasants in remote places were armed and incited against U.S. 'imperialism.' PRAC was in close touch with Spanish and German merchants in small coast towns, where supplies of fuel oil were stored. Arms smuggling went on, of course. Cedillo's old caches were placed at PRAC's disposal.

This was a repetition of the abortive Cedillo affair, a direct attempt to seize power. But the Nazis, who wanted to play safe, also backed Almazan's campaign against Avilo Camacho. For this they employed the residue of Cedillo's band. German merchants and manufacturers had to subscribe large amounts to the Almazan campaign. These sums were a sinking fund not for the campaign but for a possible revolt planned to follow Almazan's defeat—which was a forgone conclusion. Almazan publicly denounced the Nazis, probably in order to get support from the United States, but all the time *Gobernacion* had proof that he worked with the Nazis, and later on handed those proofs over to the press.

In the midst of all this, the Second World War started in Europe. And, in Mexico and the whole of Latin America, the British and French espionage apparatuses were caught napping. The British IS had exactly four men south of the Rio Grande. The French had one woman and two men.

However, the *Policia Secreta* began to show its teeth with the outbreak of the war. It became, at least during the first six months, almost impossible for the Nazis to create and infiltrate movements. They, therefore, disbanded the PRAC.

Still, they continued their work wherever and whenever they could. There can be little doubt that the tactics employed by the Almazan supporters on election day—7 July 1940—were an imitation of Nazi methods and more expert than any Mexican could have devised. Women and children were kept on the streets as a shield for the snipers, and as a heart-rending spectacle. Late in the afternoon there was a general march on the President's Palace by 'enraged' middle-class elements; it was organized in real *putsch* style. Another point no Mexican cunning would have conceived was the stationing of English-speaking interpreters, perfectly coached, along the route taken by Almazan's car-cavalcade through Mexico City. This was to impress foreign correspondents, when their cars were hailed with anti-Yankee enthusiasm, which was hardly spontaneous. Neither was the disturbance at the opening of Chaplin's *Great Dictator* spontaneous, nor the stoning of the United States Embassy upon Mr Wallace's arrival for the inauguration.

Don't say the Nazis didn't try in Mexico. They tried everything they could think of. They tried to get into power via Cedillo and later on through the PRAC. They tried to create disorder through underground movements, through the Gold Shirts, through Leon Osorio's gang, through Brito Foucher, through nameless small fifth-column groups. They organized the German colony and made it pay through the nose, and made it frightened and Gestapo-conscious. They collaborated with the machines of their Axis partners, and tried to overthrow the government, using the Falange as a lever. They collaborated with anybody in Mexico who had fascist leanings and who was willing to use guns or dynamite. They tried to interfere with the Mexican elections. Their agents kept pouring in.

But now it was war. And now—in July 1940—when it looked as though the European phase of the war were all over, and the second round—namely the one in the Western Hemisphere—might start soon, the army took a hand. The former commander of the Berlin garrison, Friedrich Karl Schleebrugge, arrived in Mexico. He was a direct envoy of Colonel Nicolai's. He was to take charge of the military intelligence. He immediately got in touch with the German ships trapped in the ports on this hemisphere, and arranged for plans of escape, or if escape was impossible, for their scuttling. The *Policia Secreta*, incidentally, immediately put him under police surveillance.

Dr Joachim H. Herstlett, Hjalmar Schacht's ambassador, who had come to Mexico in 1938 to arrange for the Mexican-German oil business and also for a little revolution in Mexico, was still at the head of non-military espionage. He was centralizing all financial affairs, supervising strategic espionage and sabotage, gathering and sifting information. As liaison officers between Herstlett and Schleebrugge, there were Rudolf Plaska and Hans Herzer, both Nicolai's agents, tried and true from their work in Poland.

Schleebrugge's right-hand man was Gerhard Henschke, who had been expelled from Central America as a result of certain ship scuttlings; other assistants of Schleebrugge were Arthur Richard Beier, head of the Gestapo in Mexico, and Paul Pliska of the Hamburg-America Line.

At present the whole Nazi machine employs several hundred first-class agents in Mexico. But the *Policia Secreta* knows them all, and they know that the *Policia Secreta* knows them.

NO SECRETS IN SOUTH AMERICA

Hitler once said to Rauschning:

> We will not only give the South Americans our capital and our enterprising spirit, but we shall convert them to our *Weltanschauung*. If anywhere democracy is senseless and suicidal, it is in South America.

Perhaps Hitler was talking in all seriousness when he spoke of 'giving' something to the South Americans. Certainly in practice it seemed quite otherwise. He seemed more interested in taking. Taking the whole of South America, as a matter of fact.

There were many reasons. South America is rich in raw materials. South America is an excellent market. South America is, from the Nazi point of view, the ideal colonial empire for a Nazi-controlled Europe. South America 'belongs' in the new order.

Naturally, economic conquest was not the final goal—it never is Hitler's final goal. All the same—the Nazis set about the economic conquest of South America with great zeal. From 1933 on, the AO sent tens of thousands of efficient salesmen, organizers, engineers, farmers, etc. to South America. The number of German-controlled industries, businesses, and banks increased steadily. It became ten times as large as the total number of German-controlled enterprises in the rest of the world. The exports of some South American countries to Germany doubled and trebled—in the case of Peru, quadrupled....

But the economic conquest was only an initial step. South America, Hitler had said, was to receive not only German capital and German enterprise, but the German *Weltanschauung*. It must be conquered militarily as well as economically. It was not only to be fitted into a place in the new order; it was to help establish this new order—that is, to help the Nazis conquer the world. For South America held not only raw materials and markets, but many strategic points whose occupation meant control of a large part of the world.

The various aims criss-crossed. Venezuela, for example, was not only the third greatest oil-producing country in the world (after the United States and the Soviet Union), but strategically it could menace Trinidad and Panama and possibly a communication line between Dakar and Brazil. After 1936, when the Germans really got busy there, Venezuelan trade with Germany increased by 78 per cent....

Patagonia. The Nazis never ceased to declare that this country belonged to no one and that they had a valid claim on this tiny, worthless southern tip of South America, because it was settled principally by German farmers. Nor did they trouble to add that whoever owned Patagonia controlled the Straits of Magellan. And if this same power could by chance seize control of the Panama Canal, or render it useless, it could erect an impassable wall around the globe. It could close the seaway from the Pacific to the Atlantic—a possibility which was none too pleasant for the United States.

The new order. There is no doubt that South America would occupy its place in this new order. But South America must be conquered first in order to establish the new order. In order to reduce the United States to a second-rate power. In order to destroy the British Empire.

It is therefore quite logical that the espionage machine of the Third Reich should concentrate its utmost forces upon South America. The whole vast territory must be combed. To wage a war against South America—whether or not it was called a war, whether or not blood was shed, whether it was waged from within or from without—to win such a war South America must be deprived of its every secret.

The work began immediately after Hitler came to power.

The conditions for military espionage in this vast terrain were extraordinarily favourable. Nicolai could have wished for nothing better. In the case of South America, no intelligence apparatus had to be organized. It was there already, in the many airlines which spanned the entire continent.

Ironically enough, they were an innocent consequence of the Treaty of Versailles, which had forbidden Germany to build planes or establish airlines. What then of the men who believed in the future of the aircraft? Were they to renounce their dreams and take up another profession? If not, they had no choice but to leave Germany.

There were, for example, a number of German officers and pilots who had gone to Colombia in 1919, immediately after the end of the First World War. Perhaps even at that time they recognized the strategic importance of this country which lay so close to the Panama Canal. In any case, under the leadership of Fritz Hammer they established the first German airline in South America, Scadta. This was the first permanent air-transport system to operate in the Western Hemisphere.

Hammer was an excellent organizer. He later established the Sedta airline in Ecuador and the Trans-Andes Line to Chile.

In 1927 the Condor Syndicate was founded, also by Germans. This line alone covers 4,000 miles of the Pacific sea coast. It traverses Uruguay to Buenos Aires, then swings West across Argentina and the Andes to Santiago (since 1935). It is connected with the German-owned Lufthansa of Peru.

Although owned entirely by Germans, Condor flew the Brazilian flag and received a subsidy from the Brazilian Government. The managing director is Ernst Hoeck, a naturalized Brazilian....

The German Lufthansa created a great network in the interior of Ecuador and touched points which the American airlines did not touch. In 1937 the Lufthansa acquired a controlling share in the Sedta line, which operated exclusively with German pilots who had been trained in Germany. By advertisements and bribery, the Sedta fought the penetration of American airlines in Ecuador. Not long ago it attempted in vain to secure a licence for plane service to the Galapagos Islands, which are situated near the Pacific entrance to the Panama Canal.

Then there was the Lloyd Aereo Boliviano, which for a long time was a purely German firm associated with the Lufthansa and the Condor Syndicate.

There was also a second airline in Argentina, the Aero Costa Argentina, nominally Argentine-owned, but controlled by Lufthansa and Condor. This airline employed mostly German pilots and German engineers.

One of the most important lines of the Lufthansa reached across Peru from Lima to the Chilean border and across Bolivia to Rio de Janeiro. These routes were not initiated until May 1938. In the spring of 1941 the Lufthansa was attempting to start a new line to the Amazon River, and another along the Pacific coast of Peru....

German planes over South America. Hundreds of German pilots have flown over South America and familiarized themselves with the terrain. Scadta for a time replaced its customary German pilots by new pilots from Germany, so that many more of them might have an opportunity to learn the air routes over South America.

Naturally, these aviators had occasion to fly over the Panama Canal a number of times.

There was a law in Brazil that at least two-thirds of the flying personnel had to be Brazilian, but that did not hamper the Germans. Condor and the other German-controlled commercial airlines hired former Germans who had been naturalized. Some six years ago Condor instituted an aerial photography section, which was commissioned by the Brazilian Government to photograph the interior of Brazil. It is an open secret that the prints of these photographs were sent to Germany. It is also an open secret that not only the Brazilian countryside was photographed, but that detailed pictures of all the South American countries were sent to Berlin.

It is also well known that many of the German lines in South America built airfields with uncommonly long runways, long enough for heavy bombers; and the workshops and fuel reserves on these fields are larger than is needed.

It is still another open secret that shortly after the outbreak of the war, two Fokker-Wulf machines of the Condor Syndicate went to spy out the position of two British warships, disobeying Brazilian regulations and flying out over the South Atlantic. While this particular attempt was discovered, there were probably many similar cases that went undetected.

Altogether, during recent years Germans commanded some 22,000 miles of air routes. One would have to be a rank optimist to assume that there are any points of strategic importance in South America which they have overlooked.

Colonel Nicolai had always been a man of thoroughness. Those who are acquainted with him and his methods will not be surprised that in recent years there was a sharp upturn in the number of spies who tried to photograph the Panama Canal and its fortifications. These spies were almost always German; those who were not could all be traced back to Germans for whom they were working—even to German diplomats.

Nor is it surprising that in the spring of 1941 the Scadta line built an airfield less than one hour's flying time from the Panama Canal. This field had underground hangars, repair shops and living quarters, and was camouflaged by a surface planted with reeds. In Costa Rica land was purchased for a cotton plantation. The Government stepped in and kindly ploughed irrigation ditches through the land; this should have been very good for the cotton, but not so good for an airfield and so the undertaking was abandoned.

There are hundreds of examples of the work of Nicolai's agents; how they meticulously studied the terrain and established themselves in the vicinity of strategic points.

For example, there is San Miguel Cozumel, on the Mexican shore of the Gulf of Mexico. A perfect submarine harbour. Mosquito Keys used to be frequented by fishermen from Cuba and Caymans. They don't go there anymore. This is where the British schooner, *Alston*, vanished in the winter of 1939. It is said that pre-fabricated submarines may be assembled on the lagoons here.

There is the German manager of the dock and fuel depot at Puerto Cabezas, Nicaragua. A German 'marine biology' expedition has been combing these waters for the last eighteen months....

And the armies? Colonel Nicolai had plenty of information on this subject. For after the end of the First World War many South American nations engaged German officers to train their armies.

Major General Wilhelm Faupel was military adviser in Argentina and Peru for nine years after the First World War. Later, General Guenther Niederfuhr came as instructor to the Argentine Army; today he is the military attaché of the German Embassy in Buenos Aires....

General Bohnstedt was for many years head of the Salvadorean military academy and official instructor of the Salvadorean Army. The founder of the SA, Ernst Röhm, was instructor of the Bolivian Army from 1925 to 1930. He came to Bolivia accompanied by a number of officers, some of whom are still there.

Needless to say, Herr von Ribbentrop arranged that the proper diplomats were sent to South America, or that those whom he permitted to remain were advised of their duties. In 1941 so many diplomats were exposed that all the German embassies, legations, and consulates in South America were clearly branded as headquarters of espionage and German agitation and propaganda. These scandals were all widely publicized; it is not necessary to list them here. Indeed, it would be far simpler to list the names of individuals who were innocent of espionage.

And, of course, Herr Rosenberg set his machine at full steam ahead in South America. He sent cultural attachés by the dozen across the Atlantic. His Ibero-American Institute in Hamburg sent flocks of engineers, architects, physicians, scientists; it arranged art exhibitions, established libraries, and in the name of culture entrenched itself wherever it could.

And then, of course, there was Herr Bohle and his AO. Bohle divided South America according to five main strategic points. These were Rio de Janeiro, Montevideo, Buenos Aires, La Paz, and Bogota.

Here were the headquarters of the territorial leaders of the AO. Usually they were the commercial attachés to the legations and therefore enjoyed diplomatic immunity. After the outbreak of the war, Bohle established a sixth strategic point in Santiago.

The AO in South America had a strong foothold through the many schools and the teachers' organizations in the German colonies, especially in Brazil.

Dr Goebbels bought out South American newspapers or bribed them or flooded them with propaganda material. One of his best instruments was the Transocean News Service, which delivered news in many countries at a purely nominal price. In Brazil alone Goebbels controlled more than half the fifteen German-language newspapers.

In Argentina he controlled twelve important dailies. Moreover it has been estimated that over 300,000 Nazi pamphlets or magazines were distributed there weekly.

In La Paz, Goebbels controlled six daily newspapers.

An instructive subject for research would be an analysis of all the political crises, uprisings, successful and unsuccessful revolutions in South America, from 1933 on. Undoubtedly it would be discovered that in every one the Nazis had participated in some manner, or at least had given the initial impulse. We must remember that the creation of inner unrest and insecurity has always been the favourite Nazi weapon.

Here we must limit ourselves to a few examples where the Nazis played a distinctly prominent part. One is the uprising of the Green Shirts in Brazil (11 May 1938), which was led by the cultural attaché of the German Embassy, Herr Henning Hans von Cossel. In this uprising there occurred what amounted to a siege of President Vargas' palace.

There is the case of German Busch Becerra, a Bolivian of German descent. Becerra, although he had never left Bolivia, was strongly under the influence of German army officers who had come to Bolivia as instructors to the Bolivian Army. After fighting in the Chaco war, for which he was decorated, he was elected President of Bolivia in 1937. In 1938 he tore up the Constitution and declared Bolivia a totalitarian State. He concluded a barter agreement with the Nazis, whose terms were overwhelmingly to German advantage. Bolivia was to deliver oil and tin and receive arms in return. In the summer of 1939 he allegedly committed suicide, the official excuse being that he had had a nervous breakdown from overwork. But it is more likely that he was assassinated by some member of the opposition.

There was the case of Patagonia.

On 30 March 1939, the Argentine newspaper *Noticias Graficas* published a sensational exposé of a Nazi espionage organization in Patagonia. The facts had been obtained from Enrique Jurges, a former friend of Röhm's and an associate of Dr Goebbels, who had resolved to revenge himself against the Gestapo for the murder of his wife. The newspaper story spoke of an espionage organization which had been founded to wrest Patagonia from Argentina, 'whose claim is invalid, based as it is on outmoded political ideas' and seize it for Germany.

This organization had seven 'strategic points': the German Embassy in Argentina, the German Chamber of Commerce, two German banks, a wool exporting firm in Patagonia, a shipping line and the German Labour Front in Argentina. The German Embassy branded the whole story a lie, and after weeks of investigation the Argentine police admitted that they could not prove the authenticity of the documents. However, the police investigation revealed other matters. For example, that the German organizations had forbidden their members to become Argentine citizens; that the SA was giving its members military training, and other similar developments which gave but cold comfort to the Argentinians.

In the summer of 1940 a parliamentary committee in Uruguay investigated certain Nazi activities.

It was proved that Nazi cells were organized in Montevideo by Simeon del Bonete and Palisando; Nazi agents 'had penetrated political life extensively; Nazis were firmly installed in the schools; there were storm troopers all over the country; all vital strategic points were being photographed; Nazi parachutists practised in Uruguayan military camps.' The German Minister directed all these activities from the Legation. Herr Fuhrmann, the head of the AO of Uruguay, was plotting to seize the mouth of the Rio Plata, to use as a base for a revolution of the 2,500,000 Germans in Argentina and Southern Brazil. The Uruguayan Army was scheduled to revolt. A temporary government was to be set up in Montevideo until Hitler could appoint a *führer* for Uruguay. Members of the opposition, anti-Nazis, Jews, and Freemasons, were to be slaughtered. Uruguay was to become an agricultural colony of the Reich.

In the summer of 1941 the Argentine Chamber disclosed a new plan to revive the old separatist movement in Patagonia. A few companies of shock troops were to attack Uruguay from Argentina. It was revealed that the influence of the Nazi agents on the police and in the ministries, schools, and press had become a definite threat. Even radio stations were being paid directly from Germany. Worse yet was the mounting influence of the Nazis among the younger army officers. Berlin had extended promises: let Argentina become a member of the Axis and she would receive Uruguay, Paraguay, part of Bolivia, and the Falkland Islands, which were held by the British but which Argentina had always claimed. In return, Patagonia was to become a German colony.

You can't say the Nazis didn't try.

PART VI
The Counter-revolution of Espionage

AWAKENING

On 18 October 1938—probably for the first time since the First World War—the name of Colonel Walter Nicolai once more came before the public eye. This happened in New York during the Nazi spy trial.

One of the accused, Guenther Gustave Rumrich,[1] a deserter from the United States Army, said in answer to the question of how he came to spy for the Third Reich:

'I read a book by Colonel Nicolai and then I wrote to him in care of the *Voelkischer Beobachter* in Berlin. I offered him my services. He answered me through an advertisement in a New York newspaper.'

The trial in which this remarkable and weird statement was made was in itself remarkable and weird enough. It was a trial full of the property of spy novels. Stories of mobilization plans stolen ... a general kidnapped ... a code written out on match boxes ... a new Mata Hari installed in Washington ... fifty American passport forms stolen....

But more remarkable and weird than that was something which heretofore no spy trial had seen. Names were named. The names of those who loomed behind these small spies who had been arrested. Eighteen persons were accused. Four of them sat before the court. The others had either made their getaway to Germany or they had never left Germany. They had remained in the background, in their offices; they had guided the work from afar.

In court these men were named. The newspapers wrote: 'Hitler's spy chiefs indicted as plotters against United States' and 'United States traces spy plot to Berlin.' Even the cautious *New York Times* remarked on June 21:

> Germany was officially named as the power responsible for the undercover force that aggressively sought to pry out the best technical military defence secrets of the United States.

Who knows how long it would have taken the United States to realize the gravity of the German espionage problem, had it not been for this improbable spy trial? Even after this trial, it was a long time before the full danger was understood.

Official Washington had understood for a long time, however, and now definite action was taken. President Roosevelt himself declared that the country must be defended against this kind of aggression. There were the first steps toward the establishment of a counterespionage organization. The FBI extended its net of agents. Between 500 and 800 operatives were to cover key positions.

But the American public failed to grasp the situation. Most people found the revelations of the trial too fantastic to be believed. Once more Hitler profited from his trick of doing the improbable—so improbable that even when the stratagem was revealed, no one believed it.

Thanks to the members of one profession who persistently fought against this popular prejudice, the majority of Americans finally began to see what was happening before their very eyes, in their own houses and places of work. The thanks are due to American reporters. When the history of the destruction of Hitler is someday written, American newspapermen will certainly have an honourable place in it. They are not only the best, but the most courageous in the world; and they have contributed to the ultimate defeat of Hitler by awakening the world to the menace. This is true of the European correspondents of American newspapers and news syndicates; it is equally true of the cub reporters who helped materially to uncover Nazi espionage in the United States. By tireless spade work they gathered detail after detail, printed disclosure upon disclosure, until slowly the public opened its eyes to what Nazi spies and their agents were about in these United States.

The Bund came into the spotlight. It was soon discovered that this was no innocuous society of eccentrics, but a thoroughgoing military organization. The Bund trained its members in camps. There was a regular SA within the Bund, the so-called OD men, whose number was officially given as 5,000; in reality they far exceeded that number. There was also a Hitler Youth, an AO, and a Labor Front in which every American of German descent had to register. Registrants had to make a monthly contribution to this Labor Front. The Labor Front often succeeded in placing its members in aircraft or munitions factories, or other places vital to the defence effort.

It was found that the Bund had camps located wherever there were nearby ports, airfields, munitions depots, aircraft factories, etc.

Gradually, almost a year and a half after the spy trial, individual German agents who had kept well under cover, began to be tracked down. There was, for example, Dr Friedrich Ernst Ferdinand Auhagen,[2] who came to the United States in 1923 as a mining engineer. After working for a time in the Pennsylvania coal fields and then in Wall Street, he became a lecturer at Columbia University. He received regularly large sums of money from Germany with which he distributed propaganda material to over 200,000 persons. For a time he edited a small magazine, *Today's Challenge*; later this became a weekly, the *Forum Observer*. The magazine was pure propaganda and was distributed free.

Auhagen travelled about the country and made speeches for Hitler and against the Jews. He lived very well on the money he received from Germany. When the State Department got after him for not having registered as a foreign propagandist, he tried to flee to Japan. He was caught, arrested, tried, and sentenced to two years in prison.

The three principal Nazi propaganda agencies in the United States, which received $750,000 annually from Herr Goebbels, were the German Library of Information, the German Railroad Information Office, and the Transocean News Service.

The German Library of Information was organized in 1936 by the German Consulate in New York. Its purpose was to supply information on present-day Germany and to distribute propaganda. For this purpose it had $450,000 a year at its disposal. The library was run directly by the German Consul and the Embassy in Washington, indirectly, of course, by the Propaganda Ministry in Berlin. *Facts in Review*, a free publication of the library, reached from 100,000 to 200,000 persons.

The director of the library was Dr Matthias Schmitz, a former instructor at Smith College. Assisting him was George Sylvester Viereck,[3] who in the First World War had been active as a pro-German intellectual. The number of employees was originally four; in the course of time it was expanded to forty-seven.

Viereck did not limit his talents to the Library of Information and to Herr Auhagen's magazine. He also claimed to be the correspondent of the *Muenchener Neuesten Nachrichten*. Before Hitler, this modest newspaper would not have dreamed of engaging a correspondent at a monthly salary of five hundred dollars. (Herr Viereck was finally arrested by the FBI on 9 October 1941. The indictment described him as the most dangerous Nazi agent in this country.)

The German Railroad Information Office remained open even after the outbreak of the war, although it was no longer permissible for Americans to travel to Germany. This office was opened shortly after the end of the First World War, to develop friendly relations between Germany and the United States. Its most precious possession was a mailing list of 125,000 names, to which were sent weekly *News Flashes from Germany*. This mailing list was available to all Nazi organizations and their sympathizers.

Finally, the Transocean News Service pretended to be a news service like AP or Havas. It was directed by Dr Manfred Zapp and Guenther Tonn. As a business enterprise it was always in the red, for it had to extend its service at any cost. It was subsidized by Berlin to the extent of some $90,000 annually.

The most important task of Transocean News Service was to flood Central and South America with pro-German, anti-Semitic propaganda. In addition, Dr Manfred Zapp was supposed to maintain relationships with the American press as a potential source of information. This was not difficult for him, since he was gifted with considerable charm and wit. But he was rather slow at learning things. It is well known that Goebbels was dissatisfied with him, and publicly stated that the man was stupid.

More dangerous than Herr Zapp—because far more intelligent—was the German journalist, Colin Ross,[4] who came to America from time to time to collect material for a book and to deliver lectures. He made excellent connections and used his 'good friends' to extract valuable information. On his last trip—early in 1939—he hired an American photographer and had him take pictures of fortifications and warships. Before Washington caught up with him, he was on his way back to Germany.

The spotlight penetrated ever more relentlessly into the shadows. One could not help noticing that since Hitler had come to power, the number of German consulates had increased steadily. And the number of employees in these consulates, and at the Embassy in Washington, increased beyond all bounds. To give but one example: in 1933 the German Consulate General in New York had 38 employees; in 1941 it had 116. By 1941 everyone in the United States knew what the German consulates were for and why they were so many of them with so many employees. Everyone knew that they were the headquarters of espionage, just as they had been in other countries; that conspiracies and sabotage were planned and executed by the consular officials.

The light of publicity was cast upon the German consuls, their agents and sub-agents; and the American public began to recognize them for what they were. Often against their own will, the people of America were compelled to see that these men were spies and conspirators and saboteurs.

There was Captain Fritz Wiedemann,[5] the successor to Manfred Killinger[6] as Consul General in San Francisco. Manfred Killinger was a notorious gangster and *Feme* murderer who was finally forced to leave San Francisco. In any case, that post had become a crucial one, and a more efficient man was needed, for the Consul General in San Francisco for some time directed all espionage on the Pacific coast and was responsible for relations with the Japanese espionage organization.

Captain Fritz Wiedemann, an old friend of the Führer's, whose superior he had been during the First World War, was far more skilful than Killinger. The personal charm which had made him a favourite of the Cliveden set made him popular in San Francisco for some time. Especially since he came out publicly against the Bund and declared that National Socialism was not good for America. This popularity of his must have penetrated into rather influential circles. For the Führer himself once wired Wiedemann congratulating him 'on your fine work in defeating repeal of the Neutrality Act.' A case which did not come to trial was that of Mrs Alice Crockett. Mrs Crockett demanded $8,000 from Wiedemann, asserting that he was the paymaster for German espionage in the United States and had already paid out more than $5,000,000 to various agents. Mrs Crockett also declared that Wiedemann had worked together with Colonel Lindbergh and Henry Ford, and that the person who paid the spies directly was none other than Princess Stefanie von Hohenlohe.

The Princess had come to America with Wiedemann and was living quietly in the vicinity of San Francisco. Nevertheless, Washington was unwilling to renew her visitor's visa, and it was said that she would be deported. The newspapers printed a great deal about the Princess' past. Then for a time not a word was heard about her. Then came tidings that she was not to be deported and that the Department of Justice had assurances of her 'co-operation.'

Baron Edgar von Spiegel,[7] Consul General in New Orleans, was also showered with some unfavourable publicity when he reprimanded and threatened an anti-Nazi journalist and tried to influence the board of trustees of a university by the offer of a small endowment. In New Orleans Spiegel was in a position to control espionage activities in the Gulf of Mexico. It was not by hazard that the man such a post was given to was a former U-boat commander.

Until very recently little attention was paid to the consul in Boston, Dr Herbert Scholz.[8] And when he did emerge into public view, there was little to reproach him with, save that he was propagandizing for Germany among the ladies of Boston society. This comparative obscurity is evidence of Dr Scholz's skill and cleverness. For the part he played was actually more dangerous and more significant than that of any other consul—possibly more important than the part of the German Ambassador in Washington. Dr Herbert Scholz was the chief of the Gestapo in the United States. Scholz had had a varied career. He was the best friend of one of the early members of the Nazi Party, Rolf Rainer. With Rainer he had belonged to Röhm's intimate circle. After Hitler took power, Rainer became Hess's adjutant and Scholz in turn became Rainer's adjutant. Their real job, however, was to attend to what the Nazis termed 'the co-ordination of business enterprises.'

The two young men called on the owners and directors of industrial concerns and other big business enterprises to inform them that they would have to play ball. In most cases the young men even brought along somebody whom they were to install as director or part owner. For this work, they netted money from both sides.

During the blood purge they just barely escaped. They fled to Bavaria, and hid out in the vicinity of the Chiemsee till it blew over. When they reappeared, Rolf Rainer was given a short prison sentence. Scholz, probably through the intervention of his influential father and of his father-in-law, who was a director of the famous German dye trust, escaped without any punishment. He then entered the foreign service. About this time he met Heinrich Himmler, who took a liking to the young man. Later, when Herbert Scholz was sent to Washington as first secretary to the Ambassador, he carried with him the instructions of Himmler. The German Ambassador used to go pale with fear whenever he had any dealings with his secretary. He knew that Scholz was sending in reports on him to Himmler.

Herbert Scholz and his wife were extremely well liked in Washington. They were invited everywhere, and it was the general belief that Scholz would someday be Ambassador, or at least Consul General in New York. His sudden transfer to Boston astonished everyone.

What lay behind this transfer has been never completely clarified. Perhaps—as some informed circles in Berlin maintain—enemies of Himmler (perhaps Göring) effected the transfer while Himmler was on vacation. Or perhaps Himmler preferred Scholz to be out of the limelight. The obscurity of Boston may have facilitated his work.

Be that as it may, it is certain that Scholz was Himmler's representative. He did no routine consular work; this was taken care of entirely by the Consular Secretary, Kurt Boehme. And, regularly, he received diplomatic mail and code telegrams from Himmler.

In July 1941, shortly after the closing of the German consulates, a story was published in New York which declared that George Johnson Armstrong,[9] a spy who had been condemned to death and hanged in England, was an agent of Scholz's. The story had it that Armstrong had been directed to Scholz through the former Austrian world champion ice skater, Fritzi Burger. Armstrong was in love with her, and she had persuaded him to help Scholz by shipping as a sailor on American boats going to Central and South America.

The story is improbable, though not on account of its romantic colour. It is improbable because Herbert Scholz did not deal directly with his spies. As the chief of the Gestapo in the United States, he was rather the man who directed and supervised spies who in turn hired, instructed, and paid their own agents.

It took a long time before the public in the United States understood what the Nazis really were, what they wanted, and that they did not scruple about methods. A long time. By the time Americans did understand, Europe was in flames, France had collapsed, and millions were labouring under the Nazi yoke. Nevertheless, even as late as the middle of 1941, the American public did not know what sort of war the Nazis were preparing against the United States. A war which might be without bloodshed, which might begin from within instead of from without. But a war, nevertheless, which like all wars had to be prepared. In a total war, a certain stage of preparation must be complete before the first shot is fired. That stage involves the thorough entangling of a country in the web of total espionage. In the United States that web has long been spun.

B4 ACQUIRES ALLIES

It took a long time, too, before England understood that this was a total war. It did not dawn on the English until just before the fall of France. But when they finally did realize it, B4 in one flash realized something else. B4 saw that the British Empire with its great net of commercial relations made an ideal vantage ground for its own total espionage.

The apparatus for total espionage already existed. It was the Ministry of Economic Warfare. This apparatus needed only to be geared to use.

The original purpose of the Ministry of Economic Warfare was to carry out the blockade. Before the invasion of Belgium and the Netherlands, there had been two phases of this work. In the first phase, the machinery of contraband control was devised and put to work. In the second phase agreements were concluded with individual firms abroad in order to speed up the procedure of control, and to negotiate war trade agreements with neutral countries. During this phase the Ministry's main efforts centred upon preventing Germany from importing raw materials by indirection, through neutral countries whose shipping the British were allowing to pass.

Then came the third phase: 'The blockade has been transferred from the seas to the quays,' as an official statement put it. The navicert system was made compulsory.

But the blockade was extended beyond the quays. Control was extended to the offices of business houses and factories throughout the world.

The Ministry of Economic Warfare was not just a group of offices in London. It had offices all over the world. To be sure, the words 'Ministry of Economic Warfare' were not lettered on the doors of these offices. Rather the offices were lodged in British—and often non-British—business houses, banks, brokers' offices. Sometimes there were no offices: simply men who had spent years in the export trade and knew all the ins and outs.

These were the men who extended the control back of the quays and saw to it that London was informed to the last detail about the export trade. It was not quite as complex as it sounds. It was no secret how much oil, copper, cotton, wool, rubber, nickel, and nickel ore Germany had imported during the last few years before the war. The countries from which these imports had originated and the firms that had undertaken the shipping were well known. Now these firms were carefully watched. The firms that were associated with them were watched. Certain people who bought grain for a firm in Athens or cotton for a firm in Rumania were watched. On the docks of New York, San Francisco, Vera Cruz, Valparaiso, and other ports appeared men who were very curious as to whether boxes which were supposed to contain toys for a Swedish firm really contained toys. And American customs officials who shared their suspicions opened the boxes....

The net was cast wider and wider.

But the Ministry of Economic Warfare did not limit itself to mere control. It intervened directly in the shooting war.

Much was known by this Ministry. Its men not only knew the sources of cotton, wool, rubber, hides and skins, nickel, lead, zinc, and jute. They knew from previous experience where these vital raw materials were received in Germany. And it was not by chance that certain factories which had large stocks of such raw materials were bombed heavily and regularly. It was not by chance that the zinc mines in Poland and later the copper mines in Yugoslavia and the synthetic rubber and oil plants in Germany were bombed.

The men in the Ministry of Economic Warfare knew other things. The British commercial houses which had traded on the Continent of Europe for many generations knew where the most important railway junctions were situated; knew about shipping on the Danube and Elbe. They gave their suggestions, and these railway lines were crippled for long spells or the shipping was tied up in the Danube. And much raw material that 'happened' to be in the bombed trains or ships was destroyed.

The Ministry of Economic Warfare knew still other things. Ironically, Germany herself supplied a certain amount of information. For years, an *Industrial Directory*, compiled with true German thoroughness, had been published annually in Germany. Nor did it fail to appear in 1940. This book listed all factories, in cities and in the vicinity of cities, along with data about the equipment of these factories, what they produced and in what quantities. It told nothing about the war industries themselves, of course, but there were more than enough leading facts. Starting from these facts, the representatives of British commercial houses on the Continent could find out a great deal. In Zurich, in Lisbon, in Madrid—they needed merely to keep their ears open. And a few eyewitnesses could learn much about what went on in the factories. The spies of the Ministry of Economic Warfare were active even in the occupied territories and in Germany herself. They were not Englishmen, of course. But they were men who had worked all their lives with the British, and they gladly retailed their information. They did not have to be asked.

And the Bombers of the RAF appeared over factories manufacturing important war goods and dropped their bombs.

Like the Ministry of Economic Warfare, the entire British IS still worked on an 'individual' basis. That is, its work was the sum total of a large aggregate of brilliant individual accomplishments. As yet no effort was made to gather all the potential forces for espionage or counterespionage which were latent all over the world.

The British IS still depended, as it had for centuries, on the talent and ingenuity of individual agents and the organizational and deductive ability of a small group of dependable officials.

The agents of the British IS were among the best in the world. They were active in Baur-au-Lac in Zurich, in the Avenida Palace in Lisbon, in the Hotel Aletti in Algiers (which since the fall of France had become the promontory for observing the movements of the Italian fleet and Pétain's fleet). But they were still only individuals. There was no mass espionage.

It must be emphasized that the agents of the British IS were not only capable and skilful; they were possessed of an almost legendary courage. As the war progressed and the situation of England seemed increasingly hopeless, while the superior might of the German war machine proved itself—the agents of the British IS became all the more aggressive, daring, and recklessly brave.

The first invasions of the European mainland by these agents began shortly after Dunkirk. They issued out of the fog in the little fjords of Northern Norway, in the thousand little inlets which the enemy could never completely control. They appeared on the cliffs in Brittany. They spoke with the inhabitants of the occupied territories, asked questions, received information, and vanished into the night. And the next day or the next week the bombers of the RAF appeared and dropped their loads over particular targets in Northern France, Belgium, Holland, Norway, where the Germans had stored oil, munitions, and spare parts for the machines of their mechanized army.

No, these agents did not lack courage. And many of them never returned from such trips. There was something magnificent about these individual battles against the mighty war machine of thousands of tanks and planes.

This was truly the imaginativeness and the courageous resolution of Lawrence. But they were still only individuals.

Still lacking was the proper conception of the war, which would have forged these separate individuals into one invincible apparatus, a machine that in its unity would surpass the few hundred IS agents that comprised it. The IS had still to learn that total war required total espionage.

It is remarkable that it took so long for this idea to penetrate. Men like Sir Robert Vansittart knew very well what Nazism was, what Pan-Germanism meant, and what the world might expect from a victorious Hitler. But an individual, even one as esteemed as Sir Robert, could not fly in the face of tradition. The ancient, honourable tradition of the British Secret Service considered war a professional matter, a trade that must be learned in long apprenticeship and a condition which was only temporary. Tradition had it that a war was either won or lost, and if it was lost, that did not mean the end of the world.

Above all the tradition dictated that an Englishman was an Englishman and a foreigner a foreigner. Sometimes the British Secret Service found it necessary to hire foreigners. But they were still alien; they were paid and mistrusted. After all, a foreigner who would sell information was no better than a traitor.

But in the critical months of the summer and fall of 1940 this fundamental attitude changed. Many things contributed to bring about this change.

Perhaps the Link affair helped. For it demonstrated to the IS that Englishmen in high places, members of the first families, could be traitors. Perhaps the split in the ranks of the French also helped. It meant a great deal that General de Gaulle had come to England, scorning the commands and decrees of the men of Vichy; and that he had gathered about him an ever-growing band of brave Frenchmen who had not lost their sense of honour. And there was the magnificent stand of one who was called the Lawrence of Syria, Colonel Philibert Collet, who turned important information over to the British. (In the summer of 1941 he finally went over to them.) Perhaps, too, the IS learned something from the German refugees, who had volunteered in the Foreign Legion in order to fight Hitler. And when Vichy gave up the struggle, many had managed to make their way to Egypt in spite of almost insuperable difficulties and perils, in order to continue the fight.

Unquestionably, the change in attitude was in part due to the activities of four German refugees in the Balkans. These four had created for the British an espionage organization which functioned splendidly. They had supplied invaluable material, and, refusing to take any money, had worked under such perilous circumstances that three of the four eventually lost their lives.

Many things contributed. And slowly the men of the IS realized that this war was more than just another war; that it could not be formally won or lost; that the fate of humanity was at stake. Slowly they understood that the basis of their old work was much too limited. They began to make contacts. They began working with eleven officers of the former Czechoslovak Intelligence Service who were now in London.

These eleven officers—who have been kept surrounded with the greatest secrecy—had fled with their most important papers on the day Hitler entered Prague. They had taken a plane, flown off into a snowstorm to cross over Germany, with the Germans in pursuit, attempting to shoot them down. Now the British IS got in touch with these men. And the Czechoslovak secret service men had interesting suggestions to offer. They spoke of the peoples in the occupied territories. They suggested that the British IS open its eyes and look around. It had all the allies it wished. It had millions of allies throughout Europe.

TWILIGHT

German tanks advanced further and further, German troops followed and took possession of more and more of the Continent of Europe. The German base widened from day to day.

Colonel Nicolai and his associates had to follow; the base of German espionage also widened from day to day. In every newly conquered country the German espionage apparatus not only reaped a rich harvest of new information, but also found new human material and new connections. No time was lost in putting all this to use.

The collaboration with Spanish espionage was most fruitful and involved the least friction. This collaboration had been in force since 1936. The liaison man was the millionaire, Juan March, an old acquaintance of Herr von Stohrer's and Canaris', who in the First World War had been a smuggler, war profiteer and paid German agent. During and after the Spanish Civil War this man had headed his friend Franco's Naval Intelligence.

Then there was General Martinez Anido, who had already founded the organization of his *pistoleros*, a kind of Gestapo, under Primo de Rivera. Finally there was the service headed by Emilio Mola, the Army Intelligence, which was none too reliable.

In France there was no chance of working with the old espionage machine. As far as the Germans were concerned, this whole apparatus had been wiped off the face of the earth.

On the other hand, the excellent news Service of the Havas agency was still very alive. The Nazis seized it. They allowed it to sell its service at low prices, like Transocean; in certain places, particularly South America, they even gave away the service for nothing in order to maintain certain contacts and if possible exploit these even further. Many of the Havas employees refused to propagandize and spy for Germany. These quit their jobs. But others remained.

The espionage apparatus of the AO took possession of the many organizations of French waiters and chefs throughout the world. Or rather, it tried to take possession of them, for it frequently made no headway at all. These unheroic and rather poor Frenchmen resisted with a strength none had foreseen. They did not want to spy for Germany; they spat into their fires and cursed and hoped that Germany would be crushed quickly.

German espionage also had little success in its recruiting among the Frenchwomen who worked mainly in America as hairdressers, manicurists, etc.

On the other hand, the French Embassy in Washington did not reduce its personnel after the fall of France. On the contrary, its personnel grew, very much after the manner of the German consulates and embassies after Hitler came to power.

Once more it was the excellent *New York Herald Tribune* which started an investigation of its own to find out just how far the French Embassy was working for Vichy and how far for Berlin. It named names. There was Colonel Georges Bertrand-Vigne, the counsellor of the Embassy, who had come to the United States with Henri-Haye. There was the former press attaché, Captain Charles Brousse, who stayed in Washington and had some excellent contacts with Messrs Heribert von Strempel and Ernst Ostermann von Roth, of the German Embassy. And there was, finally, the mystery man, Monsieur Jean Musa, who, though generally believed to be the private secretary of the Ambassador, lived in New York. Once upon a time he had been a waiter in New York; now he seemed to have money enough to have suites in some of the most expensive hotels. The *Herald Tribune* suggested that there was some connection between the Ambassador and Monsieur Musa on the one hand, and certain agents of the Paris police who were doing espionage work in the United States, on the other. Incidentally, Henri-Haye was quite indignant about the revelations, and explained that the activities of his friends were harmless and legal.

In this connection one cannot fail to notice the presence of Camille Chautemps,[10] who appeared rather suddenly in Washington and was termed by those in the know the unofficial ambassador of Vichy. There can be little doubt that his main function was that of an 'observer.' Unfortunately, there can be no doubt that now and then he has had access to extremely valuable information in certain United States Government departments—valuable for Hitler.

It has even been said that M. Chautemps, whose political past indicates that he would stop at nothing, and who has been publicly accused of almost everything without ever venturing a denial, has had a hand in arranging for German spies to come and live in French Guiana. Whatever the truth, it is well known to the British Intelligence Service that all the facilities of the French Intelligence Service in French Guiana have been placed at the disposal of the Germans.

Which is just one of many cases. Another one is that of General Henri Fernand Dentz, who definitely did espionage work for the Nazis in Syria, and who very definitely must be called a full-fledged Nazi agent.

It was noticed that certain big industrialists, the owners of prosperous French businesses, suddenly appeared in the United States and made a great show of being anti-Hitler. Yet it was obvious that only through special immunity had they been able to leave France without forfeiting some of their property. Nor did they ever encounter any difficulty returning to the France from which they claimed they had fled.

For example, one day M. Pierre Massin appeared in New York, where he was associated with the firm of Henry à la Pensée. Massin had been one of the leading anti-Semites in Paris. He had been praised in the newspaper, *Au Pilori* (compared to which Streicher's *Stuermer* reads like a child's primer) for his work as president of the *Féderation des Comités du Haut Commerce de Paris*. Now he appeared in New York, and when the immigration authorities first took him to Ellis Island, he protested vigorously and declared that he was not at all anti-Semitic, that his best friends were Jews, and that he was happy to be out of France, from which he had barely escaped, and so on. The American authorities believed that he had barely escaped, although he came with an amazing array of baggage. He was finally admitted. Shortly afterward he returned to France. He was unable to complete his second voyage to the United States because the British were less gullible than the American officials had been, and took him off the ship at Bermuda.

And how about Armand Gregoire, the Paris lawyer who a short time ago arrived in New York? He was once one of the leading men of the Francists, the French fascist and anti-Semitic party. Needless to say, he could not have got out of France without the permission of the German authorities. Needless to say, he couldn't have taken any money out without their permission. M. Gregoire had been one of the good friends of Otto Abetz. But now he is 'no longer interested in politics.' Now he has come to the United States strictly on private business.

While the espionage web was thus engulfing Europe, things were not going too well in South America. A number of South American countries had concluded that perhaps it was not to their interest to harbour the Germans and their airlines.

There was Colombia, which was so important to German espionage, with its Scadta line. In Colombia some eighty German pilots and German employees were abruptly discharged, although they received large compensatory stipends. It was a considerable change, even though a number of the old employees of the line lingered in the vicinity of the east coast of Colombia and became 'farmers.' Others organized a temporary unscheduled air transport service. In Peru the Government suddenly closed the doors of the Lufthansa and the Transocean News Service. Simultaneously American naval, army, and air missions were invited to train the armed forces of the country.

During the first part of 1941 the Germans were completely driven out of the Aereo Boliviano; the Government itself took over the German shares.

The German air mastery of South America was therefore broken. Nor was it any consolation for the German espionage apparatus to know that the United States was behind all these moves. By advancing comparatively small credits to the South American Governments, the United States had made these transactions possible. The result was that Pan-American Airways gained ground. The Germans were chased from realms other than the air. Everywhere, in all the South American nations, there was felt a mounting reaction to the German influence.

In the Nicaraguan Congress a bill was introduced to prohibit all subversive action or propaganda, in no matter what form, against the principles of democracy. Paul Ernst Strobelt, the head of the Nicaraguan Gestapo, was deported. At about the same time, Mexico expelled a Nicaraguan political exile, General Oberto Hurtado, a member of Nicaragua's Nazi Party who had written the German Minister in Mexico, 'I have enough arms, but I need planes.' Planes for a revolt. And needless to say, crated Messerschmitt fighters had already arrived, though Hurtado could not get possession of them.

In Chile a bill was drafted by July, providing for the dissolution of the Popular Socialist Vanguard, the Chilean Nazi Party. Early in August, the Government started an investigation of Nazi activities and the Minister of the Interior soon announced that a Nazi plot had just been foiled at the last minute. Six prominent leaders of totalitarian activities were already under arrest. Raids were organized in all the districts where Germans were powerful, and numerous compromising documents were seized. Also discovered were extensive caches of arms. Some newspapers bluntly demanded the ousting of the German Ambassador, Wilhelm von Schoen.

In Peru the expulsion of Karl Deterding, an employee of the Peruvian Insurance Company and the Nazi Gauleiter for Peru, was demanded.

In Cuba, the police confiscated a truck full of documents, pictures, and maps. Among them there was found a list of the most important members of the Falange in Cuba and definite proof that these Falange members operated as fifth columnists. There were also communications from Dr Goebbels to these Falangists and some letters referring to German U-boats near Cuba. Furthermore, there were maps of Cuban fortifications and plans for the construction of airfields. The Falange leaders were arrested.

At the same time three Nazis and a Swiss were arrested for spying out convenient landing places—just in case. And steps were taken to halt the suspicious activities of some Japanese fishermen—a mere five hundred of them.

That was by no means all. By July and August, 1941, scarcely a day went by without a few Germans' being arrested for 'suspicious activities.' According to the able Colonel Manuel Benitey, Havana police chief, it was just about zero hour. He had created an anti-espionage bureau which had done admirable work. According to him and his agents, German and Italian spies did not work directly, but mainly through the Falange. 'The Spanish Falange is our chief problem,' he declared.

In the middle of August the Cuban Minister of State declared that practically all Axis consulates in Cuba had been closed. All except the Nazi consular office at Santiago de Cuba.

In Buenos Aires the *Accion Argentina*, a non-political association of 800,000 members, called for strict measures against totalitarian propaganda, demanded the closing of clubs, schools, labour associations, etc., which were supported by anti-democratic groups, and asked for immediate safeguards against subversive activity on the part of diplomatic and consular representatives of totalitarian governments.

In Venezuela, Nazi oil workers were discharged; the companies organized patrols against sabotage. German seamen stranded in Venezuela were restricted in their movements.

In Bolivia the Nazis played for big stakes. The Bolivian military attaché in Germany was Elias Belmonte Pabon, who had been Minister of the Interior under German Busch. The Nazis had been in league with him for a long time; everyone in La Paz knew that Pabon was slated to be the future dictator of Bolivia.

In the summer of 1941 the Nazis apparently thought the time was ripe. Perhaps, too, they were impatient to strike so as to recover the ground they were losing in other South American countries. But before they could take action the plot was discovered, and there was ample proof that it was headed by German Ambassador Ernst Wendler.

The incriminating documents that were seized came mainly from the hand of Major Pabon. They showed clearly that the details of the plot had been settled at the conference in March 1941, a conference called by Hjalmar Schacht's envoy, Kurt Rieth, the former German Minister to Austria.

In La Paz a number of officers, some of them generals, were arrested for complicity in the plot. Pabon was dismissed outright; Herr Hermann Schroth, a German citizen and former manager of the Lloyd Aereo Boliviano, was arrested. Herr Paul von Bauer, former director of this airline and then for some time adviser to the line, was deported. It was proved that he had made several secret flights to the Panama Canal Zone.

Also arrested was the former Bolivian Minister of Finance, Victor Paz Estensoro, who had promised to deliver the oil fields of Bolivia into the hands of the Nazis. He had been leader of the National Revolutionary Movement, which was now dissolved. Four Bolivian newspapers under Goebbels' domination were banned. The second headquarters of the uprising was the town of Cochabamba. The German Consul there was arrested.

German Minister Wendler and his staff tried to go to Chile. But the Chilean Government declared him *persona non grata* and they sadly had to set out for Japan.

In consequence of the events in Bolivia, the Argentine police raided the Brown House in Buenos Aires, the *Edificio Naco Germanico*. They found papers and correspondence which indicated that Germany had had a hand in the outbreak of the border hostilities between Peru and Ecuador.

Another find was a short-wave radio set in which were hidden code messages from the German Ambassador, von Thermann. The radio set and the messages were destined for Peru. The German Ambassador protested vigorously the confiscation of the radio, but made no mention of the messages. Herr von Thermann declared he would resign his post if he did not receive satisfaction. He finally got back his short-wave set, but the messages were kept and the police set about deciphering them. At the same time sentiment against von Thermann was growing in Buenos Aires, and influential groups in Congress began demanding his expulsion.

By this time important evidence had already been uncovered that in spite of the Presidential decree of May 1939, the Argentine Branch of the Nazi Party was still operating under various guises. Very shortly afterwards, Miguel Culaciati, Minister of the Interior, decided to suppress the 'Superior Council of Argentine Nationalism,' which was nothing but a front for Axis espionage and propaganda. An investigation of a Nationalist plot in the city of Parana produced evidence that a German military organization existed there. It was promptly suppressed. A few days later the Congressional Committee investigating anti-Argentine activities announced the discovery of a blacklist drawn up by the Gestapo which contained the names of some three thousand persons 'unfriendly to Germany.' At about the same time it was disclosed that the German Embassy received more mail, and especially more parcels and packages, than any other Embassy or Legation in Argentina. In 1940 alone it had received 1,300,000 letters and packages, weighing 61,600 pounds and bearing postage worth $27,400.

The congressional committee, after sifting enormous amounts of material, finally came to the conclusion that Ambassador Edmund von Thermann had abused his diplomatic immunity and—as a sideline—more or less directed the entire espionage activities of the Nazis and of the fifth column in Argentine. There was great excitement as to whether the parliament should officially demand the recall of Herr Thermann. The Supreme Court declared that there was enough evidence to expel the envoy. Finally, it was decided not to demand the expulsion officially because it was surmised that after the public debate of von Thermann's ethics, he would be morally compelled to leave the country anyhow.

Strangely enough, though von Thermann had threatened to resign earlier, he now sat pat. Even when a few weeks later—in September 1941—Nazi sympathizers were arrested all over Argentina, when officers of the air corps were revealed as spies and army airports were occupied by the police. At this writing he is still German Ambassador to Argentina.

Berlin meanwhile tried to represent the whole Bolivian scandal as a frame-up by the United States, and the ministers and ambassadors in all the South American States were instructed to give this explanation to the governments to which they were accredited.

Meanwhile, in Paraguay a presidential decree was issued invoking the death penalty for any attempt to bring about the transfer of Paraguayan territory to any other power. The same punishment awaited those who incited another country to make war on Paraguay. Twenty-five years imprisonment was to be the penalty for all who tried by force and violence to overthrow the Constitution.

In Colombia the Government took steps to eliminate the totalitarian influence from the schools. In this enterprise it was interrupted by the discovery of an army plot instigated by the Nazis. A large number of people were arrested. The official radio declared that the Nazis had tried to undermine the army. The House of Representatives met in a closed session.

In Mexico the closing of the fifteen German consulates was ordered for 1 September, after Germany had asked the recall of the Mexican vice-consul in Paris and the closing of the Mexican consular offices in Norway, Holland, France, and Belgium.

In Panama there was finally a *coup d'état* and President Arnulfo Arias, who had been known for his Nazi sympathies, fled to Havana. A new Government was formed, guaranteeing Washington every co-operation in defence of the Panama Canal.

But the severest blow against Nazi espionage in Central and South America, and indeed against all the Axis activities there, was the issuance of a blacklist containing the names of some two thousand Latin-American firms with Axis connections. This blacklist was distributed by the Office of the Co-ordinator of Commercial and Cultural Relations Between the American Republics, headed by Nelson Rockefeller. A very short time after the distribution of this list in Latin America, it was estimated that business firms and agencies connected with the Axis had lost more than one thousand United States accounts. And the list is constantly being expanded. No wonder that an authoritative German spokesman, commenting on the blacklist, said that President Roosevelt was acting 'as though he were already in the war.'

In Portugal, too, the machine was no longer running smoothly. The most important of Nicolai's agents there, Fred Lang—a man who looked Latin rather than German and spoke five languages fluently—was sending rather doleful reports to Berlin. Since the winter of 1940, too much had been happening which took the German agents by surprise.

For example, there was the police raid on the building of the Café Palladium in the Avenida da Libertade. In the back rooms of this building were piled tens of thousands of propaganda leaflets and pamphlets in many languages, which had just been wrapped for shipment to North and South America. The material was confiscated.

One day the police even appeared at the offices of the Sitmar Travel Bureau. In the cellar and in the living rooms above they found extensive stores of arms. Herr Lang was forced to appeal to the German Minister, who applied so much pressure that the affair was finally hushed up; not even the newspapers got wind of it. The Nazis explained that the arms were being stored only temporarily and would be shipped abroad in the near future.

In fact, the Portuguese police were not permitted to confiscate the weapons.

Even more unpleasant for the Germans was the burglary of the home of Herr Grimmeisen, who lived on the Herculanum. Herr Grimmeisen was a private person, a businessman with no official status. As soon as he discovered the burglary he raised a terrific fuss. The police who came to the scene imagined that millions must have been stolen. But when he was asked to list the stolen goods, he stammered some hasty excuses. The loss was really not so large, he said. He seemed to be sorry he had called in the police at all.

He could not very well have admitted what had been stolen. It would have been highly embarrassing for him to say that irreplaceable documents had been stolen. And how could he have said that he suspected the British businessman who lived on the floor above him; or that he thought this Englishman was an agent of the British IS and that the documents were probably already on their way to London? For then he might have had to answer some unpleasant questions himself.

Fred Lang and his assistants found it utterly impossible to get information about ships sailing to England. It was most disconcerting. Lang had so many good connections, particularly with the International Police. He had so many friends in and around Lisbon. But all these connections were of no avail. The departure of English and Allied shipping for England was cloaked in such secrecy that the German espionage machine has to this day been unable to spy out a single one.

Egypt seemed to be a paradise for the agents of German espionage. Egypt had not declared war, and it was unlikely to do so. It was not hard to evade Egyptian laws. The British IS as well as the British Army in Egypt had their hands tied. They were well aware that the Germans had set up an espionage apparatus; they knew some of the agents; but they had no power to make arrests.

It was therefore all the more distressing to the Germans that despite these favourable conditions and despite the valuable information floating around in Egypt and the surrounding territory, they could not get anywhere. The Egyptian populace stood in their way. The Egyptians—particularly the younger Egyptians—actually organized themselves into counterespionage regiments. They followed after the German agents whom the British pointed out, kept them under observation every moment and so prevented any real work.

And what of the Irish, who had seemed so promising? To be sure, the German Intelligence Service had several hundred Irish agents in England. The prearranged plan was for some of these agents to make occasional trips to Ulster, thence across the border illegally into Eire. Once in Eire it was easy to get in touch with the German Consulate in Dublin.

The plan was first-rate. The only hitch was that Scotland Yard found out about it. Many of the Irish agents set out for Ulster, but hardly any returned from their journey. The ever-dwindling army of spies finally was faced with the choice of making the trip against overwhelming odds, or remaining in relative safety in England; most of them took the prudent course. And the German Consul in Dublin wondered why no one came to see him.

The enthusiasm of Herr Ott's reports must have flagged. At any rate, he no longer spoke so cheerfully of his personal acquaintances in Tokyo.

He did not admire the Japanese espionage system as much as had his chief, Rudolf Hess. And his opinion of the Japanese was quite at odds with that of Professor Haushofer. He felt that the Japanese were deficient in imagination and creative spirit. And that meant that in the field of espionage they did not exercise the best judgment.

By now Ambassador Ott had begun to find out—and he made no secret of his discovery—that Japanese spies were persistently being victimized. They paid enormous sums for statistical works and other material which they could have bought for a few yen in any book store. You had only to hint that it was confidential information. They could not distinguish between important and worthless information, between a vital plan and a minor suggestion. They used up not only great sums of money but a great many agents, and made little progress in the countries where progress counted.

Moreover, their racial traits and their reputation as spies meant a great initial handicap. For example, it was impossible for them to get jobs in an arsenal, a naval dockyard, or at any plant working on vital strategic projects. And any foreign person working on such jobs who was seen to associate with Japanese immediately became suspect and subject to investigation.

What particularly troubled Ott was that the Japanese could get not a scrap of information out of Russia. It may properly be assumed that from the summer of 1940 on, the Germans sent ever more urgent requests for material on the Soviet Union. This question will be discussed later, as well as Ott's opportunities to satisfy his Berlin superiors.

In brief, Ott was none too well off. He was getting an enormous quantity of information, but its quality was miserable. Therefore, in the early part of 1941, he decided on a new form of collaboration. It resembled the collaboration that Himmler's assistant, Heydrich, had worked out in Italy. Ott decided to do his own organizing and not to depend upon the Japanese system. And he was through with asking for the information he needed, he was going to demand it. Or else....

He reorganized his apparatus quite as though he were in the country of a potential enemy instead of an ally. He increased the Embassy staff to two hundred and fifty persons. He had the Embassy guarded day and night by storm troopers with hand grenades. He called a meeting of the hundred and thirty-eight newspaper correspondents whom Goebbels had sent to Japan and arranged that these correspondents should report to him, the Ambassador, instead of to their newspapers. (Incidentally, there were only about twelve correspondents of British and American newspapers and news agencies in Tokyo.)

He sent for technicians and specialists, as well as pilots and engineers, from Germany and settled them in the Japanese Air Force, the Japanese war industries, and the Japanese Army. He organized the tourists, waiters, and chambermaids. He set up a short-wave station on the roof of the Embassy.

And then he resolved to do something himself about the Russian matter. He sent one of his best men, Guenther Friedrich Kaufmann, to Shanghai. Kaufmann was to get in touch with White Russian circles there. He was to convince these circles that Hitler intended to restore the Czarist regime in Russia. Vladimir Romanoff, the son of Grand Duke Cyril and the great-nephew of the last Czar, was to become the new Czar.

Herr Kaufmann, who had been very efficient in Tokyo, was not so efficient in Shanghai. Perhaps it was his weakness for hard drink. While drunk he talked too much. Among other things, he remarked that Japan was full of Russian spies; that every member of the large Communist Party of Japan spied for the Soviet Union. For every Communist the police dispatched, ten new Communists sprang up. On the other hand, the Japanese couldn't manage to smuggle their agents into the Soviet Union. And Kaufmann added that his chief, Herr Ott, was very much disturbed by this, because Berlin was clamouring for more information on Russia.

It is doubtful that Herr Kaufmann got much useful information in Shanghai. The White Russians did not take to him, for though they hated Stalin, they had no love for the Nazis and did not trust them.

Herr Kaufmann was not the only failure. The efforts of German espionage to smuggle agents into the Soviet Union from Central Europe and the Balkans also failed. And when there was an occasional success, the agent was never heard from again. The few who were heard from had no information of value. For it is apparent that the German General Staff did not have correct intelligence on Russia when it began its Russian attack on 21 June 1941.

Had Colonel Nicolai failed?

Someone had failed. Somewhere in the espionage machine a wrench had been thrown into the works. There is no other explanation for the sense of uncertainty that pervaded leading German circles immediately after the outbreak of the Russian war. This feeling was in sharp contrast to the cocksureness they had felt before the invasion of Belgium, Holland, and France. Perhaps it was because Rudolf Hess was no longer there to lead the Liaison Staff.

STORY OF A STRANGE FLIGHT

On the evening of 10 May 1941, Rudolf Hess took off from the field of the Messerschmitt plant at Augsburg, Bavaria, in a new type of reconnaissance plane. He did not choose the most direct route to Dungavel Castle, the estate of the fourteenth Duke of Hamilton, but one which avoided German air patrols. A few thousand feet above his goal he bailed out. He was found with a broken ankle, covered by his parachute.

The world was stunned. After all, Hess was the leader of the National Socialist Party, second only to Hitler, and was supposed to become the Führer in case of Hitler's and Göring's death. On the other hand, he had not played a big role since Hitler had come to power, not at all a role equal to his position within the Party, and not to be compared with the roles played by Göring, Goebbels, Ribbentrop, Ley. He had almost disappeared into the background. Occasionally you saw his picture, the picture of a tall man of athletic build, with an angular face, a hard mouth, square jaw, with dark hair and heavy, bushy eyebrows. But you heard little about him.

Why, then, had he gone to Scotland?

Immediately, every sort of rumour sprang up. Some said that Hess had fled from the Nazis, either because he thought they were doomed, or because he did not like the treaty with Russia, or because he was having personal difficulties with the Gestapo. From Germany came the news that Hess was mentally unbalanced, and that he had taken off evidently without knowing what he was doing. It did not diminish the general confusion when no official statement about the Hess affair was given out either by the British Government or by the Führer. For some time it seemed as though nobody really knew exactly why Hess had taken off for Scotland.

In London a few men knew. But not the members of the British Cabinet. Only the officials of B4 knew why Hess had come. As to the rest of the world, it was completely in the dark about the real facts behind the flight. Even the FBI, which at that time had established excellent sources abroad, did not learn the story before the end of June.

It all started with those letters, supposedly from members of the English Link movement, sent to Berlin via Lisbon. It was with a view to Nazi psychology that those letters had been composed. During the spring of 1941 they had become more and more urgent. They left not the slightest doubt that the Nazis had many potential friends in England who were eager to collaborate. Again and again the letters insisted that all that was needed was a signal. Some grand gesture to break the ice. Some act that would start the thing going.

An act. It needed no more than this word to decide men like Rudolf Hess. After all, the original, simon-pure Nazis preferred deeds to cautious consideration. That is how they had started the beer-cellar *putsch*. That is how they had disposed of the inner opposition. That is how they had overwhelmed Europe.

Hess had acted before 10 May ... about three weeks earlier when he visited General Franco in Madrid. During this visit, on 22 April—a visit which was first officially commented on and then officially denied by the Nazis—he started putting out feelers. Perhaps he even intended to talk over the whole question with the British Ambassador, Sir Samuel Hoare. There are some who say he did talk to Hoare, but, as was later proved beyond doubt, no such conversation took place.

Hess tried something much more picturesque. He got in touch with the Commander of Gibraltar and proposed to come to Gibraltar to discuss a matter of importance. The Commander, who had not been informed by the gentlemen of B4 in London what it was all about, replied that if Hess appeared at Gibraltar, he would have him shot.

Thereupon, Hess sent one of his two personal adjutants to Lisbon. The adjutant took a room in the Avenida Palace, the international hotel near the railway station, where most Americans stay. There was a conversation at the bar of the Avenida Palace, a second one later on in the lobby of the Hotel Metropole on the Rossio Square, and finally a third at the Café Chiado, in the Rua Garett. That same night the adjutant flew back to Madrid. He was able to give an interesting report to the Deputy Führer.

So much the gentlemen of B4 knew. Still, nobody could have been more astonished than they, when instead of some minor official for whom they had laid the trap, Rudolf Hess himself fell into it.

That was when Mr Winston Churchill entered the picture. The Prime Minister did not remain mystified very long. During the very night when Hess was arrested, he received a visit from two men of B4. The conference was a short one. According to the few well-informed persons, it ended somewhat abruptly when Winston Churchill flew into such a fit of rage that the intelligence men retired hastily.

What had got Winston Churchill so excited was not the fact that there were a number of men in England who even in the midst of the war were still corresponding with the Nazis and trying to overthrow his government. After the Link business and after other similar experiences, the old sceptic did not need the arrival of Hess to convince him that such men existed. It was only when the B4 officials told him that those letters had been written by their agents, and that none of the people whose names were used knew anything about them, that the fireworks started.

Of course Churchill would never have given his approval to such a dangerous game. Now, when he considered the situation, he could not help but see certain possibilities. And he would not have been Winston Churchill had he not taken a hand in the game. He first had stated that he himself would interview Hess. Now he decided against it. Hess must be made to believe that the conspiracy was still going on, in spite of his arrest and, of course, behind Churchill's back. And so Ivone Augustine Kirkpatrick went to Scotland to see Hess. Kirkpatrick, after a diplomatic career in Rio de Janeiro, Rome, and the Vatican, had been in Berlin from 1933 to 1938, starting as First Secretary in the British Embassy and later as chargé d'affaires. He knew Hess very well. Needless to say, he had no idea how many letters he had written to Hess lately—before B4 informed him.

In any case, the British gave full publicity to Kirkpatrick's conversation with Hess, which could easily have been kept secret. Then, a few days later, Kirkpatrick flew to Ireland. This trip was also mentioned in the press, although in wartime the movements of important personages are not usually made public. The newspapers even spoke of a mission. In Dublin, Kirkpatrick, armed with a letter from Hess, met with members of the German Embassy. This has definitely been confirmed by reliable British sources.

Of course, since the message was coded, nobody—neither the British Secret Service nor Kirkpatrick—could be quite sure what. Hess had written.

And what was happening in the meantime in Berlin?

The men in London and in Washington who know the whole story know, of course, only how the trap was set and how it was sprung. But since, after Hess's visit to Madrid, there was never any sign of hesitation on the part of the Nazis, it may be assumed that the Führer had approved of the whole fantastic plan. At least that is what the men in London and Washington think.

Colonel Nicolai must have known about the project weeks, maybe months before. He must have known about the exchange of letters via Lisbon. Off-hand one would say that the entire scheme was not made to order for the mind of a Prussian officer. But after all, the Nazi mind was in control of the Liaison Staff.

And no matter how Colonel Nicolai, how Canaris and the rest of the officers and the representatives of the War Ministry in the Liaison Staff felt about the Hess adventure, they must have consented at last. Because, as later events proved, they were waiting for Hess to send them a certain sign. And when it came, they acted.

There must have been a few days of panic in the Liaison Staff when for some time Hess was not heard from at all, and when at last it came out that he was in the hands of the British Government. But even in those panicky days, the Nazis never lost their heads, and everything they did in connection with the Hess flight served only one purpose. No matter how contradictory their explanations were, they were all intended to prevent Churchill from finding out why Hess really had come and what he was trying to accomplish.

If one views the German statements after the Hess flight from this angle, they become completely logical. It was excellent psychology not to make any statements at all in the beginning, thereby creating the impression that Hess had taken off without the permission or even the knowledge of the Führer. When it was finally declared that Hess was mentally ill, this again seemed to prove that Hitler was surprised at Hess's flight. When it was hinted that Hess's wife and his intimate friends had been arrested, the impression was strengthened that Hitler believed Hess to be disloyal.

In short, Berlin did everything possible to confuse the issue. That was not without danger, since not only the world at large was confused, but the German population as well. Which made it necessary for Dr Goebbels to organize hurriedly a house-to-house canvass to quiet the apprehensive Germans.

Berlin must have been delighted when the first rumours sprang up that Hess had 'talked'; when the world fell for the story that Hess no longer could stand the pro-Russian policies of Hitler. So Hess had talked? The more he talked, the better. The more rumours, the better. Nobody would think of the real motives for the flight.

One must admit that the British played their cards cleverly. On 5 June, Sir Stafford Cripps, British Ambassador to Russia, left Moscow and went to Stockholm. Three days later it was rumoured in Stockholm that Cripps probably would not go to London but would make his report to the Foreign Office direct from Stockholm and then return to Moscow. There must have been a good deal of laughter in Berlin circles. They were not going to be caught by such a stupid trick. They knew that if any important secret negotiations were under way, Cripps would never have left Moscow. And they were not at all surprised, were, in fact, delighted when a few days later, on 15 June, word came from London that Cripps would not return to Moscow at all.

On 22 June, Hitler marched. That was three and a half weeks after Kirkpatrick's visit to Dublin.

And then Berlin waited in breathless suspense. Would there be a revolution in Scotland? Would Churchill fall? For twenty-four hours the suspense lasted. Then Churchill spoke.

And then Berlin knew that Rudolf Hess had fallen into a trap and that a great gamble had been lost. The first major defeat of the German espionage machine was a *fait accompli*.

FBI

The fight for the United States continued. In the summer of 1940 drills were held at the Bund Camp in Andover, N.J. Five of the men who had taken part in these drills returned to their jobs at Picatinny Arsenal—the biggest in the United States. Twelve held positions in the National Guard. Three were at the Hercules Powder plant in Kenvil.

On 12 September 1940, there was an explosion at the Hercules Powder Company at Kenvil, NJ. There were 52 victims, 50 wounded. That same week there was a blast at the Picatinny Arsenal. Two dead.

25 September 1940: Explosion at the Pennsylvania Industrial Chemical Company at Clairton, near Pittsburgh, PA.

5 October 1940: Explosion and fire at a chemical plant in Terre Haute, Indiana.

30 October 1940: Fire destroyed part of the new War Department Building at Washington. Near the burned buildings was the headquarters of the Signal Corps, which sends code messages. As a result of this fire, documents belonging to the Secret Service were damaged or threatened with destruction.

11 November 1940: Fire destroyed about $200,000 worth of military equipment stored in a wing of the Atlanta Auditorium.

12 November 1940: In less than fifty minutes three formidable explosions occurred at Woodbridge, NJ. Two buildings of the United Railway and Signal Corporation were destroyed. The plant was making torpedoes for the government. At Newcastle, PA an explosion destroyed the village of Edinburgh and the Burton Powder Works of the American Cyanamid and Chemical Corp. At Allentown, PA there was an explosion at the plant of the Trojan Powder Co.

17 November 1940: Explosion at Bridgeville, near Pittsburgh, destroying half of a large building of the American Cyanamid and Chemical Corp. This was the third explosion in this company's factory in a week.

22 November 1940: Explosion destroyed the huge refinery No. 4 of the Lion Oil Refining Co. at Eldorado, Arkansas.

28 November 1940: Explosion destroyed a warehouse at Yakima, Washington.

28 November 1940: Explosion destroyed the factory of the Dupont Company of Tacoma, Wash., where black powder was stored.

20 November 1940: A fire at Los Angeles destroyed a factory making aircraft parts.

2 December 1940: Explosion of a ton of dynamite at Tacoma, Wash.

13 December 1940: A huge reservoir containing 10,000 gallons of gasoline blew up at the Canton (Ohio) Oil Refining Company.

14 December 1940: Fire at the Oil Refinery of the Southport Petroleum Company, Texas City, Texas.

30 March 1941: United States authorities took possession of thirty ships of the European Axis powers lying in American ports. Twenty-seven had been put out of commission. There was no doubt about sabotage.

31 May 1941: A fire on the New Jersey waterfront destroyed $25,000,000 worth of warehouses, freight cars, docks, livestock, food supplies, including material destined for Great Britain.

1 June 1941: At the Boeing Aircraft Plant at Vancouver, BC the centre portion of the assembly plant and the administration building were destroyed by fire.

2 June 1941: A four-motored Consolidated Bomber being prepared for delivery to England crashed in the San Diego Bay. The controls had jammed. A spokesman for Consolidated stated that they had been tampered with.

4 August 1941: At the Majestic Tool and Manufacturing Corporation in Detroit about four hundred micrometers and other precision instruments were stolen. Since this robbery greatly delayed and endangered the manufacture of machine tools for defence industry, an official declared that sabotage was more than likely.

12 August 1941: Saboteurs poured sand into the oil-cups of the powerhouse machinery in the American Brake Shoe and Foundry Company in Mahwah, NJ. The plant was producing railway castings, aerial bomb casings, and other defence material, especially test bombs ordered directly by the War Department.

Walter Winchell wrote that after the New Jersey waterfront fire you could hear in the streets of Yorkville: 'That was our answer to the closing of Camp Nordland.'

It was generally assumed that the fire was a result of sabotage.

But the official statement of the FBI did not mention sabotage. Official statements must be cautious, of course. Naturally, sabotage could not be proved a few days after the fire, unless someone made a confession. In the case of the Hercules Powder Company explosion there was also no official insinuation of sabotage. Explosions of this kind have one characteristic in common: their origin is extremely difficult to determine. In the famous case of the Black Tom explosion the evidence was not forthcoming for ten years.

The FBI declared there was no evidence of sabotage in the New Jersey fire. But that statement was for the record. As to the private opinion of J. Edgar Hoover and his men, that might be another story.

They had expected something of the sort. On the day of the New Jersey fire they had received information which enabled them to safeguard many factories, bridges, warehouses, etc. in the United States by increasing the number of guards.

The FBI would be likely to declare that there was no evidence of sabotage because it abstains from making accusations which it cannot fully prove. But this does not mean the FBI was blind to what it was fighting, and to the weapons of its unscrupulous adversary.

J. Edgar Hoover had known for a long time that with the war the number of German agents in the United States had increased constantly, and that not a day passed without new agents filtering in. He knew, too, where these agents were located. For one thing it was plain that in spite of the war and the cutting off of travel to Germany, the Hamburg-America Line and North German Lloyd had both increased their personnel. In Chicago they had even had to rent new and larger quarters. And the German

Railroad Information office had also hired new men throughout the country.

The FBI knew—as the State Department informed the Senate Judiciary Committee on 16 June 1941—that in this Second World War there were more spies and saboteurs in the United States than there had been during the First World War.

And there was scarcely a day when these spies and saboteurs stood idle. Assistant Attorney General Thurman Arnold declared he had proof that the Axis was thoroughly informed about all defence plans and all ship movements 'through dummy marine and fire insurance companies operating in the United States.'

And Representative Dies secured sensational material which proved that the Bund was to be a kind of vanguard for Hitler's Blitzkrieg.

The events in Camp Nordland had shown only too clearly how right he was. 'That was our answer to the closing of Camp Nordland,' the Yorkville Nazis had said after the Jersey fire.

The State Police had come to Camp Nordland the day before the fire. When they were seen approaching, a Bund member, Paul Huissel, hurried to one of the rooms to tear up certain papers. It developed that Huissel was an American citizen who had emigrated from Germany fourteen years before.

The bits of paper, which the G-men pasted together, listed addresses of Bund members and of German consuls. Huissel, a Nazi by conviction, was asked by one of the G-men why he had become naturalized. His answer was typical: 'As a citizen I can talk freely and say anything I want without fear,' he said. 'If I had not become a citizen I would be subject to alien laws.'

And talking freely was not the only thing a citizen could do with less risk than an alien. Spying also was easier for a citizen than for an alien....

J. Edgar Hoover had for years anticipated a general attack on the United States by the German espionage and sabotage machine. He had been working day and night to improve the defence apparatus of the United States. In recent years literally hundreds of conferences with local police forces throughout the United States had taken place.

For some time the FBI had been instructing local policemen in scientific methods of fighting espionage, sabotage, and all other threats to national defence. The most modern methods for protecting great industries against sabotage were studied and taught. The whole thing was on a national basis.

President Roosevelt had played a decisive role in this development. He had seen to it that all information on espionage, counterespionage, sabotage, subversive activities, and violations of the neutrality laws were forwarded to the FBI. The co-operation of local police authorities with the FBI was a voluntary matter because there were no laws to bind them. But the voluntary basis was sufficient.

All this was covered by the 'FBI Law Enforcement Officers' Mobilization Plan for National Defence.' The army at Hoover's command through this co-operation amounted to 150,000 men.

Assisting Hoover was his trusted old associate, Hugh M. Clegg, assistant director of the FBI, who had taken over the leadership of the National Defence Investigation Unit.

Mr Clegg was not only an extremely competent official in national affairs, but one who appreciated the necessity for international co-operation in counterespionage. Therefore, early in 1941 he went to England, where he had conferences with Scotland Yard officials to discuss closer co-operation in counterespionage.

A further provision for co-operation was contained in secret clauses of the Act of Havana (22 July 1940), which dealt with joint protection against direct or indirect invasion. This act provided for a permanent exchange of information pertaining to counterespionage among the nations of the hemisphere.

On 16 June 1941 the United States struck its first great blow against the German espionage machine.[11] In a note to the German *chargé d'affaires* in Washington the United States ordered the closing of all twenty-four German consulates, as well as the German Library of Information, the German Railroads Information Office and the Transocean News Service. The reason given was 'activities of an improper and unwarranted character.' Mr Sumner Welles did not go into details; he merely said that the agencies closed had acted in a manner 'inimical to the welfare of this country.'

This step made an international stir, for it was recognized everywhere as the preliminary before the official diplomatic break. Nor was it the last step.

Perhaps the FBI had had something to do with the closing of the German consulates. Now it struck again. At the end of June it arrested twenty-nine persons whom it accused of spying for Germany and the Axis. The FBI had followed some of these persons for more than two years, slowly and patiently gathering evidence of espionage. Their patience was indeed rewarded as was proved during the trial against some members of the spy ring which opened on 3 September 1941, in Brooklyn. Some of the G-men had even posed as German spies, sending radio messages to Germany which contained information of no value, military or otherwise. The story of their activities and of the credulity of some of the Nazi spies was reminiscent more of a musical comedy than of a serious plot. But it was a serious plot. Some of the arrested persons were employed by the American shipping lines engaged in traffic to Europe and to South America. Some of them were even employed in plants manufacturing equipment vital to the national defence. They had not sent their information directly to Germany, but to South American German consulates and other intermediaries. The Little Casino

Bar Restaurant in Yorkville had been their chief meeting place. J. Edgar Hoover declared, 'This is one of the most active, extensive and vicious groups we have ever had to deal with.'

Among the prisoners was the brother of James Wheeler-Hill, who for a while had been the Führer of the Bund—in the interlude between the arrest and conviction of Fritz Kuhn and his own arrest and conviction.

The leader of the espionage ring was, according to the FBI, Frederick Joubert Duquesne,[12] a Frenchman, born in Cape Colony. He was sixty-three, had fought against England during the Boer War, and had spent his whole life as a spy against England. He was an old agent of Colonel Nicolai's, who must have been deeply affected by his arrest. During the First World War he had lived in South America. While there he is said to have planted bombs on British ships, which then exploded in mid-ocean and sank without a trace.

During the next few days more persons implicated in the plot were arrested. And since then many more persons suspected of working as German spies, though not within the big spy ring, have been detained. The last one (before this book went to press) was a German-born car washer by the name of Euke Hard Dierken, who was charged with having tipped off the German authorities about the movements of British ships.

But perhaps more important than the arrest of these few agents was the fact that the United States authorities did not attempt to gloss over who bore the real guilt. 'Although no legal action is contemplated against that Government, it would have been a sham and a pretence not to have named the Reich,' an official of the Department of Justice explained when the German Government was officially denounced as a conspirator in a world-wide espionage scheme against the United States. This was on 15 July 1941.

A week later, on 22 July, the Senate passed the anti-spy bill for the navy, 41 to 14. Previously Senator David I. Walsh, Chairman of the Naval Affairs Committee, had given an account of many hitherto unknown acts of sabotage in the navy. He declared among other things that the headquarters of espionage against the navy was located in San Francisco. Of those employed at the Mare Island Navy Yard, some four hundred men were suspected. The bill authorized the expenditure of one million dollars for a secret detective force to combat espionage in the navy. Soon afterwards the City of New York prohibited the use of cameras by passengers on Staten Island Ferry boats.

The closing of the German consulates dealt a heavy blow to the effective functioning of the German espionage apparatus. But it did not destroy it.

During the First World War things had been different. Once the hands of von Papen, von Rintelen, and von Ribbentrop had been tied, the German espionage machine in the United States was smashed. The numerous pro-

German German-Americans of that period were not sufficiently organized to take over the helm; and probably they never would have been amenable to such organization. For at that time they were split up into the most various allegiances and party factions, like the Germans living in all other countries.

This was the essential difference between then and 1941. The Nazis would permit no splits among the German-Americans. They were all organized, and they all had to fulfil their assigned tasks. The apparatus of the AO was so designed that the functionaries, particularly those who directed espionage and sabotage, occupied no official positions. Group leaders were simply private persons, almost always American citizens, engaged in some respectable trade or profession: doctors, businessmen, engineers.

There was no reason why their work should be impaired by the closing of the consulates. Instead of sending their material to the consulates, they could send it to the Ambassador. And if this was out of the question, there were still the Italian Ambassador, the Japanese Ambassador, and the ambassadors and envoys of France, Spain, and some occupied countries. Finally, they were still in touch with the German legations and consulates in South and Central America (with whom they could also communicate through coded short-wave messages). And there were also the Foreign Office Gestapo agents stationed in the southern part of the hemisphere.

The strength of the German espionage apparatus lay in its ability to shift from legality to illegality at a moment's notice. The experiences of the World War, in particular the von Papen affair had shown Colonel Nicolai, Ludendorff, and the whole German General Staff that it was too risky to put all their eggs in one basket. It had also shown them that in the long run no good would come of espionage work carried on or directed by diplomatic officials.

Legal and illegal, above ground and underground—this double game was the secret of the German espionage machine. On the one hand the embassies, consulates, and the entire official personnel; on the other hand the almost unknown AO. This was the reason why this espionage machine was so hard to detect, and even harder to destroy. For the machine was so flexible that the loss of a single part was no loss; a spare part was at hand to fill the gap.

The only action that could put down this total machine was total annihilation.

To be sure, Washington had not progressed so far by the summer of 1941. The AO had not yet been attacked; the representatives of the German Labour Front had not been touched; the Hitler Youth, the teachers' association and the innumerable other German organizations still went unscathed.

And neither had German journalists been touched. There were quite a few of them in the United States, receiving disproportionately high salaries and exceedingly high expense accounts. Not much is heard about them because they deliberately avoid the limelight, or any contact with even the most casual legitimate sources of a newspaper man's information. Just to name a few: Rudolf Mattfeldt in Washington; Paul Scheffer, Margret Boveri, August Halfeld, and Herbert Gross in New York; not to speak of a couple of entirely phony, so-called movie correspondents in Hollywood.

The Japanese consulates were still open, and one need not be unduly perspicacious to guess that German espionage made use of them. Informed sources knew as early as June, 1941 that the number of Germans one ran into at the Japanese Consulate General in New York was constantly growing. We can, of course, only guess as to how far the co-operation of the Axis partners went in this respect. But there is little doubt that until their funds were frozen, the Japanese had to 'finance' German espionage; that steady communication went on between Japanese official representatives and the heads of German espionage—not necessarily direct, however; they could always work through the Japanese businessmen in the big cities of the United States.

Furthermore, it is probable that the many Japanese shipping offices and agencies now went to work for the Germans—not only in the United States, but also wherever in South America the Germans were being watched closely.

The same thing goes for the Spanish Falangists who are doing propaganda and espionage work for the Nazis not only in Latin American countries, but in the United States as well. Lately they have become extremely cautious in order to avoid 'publicity.'

And how many openings German espionage still possesses in the United States—at least at the time this book is being written! With how many persons does it keep in closest touch, persons whom no one would suspect of earning their living as spies?

Shadows of the last World War. It is strange, how all the clues remind one of the First World War. The spies... the sabotage.... In the last war there was even an organization financed by von Papen and headed by his stooges: the National Labour Peace Council. This organization wanted to keep America out of the war.

There are so many parallels....

In September 1940 a mass meeting was held in Chicago sponsored by what seemed to be reputable American organizations. Its purpose was to keep America out of the war and the chief speaker was none other than Charles Lindbergh. After months of painstaking investigation it has now been established that the prime mover behind the 'American patriotic rally' was one Ernest Ten Eycken, and that this man was an official of the *Einheitsfront*, a powerful clandestine Nazi organization in Chicago. But few people knew that Ten Eycken is also connected with the engineering firm of H. A. Brassert & Co., of Chicago and New York. The man for whom this firm is named is Herman Alexander Brassert,[13] incidentally an American citizen born in England of German parents. He is the man behind the *Hermann* Göring *Werke*—the huge combine of steel plants that Hitler's Number 2 man acquired through the simple device of confiscations and 'gifts' of shares. Brassert, one of Göring's closest advisers and confidants, is also the head of a dummy Berlin corporation in which the wily *Reichsmarschall* has concealed a goodly portion of his personal fortune from the prying eyes of his rival—Gestapo Chief Heinrich Himmler.

Brassert, then, who directs the German steel industry also maintains a large American organization. Known to be among America's foremost steel engineering firms, this organization, entrenched in defence projects, knows details of vital American defence secrets....

Keep America out of the war. Of whom does that remind us?

Strangely enough, of Walter H. Schellenberg, the head of the AO in the United States, little was heard. Around the middle of July, 1941, a warrant for his arrest had been sworn out by the immigration authorities. It could not be served, however, because Herr Schellenberg could not be found. Not until 21 July were his whereabouts divulged. He had left on board the *West Point* for Lisbon on 15 July. On the official list of those who had departed on the *West Point*, which was given out by the State Department six days after the *West Point* sailed, Schellenberg was listed on Page 7—an official of the German Consulate General in New York. The State Department was asked why he had been given diplomatic status. It replied that the German Embassy had claimed he was a consular financial expert on the Dawes and Young loans.

So Herr Schellenberg had left, together with Kurt Rieth and the employees of Transocean and all the German consuls. Needless to say, he had never had anything to do with the Dawes and Young loans.

But hadn't he always' insisted that he was an American citizen? Perhaps he had lied. Or perhaps he was an American citizen and nevertheless....

Whatever the case, he is no longer among us. The last time Walter H. Schellenberg was seen in public was on Friday, 22 March 1941, in New York City. He was sitting on the platform in Madison Square Garden at the big Lindbergh-Wheeler rally of the America First Committee. On the platform!

He smiled benignly throughout the proceedings, and occasionally waved a small American flag.

THE UNKNOWN SOLDIERS OF ESPIONAGE

I don't think that Colonel Walther Nicolai is sleeping very well these nights. Perhaps, after all, it had been Rudolf Hess who assured the smooth functioning of the entire espionage system, who had unified the work of the many heterogeneous elements.

During the first weeks of the Russian war there were many rumours about arrests and suicides of prominent Nazis. These reports were quickly denied. The rumours themselves do not matter; the significant thing is that such rumours could arise. The atmosphere had changed. Confidence had vanished and a sense of nervousness had become widespread. The reaction of the world to these rumours of suicide and arrest was that the men concerned—Göring, Haushofer, Udet—had warned against the Russian campaign and thereby had incurred Hitler's anger. This seems illogical. It is probable that they incurred Hitler's anger (whether they were arrested or not) because they had not given warning. In other words, because they were not correctly informed.

The Russian adventure itself (no matter how it ends) was handicapped from the start by the lack of reliable and complete military intelligence. Compared to the information which had been available before the invasions of Holland, Belgium, France, and the others, it was really a plunge into the dark. Even Hitler admitted that in his speech of 3 October 1941. 'We had no idea how gigantic the preparations of this enemy were...,' he said.

Worse still, German espionage agents working in the Soviet Union were no longer heard from after the war began. With good reason. They had been shot on the first day of the war. The world at large did not hear this until August, when Moscow released the news....

And so, while the German Army for the first time was marching into the unknown, into a country which had not been initially conquered by total espionage, in the West and the North incomprehensible and unpleasant events were taking place.

Especially in France, the counterespionage apparatus which was in the hands of the Gestapo, proved inadequate. How disastrous the situation must have become is indicated by the fact that by the beginning of August the entire counterespionage in the occupied territories was taken out of the hands of the Gestapo and turned over to the War Ministry, that is, the army. This was first revealed on 21 August, when six thousand 'Jews' were arrested in Paris. The Commander of Paris, General Heinrich von Stuelpnagel, was mentioned casually in the press as the director of the action. While he was 'acting,' there was a great deal of quarrelling backstage as to who was to blame. Heinrich Himmler is said to have considered a purge of the Gestapo agents working in France. At the same time he demanded the recall of Otto Abetz to 'explain' the anti-Nazi sentiments of the French.

And day and night, more and more British bombers dropped their charges over the occupied territories and the cities of Germany. Could chance have led them to the spots where they dealt the severest blows to Germany? Why were they firing storehouses that had just been filled with munitions? Why were they destroying factories which were making a delicate and vital aircraft part? Why were they striking at the very railway lines which were at the moment so sorely needed for bringing up supplies to the new front? Were the British so confoundedly lucky, or had the ever-broadening base of the German machine made it more vulnerable?

During these days it must have seemed to Colonel Nicolai that all Europe had become one vast counterespionage organization.

I don't think that Colonel Walther Nicolai is sleeping very well these nights. And I believe I can guess what he is thinking while he lies awake at night, or what he dreams in his troubled sleep.

Simple children's drawings. Toy balloons. Church bells. Schoolchildren counting the cars in a train and the number of trains. A cripple's wooden leg.

For Colonel Nicolai must surely be thinking of Belgium, these last months—the Belgium of 1914 to 1918; of the Belgium that hated the German Army of Occupation; the Belgium which invented a thousand new devices for informing the Allies about the movements of German troops, about their plans, their strength and their weaknesses.

Toy balloons bearing important messages which a favourable wind carried to the French trenches. Silly child's scribblings and drawings which were really a complex code. Hundreds, thousands of schoolchildren standing near the railway tracks, counting the trains and cars so that the Allied Command might have precise information about the disposition of German troops. Thousands of devices which could spring only from the minds of a people filled with rage and defiance. The years between 1914 and 1918 were a nightmare for Colonel Nicolai.

And now—now it must seem to him as if the same thing were happening all over again. As if the old, forgotten anxiety dream were returning.

The German High Command had no illusions when for the second time in twenty-five years it invaded the small, defenceless, neutral countries. It could not fail to know that the population of these countries would not receive the conquerors with open arms. It had to reckon with hatred, violence, and passive resistance. Perhaps it had not reckoned with quite so much hatred, but even at that the problem was not too difficult. An unarmed people, a people without an army, without fortifications, a people whose women and children were always at the mercy of the enemy's guns—such a people were not a problem for the German Army. The Gestapo would take care of that.

The Gestapo could handle these people who refused to love the Germans; that was what the Gestapo was for.

The Gestapo lost no time in getting down to work. It moved into each newly occupied territory right with the German troops. The Gestapo did not shirk work. It did its best. But it had not reckoned on so much hatred and so much resistance.

In Poland, public hangings became a daily spectacle. The Gestapo agents no longer bothered to give reasons; they did not wait for trials or court martials. They strung their victims up.

In Czechoslovakia, resisters were shot. Stood up against the wall and shot. 'Restoration of order.' Any Czech brought before a military court on charges of murder, revolt, open violence, or serious property destruction could be either acquitted or sentenced to death. He was always sentenced to death.

In Norway, concentration camps. Torture. Starvation for those who closed their hearts to the Germans.

During September and October 1941 the executions in the occupied territory mounted terrifically. Lately, hardly a day has passed without hundreds of arrests and dozens of assassinations. Even the Nazis have admitted officially hundreds of executions. The true figure can only be guessed.

Nevertheless it was difficult to handle these strange foreigners. The punishments seemed to make no impression upon them. In Norway they became increasingly hostile, increasingly contemptuous. In Holland they wore insignia which had been forbidden. They allowed the Germans to rip these off their clothing, but they refused to take them off themselves. In Poland they formed bands which engaged in guerrilla warfare. In Athens they took the swastika flag down from the Acropolis. In France they became deaf and dumb and seemed not to notice when a German soldier spoke to them.

All this was none too pleasant. But it was not yet the worst. These people who would not like the German soldiers began to spy. Espionage! Aid to the enemy! Now the Gestapo threw its whole might into the struggle. Some culprits were found, convicted, sentenced.

Four Danish aviators were caught in a Berlin airport, about to take off for Portugal. Espionage. Fourteen years imprisonment. Still, Denmark was a friendly nation.

In Bergen, Norway, ten Norwegians were condemned to death and seven others given long prison terms because they had spied for England, sending some eighty military reports by radio to the British.

In the Hague forty Dutchmen were taken before a military court on charges of sabotage and giving information to the enemy. They were also charged with membership in a large organization which plotted espionage and sabotage.

The Vichy regime published a proclamation that any Frenchman who in any manner aided or attempted to aid a British flier would be condemned to death by a German military court.

In Munich eleven prominent Poles were tried for delivering military secrets to Great Britain. They had assisted more than one hundred pilots and technical specialists to escape from Nazi-occupied Poland via Romania to England. The Germans asserted that these men had carried with them vital military secrets.

In Amsterdam eighteen Dutchmen were sentenced to death by a German military court for espionage and sabotage.

In France the Nazis interned 24,000 British women and children under inhuman conditions because they hoped thereby to detect those who had been practising espionage in France. They were finally released when it was discovered that espionage activity had not diminished at all.

In Belgium a man of seventy years, together with his sixty-eight-year-old wife and their thirty-four-year-old daughter were sentenced to death without possibility of appeal for having sheltered a British flier who had crashed. The German military court declared that 'the humane motive put forward by the accused cannot be taken into consideration.'

In Yugoslavia, the Nazis were forced to shoot and hang thousands in order to prevent sabotage. Turkish sources have recently put the number of such executions at 80,000.

All over France the promises of money to be paid out to those who informed on saboteurs rose steadily. In one case of railway sabotage, the reward, which had been a hundred thousand francs in June 1941, was increased to one million francs in August. Not that it did any good.

In Czechoslovakia Himmler had a splendid idea. He created an office whose agents were to entrap young Czechs, promising to smuggle them out of the country to the Czechoslovak Army abroad. When a young Czech took the bait, he was immediately reported to the Gestapo.

But this office did not last long. Its agents were often attacked at night and badly beaten.

The Gestapo was soon forced to recognize that it was powerless. Here were people who not only refused to love the Germans, but who lost all fear of death after a short period of German rule. The cases of espionage and sabotage increased. It became more and more uncanny. The German authorities felt that they were sitting on a volcano.

Colonel Nicolai was not the only one who lost sleep during these months.

In 1916 Colonel Nicolai had tried to prevent espionage by forbidding the Belgians to move from town to town. For a time this helped, because the information that was gathered could not be delivered to the Allies.

Now, a similar step was taken in all occupied territories. No one was permitted to go even from one village to the next. In Slovakia, 20,000 gypsies were compelled to settle down in one place. For six hundred years they had been wanderers, but the Germans feared that in their roaming they would be able to secure and transmit information.

The restrictions on freedom of movement were even extended to Swiss and American consular officials.

All this had a strangely confusing and depressing effect on the Germans themselves. They no longer felt as secure as they had once felt. A kind of war of nerves was now being levelled against them, and this war of nerves was taking a toll. And as the restrictions on the populations in the occupied territories grew more severe, the work of the German garrisons increased. They had more work and they knew they were hated, and they began to realize that it was dangerous to go out in the streets alone, especially at night.

The German soldiers did not actually come down with nervous breakdowns—but every one of them felt clearly that things had taken a turn for the worse.

They were surrounded by spies. By spies who for some unknown reason appeared to be strong and invulnerable. It seemed as though these spies had something the Germans lacked. Yet they were really nothing but snipers, ambushers, contemptible stalkers in the night.

But the German soldiers could not summon up contempt for them. On the contrary, they seemed superior; and their stature seemed to grow daily.

And they were everywhere ... everywhere....

In Czechoslovakia they set up a secret radio which nightly sent valuable information to the British on developments behind the German lines.

In Holland they founded a secret society, 'The Beggars,' which passed a death sentence upon traitors to the Dutch cause and found ways and means to execute the guilty.

In Poland, every day saw new acts of sabotage by the armed guerrillas.

In Belgium, British agents who had landed by parachute and in small boats, were sheltered by the populace and assisted to escape.

In Bohemia a military train was stopped by fake signals and when the guard troops got out to stretch their legs, saboteurs crept aboard the train and cut the cables and bolts securing tanks on the flat cars.

In Czechoslovakia a munitions factory was blown up. The force of the explosion was felt sixty miles away, and the sky was lighted by the flames all night long.

Polish couriers repeatedly managed to make their way through the occupied territories to London to report to General Sikorski. Most of these couriers were girls who often arrived half dead of cold, with frostbitten fingers and toes.

In Northern France a matchbox-sized radio transmitter was built.

In Czechoslovakia there was a sharp upsurge in the number of railway accidents.

In Poland there was a secret newspaper. Dozens of times the German authorities proclaimed they had found the editors and the printing press. But the next day the newspaper appeared anew.

Saboteurs. Spies. Millions. All Europe was seething with them.

During those months the Nazis who had invented and constructed the machinery of the fifth column—Nicolai, Bohle, Himmler, Rosenberg, Goebbels—must have thought of the times when their own work was in its first stages. If the clock could be turned back, perhaps they would never have loosed this monster upon the world.

For the monster had turned against them. The peoples who had been betrayed by traitors within their own ranks, who had been overwhelmed by total espionage, had now themselves become a fifth column—a vast fifth column which was gripping Europe.

And this fifth column waited patiently for the other columns to march in through the gates—like General Mola's original fifth column in Madrid, instructed to wait until the other four columns were hammering at the gates of the city, and then to launch the war from within.

Now the other columns were already on the march. Or rather, they were on the wing, every night, and every day also; taking off from England, flying over the Continent and dropping their bombs. And these columns seemed to work very well with the great fifth column on the European Continent, for how else did the British always drop their bombs where they would hurt the Nazis most?

Spies. A continent of spies. Nicolai, Himmler, Goebbels, and the others must have wondered how something so powerful could arise without being organized; that it could stride on without a führer to guide it. That such a fifth column could spring spontaneously out of the earth overnight....

And now it spread out over Germany herself. The Nazis had lured or forced tens of thousands of Belgians, French, Poles, and Czechs to Germany and put them to work there. Perhaps that was a mistake. Perhaps the ever-increasing sabotage in the Reich was due to these aliens.

Or perhaps it was the opposition within Germany, the opposition which had gone underground eight years ago—buried but not dead. Perhaps the men of this opposition were responsible for the sabotage; perhaps they were partly responsible for the accuracy and the foreknowledge of the British bombers over Germany.

Spies. Everywhere. Europe was full of them.

On dark nights little English speedboats shot across the Channel, landed somewhere on the French or Belgian coast. IS agents sprang out, were met by a few men or women, held brief conversations, scribbled a few notes, nodded, and vanished once more into the night.

Airplanes fly over Holland. A man drops from the plane; a parachute blooms open. Slowly the parachute sinks down. A German guard hurries to the spot where it has landed. When he arrives he finds three Dutch peasants. One of them is without a jacket, one without a shirt, the third is without shoes or trousers. No, they insist, they saw no parachute descending.

Three German officers stop an automobile on the Champs Élysées in Paris. They order the driver to take them to a certain place in the city suburbs. A plane is standing ready, guarded by German soldiers. They get in and take off. Half an hour later the German guards learn that they have allowed three British agents to escape.

In Oslo and Trondheim and many small towns along the Norwegian coast, Norwegians keep their eyes open and remember all they can about the number and equipment of German soldiers, the type of planes, and so on. At night they tell their neighbour what they have learned, and he in turn tells his neighbour. Finally a fisherman gets the story, and then he rows out to sea. At sea he meets a motorboat; there is a short conversation and then he returns. If he is caught—firing squad. But few are caught.

Sometimes, too, a fishing boat sets sail with its hold crammed with young men who want to go to England and fight to liberate their country.

Concealed radio transmitters in Holland inform the RAF where to fly; inform them of troop concentrations, ammunition dumps, and camouflaged airfields.

In Belgium two soldiers are attacked at night in a deserted street and beaten to death. Their bodies are found the next morning, stripped. English agents are now wearing those uniforms.

Young Frenchmen hike through France during the night. They want to get to England, to de Gaulle. A few of them obtain a German 'E' boat and hurtle across the Channel, their flight covered by British planes.

In Czechoslovakia, fires suddenly break out in the vicinity of airfields lined with Heinkels and Messerschmitts.

In Poland another secret radio directs the British pilots. The day after the fliers had been there, the station came on the air again. There was a message congratulating the fliers, and the words: 'If you do not hear from us for a little while, do not worry, we will be back.'

In France, the Nazi authorities abandoned their practice of requisitioning a certain number of houses for their officers and men and forcing the inhabitants to leave within a few hours. The RAF seemed to have an uncanny knowledge of where those houses were. The Germans finally adopted the resort of quartering their men with French families; they were safer that way.

In Brittany the Germans arrested six priests who had helped British agents escape across the Channel in small boats.

During the raid on the Lofotens,[14] the British caught between ten and twenty ships, an extraordinary number. They must have had some very accurate information.

In Berck-sur-mer, in Northern France, forty British parachutists descended. They were awaited by French sympathizers, and British agents and taken to a near-by airport where they disposed of the few guards and destroyed thirty machines, took forty prisoners and recrossed the Channel again in motor torpedo boats which were waiting along the coast. All was carried out with the utmost precision.

Spies. Spies. The Nazi Army is surrounded by spies. It is encircled by espionage. The German advantage has been overcome. The ten years head start of total espionage has been overcome. Now the world knows. The world will not be taken by surprise any longer.

Counterespionage has become total.

Spies. Europe is full of spies. Today they are still there, fifth columnists lined up against the fifth column of the underworld.

Some day they will be soldiers. The Unknown Soldiers of tomorrow.

Chronology

1932

June: Formation of the Gestapo. Colonel Nicolai goes to Munich.

December: Hess becomes head of the political police of the Nazi Party.

1933

January: Hitler comes to Power.

February: Goebbels becomes Minister of Propaganda.

March: The OGPU arrests a number of Vickers engineers.

April: Foundation of the Nazi spy organization, the Friends of the New Germany, in New York.

May: Rosenberg visits London.

August: French engineer arrested on the way to Germany with the plans of the Maginot Line.

October: Saar Government protests to the League of Nations concerning German espionage in France.

November: German storm trooper sentenced by Czech court to four years' imprisonment for espionage.

December: Hess becomes Minister Without Portfolio.
Himmler appointed Chief of the Gestapo.

1934

February: Ernst Wilhelm Bohle becomes chief of the AO.

June: Hitler's blood purge. General Bredow, former espionage chief of the *Reichswehr*, killed.

July: Three German spies arrested in Metz, France.
Hess founds the Liaison Staff.

1935

February: Hitler assumes the right to invoke the death penalty in treason cases.

The French Government arrests Baron von Radowitz as a member of an international spy ring.

March: The Czech Government arrests three German students of Prague University on charges of spying for the Germans. At Brest the French Government arrests Lydia Oswald, a dancer, and a French naval officer. The dancer confesses that she has spied for Germany.

April: In Liège, Belgium, a Polish girl spy is arrested for selling military devices to German agents.

Four Czech officers and sixteen civilians arrested as members of a spy ring in Prague.

June: Ribbentrop goes to London as Ambassador Extraordinary. In Strasbourg, a barmaid is convicted as a German spy.

August: Non-commissioned officers of the Metz garrison in France arrested on charges of spying for Germany. Abetz starts his activities in France.

November: Twenty-eight persons in Prague, including a major in the Czech Army, arrested as part of a German spy ring. The Czechs accuse the Berlin radio of having tried to warn the conspirators.

Gold Shirt uprising in Mexico City suppressed.

In England Dr H. Gortz, a chemist, is arrested as a spy for Germany.

December: Four Belgians arrested in Liège for activities on behalf of Germany.

1936

March: Formation of the German-American Bund in the United States.

May: Election victory of Leon Degrelle, Belgian fascist leader and German agent.

German espionage headquarters discovered in Prague. Memel police report discovery of a spy plot financed by the German Consulate.

July: Three French socialites convicted of delivering military and diplomatic secrets to Germany.

Lieutenant Commander John S. Farnsworth arrested on charges of selling United States naval secrets to Japan. Harry Thomas Thompson convicted of espionage.

August: German Library of Information opened in New York.

September: Beginning of the German 'tourist' spy campaign.

October: German spies arrested in Barcelona.

November: Former German army lieutenant convicted in Paris of spying.

1937

February:	Bohle's organization included within the Foreign Office.
April:	Police uncover a German-Italian spy ring in Madrid. Fifty-five persons arrested.
May:	Senator Nye and Rep. Bernard charge a group of Spanish Nationalists with activities in the United States on behalf of Franco. Ask a Congressional investigation.
August:	Secret information service discovered in London, organized by the Nazis among journalists and domestics.
September:	*Cagoulard* uprising in France.
October:	Espionage conference of the Axis powers under the direction of the German, Italian, and Japanese Ministers in Mexico City.
November:	Dr Carmen Calero and accomplices are arrested in Mexico City for attempted sabotage and assassination.
December:	U.S. Navy acts to declare the California region between San Diego and Mexicali a proscribed area for plane flights. Move linked to Japanese espionage activities.
	United States authorities seize letters on the Japanese liner, *Tatsuta Maru*, and on three other vessels. Postal law violations alleged.
	Bill for the deportation of alien spies introduced in the U.S. Senate.

1938

February:	Ribbentrop becomes German Minister of Foreign Affairs. Spy ring in the U.S. Army bared. G. G. Rumrich and E. Glaser, soldiers, J. Hoffmann, a German hairdresser on the SS *Europa*, and Werner Voss, an aircraft mechanic, held in New York City. Passport frauds, attempts to obtain military secrets, and a plot to kidnap Colonel H. W. T. Eglin revealed. Psychological Laboratory starts work as an official part of the German War Ministry.
April:	French Government starts deporting undesirable aliens in order to stamp out espionage.
May:	Mrs. J. W. Jordan, member of a German spy ring operating in the United States and England, convicted in Scotland of violating the Official Secrets Act.
	Cedillo uprising, backed by German arms and money, in Mexico.
	German agent sentenced in France for helping a spy escape to Germany.

Espionage Chief Stohrer goes to Madrid as German Ambassador.

Green Shirts attempt uprising in Bolivia.

June: Theft of important documents from HMS *Osprey* (Great Britain).

July: Fritz Kuhn, führer of the German-American Bund, declares that spies ought to be shot.

August: H. Oldofredis, a German spy, expelled from Argentina.

October: Arnold Gingrich tells Congress that the German secret police have a United States espionage unit.

The Nazis take over the Foreign Bureau of the Spanish Falange.

Italian and German army personnel ousted from Canal Zone.

November: Germans and Danes arrested in Denmark for spying. Consul Von Pflugk-Hartung said to be the key man.

December: France limits permits for foreigners traveling in the Maginot Line zone.

Spanish Loyalist Government sentences two hundred spies to death. Press asks public to aid anti-spy campaign.

1939

January: Wiedemann is sent to San Francisco as German Consul.

Senator Smathers charges that German employees of United States consular offices are part of a spy system. Offers bill to end evil.

February: Holleuffer starts the Nazi Party in Mexico.

March: Mexican officials hold eight spies, mostly Germans, including Baron Holleuffer and P. Garbinsky.

Mexican press reports papers found on Garbinsky reveal operations against the United States and British Honduras.

Attorney General Murphy reports Federal Departments cooperating in anti-spy drive.

April: Documents are published in Buenos Aires on plot to organize Nazi espionage in Patagonia.

British try Irishman on charge of selling secret plans of arms plants to the Germans. German Consul in Liverpool involved.

Bill reported to House of Representatives increasing the penalty for peacetime espionage.

June: Attorney General Murphy announces special precautions at Pacific Coast aviation plants. Sabotage cited.

German spy ring in Belgium exposed.

French Premier Daladier exposes great German-French spy ring in Paris. Several French journalists arrested. Otto Abetz leaves Paris hastily. Baroness von Einem and Elizabeth Buettner escape.

July:	German circus clowns arrested as spies in Bucharest.
August:	U.S. Department of Justice sets up counterespionage offices in the Canal Zone, Puerto Rico, and Alaska.
September:	FBI reports on German-American Bund activities in the Philadelphia area. U. S. Army officers involved.
	Link, pro-German British organization, dissolved.
November:	Munich beer-cellar bombing. Hitler escapes assassination.
	Two operatives of the British Intelligence Service kidnapped from Holland by the Germans.

1940

January:	Councillor Roos of Alsace-Lorraine executed as German spy leader.
	Sabotage plot discovered in Great Britain to cripple railways, public works, communications, and bridges.
February:	Three German spies sentenced to death in France.
	Turkey dismisses German experts in defence industries.
	Netherlands army sergeant arrested in a round-up of persons alleged to have sent messages to Germany on ship departures.
	Uruguay tries to locate secret radio stations which are reporting movements of British warships to the Germans.
March:	First German woman spy executed in France.
April:	German journalist arrested in Stockholm as a spy.
	Two German spies killed under the Triumphal Arch in Bucharest.
	German espionage activities discovered in Yugoslavia.
May:	Professor von der Osten and four other Germans arrested as spies in Istanbul.
	Dr Westrick arrives in the United States.
	Sir Oswald Mosley arrested in Great Britain.
	German American Bund linked with news leakage of convoy departures from Canada.
June:	German-French spy ring arrested by Minister Georges Mandel in France.
	Nazi conspiracy in Uruguay discovered.
July:	Schleebrugge comes to Mexico.
August:	Westrick expelled from the United States.

September:	Series of sabotage acts in the United States begins with the explosion of the Hercules Powder Company plant in New Jersey.
October:	Heydrich takes over the OVRA.
November:	Dies reports his committee has evidence that Axis agents in the United States are working to sabotage aid to Britain.

1941

March:	In Santiago, Chile, Dr Kurt Rieth, Nazi spy chief, calls a conference of the German Ministers to Argentina, Chile, Peru, and Bolivia to organize further espionage activity in South America.
April:	Hess goes to Madrid to have a conference with Franco.
	Peru seizes the German airlines and closes Transocean News Agency.
May:	Hess flies to Scotland.
	Dr Kurt Rieth arrives in the United States.
	Arrest of German spies, Auhagen and Rieth, in the United States. Transocean News Service managers, Zapp and Tonn, also arrested in New York as Nazi agents.
June:	German spy ring in New York arrested.
July:	Closing of German consulates in the United States.
	Anti-spy bill for the U.S. Navy.
	Nazi plot in Bolivia discovered. German Minister Wendler expelled.
	Nazi plot in Argentina discovered.
August:	Nazi plot in Chile foiled.
	Nazi plot in Iran foiled.
	Argentina arrests 36 Nazi spies. The Argentine Congressional Committee charges that the German Embassy in Buenos Aires has trained and disciplined 45,000 Nazis.
September:	All German consulates in Mexico closed.
	Nazi spy trial opens in Brooklyn, New York
	Japan closes travel office in New York.
	French Fascist leader, Armand Gregoire, arrives in New York on a secret mission.
	Thirteen Nazi spies arrested in Chile.
	Argentina arrests Nazi sympathizers in the army and occupies airports. Attempted revolt put down.
	Reinhard Heydrich appointed Reich protector in Bohemia and Moravia.
	German agent George Sylvester Viereck indicted and seized in New York City.

Endnotes

Part I

1. Walter Nicolai, (1873–1947). Walter Nicolai was the son of a Prussian Army Captain and studied from 1901 to 1904 at the War Academy in Berlin. He was appointed as Chief of the Intelligence Service of the German High Command to Russia. He spoke fluent Russian. Nicolai was considered ultra-conservative, monarchist, and non-political. In 1906, Nicolai began his career in *Abteilung* IIIb, when he took over the news station in Königsburg. He built up the station to be a major centre for espionage against the Russian Empire. Nicolai led the German secret service between 1913 and 1919. After the end of the First World War Nicolai retired as a colonel. His deputy and later successor in 1920 was Major Friedrich Gempp. In his postwar years, Nicolai published two books about his activities. Under Nazi Germany, he belonged to the expert advisory board of the Imperial Institute for the History of the New Germany. At the end of the Second World War, Nicolai was arrested by the Soviet NKVD, deported from Germany, and interrogated in Moscow. He died while in custody on 4 May 1947 at the Hospital of Moscow's Butyrka Prison.
2. Franz Joseph Hermann Michael Maria von Papen, (1879–1969). Von Papen was expelled from the USA during the First World War and later served as an officer, first on the Western Front and later in Palestine. He entered politics and was a member of the parliament of Prussia in 1921–32. Von Hindenburg appointed him Chancellor, but the cabinet he formed with the assistance of General Kurt von Schleicher was weak; by 1933 he was replaced by Hitler, himself becoming Vice-Chancellor. Hitler and his allies quickly marginalised von Papen and the rest of the cabinet. During the 'Night of the Long Knives', General von Schleicher was gunned down along with his wife, but von Papen managed to survive. He was later sidelined by being made Ambassador to Austria. Hitler dismissed him from his mission in Austria in 1938, and he later served as Ambassador to Turkey in 1939–44. At Nuremberg he was acquitted, but a later de-Nazification court sentenced him to eight years' hard labour. Von Papen was released on appeal in 1949.
3. Horst von der Goltz, (born Franz Wachendorf in 1884). Von der Goltz was a counterintelligence agent during the First World War. His autobiography, *My Adventures as a German Secret Service Agent*, was published in 1918. He died in the USA, date unknown.

4. Captain Franz Dagobert Johannes von Rintelen, (1878 –1949). Rintelen was sent to the neutral United States in 1915, at age 38, on a false Swiss passport in the name of Emil V. Gasche, the surname appropriated from his brother-in-law. Von Rintelen worked with a chemist, Dr Scheele, to develop time-delayed incendiary devices known as pencil bombs, which were then placed in the holds of merchant ships trading to Britain to cause fires in the ships' holds so that the crew would throw the munitions overboard. After imprisonment in the USA he returned to Germany in 1920, a forgotten man. He moved to England, where he died on 30 May 1949.

5. Kurt Ferdinand Friedrich Hermann von Schleicher, (1882–1934). Schleicher rose to power as a close advisor to President Paul von Hindenburg. Seventeen months after his resignation, he was assassinated by order of his successor, Adolf Hitler, in the Night of the Long Knives.

6. The *Feme* murders were a series of against right-wing assassinations of opponents who were deemed to be traitors to Germany during the turbulent period 1919–1923. The victims included Germans suspected of espionage for the Allied Commission charged with enforcing the provisions of the Treaty of Versailles. In an attempt to conceal their military build-up the *Reichswehr* tried suspected spies *in absentia* and assassinated those who were deemed to be spies. The term *Feme* or *Femegerichte* comes from the name given to a form of vigilantism practised in Germany during the Middle Ages.

7. Ernst Julius Guenther Röhm, (1887-1934). Röhm joined the German Workers' Party, which soon became the Nazi Party. He also met Hitler and they became political allies and close friends. Following the Beer Hall *Putsch*, Röhm was found guilty, but was granted a conditional discharge. At Landsberg Prison in April 1924, Röhm was given full powers by Hitler to rebuild the SA in any way he saw fit. By August 1933, Röhm and Hitler were so close that he was the only Nazi who dared address Hitler as 'Adolf,' rather than 'mein Führer'. Despite this friendship, Röhm represented a challenge to Hitler, who by now desired the support of the army. In the 'Night of the Long Knives' on 30 June 1934, Röhm and the entire leadership of the SA was purged, Röhm was shot in the chest at point-blank range.

8. Joseph Goebbels, (1897–1945). Goebbels came into contact with the Nazi Party in 1923 during the French occupation of the Ruhr; he became a member in 1924. He rose to power in 1933 along with Hitler and was appointed Propaganda Minister. One of his first acts was the burning of books. He exerted totalitarian control over the media, arts and information in Germany. Goebbels remained with Hitler in Berlin to the end; after Hitler's suicide, Goebbels succeeded him as Chancellor, but along with his wife Magda, he killed their six young children and then committed suicide.

9. Heinrich Luitpold Himmler, (1900–1945). Himmler joined the Party in 1923 and the SS in 1925. In 1929, he was appointed *Reichsführer-SS* by Hitler. Himmler developed the SS into a powerful group with its own military, and following Hitler's orders, he set up and controlled the Nazi concentration camps. From 1943 onwards, he was both Chief of German Police and Minister of the Interior, overseeing all internal and external police and security forces, including the Gestapo. On Hitler's behalf, Himmler formed the *Einsatzgruppen* and built extermination camps. Late in the war, Hitler gave Himmler command of the Army Group Upper Rhine and the Army Group Vistula; he failed to achieve his assigned objectives and Hitler replaced him in these posts. Shortly before the end of the war, without Hitler's knowledge, Himmler attempted to open peace talks with the Western Allies. Hearing of this, Hitler dismissed him from all his posts in April 1945. Himmler was arrested by British forces and he committed suicide with a

cyanide capsule on 23 May 1945.

10. Rudolf Hess, (1894-1987). After hearing Hitler speak for the first time in May 1920, Hess became completely devoted to him. He joined the fledgling Nazi Party in 1920 as one of its first members and commanded an SA battalion during the Beer Hall *Putsch*. Hess served seven and a half months in Landsberg Prison and acted as Hitler's private secretary there, transcribing and partially editing *Mein Kampf*. He rose in Hitler's estimation and on the eve of the invasion of Poland, Hitler announced that should anything happen to both him and Göring, Hess would be next in the line of succession. On 10 May 1941 he flew solo to Scotland in an attempt to negotiate peace with the United Kingdom, where he was arrested and became a prisoner of war. Hess was tried at Nuremberg and sentenced to life imprisonment, which he served at Spandau Prison, Berlin.

11. Karl Ernst Haushofer, (1869–1946). Haushofer, was a general, geographer and geo-politician. Through his student Rudolf Hess, Haushofer's ideas influenced the development of Adolf Hitler's expansionist strategies, although Haushofer denied direct influence on the Nazi regime. Under the Nuremberg Laws, Haushofer's wife and children were categorized as *mischlinge*. His son, Albrecht, was issued a German Blood Certificate through the help of Hess. After the 20 July 1944 plot to assassinate Hitler, Haushofer's son Albrecht (1903–1945) went into hiding but was arrested on 7 December 1944, and put into the Moabit prison in Berlin. During the night of 22–23 April 1945, he and other selected prisoners, such as Klaus Bonhoeffer were walked out of the prison by an SS-squad and shot. Haushofer himself was imprisoned in Dachau concentration camp for eight months but survived. Karl Haushofer was interrogated by the Allied forces to determine whether he should stand trial at Nuremberg for war crimes, but it was determined that he had not committed any. On the night of 10–11 March 1946, Haushofer and his wife committed suicide in a secluded hollow on their Hartschimmelhof estate at Pähl/Ammersee.

12. Hermann Göring, (1893-1946). Göring fought in the First World War, initially in the infantry and then as a fighter pilot, finally commanding the famous Richthofen squadron. A member of the party from its early days, he was wounded in 1923 during the failed Beer Hall *Putsch*. He suffered from a lifelong addiction to morphine after being treated with the drug for his injuries. He founded the Gestapo in 1933 and was appointed Commander-in-Chief of the Luftwaffe in 1935. At Nuremberg he was sentenced to death by hanging, but committed suicide by taking cyanide the night before his execution.

13. Eugen Ott, (1889–1977). Ott was adjutant to General Kurt von Schleicher until his assassination during the night of the long knives. Shortly after Hitler came to power he was sent to Tokyo as military attaché at the German Embassy (1934). He was then appointed as ambassador to Japan during the early years of the War. In early September 1940, Heinrich Georg Stahmer arrived in Tokyo to assist Ambassador Ott negotiate the Tripartite Pact with Japan. Stahmer would later replace Ott as ambassador when Richard Sorge, who had been working for Ott in Japan as an agent for the *Abwehr*, was unmasked as a spy for the Soviet Union in Japan in late 1941. Ott left Tokyo and went to Peking for the remainder of the war. Interestingly Riess does not mention Sorge, and it seems that the Nazis kept this under wraps. Sorge is most famous for his service in Japan in 1940 and 1941, when he provided information about Hitler's plan to attack the Soviet Union, although he did not succeed in finding out the exact date of the attack. In mid-September 1941, he informed the Soviet command that Japan was not going to attack the Union in the near future, which allowed the command to transfer 18 divisions, 1,700 tanks, and over 1,500 aircraft from Siberia and the Far East to

the Western Front against Nazi Germany during the most critical months of the Battle for Moscow. A month later Sorge was arrested in Japan on the counts of espionage. He was tortured, confessed, tried, and hanged in November 1944.

14. Wilhelm Franz Canaris, (1887–1945). Canaris joined the German Imperial Navy in 1905 and served during the First World War. In 1935 he was made head of the *Abwehr*, Germany's official military intelligence agency. Later that year, he was promoted Rear Admiral. In 1938, with the support of MI6, Canaris devised a plan to assassinate Hitler, precipitating the dissolution of the entire Nazi Party before the invasion of Czechoslovakia, but nothing came of this. The assassination of Heydrich in Prague, organised by MI6, was done in part to preserve Canaris in his important position. Evidence mounted that he was playing a double game, and at the insistence of Himmler, who had suspected him for a long time, Hitler dismissed Canaris in February 1944, replacing him with Walter F. Schellenberg. Canaris was put under house arrest, preventing him from taking any direct part in the 20 July plot. Himmler kept Canaris alive for some time because he planned to use him secretly as a future contact with the British. When Himmler's plan failed to materialise, he received Hitler's approval to send Canaris to his death. He was humiliated before witnesses and then led to the gallows barefoot and naked on 9 April 1945. Riess was obviously unaware that Canaris was a British double-agent.

15. Hanns Oberlindober, (1896–1949). Oberlindober was severely wounded in 1918 and retired from the army. He was awarded the Iron Cross awarded both classes. He was a Nazi (NSDAP) member of the Reichstag from 1930. In 1934 Oberlindober managed the NSDAP office for war victims and he organized meetings of veterans of the First World War which enabled him to maintain relations with British and French veterans' organizations. At the end of the War Oberlindober was captured by the Americans. In 1948, he was extradited from the U.S. prison at Poland, where he died in a Warsaw hospital in 1949.

16. George Kynaston Cockerill, (1867–1957). Cockerill was a British Army officer retiring as Brigadier General Sir George Kynaston Cockerill CB. During the First World War he had served in the War Office, first as Sub-Director of Military Operations, then as Deputy Director of Military Intelligence and Director of Special Intelligence. It is probably this that leads Riess to make his assumption. The tradition in the Secret Intelligence Service (SIS)—commonly known as MI6—had been for the 'head' to be referred to as 'C' (not 'M' as used by Ian Fleming for his James Bond books). The 'C' after 1923 had actually been Admiral Sir Hugh 'Quex' Sinclair. Sinclair died in 1939, after an illness, and was replaced as 'C' by Lt-Col. Stewart Menzies, (1890–1958) who remained in post until 1952. When the Second World War began, SIS expanded greatly. Menzies insisted on wartime control of codebreaking, and this gave him immense power and influence, which he used judiciously. By distributing the Ultra material collected by the Government Code & Cypher School, for the first time, MI6 became an important branch of the government. Extensive breaches of Nazi *Enigma* signals gave Menzies and his team enormous insight into Adolf Hitler's strategy, and this was kept a closely held secret, not only during the war, but until as late as 1974. The Nazis had suspicions, but believed *Enigma* to be unbreakable, and never knew during the war that the Allies were reading a high proportion of their wireless traffic. Menzies kept Prime Minister Winston Churchill supplied daily with important Ultra decrypts, and the two worked together to ensure that financial resources were devoted towards research and upgrading technology at Bletchley Park, to keep pace with Nazi coding refinements, as well as directing talented workers to the massive effort, which employed nearly 10,000 workers by 1945. Bletchley's efforts were decisive in the battle against Nazi submarine warfare, which was severely threatening

trans-Atlantic shipping, particularly in the first half of 1943. Britain, which was cut off from Europe after mid-1940, was almost completely dependent on North American supplies for survival. The access to Ultra was also vitally important in the battle for Normandy, leading up to D-Day in June 1944, and afterwards. Menzies, who was promoted to major-general in January 1944, also supported efforts to contact anti-Nazi resistance, including Wilhelm Canaris, the anti-Nazi head of Abwehr, in Germany. Prime Minister Winston Churchill was kept informed of these efforts throughout the war, and information from and about the Nazi resistance was exploited tactically. Menzies coordinated his operations with Special Operations Executive (SOE), British Security Coordination (BSC), Office of Strategic Services (OSS) and the Free French Forces. After the war, Menzies reorganised the SIS for the Cold War and absorbed most of SOE.

17. Alfred Duff Cooper, (1890–1954). Alfred Duff Cooper, 1st Viscount Norwich GCMG DSO PC, known as Duff Cooper, was a politician and diplomat. Cooper was Financial Secretary to the War Office in 1931, then as Financial Secretary to the Treasury in 1934. In 1935 he was appointed to the Cabinet as War Secretary and promoted again to First Lord of the Admiralty in 1937. He was the most public critic of Neville Chamberlain's appeasement policy inside the Cabinet and resigned the day after the 1938 Munich Agreement was signed with Hitler. He re-entered the Cabinet as Minister of Information under Winston Churchill, but after a controversial appointment as Resident Cabinet Minister in Singapore in 1941, he did not play a major role in the direction of the war until appointed the British Government's liaison to the Free French in 1943. He subsequently became the British ambassador to France in 1944. He left office in 1947 and was knighted. In 1952 he was created Viscount Norwich in recognition of his political and literary career.

18. Leslie Hore-Belisha, (1893–1957). Hore-Belisha was controversially appointed by Neville Chamberlain as Secretary of State for War replacing Duff Cooper. Many took to nicknaming him 'Horeb-Elisha' or 'Horeb' as a pun on his race. (Horeb is mentioned in the Hebrew Bible as the place where the golden calf was made and to which Elijah fled). Pressure mounted on Chamberlain to remove Hore-Belisha from the Cabinet at the earliest opportunity. Convinced that war was looming, Hore-Belisha sought permission to introduce conscription in 1938 but was rebuffed by Chamberlain, who would not agree to increased defence spending. Senior Conservatives believed that Hore-Belisha was more concerned about the fate of Jewish people abroad than of Britain itself, such that he wanted Britain to wage war against Germany with the sole intention of protecting European Jews. Despite strong political and public opposition, in early 1939 he was finally allowed to introduce conscription. In January 1940, the government caved-in to popular opinion and Hore-Belisha was dismissed from the War Office. Instead, the Prime Minister offered him the post of Presidency of the Board of Trade. Hore-Belisha refused this demotion and resigned from the government. Due to the sensitive nature of the disagreements, many MPs and political commentators were bewildered as to why the dismissal had taken place, and Hore-Belisha's formal statement to the Commons left them little wiser. A common belief was that Hore-Belisha's bold reforms at the War Office had been opposed by the established military commanders.

19. Robert Gilbert Vansittart, (1881–1957). Vansittart was Principal Private Secretary to the Prime Minister from 1928 to 1930 and Permanent Under-Secretary at the Foreign Office from 1930 to 1938 and later served as Chief Diplomatic Adviser to the British Government. Vansittart was closely involved in intelligence work. In 1940, Vansittart sued the American historian Harry Elmer Barnes for libel for

an article Barnes had written in 1939 accusing him of plotting aggression against Germany in 1939. During the war, Vansittart became a prominent advocate of an extremely hard line with Germany. His earlier worries about Germany were reformulated into an argument that Germany was intrinsically militaristic and aggressive. *In Black Record: Germans Past and Present* (1941), Vansittart portrayed Nazism as just the latest manifestation of Germany's continuous record of aggression from the time of ancient Rome. Therefore, after Germany was defeated, it must be stripped of all military capacity, including its heavy industries. The German people enthusiastically supported Hitler's wars of aggression, just as they supported the Franco-Prussian War in 1870 and the First World War in 1914. So they must be thoroughly re-educated under strict Allied supervision for at least a generation. De-Nazification was not enough. The German military elite was the real cause of war, especially the 'Prussianist' officer corps and the General Staff: both must be destroyed.

20. It would be interesting to know where Riess got this from. He named SIS as 'Special Intelligence Section', was this just a guess? As for 'B4' he got that wrong as it was actually the branch of the Security Service that was responsible for Soviet counter-espionage.

Part II

1. Colonel Maurice-Henri Gauché was head of the *Deuxième Bureau* from 1937 to 1940. He was originally an infantry officer. One British general who knew him said he was 'a pleasant though ponderous officer … who had an extraordinary affection for a tame parrot. He was of medium height, but thick set with greying hair cropped short … and an intelligent twinkle in his eyes, which peered through pince nez so precariously that it seemed as if a sneeze might dislodge them.'

2. The *Cagoulards* were members of a French fascist organization in the 1930s called the Secret Committee of Revolutionary Action. They received the name *Cagoulards* from the French word *cagoule*, a hood with openings for the eyes, worn by members of the organization at secret meetings. The *Cagoulards* were secretly supported by certain groups among the French bourgeoisie and the reactionary military. The organization maintained arms caches, was responsible for bombings and arson, and committed acts of terrorism against democratic political figures. After the occupation of France by fascist Germany in 1940, many *Cagoulards* became active collaborationists and supporters of the Vichy regime.

3. John Semer Farnsworth, (1893–1952). Farnsworth was a former United States Navy officer who was convicted of spying for Japan during the 1930s. He was identified as Agent K in radio messages intercepted by the Office of Naval Intelligence (ONI). On 27 February 1937, Farnsworth was sentenced to four to twelve years in prison for conspiring 'to communicate and transmit to a foreign government—(Japan)—writings, code books, photographs and plans relating to the national defence with the intent that they should be used to the injury of the United States'. He served an eleven-year prison term and died in Manhattan in 1952.

4. William Lonkowski, (b. 1893). Lonkowski was an aero-engineer in the First World War who went on to become an *Abwehr* agent. One of his first assignments was assessing France's aircraft capacities in 1922. William Lonkowski arrived in the United States on 27 March 1927. He obtained employment at the Ireland Aircraft Corporation on Long Island, New York and began to develop a spy ring among the plant's German-American workers. Two key individuals he recruited

were Otto Voss and Werner Gudenberg who would eventually move on to other defence plants expanding the reach of the spy ring. Eventually Lonkowski's network of spies could deliver almost overnight any secret ordnance plan the *Abwehr* requested. Lonkowski left Ireland Aircraft Corporation and developed a new cover for his spying activities by becoming a correspondent for the German aviation magazine *Luftreise*. Lonkowski's activities were finally uncovered on 25 September 1935 when he was stopped by a customs official as he was boarding the ocean liner *Europa*. A customs official saw Lonkowski was carrying a violin case and asked to see it solely because of his interest in violins. Upon opening the case the customs official saw aircraft drawings under the instrument. Lonkowski was interviewed by military intelligence and explained these drawings were necessary for him to write his aviation articles. He was told to come back in three days for further questioning. The next day Lonkowski fled to Canada and boarded a German freighter back to his homeland. Hitler rewarded him with a major position in the Air Ministry.

5. Some sources say the *Europa*, some the *Bremen*.

6. Ignatz Theodor Griebl, (b. 1899). Griebl was a German-American physician and spymaster based in Yorkville, New York. Griebl was born in Bavaria in 1899 and served as an artillery officer during the First World War. He was wounded on the Italian front where he met his future wife, Austrian nurse Maria Ganz. He studied medicine at the University of Munich and arrived in the United States in 1925 where the new doctor and his wife started a practice in Bangor, Maine. In 1928 they moved their practice to the German-American community of Yorkville, New York specializing in obstetrics. He took American citizenship and became an officer in U.S. Army medical reserve. On 3 March 1934 he contacted Joseph Goebbels by letter offering his services to spy for Germany. Goebbels forwarded the information to the Gestapo which at the time was assembling an international group of police spies and informants. The Gestapo turned the lead over to its Maritime Bureau which had a network of couriers aboard German ocean liners. Dr Griebl began his spy ring by recruiting from the pro-Hitler group 'Friends of New Germany' which he had joined in 1933. Here he first recruited Axel Wheeler-Hill and Oskar Karl Pfaus who on their own would become involved in larger spy rings. Back in Bangor, Maine, Dr Griebl recruited an old friend who worked as an engineer at the Bath Iron Works obtaining a blueprint copy of a newly designed warship. In October 1934 William Lonkowski who had been spying for the *Abwehr* in American since 1927 called upon Dr Griebl and both agreed to combine their resources. Eventually the spy ring he developed in America was compromised and Dr Griebl was brought in by the FBI and given a polygraph examination. The FBI was satisfied with his polygraph results and he was released. On 10 May 1938 Dr Griebl escaped to Germany aboard the ocean liner *Bremen*.

7. Georg Gyssling, (1893–1965). Gyssling was German consul to the United States from 1927 until 1941; from 1933 in Los Angeles. He was member of the Nazi Party from 1931. Gyssling had a specific brief to monitor the activities of the studios. He watched films and dictated scene-by-scene requests for cuts. In June 1939 MGM gave ten Nazi newspaper editors a tour of its studio in Los Angeles, and during the 1930s hardly any Jewish characters appeared in Hollywood films. Gyssling was extremely diligent in his duties. Before Hollywood actually 'woke up' to what was happening in the Third Reich it effectively had a financial pact with Hitler and danced to his tune. The Nazis could also prevent movies from being made and one Hollywood film about Hitler's treatment of the Jews was never produced due to Nazi pressure. In 1933 the Hollywood screenwriter, Herman Mankiewicz, who wrote *Citizen Kane*, came up with a script about Hitler's persecution of

the Jews in which he predicted that this would lead to the killing of the Jews. Gyssling told studio executives that if any studio made this picture then all of the Hollywood studios would be banned from the German market. Hollywood failed to fully grasp the significance of the rise of Nazism in Germany, even though the American motion picture industry was largely in the hands of Jewish Americans. They underestimated the Nazis, assuming that the national socialists were a passing phenomenon. The bubble burst when Germany's propaganda minister, Joseph Goebbels, seized control of the film industry and began dismissing Jews *en masse*. With Goebbel's coup, Hollywood could no longer be sanguine or naive about the Nazi regime. Nonetheless, Hollywood continued doing business with Germany, going as far as submitting to its new censorship rules forbidding 'cheerful' Jewish characters in films. Hollywood studios from Universal to Paramount maintained offices throughout Germany, particularly in Berlin, Düsseldorf and Frankfurt, since the German market was too lucrative to abandon. Warner Brothers—not willing to abide by moral cowardice—closed its German office on principle at the end of 1933, becoming the first Hollywood studio to do so. United Artists, Universal, RKO and Columbia followed suit, but Paramount, Fox and MGM continued their operations. Shortly after *Kristallnacht*, in November 1938, Gyssling accompanied Leni Riefenstahl around Los Angeles, but the reception she received was chilly. Upon her return to Europe, she complained, 'I was welcomed everywhere in the United States but in Hollywood—where the film industry is controlled by Jews and anti-Nazi leagues.'

8. Hermann Max Schwinn, (b. 1905). Schwinn was born in Hamburg and emigrated to the United States in 1924 living for a period in Canton and Akron, Ohio. A few years later he moved to Los Angeles and became active in the organization the 'Friends of New Germany'. In the mid-1930s he was appointed the Western Director of the German American Bund. He lost his citizenship in 1940. At that time he was replaced as Western Director of the Bund by Carl Woeppelmann. He was a defendant in the Great Sedition Trial of 1944. At the time of the trial he was being held as an enemy alien.

9. Heinz Heinrich Spanknöbel, (1893–1947). Spanknöbel was a German immigrant who formed and led the pro-Nazi 'Friends of New Germany'. In May 1933, Rudolf Hess gave Spanknöbel authority to form an American Nazi organization. Shortly thereafter, with help from the German consul in New York City he formed the 'Friends' by merging two older organizations in the United States, 'Gau-USA' and the 'Free Society of Teutonia', which were both small groups with only a few hundred members each. The 'Friends of New Germany' was based in New York but had a strong presence in Chicago. The organization led by Spanknöbel was openly pro-Nazi, and engaged in activities such as storming the German language *New Yorker Staats-Zeitung* with the demand that Nazi-sympathetic articles be published, and the infiltration of other non-political German-American organizations. One of the 'Friends'' early initiatives was to counter, with propaganda, a Jewish boycott of businesses in the German neighbourhood of Yorkville, Manhattan. In an internal battle for control of the 'Friends', Spanknöbel was ousted as leader and subsequently deported in October 1933 due to the fact that he had failed to register as a foreign agent. At the same time, Congressman Samuel Dickstein's investigation concluded that the 'Friends' represented a branch of German dictator Adolf Hitler's Nazi Party in America. He was subsequently arrested in Dresden by the NKVD on 4 October 1945 and died of starvation in Soviet captivity.

10. Fritz and Peter Gissibl and their brother Andrew were early Nazis in the United States. They formed a society named 'The Free Society of Teutonia', and it was

one of the earliest National Socialist organizations to appear in America. They made their headquarters in Chicago and from there they set about recruiting ethnic Germans who supported German nationalist aims. The Teutonia Society initially functioned as a club, but soon raised a group of militants based on the SA and, with membership increasing, became vocal critics of Jews, communism and the Treaty of Versailles. Alongside this however it retained a social function, with Teutonia Society meetings frequently ending up in heavy beer-drinking sessions. The group changed its name to the 'Nationalistic Society of Teutonia' in 1926, at which point Peter Gissibil was advising members to also seek Nazi Party membership. The group gained a strong, if fairly small following, and was able to establish units in Milwaukee, St Louis, Missouri, Detroit, New York City, Cincinnati and Newark, New Jersey. The group's treasurer was Fritz Gissibil, who was also the main Nazi Party representative in the United States and who regularly collected money for the Nazis through the Society. A 'thank you' letter from Adolf Hitler to the Society caused a stir during the Second World War when the Gissibil brothers were brought to trial following an FBI investigation.

11. Walter Kappe, (1904–1944). Kappe arrived in the United States in 1925 and worked in a farm implement factory in Kankakee, Illinois. Later he moved to Chicago and began to write for German language newspapers. Kappe was fluent in English and later became the press secretary for the German American Bund. He founded their paper *Deutscher Weckruf und Beobachter* and its predecessor *Deutsche Zeitung*. In 1936, when the German American Bund was established, Kappe organized the AV Publishing Company and five other Bund corporations. Fritz Kuhn ousted Kappe from his position in the Bund seeing him as a dangerous rival. In 1937, Kappe returned to Germany, where he was attached to *Abwehr* II (the sabotage branch of German intelligence) where he obtained a naval commission with the rank of lieutenant. He was chosen by the Nazis to launch a sabotage operation against America shortly after the attack on Pearl Harbor. Known as *Operation Pastorius*, Kappe recruited men for the mission by reviewing records from the *Ausland Institute* (German Foreign Institute) of those who were paid to return to Germany from America. He established a sabotage school on the outskirts of Berlin to train the new recruits. Once the sabotage network was established and transferred to America, Kappe planned to slip into the U.S. with a new identity and direct operations. On 13 June 1942, Richard Quirin, George John Dasch, Heinrich Harm Heinck and Ernst Peter Burger landed on a beach near Amagansett, Long Island, New York on a U-boat. A similar group landed on Ponte Vedra Beach, near Jacksonville, Florida, on 17 June 1942. *Operation Pastorius* was a complete failure: all seven landed agents were arrested within days, five were executed and two were jailed. Kappe did not join them in the end; he remained in Germany. It is believed that Kappe eventually died fighting the Russians on the Eastern Front in 1944.

12. Walter H. Schellenberg, (b. 1894). Little is known of Schellenberg other than the fact that he was born in Wiesbaden. He arrived on board the SS *Europa* and immigration records show his date of arrival as 6 June 1935. He worked for Robert Meyer and Co., of New York. He arrived for a second time also on board the SS *Europa* on 15 October 1936 actually in the company of his employer Mr Robert Meyer. He is not to be confused with Walter F. Schellenberg of the German Secret Service. It is known that he was involved in the 'America First' movement and that he was an SS officer named Walther Schellenberg, a hardened veteran of the Struggle for Power and of the *Freikorps*. He had sat on the podium with its leaders at an 'America First' rally in New York, before returning to Germany.

13. Fritz Julius Kuhn, (1896–1951). Kuhn was born in Munich and earned an Iron Cross as a German infantry lieutenant. He moved to the United States and, in 1934, he became a naturalized citizen. In March 1936, the German American Bund was established in Buffalo, New York and Kuhn as its *Bundesführer*. Kuhn was initially effective as a leader and was able to unite the organization and expand its membership but came to be seen simply as an incompetent swindler and liar. One of his first tasks was to plan a trip to Germany with 50 of his American followers. The purpose was to be in the presence of Hitler and to witness personally National-Socialism in practice. At this time, Germany was preparing to host the 1936 Olympics. Kuhn anticipated a warm welcome from Hitler, but the encounter was a disappointment. This did not stop Kuhn from elaborating more propaganda to his followers once he returned to the United States about how Hitler acknowledged him as the 'American Führer'. In 1938 Congress passed the Foreign Agents Registration Act requiring foreign agents to register with the State Department. The negative attention to the American Nazis was not to Hitler's liking, who wanted the Nazi Party in America to be strong, but stealthy. Hitler wanted the U.S. to stay neutral throughout the war. Any American resentment towards the Nazi Party was too dangerous. Unfortunately for Hitler, Kuhn was only looking to stir more attention from the media. On 1 March 1938, the Nazi government decreed that no German national 'Reichsdeutsche' could be a member of the Bund, and that no Nazi emblems were to be used by the organization. Undaunted, on 20 February 1939, Kuhn held the largest and most publicized rally in the Bund's history at Madison Square Garden in New York City. Some 20,000 people attended and heard Kuhn criticize President Roosevelt by repeatedly referring to him as 'Frank D. Rosenfeld', calling his New Deal the 'Jew Deal' and denouncing what he believed to be Bolshevik-Jewish American leadership. In 1939, seeking to cripple the Bund, New York City Mayor Fiorello La Guardia ordered the city investigate the Bund's taxes. It found that Kuhn had embezzled over $14,000 from the Bund, spending part of that money on a mistress. District Attorney Thomas E. Dewey issued an indictment and won a conviction against Kuhn. On 5 December 1939, Kuhn was sentenced to two-and-a-half to five years in prison for tax evasion and embezzlement. Despite his criminal conviction for embezzlement, followers of the Bund continued to hold Kuhn in high regard, in line with the principle of *Führerprinzip* common to all Nazis that the leader has absolute power. Kuhn's citizenship was cancelled on 1 June 1943 while he was still in prison. Upon his release, after spending 43 months in state prison, Kuhn was re-arrested on 21 June 1943 as an enemy agent and interned by the Federal government at a camp in Crystal City, Texas. After the War, Kuhn was sent to Ellis Island. He was deported to Germany at some point after September 1945. On arriving in West Germany he was imprisoned, but released shortly before his death.

14. Hans-Heinrich Dieckhoff, (1884–1952). Dieckhoff was ambassador to the United States from 1937 to November 1938. He was recalled in direct tit-for-tat response to the American recall of its ambassador in protest over *Kristallnacht*. He was the last to occupy the post until after the war. In 1943 he assumed the post of ambassador to Spain. Dieckhoff was interrogated after the war and was called to testify at the Nuremberg trials, but he was never formally charged with any crime. Dieckhoff was related through marriage to Joachim von Ribbentrop, being the brother-in-law of Ribbentrop's sister.

15. Leopold von Hoesch, (1881–1936). Von Hoesch was a career diplomat who was appointed to France in 1923. In 1932 Hoesch was transferred to London, where he remained until his death. He was well liked by most British statesmen, including

Anthony Eden. By 1934, Hoesch was beginning to challenge Hitler indirectly, sending communiqués to Konstantin von Neurath, Foreign Minister, detailing his distrust of Ribbentrop whom Hitler had appointed to serve as Commissioner of Disarmament Questions. The relationship between Hoesch and Hitler continued to sour as Ribbentrop gained more power within the German hierarchy. Before Hitler could take action against him, Hoesch died of a heart attack on 11 April 1936. Von Hoesch was honoured with a large British-ordered funeral cortège in which his flag-draped coffin was escorted to Dover where a 19-gun salute was fired as his body was transferred to the British destroyer HMS *Scout* for transport back to Germany. Contrary to Riess's comment, there is no evidence that he committed suicide.

16. Ulrich Friedrich Wilhelm Joachim von Ribbentrop, (1893–1946). Ribbentrop was first introduced to Hitler in 1928 and became a secret emissary between him and von Papen. From the start, Ribbentrop was Hitler's favourite foreign-policy adviser. In August 1936, Hitler appointed von Ribbentrop Ambassador to Britain with orders to negotiate the Anglo-German alliance, but this came to nothing. In 1938 he succeeded von Neurath as Foreign Minister and his most successful moment came with the signing of the Non-Aggression Pact with Russia in August 1939. He was against the attack on the USSR in 1941 and passed a word to a Soviet diplomat: 'Please tell Stalin I was against this war, and that I know it will bring great misfortune to Germany.' As the war progressed Hitler found Ribbentrop increasingly tiresome and sought to avoid him; his position weakened further when many old Foreign Office diplomats participated in the 20 July 1944 assassination attempt on Hitler. In April 1945, Ribbentrop attended Hitler's 56th birthday party in Berlin. Three days later, he attempted to meet with Hitler, only to be told to go away. This was their last meeting. He was arrested after the war, tried at Nuremberg, and executed in 1946.

17. Montagu Collet Norman, (1871–1950). Norman was a banker, best known for his role as the Governor of the Bank of England from 1920 to 1944. He was a close friend of the German Central Bank President, Hjalmar Schacht, who was a supporter of Adolf Hitler and the Nazi Party, and served in Hitler's government as President of the Reichsbank and Minister of Economics. As such, Schacht played a key role in implementing the policies attributed to Hitler. Norman was also so close to the Schacht family that he was godfather to one of Schacht's grandchildren. Both were members of the Anglo-German Fellowship and the Bank for International Settlements. In 2013 it came to light in a newly digitally published history that the Bank of England—under Norman—had helped the Nazis sell gold looted from Czechoslovakia in March 1939. The documents put Norman right at the heart of the decision, raising fresh questions about his suspected Nazi sympathies.

When Mark Carney took over as Governor of the Bank of England in 2013, one of his first acts was to remove Norman's portrait from the Board Room.

18. Sir Nevile Meyrick Henderson KCMG, (1882–1942). Henderson was Ambassador of the United Kingdom to Nazi Germany from 1937 to 1939. After returning to London Henderson asked for another ambassadorship, but was denied. He wrote *Failure of a Mission: Berlin 1937–1939*, which was published in 1940, in which he spoke highly of some members of the Nazi regime, including Hermann Göring, but not von Ribbentrop. He had been on friendly terms with members of the Astors' Cliveden set, which also supported appeasement. He died on 30 December 1942 from cancer which he had been suffering from since 1938.

19. Sir Horace John Wilson, (1882–1972). Wilson was a British Government official who had a key role in the appeasement-oriented ministry of Neville Chamberlain. He was present at the Munich conference of September 1938.

20. Robert Anthony Eden, (1897–1977). Eden was Secretary of State for Foreign Affairs 22 December 1935—20 February 1938, 22 December 1940—26 July 1945 and 28 October 1951—7 April 1955. He was Prime Minister 6 April 1955—10 January 1957. His resignation in February 1938 was largely attributed to growing dissatisfaction with Chamberlain's policy of appeasement.

21. Kurt Schuschnigg, (1897–1977). Schuschnigg was Chancellor of the Federal State of Austria, following the assassination of his predecessor, Engelbert Dollfuss, in July 1934, until Hitler's annexation of Austria in March 1938. He was opposed to Hitler's ambitions to absorb Austria into the Third Reich. After the invasion by Nazi Germany, he was arrested by the Germans, kept in solitary confinement and eventually interned in various concentration camps. He was liberated in 1945 by the advancing United States Army and spent most of the remainder of his life in the United States.

22. Frank Sanborn and his brother Walter arrived in Mexico City on 19 June 1903 from California. And they soon opened Mexico's first soda fountain. During the Mexican Revolution, troops of Emiliano Zapata used a Sanborns branch as a rendezvous point and gathering place. Photographs from the period show Zapatista soldiers enjoying their first restaurant meal at Sanborns' lunch counter, leading to the Sanborns slogan 'Meet me at Sanborns'. In 1919, Walter Sanborn, tired of Mexico's political turmoil, returned to the U.S. and left the management of the company to his brother Frank. At this same time Sanborns acquired its most famous branch location, the sixteenth-century House of Tiles, the *Casa de los Azulejos*, a major Mexico City tourist attraction and national monument. In 1946, Frank Sanborn sold his interest in Sanborns to fellow pharmacist Charles Walgreen Jr. of Chicago.

23. Nicolás Rodríguez Carrasco, (1890–1940). Carrasco fought alongside Pancho Villa during the Mexican Revolution but deserted him in 1918. After the revolution he moved to the right and joined several racist, anti-semitic organizations. In 1929 he supported the presidential campaign of José Vasconcelos. Vasconcelos lost the election and then claimed it had been rigged, after which he fled the country. Rodríguez went over to the other side and supported Elías Calles, former president and the strongman of Mexico at that time. Under the protection of Calles Rodríguez founded the green shirts but in 1932 they were disbanded by president Abelardo L. Rodríguez . In 1933 Carrasco founded another fascist organization, the Gold shirts, which became more successful. After Calles' deportation in 1936 Rodríguez lost his protector and in August of the same year he was arrested and deported. Rodríguez moved to Texas where he was joined by many of his gold shirts and sought cooperation with American fascists such as the Silver shirts of William Dudley Pelley. In 1938 he attempted an unsuccessful attack on Mexico. After this failed attempt he was continuously monitored by the Mexican and American secret services and unable to organize any new actions. He died in 1940.

24. Waldemar Pabst, (1880–1970). Pabst was a far right anti-communist activist in both his homeland and Austria. As a serving officer Pabst gained notoriety for ordering the executions of Karl Liebknecht and Rosa Luxemburg in 1919 as well as for his leading role in the coterie of ultra-nationalist conspirators around Wolfgang Kapp. In Austria he played a central part in organising rightist militia groups before being deported due to his activities. Pabst subsequently faded from public life in Nazi Germany as he was never more than loosely associated with the Nazis.

25. Wilhelm Emanuel Freiherr von Ketteler, (1906–1938). Freiherr von Ketteler was a German diplomat, mainly known as one of the young conservative opponents of Nazism in 'Edgar Jung-circle' and close associate of Hitler's Vice-Chancellor and Ambassador to Vienna, Franz von Papen. He disappeared on 14 March 1938

and his disfigured body was discovered several weeks later in the Danube near Hainburg, fifty kilometres downstream from Vienna. He was later identified from his signet ring.

26. Charles André Joseph Marie de Gaulle, (1890–1970). At the time that Riess wrote this book in 1941 Charles de Gaulle was relatively little known. After the collapse of the French Army de Gaulle went to Bordeaux, which was the temporary wartime capital following the fall of Paris. On learning that Marshal Pétain had become Premier on 16 June 1940 and was planning to seek an armistice with Nazi Germany, de Gaulle and other officers rebelled against the new French Government. On the morning of 17 June, de Gaulle and a few senior French officers flew to England. De Gaulle strongly denounced the French Government's decision to seek armistice with Germany and immediately set about building the Free French Forces from the soldiers and officers deployed outside France or who had fled France with him. On 18 June, de Gaulle delivered a radio address via the BBC Radio service; the talk was authorized by Churchill.

Part III

1. Although Haushofer accompanied Hess on numerous propaganda missions, and participated in consultations between Nazis and Japanese leaders, he claimed that Hitler and the Nazis only seized upon half-developed ideas and catchwords. Furthermore, the Nazi party and government lacked any official organ that was receptive to geopolitik, leading to selective adoption and poor interpretation of Haushofer's theories. Ultimately, Hess and Konstantin von Neurath, Nazi Minister of Foreign Affairs, were the only officials Haushofer would admit had a proper understanding of geopolitik. Haushofer was never a member of the Nazi Party, and did voice disagreements with the party, leading to his brief imprisonment. Haushofer came under suspicion because of his contacts with left wing socialist figures within the Nazi movement led by Gregor Strasser. His son was implicated in the 20 July 1944 plot to assassinate Hitler and was executed by the Gestapo.

2. Ernst 'Putzi' Hanfstaengl, (1887–1976). Hanfstaengl had an American mother and was brought up and educated in the USA where, in 1920, he married Helene Elise Adelheid Niemeyer. He returned to Germany in 1922 and soon became one of Hitler's most intimate followers. For much of the 1920s Hanfstaengl introduced Hitler to Munich's high society and helped polish his image. He also helped to finance the publication of *Mein Kampf*, and the Party's official newspaper, the *Völkischer Beobachter*. Hanfstaengl wrote both Brownshirt and Hitler Youth marches, based on his memories of Harvard football songs; he later claimed that he devised the chant '*Sieg Heil*'. Several disputes arose between Hanfstaengl and Goebbels which led to him being removed from Hitler's staff in 1933. He and Helene divorced in 1936. Hanfstaengl fell completely out of Hitler's favour after he was denounced by Unity Mitford, a close friend of both the Hanfstaengls and Hitler. He moved to England where he was imprisoned as an enemy alien after the outbreak of the War. In 1942 he was turned over to the U.S. and worked for President Roosevelt's 'S-Project', revealing information on approximately 400 Nazi leaders.

3. Arthur Seyss-Inquart, (1892– 1946). Seyss-Inquart was an Austrian Nazi politician who served as Chancellor of Austria for two days—11 March to 13 March 1938—before the Anschluss annexation of Austria by Nazi Germany, signing the constitutional law as acting head of state upon the resignation of President Wilhelm Miklas. During the War he served the Third Reich in the General

Government of occupied Poland and as Reichskommissar in the Netherlands. At the Nuremberg trials, he was found guilty of crimes against humanity and sentenced to death. He was hanged on 16 October 1946, at the age of 54, together with nine other Nuremberg defendants. He was the last to mount the scaffold.

4. Petar Kosić, (1881–1949). Kosić was a senior officer of the Serbian Army and an army General of Yugoslavia . In January 1940 he was appointed Chief of Staff for and was removed from his post by a military coup on 27 March 1941. During the War he campaigned abroad against the national liberation movement. On the way back to Belgrade he was arrested on 15 February 1949 and died on 18 May in 1949 following a lengthy hunger strike.

5. Milan Nedić, (1878–1946). Events were moving so fast in 1941 when Riess was writing this text, that Riess was not aware, when sending his text to be typeset, that the situation had changed. On 29 August 1941 Nedić accepted the post of the prime minister in the Nazi-controlled government called the Government of National Salvation. In short, Nedić became a Serbian Nazi collaborator. He remained prime minister of a Nazi-installed Serbian puppet government until 1944. After the war, the Yugoslav Communist government imprisoned him. In 1946 they reported that he had suddenly committed suicide by jumping out of a window.

6. Petar Pešić, (1871–1944). General Pešić had been Chief of the General Staff 1921-22.

7. Heinrich Otto Abetz, (1903–1958). Abetz was interested in strengthening Franco-German relations and in his twenties he started a Franco-German cultural group for youths—the Sohlberg Congress—along with Jean Luchaire. The group brought together a hundred German and French youths of all professions, social classes, political leanings, and religious affiliations. The group held their first conference in the Black Forest and were frequently convened around ski slopes, campfires, and in hostels. In 1934 the Sohlberg Circle was reborn as the Franco-German Committee (*Comité France-Allemagne*), which included Pierre Drieu la Rochelle and Jacques Benoist-Mechin. An ardent Francophile, Abetz married Luchaire's French secretary, Susanne de Bruyker, in 1932. Abetz joined the Nazi Party in 1937 and in the same year he applied for the German Foreign Service. From 1938, he was representing Germany in Paris but was deported from France in June 1939 following allegations that he had bribed two French newspaper editors to write pro-German articles. He was present in Adolf Hitler's entourage at the fall of Warsaw, and served as a translator for the Führer. He returned to France in June 1940 following the German occupation and was assigned by Joachim von Ribbentrop to the embassy in Paris. He advised the German military administration in Paris and was responsible for dealings with Vichy France. In May 1941 he negotiated the Paris Protocols to expand German access to French military facilities. He left France in September 1944 as the German armies withdrew.

8. Stephanie Julianne von Hohenlohe, (1891–1972). Stephanie von Hohenlohe was a Hungarian national who relocated to London following her divorce from Prince Friedrich Franz von Hohenlohe-Waldenburg-Schillingsfürst. She was suspected of having acted as a spy for Germany during the 1930s and developed close connections among the Nazi hierarchy. She was also well connected in English society most notably with Harold Sidney Harmsworth, 1st Viscount Rothermere, and promoted British support for Germany while living in London from 1932. In England, Princess Stephanie acted as a courier, passing secret messages among high-ranking English people who were sympathetic to the Nazi regime. In 1937 she arranged for Lord Halifax to travel to Germany and meet Göring. She was

also instrumental in arranging the visit that year to Germany of Edward, Duke of Windsor and his wife Wallis, The Duchess of Windsor. In 1937 Princess Stephanie began an affair with Fritz Wiedemann, a personal aide to Hitler. When Wiedemann was appointed to the post of German Consul-General in San Francisco, she joined him in the United States in late 1937 and stayed for a time, returning to Europe the following year. In 1938, the Nazis confiscated the property of Austrian Jews, including the Leopoldskron castle in Salzburg, which had been owned by theatre director Max Reinhardt. Some reported that Göring gave Princess Stephanie the property; other sources say she leased it, or was charged by Göring with developing the estate as a guest house for prominent artists of the Reich and to serve as a reception facility to Hitler's Berghof home. She returned to England in 1939, but after war was declared she left the country, fearful of being interned and travelled to the United States returning to her former lover Fritz Wiedemann in San Francisco. On her arrival she was placed her under security surveillance by the FBI. After the attack on Pearl Harbor she was arrested by the FBI and interned in the United States as an enemy alien. She provided information to the Office of Strategic Services which was used in a 1943 report on the personality of Adolf Hitler. In May 1945 she was released on parole and returned to Germany, where she cultivated influential connections in post-war German society.

9. Max Reinhardt, (1873–1943). Reinhardt was an Austrian-born American theatre and film director, intendant, and theatrical producer. With his innovative stage productions, he is regarded one of the most prominent directors of German-language theatre in the early twentieth century. In 1920, he established the Salzburg Festival with the performance of Hofmannsthal's *Jedermann*.

10. Sir Oswald Mosley, (1896–1980). Mosley was the founder of the British Union of Fascists (BUF). He was also MP for Harrow from 1918 to 1924, and for Smethwick from 1926 to 1931. Although well-funded from his own private fortune—and probably also from Germany—Mosley appealed to few British voters. After the death of his first wife Cynthia from peritonitis in 1933 he married his mistress Diana Guinness, *née* Mitford, (1910–2003). They married in secret in Germany on 6 October 1936 in the Berlin home of Joseph Goebbels. Adolf Hitler was one of the guests. Mosley was interned in 1940 and the BUF was proscribed. He was released in 1943 and being unwelcome in England he moved abroad in 1951 spending most of the remainder of his life in France.

11. George Geoffrey Dawson, (1874–1944). Dawson was editor of *The Times* from 1912 to 1919 and again from 1923 until 1941. Dawson was close to both Stanley Baldwin and Neville Chamberlain. He was a prominent proponent and supporter of appeasement policies, after Adolf Hitler came to power in Germany. He was a member of the Anglo-German Fellowship and under his editorship *The Times* forbade any mention of German anti-semitism during the pre-war years when the Nazi Party ruled Germany. He was opposed to Zionism. Dawson was also a lifelong friend and dining companion of Edward Wood, later Lord Halifax, who was Foreign Secretary 1938–1940. He promoted the policies of the Baldwin and Chamberlain governments of the period 1936–1940.

12. Charles-Marie-Photius Maurras, (1868–1952). Maurras was the main inspiration and organizer of *Action Française*, a publication and political movement that was monarchist, anti-parliamentarist, and counter-revolutionary. Maurras' ideas greatly influenced National Catholicism and his views anticipated some of the ideas of fascism. Although in June 1940 articles in *Action Française* signed by Maurras, Léon Daudet and Maurice Pujo praised General Charles de Gaulle, Maurras quickly came to acclaim the end of the Third Republic, replaced by Marshal Philippe Pétain's Vichy France, as a 'divine surprise'. Maurras argued

for a policy of *France d'abord* (France First), whereby France would restore itself politically and morally under Pétain. This position was contrasted to the attitude of the Gaullists, who fled France and continued the military struggle. Maurras was arrested in September 1944 with Maurice Pujo, and indicted by High Court of Lyon for 'complicity with the enemy' on the basis of articles published by Maurras since the war. Maurras was sentenced to life imprisonment and deprivation of civil liberties. He was automatically dismissed from the *Académie française*. Maurras was released in March 1952 to enter a hospital, assisted by the writer Henry Bordeaux, who repeatedly asked President of the Republic Vincent Auriol to pardon Maurras. Although weakened, Maurras collaborated with *Aspects de la France*, which had replaced the outlawed review *Action Française* in 1947. He was transferred to a clinic in Tours, where he soon died.

13. Henri Philippe Joseph Pétain, (1856–1951). Due to his military leadership in the First World War Pétain was viewed as a national hero in France. In March 1939 Pétain became the French ambassador to Spain. When the War began in September Pétain turned down Daladier's offer to join his government. With the imminent fall of France in June 1940, Pétain was appointed Premier of France by President Lebrun at Bordeaux, and the Cabinet resolved to make peace with Germany. The entire government subsequently moved briefly to Clermont-Ferrand, then to the spa town of Vichy in central France. His government voted to transform the discredited French Third Republic into the French State, an authoritarian regime. After the war, he was tried and convicted for treason. At the end of Pétain's trial, although the three judges recommended acquittal on all charges, the jury convicted him and sentenced him to death by a one-vote majority. Due to his advanced age, the Court asked that the sentence not be carried out. Fearing riots at the announcement of the sentence, de Gaulle ordered that Pétain be immediately transported to Fort du Portalet in the Pyrenees. The government later transferred him to the Fort de Pierre-Levée citadel on the Île d'Yeu, a small island off the French Atlantic coast where he died in 1951.

14. Ernst Wilhelm Bohle, (1903–1960). Bohle was the leader of the Foreign Organization of the NSDAP from 1933 until 1945. He was born in Bradford, England, the son of Hermann Bohle, (1877–1943), a college teacher and engineer who had emigrated to England several years earlier. In 1906 Bohle went with his family to Cape Town where his father was appointed to a professorship of electrical engineering, and attended a high school there. Bohle studied political sciences and business administration in Cologne and Berlin and graduated in business management at the *Handelshochschule*, Berlin, 1923. Bohle joined the NSDAP in 1932 and in the following year he entered the SS at the rank of SS-Brigadeführer. He was promoted further to SS-Gruppenführer) in 1937 and SS-Obergruppenführer in 1943. In December 1931 he became an assistant tof Hans Nieland, the leader of the *Auslands-Organisation* responsible for South and South-west Africa and later North America. This unit had been founded on 1 May 1931 in Hamburg by Gregor Strasser who appointed Nieland as the Chief. After Nieland resigned on 8 May 1933 Bohle took over the leadership with the rank of Gauleiter. Bohle's father Hermann was *NSDAP/AO Landesgruppenleiter* in the Union of South Africa from 1932 until 1934 and he was president of the Berlin-based *Deutsch-Südafrikanischen Gesellschaft*. Bohle was also a confidant and on the staff of Rudolf Hess until Hess's flight to Scotland in 1941. Bohle was tried at one of the Nuremberg follow-up trials. He was sentenced to five years on 11 April 1949, but was pardoned by U.S. High Commissioner John J. McCloy on 21 December 1949.

15. Kurt Wermke, (b. 1905). Wermke was NSDAP party member 305113 and SS member 276292. He was promoted SS-Sturmbannführer on 20 April 1936. Little else is known about him apart from the fact that he was still alive in October 1944

as a SS-Sturmbannführer attached to RHSA (*Reichssicherheitshauptamt*—the Reich Security Office). He worked in the harbour service and seafarer section. This section of which Wermke was head of was section 9: *Amt Seefahrt* (*mit den unterstellten Abschnittsleitungen*) 1: Weser-Ems (Bremen); 2: Westliche Ostsee (Kiel); Östliche Ostsee (Stettin).

16. This was almost certainly William L. Shirer, (1904 –1993). Shirer was an American journalist and historian. He became known for his broadcasts from Berlin during the Third Reich and through the first year of Second World War. William Shirer was the CBS radio's foreign correspondent in France and Germany from 1925 to 1945. *Berlin Diary* was published in 1941, but his greatest achievement was his 1960 book, *The Rise and Fall of the Third Reich*.

17. Georg Wilhelm 'G. W.' Pabst, (1885–1967). Pabst was an Austrian theatre and film director. He began his career as a stage actor in Switzerland, Austria and Germany. In 1910, he travelled to the United States, where he worked as an actor and director at the German Theatre in New York. Pabst's early and most famous films concern the plight of women. Pabst abandoned his Hollywood career to return to Austria in 1938 to take care of 'family business', he said later, but other pressures may have been applied. During the Second World War he made two films in Germany, *Komödianten* (1941) and *Paracelsus* (1943). In 1955 he directed the first post-war German feature film to feature the character of Adolf Hitler, *The Last Act*.

18. Riess is being unfair here and unnecessarily whipping up hysteria where none was needed. Obviously he had to hype his book, but clearly not all of his 'facts' are accurate. He was almost certainly referring to Kirsten Malfrid Flagstad, (1895–1962). Flagstad was a Norwegian opera singer and a highly regarded Wagnerian soprano. She ranks among the greatest singers of the twentieth century and many opera critics called hers 'the voice of the century.' Having received repeated and cryptic cablegrams from her husband, the Norwegian industrialist and timber merchant Henry Johansen—probably under Gestapo pressure—and who had returned to Norway a year and a half earlier, Flagstad was forced to consider leaving the United States in 1941. Though dismissing the political implications of the departure of someone of her fame from the United States to German-occupied Norway, it was nonetheless a difficult decision for her. She had many friends, colleagues, and of course many fans all over the US. Even more importantly, her 20-year-old daughter Else had married an American named Arthur Dusenberry. She returned to Norway via Lisbon, Madrid, Barcelona, Marseille, and Berlin in April 1941. Though during the war she performed only in Sweden and Switzerland, countries not occupied by German forces, this fact did not temper the storm of public opinion that hurt her personally and professionally for the next few years. Her husband was arrested after the war for profiteering with his timber business during the occupation. This arrest, together with her decision to remain in occupied Norway, made her unpopular, particularly in the United States. In defence of her husband, Henry Johansen, it should be noted that after his death it was revealed that during the occupation he was arrested by the Gestapo and held for eight days. Also, one of Johansen's sons by his first marriage, Henry Jr, had been a member of the Norwegian underground throughout the war.

19. From 1925 to 1930 Fritz Fischer had run a theatre in the United States as a manager, singer, actor and cabaret artist where he earned enormous sums. He then returned to Germany and took over a Dresden theatre, but after two years he went bankrupt. In 1937 he came to Munich from the Berlin Scala and took over the refurbished Staatstheater am Gärtnerplatz. This building had been slated for demolition but instead there was a major renovation and it reopened on 20

November 1937 with a performance of *Die Fledermaus*, with Adolf Hitler among the guests. Ernest Pope in his book *Munich Playground* refers to Fischer as 'sleazy'. Hitler liked to go to Fischer's Staatstheater to see Franz Lehar's *Die lustige Witwe* with scantily dressed dancers. In fact Fischer's success with *Die lustige Witwe* (The Merry Widow) brought Hitler to the theatre on five occasions to watch the 'Can Can chorus'. In 1944 he was drafted into the *Volkssturm*, and he poured a bottle of Dettol over the knee saying he was unable to fight! He prepared in secret a new programme for the occupying U.S Army. However, the invading combatants had no understanding of nude ballet and sent Fischer to a detention centre. He retired in 1953.

20. Herman Esser, (1900–1981). Esser entered the Nazi party with Hitler in 1920 and became the editor of the Nazi paper *Völkischer Beobachter* and a Nazi member of the Reichstag. In the early days of the party, he was Hitler's *de facto* deputy. Esser was a renowned pervert; he was suspended from the party after a scandal where he sexually assaulted the underage daughter of a businessman. Even Hitler said of him: 'I know Esser is a scoundrel, but I shall hold on to him as long as he is useful to me.' From 1939 to the end of the war he served as the undersecretary for tourism in the Reich propaganda ministry. He was imprisoned twice and died in 1981.

21. Eugen Hadamovsky, (1904–1945). Shortly after Hitler's rise to power Hadamovsky served as the National Programming Director for German radio. He served in a variety of other posts during the War. On 12 June 1942 he was appointed head of the personnel department in the Ministry of Propaganda (*Reichspropagandaleitung*), but due to personal differences with Goebbels he was removed from the management of the radio and his career went into decline. In November 1943 he was sento to serve in the Wehrmacht . On 20 October 1944 he enlisted in the Reserve Forces with the rank of SS Obersturmführer; on 13 January 1945 he was appointed as the company commander 7 Grenadier Regiment of the 4th SS Police Grenadier Division of the SS . He died on 1 March 1945 during a counter-attack on the village Hëlkevize in Pomerania, occupied by Soviet troops .

22. Hans von Voss, (1875–1966). Von Voss's son, Hans-Alexander von Voss, (1907–1944) was one of the conspirators in the assassination attempt against Hitler, 20 July 1944. He committed suicide 8 November 1944.

23. Theodor Habicht, (1898–1944). Under orders from Hitler Habicht was sent to Austria in 1931 as *Landesinspekteur* to oversee the reorganization of the Austrian Nazi Party. Habicht was deported in 1933 after the Austrian government decided to ban the Nazi Party. In response Habicht set up a leadership-in-exile in Munich which directed a campaign of terror against the Dollfuss regime which culminated in a failed coup attempt in the murder of Dollfuss in July 1934 under the command of Austrian SS leader Fridolin Glass. His reputation partially restored, Habicht returned to a more important role in the Nazi Party in 1939 when he was appointed Undersecretary in the Foreign Department of the Nazi Party. As part of his duties he was sent to Norway in 1940 to investigate the organization of government in the newly occupied territory where he called for the removal of the Quisling government and its replacement with an administrative council. Hitler again lost faith in Habicht and his plans were rejected. He was then ordered into the Wehrmacht spending the remainder of his life on the Eastern Front where he died in action.

24. Engelbert Dollfuss, (1892–1934). Dollfuss rose from the position of Minister for Forests and Agriculture to Federal Chancellor in 1932 in the midst of an Austrian political crisis. In early 1933 he forced the closure of the parliament, banned the Austrian Nazi party and assuming dictatorial powers. Dollfuss was assassinated

as part of a failed coup attempt by Nazi agents in 1934. His successor Kurt Schuschnigg maintained his regime until Adolf Hitler's annexation of Austria in 1938.

25. Maximilian Ronge, (1874–1953). Ronge was the last director of the Evidenzbureau, the directorate of military intelligence of the Austro-Hungarian Empire. Ronge played a key role in the 1913 exposure of Alfred Redl as a double agent. Ronge retired in 1932, but was recalled to duty in the following year as director of the *Staatspolizeiliches Sonderbüro*. In 1934, Ronge was posted to the chancellery in the Dollfuss regime; his counter-espionage staff was however unable to prevent the assassination of Dollfuss by Nazi agents in the same year. When Ronge refused to join the SS after Austria's Anschluss to the German Reich in 1938, he was arrested and deported to the Dachau concentration camp. From prison, Ronge wrote a 'declaration of loyalty' to Wilhelm Canaris when the latter was promoted to Vice Admiral, upon which he was released in August 1938. During the War Ronge lived in Vienna. After the war he supported the American troops in allied-administered Austria in the creation of a new intelligence service.

26. Alfred Redl, (1864–1913). Redl was an Austrian officer who rose to head the counter-intelligence efforts of Austria-Hungary. He was one of the leading figures of pre-First World War espionage. He used advanced technology, for the time, to ensnare foreign intelligence agents. But he was himself a paid spy for the Russians.

27. Alfred Gerstenberg, (1893–1959). Gerstenberg was a German *Luftwaffe* general. During the First World War he flew as an observation pilot. In 1916 he joined the Richthofen Squadron led by Manfred von Richthofen and in October 1917 his plane was shot down and he suffered a heavy injury. After the war he served in several cavalry units, retiring in 1926. He rejoined the *Luftwaffe* in 1934 and after 1938 served as *Luftwaffe* attaché at embassies in Warsaw and Bucharest. From 1942 to 1944 Gerstenberg served as the commanding general of *Luftwaffe* in Romania setting up a defence zone around the oil refineries in Ploiești, the largest single source of oil for Nazi Germany. On 28 August 1944 he surrendered to the Russians and was kept in captivity until October 1955.

28. William L. Shirer in *The Rise and Fall of the Third Reich* seems to assume that the 'accidental' landing was genuine and that the Nazi authorities were forced to change their plans.

29. Documents released in 2011 suggest that the man who helped secure an independent Ireland, Eamon de Valera, Head of government in Ireland from 1932 to 1948, covertly co-operated with Britain to crush the IRA. Tensions came to a head when the IRA began bombing mainland Britain in early 1939. Under what was called the Sabotage or 'S-Plan', British cities including London, Manchester, Birmingham and Coventry were targeted by IRA explosive teams. In one attack on Coventry five people died and 70 more were injured. De Valera's government regarded IRA attacks against Britain as a threat to the Irish state itself. With war looking likely, De Valera was determined that Ireland should remain neutral. He knew that a hard rump of Republicans would never countenance being allied to the 'old enemy' Britain, and such an alliance could push Ireland into another bloody civil war. But he also knew that, if his country was seen as a threat, London might decide to invade. In 1939, as the documents show, De Valera's government asked for assistance from London in smearing IRA chief of staff Sean Russell as a communist agent. De Valera was worried that those executed at British hands might become martyrs at home. But he had no such qualms over those convicted of bombings in Ireland. In fact, De Valera's government executed more IRA members than Britain and even borrowed the UK's most famous executioner, Albert Pierrepoint, to hang one of them. During the war, Dublin went on to intern

more than 1,500 IRA suspects, and several died while on hunger strike in Irish jails. As a result, the IRA began to look to Nazi Germany for help. Not long after the first bombs had gone off in Britain, Sean Russell and IRA head of explosives Jim O'Donovan, went to Berlin for a meeting with German military intelligence, the *Abwehr*. At that point, Hitler refused to fund their 'S-Plan' bombing campaign because of fears of provoking conflict with Britain. But, once war had broken out, he did agree to send money, transmitters and spies to Ireland. Many of the latter proved somewhat inept. In July 1940, three German spies—one of them an Indian national—capsized before landing in Ireland. Two of them could not speak English and the Indian agent stood out in rural Ireland. After finally making it ashore, one asked a policeman if they were anywhere near Cork. All three were promptly arrested. Gerard O'Donovan, the son of one IRA saboteur, Jim O'Donovan recalled his time as a child near Dublin: 'There was a room off the dining room where there was a radio transmitter. A man used to come every Saturday and send messages to Germany on that radio... and we children used to call (him) Mr Saturday Night.' Jim O'Donovan died in 1979 without, according to those who knew him, any regrets about his involvement with the Nazis.

30. Hermann Görtz was one agent. He parachuted into Ballivor, County Meath, Ireland (*Operation Mainau*) on 5 May 1940 in an effort to gather information. He moved in with former IRA leader Jim O'Donovan. His mission was to act as a liaison officer with the IRA and enlist their assistance during a potential German invasion of Britain. However, he soon decided that the IRA was too unreliable. On landing, he lost the 'Ufa' transmitter he had parachuted with. Görtz, attired in a *Luftwaffe* uniform, then walked to Dublin. He was not apprehended despite calling into a Garda barracks in Co. Wicklow, asking for directions to Dublin. Görtz made it to Dublin and a 'safe-house' at 245 Templeogue Road, Templeogue. In May 1940 the Irish police raided the home of an IRA member of German descent, Stephen Carroll Held, who had been working with Görtz, at his house at Blackheath Park, Clontarf. They confiscated a parachute, papers, Görtz's First World War medals, and a number of documents about the defence infrastructure of Ireland. The confiscated papers included files on possible military targets in Ireland, such as airfields and harbours, as well as detailed plans of the so-called 'Plan Kathleen'. This was an IRA plan for the invasion of Northern Ireland with the support of the German military. Held had brought this plan to Germany prior to Görtz's departure but his superiors had dismissed it as unfeasible. Görtz went into hiding, staying with sympathizers in the Wicklow area and purposefully avoided contact with IRA safehouses. He remained at large for a total of eighteen months. When another IRA member, Pearse Paul Kelly, visited Görtz's hiding place in Dublin in November 1941, police arrested them both. Görtz was interned until the end of the war. He was first detained in Mountjoy Prison but later moved to Custume Barracks, Athlone with nine others. Görtz was released from jail in Athlone in August 1946. He went to live in Glenageary. He was rearrested the following year and served with a deportation order by the Minister for Justice. He claimed to have been in the SS rather than a lieutenant in the *Luftwaffe* in an attempt to prevent his deportation but this claim was disproved by Irish Military Intelligence (G2) which also 'promoted' him to Major when sending him messages allegedly from Germany. On Friday 23 May 1947 he arrived at the Aliens' Office in Dublin Castle at 9.50 a.m. and was told he was being deported to Germany the next day. Although it had been stated to him that the Irish government had specifically requested that he not be handed over to the Soviets, he committed suicide.

Part IV

1. This sensational story from Paris led to the expulsion of Nazi Otto Abetz and the arrest of 150 French reporters. The *Deuxième Bureau* revealed Abetz had spent 350,000,000 francs in bribes to the French press between May and November, 1938. Julien Poirier, advertising manager of the reactionary *Le Figaro*, had accepted 3,500,000 francs from Abetz. Aubin, news editor of *Le Temps*, received 1,000,000 in return for military information. Police were reportedly searching for Pierre Gaxotte, editor of the right-wing *Je Suis Partout* and Ferdinand de Brinon, editor of the financial paper, *L'information*. Daladier, using his emergency powers, announced that henceforth the French press would be censored.

2. Jeans Gaston Claire Amourelle, (1907–1940). Amourelle was arrested for espionage. After his trial he was imprisoned. On 22 June 1940, the day the French were humiliated into signing the armistice at Compiègne, he was dragged from prison and shot alongside three saboteurs at dawn on the Verthamon firing range, in Pessac.

3. Baroness Gerta Louise née Riess von Scheurnschloss, an officer's daughter from Kassel, led a lavish lifestyle between Berlin and Paris. Gerta married William von Einem, military attaché of the Austro-Hungarian embassy. Before her marriage she had given birth to Gottfried von Einem, (1918–1996) who became a well-known Austrian composer. Gottfried's natural father was a Hungarian aristocrat Count László von Hunyadi. William von Einem adopted Gottfried. On 28 September 1938 twenty-year-old Gottfried von Einem was having breakfast at the Adlon Hotel in Berlin, when three Gestapo officers burst in and arrested him. He was taken to Gestapo headquarters at Prinz-Albrecht-Strasse and interrogated for several hours before being released. Einem had no idea why he had been singled out, but he glimpsed a piece of paper lying on a Gestapo officer's desk, which had been signed by Heydrich, the chief of the secret police. It read: 'Taken into protective custody for suspicion of having betrayed his country, and high treason.' The Gestapo came for Einem again, repeatedly, sometimes keeping him for several days. His entire, not inconsiderable, assets were confiscated, most of which he co-owned with his mother, Baroness Gerta Louise von Einem, who had been arrested along with him. If young Baron von Einem, after weeks of intermittent grilling at Gestapo headquarters, still did not know the formal reasons for the charges, he knew he was guilty by association, for he was extremely close to his mother. Einem had a colourful family history; in comparison with other members of his generation, his was an unconventional upbringing, and his mother was exotic. His father, Baron William von Einem, a general under the Habsburg monarchy, had been posted to the Austro-Hungarian embassy in Bern, where Gottfried was born in 1918. What the son found out only later from Gestapo officials was that his real father was not William but the Hungarian Count Laszlo von Hunyady, a former Habsburg colonel, also stationed in Bern. Gottfried's beautiful mother, who was descended from the Hessian nobility, had been in the habit of travelling to Africa with him to engage in lion-hunting safaris, always taking along an upright piano, for the count adored music no less than Gerta Louise and played the piano well. On one of these outings sometime in the 1920s, the count was torn apart by a severely wounded lion on the shores of the Nile near Khartoum. Happily, by that time Gottfried had been adopted by the forbearing Baron William.

   With these facts in mind one wonders if the exotic baroness had been blackmailed into espionage by the Gestapo? Information from Professor Michael H. Kater, *The Twisted Muse: Musicians and Their Music in the Third Reich*.

4. It is known that the baroness was still alive in 1949 when she made a claim for some property in Austria to the U.S. Allied Commission for Austria.

5. Georges-Étienne Bonnet, (1889–1973). Bonnet was a leading figure in the Radical Party. In April 1938, following the fall of the second Blum government, Bonnet was appointed Foreign Minister under Daladier as Premier. He was a staunch supporter of the Munich Agreement in 1938 and was firmly opposed to taking military action against German expansion; for the most part, he preferred to follow a course of appeasement. Bonnet was widely respected for his intelligence but often inspired great mistrust in others, in part because of his highly secretive methods of working and his preference for verbal as opposed to written instructions. During his time as Foreign Minister, Bonnet was distrusted by the British, Daladier and senior officials in the Quai d'Orsay, all of whom suspected that he was in some way not quite being honest with them. After the German aggression against Poland began on 1 September 1939, Bonnet continued to argue against a French declaration of war and instead urged that the French take up Mussolini's mediation offer. On 3 September 1939, Britain declared war on Germany, which had the effect of resolving the debate in Paris and Daladier finally succeeded in having the French declaration of war issued later that same day. For a week after the war was declared, Daladier avoided having the cabinet meet to ensure that Bonnet would not have a chance to put forward his views about seeking peace with Germany. Bonnet supported the Vichy government and served on the National Council from December 1940, but the council never met, and his role in Vichy was small. Bonnet spent most of the War living on his estate in the Dordogne and attempting to secure himself an office in Vichy. He was later to claim to have been involved in the Resistance. According to Gestapo records, Bonnet contacted the Germans in February 1941 to see if it were possible that the Germans might pressure Laval to include him in the Cabinet, and again in June 1943 to reassure them that he had no intention of leaving France to join the Allies. After the War he eventually returned to parliament and published his memoirs, but essentially his reputation was tarnished. Riess seems to have compelling evidence that Bonnet was compromised by the Nazis, even so he shrugged it off after the War when no-one in France was particularly interested in talking about the War and France's humiliation.

6. The firm Aktiebolaget Cryptograph or Cryptograph Incorporated was a company owned by Avid Gerhard Damn, who invented cipher machines of his own. This was enhanced by Boris Caesar Wilhelm Hagelin, (1892– 1983) who simplified and improved one of Damn's machines, much to the liking of the Swedish army, who placed a large order with the Damn firm. After Damn's death in 1927, Hagelin ran the firm. Later he developed the M-209, which became so successful that in the early 1940's more than 140,000 were manufactured. The royalties from this alone made Hagelin the first to become a millionaire from cryptography. It is not clear if Riess's assertion that the Company was bought by a German bank is correct. It appears that at the beginning of the War, Hagelin moved from Sweden to Switzerland, all the way across Germany and through Berlin to Genoa, carrying the design documents for the company's latest machine, and re-established his company there (it still operates as Crypto AG in Zug). That design was small, cheap and moderately secure, and he convinced the U.S. military to adopt it. Many tens of thousands of them were made. Of course, the Germans also had their own machine—Enigma.

7. Georges Mandel, (1885–1944). Born as Louis George Rothschild in Chatou, Yvelines, Mandel was the son of a Jewish tailor from Alsace. Mandel began his working life as a journalist but Clemenceau later brought him into politics as his

aide and he helped Clemenceau control the press and the trade union movement during the First World War. Mandel served as Minister of Colonies from 1938 to 18 May 1940, when Premier Paul Reynaud appointed him Minister of the Interior. He opposed the Armistice and on 16 June 1940 in Bordeaux, Mandel was arrested but released shortly afterwards. Shortly thereafter, the British general Edward Spears, Churchill's military liaison officer, offered Mandel the chance to leave on his plane, together with Charles de Gaulle. Mandel declined, saying: 'It would look as though I was afraid—as if I was running away.' Mandel was arrested on 8 August 1941 in Morocco by General Charles Nogues on the orders of Pierre Laval, Prime Minister of the Vichy government. He was conveyed to the Château de Chazeron via Fort du Portalet, where Paul Reynaud, Édouard Daladier and General Maurice Gamelin were also being held prisoner. Churchill tried unsuccessfully to arrange Mandel's rescue. He described Mandel as 'the first resister' and is believed to have preferred him over Charles de Gaulle to lead the Free French Forces. Following pressure from the Germans all four were sentenced to life imprisonment on 7 November 1941. In 1944 the German Ambassador, Otto Abetz suggested to Laval that Mandel, Blum, and Reynaud should be executed by the Vichy government in retaliation for the assassination of Philippe Henriot, Minister of Propaganda, by the Algiers Committee, the Communist Maquis of the Resistance. Mandel was returned to Paris on 4 July 1944, supposedly as a hostage. While being transferred from one prison to another, he was captured by the Milice, the paramilitary force. Three days later, the Milice took Mandel to the Forest of Fontainebleau, where they executed him. He was buried at Passy Cemetery.

8. Again Riess makes a sweeping statement, but his accuracy on this point is highly doubtful and many files, if not most files, fell into the hands of the Nazis. During the War, various Nazi agencies competed for the plunder of occupied Europe's archival heritage—from key documentation of military intelligence (such as *Deuxième Bureau*) and government security agencies to trade-union records, files of Masonic lodges and Jewish Communities, and personal papers of prominent individuals. At the War's end, the victorious Red Army found some of the most important Nazi hideouts. Many of Europe's captured archives were seized a second time and rushed to Moscow on Beria's orders, where they remained in secret for almost half a century. When the Russian Federation was admitted to the Council of Europe in 1996 it promised to expedite 'the return of property claimed by Council of Europe member States, in particular the archives transferred to Moscow in 1945.' Since then only five instances of archival returns have been finalised on the basis of the new Russian law—four handled diplomatically to France, Belgium, the Netherlands and Luxembourg, and a fifth, the Rothschild family papers from Vienna, as the first instance of a private family arrangement.

Part V

1. Hjalmar Horace Greeley Schacht, (1877–1970). Schacht was an economist, banker, liberal politician, and co-founder of the German Democratic Party. He served as the Currency Commissioner and President of the Reichsbank under the Weimar Republic. He was a fierce critic of Germany's reparation obligations following the Treaty of Versailles. In 1934 Hitler appointed Schacht as his Minister of Economics and Schacht supported public works programmes, most notably the construction of autobahns to alleviate unemployment. He disagreed with what he called 'unlawful activities' against Germany's Jewish minority and in 1935 made a speech denouncing Julius Streicher. He objected to high military spending,

and thereby came into conflict with Hitler and Göring. In November 1937 he resigned as Minister of Economics, but remained President of the Reichsbank until Hitler dismissed him in January 1939. He had no role during the war and was imprisoned after the 20 July 1944 plot. He was tried at Nuremberg and acquitted.

2. Helmuth Wohlthat, (1893– 1982). Wohlthat served as an officer in the cavalry in the First World War and from 1929 to 1933 he lived in the U.S. and continued his studies of political science at Columbia University in New York. During his stay in the U.S., he married a German-American teacher. In 1934 he served under Hjalmar Schacht in the Reich and Prussian Ministry of Economics as Assistant Secretary of State. In 1938 he moved to the Prussian State Ministry and as Secretary of State in the Ministry of the 'Four Year Plan' under Hermann Göring. On 23 March 1939, he concluded the 'Wohlthat Treaty' in Romania in relation to the petrochemical industry. After the occupation of the Netherlands Wohlthat was commissioner at the Nederlandsche Bank in Amsterdam. After the war Wohlthat occupied various supervisory board posts in the private sector.

3. Max Ringelmann cannot be found and this is reference is doubtful. The German consul who received his accreditation from the British authorities on 30 November 1937 was Wilhelm Melchers, (1900–1971). On his return to Germany Melchers made a career as a leading Middle East expert of the Foreign Office when he took over the Orient Unit in the Political Department of the Foreign Office.

4. Baldur Benedikt von Schirach, (1907-1974). Von Schirach had an American mother and English was his first learnt language. He married Henriette Hoffmann in 1932, daughter of Heinrich Hoffmann, Hitler's personal photographer and close friend. Through this relationship, von Schirach became part of Hitler's inner circle. In 1931 he became a Youth Leader and in 1933 he was made head of the Hitler Youth. He fell into disfavour with Hitler in 1943, but remained at his post. He surrendered in 1945 and was one of the officials put on trial at Nuremberg. He was one of only two men to denounce Hitler. On 1 October 1946, he was found guilty of crimes against humanity for his deportation of the Viennese Jews. He was sentenced to twenty years' imprisonment at Spandau, and was released in 1966.

5. Fritz Konrad Ferdinand Grobba, (1886–1973). Riess has some of his details the wrong way around. Grobba was appointed as the German Ambassador to Iraq in October 1932 and was sent to Baghdad. He was able to speak both Turkish and Arabic. He frequently spoke of Arab nationalism and of ousting the British from the Middle East. Grobba purchased a Christian-owned newspaper, *The Arab World* and serialised an Arabic version of *Mein Kampf*. Grobba also convinced King Ghazi to allow Germany to send 50 German officers to Iraq for war games. He then convinced the King to accept German 'research expeditions' to Iraq. Unlike the Iraqis, the Germans did not return home and, instead, they stayed in Iraq long-term. Grobba enthusiastically supported a virulently anti-British group of Iraqi officers called the 'Circle of Seven.' In time, these men represented real power as successive Iraqi governments sought the support of the military for survival. In 1938, a main British pipeline in Iraq was attacked and set on fire by Arabs. When this attack was found to be connected to Grobba, he was forced to flee to Saudi Arabia and in 1939 his emissary was reported to be seeking arms in Germany. From November 1938 until September 1939 Grobba was also the German Ambassador to the Kingdom of Saudi Arabia. After the onset of War the Kingdom of Iraq deported German officials and broke off diplomatic relations with Germany. However, contrary to Article 4 of the Anglo-Iraqi Treaty of 1930, the then Prime Minister Nuri Said chose not to have Iraq declare war on Germany. From October 1939 until May 1941 Grobba served in the German foreign ministry in Berlin. On 2 May 1941, after much tension between the Rashid Ali government

and the British, the besieged forces at RAF Habbaniya under Air Vice-Marshal H. G. Smart launched pre-emptive air strikes against Iraqi forces throughout Iraq and the Anglo-Iraqi War began for real. On 3 May, German Foreign Minister Joachim von Ribbentrop persuaded Hitler that Dr Fritz Grobba be secretly returned to Iraq to head up a diplomatic mission to channel support to the Rashid Ali regime. Grobba's mission was to be sent to Iraq along with a military mission commanded by the *Oberkommando der Wehrmacht,* or OKW. The military mission had the cover name 'Special Staff F' (*Sonderstab F*) and it included a *Luftwaffe* component and was commanded by General Hellmuth Felmy. Grobba with *Fliegerführer Irak* reached Baghdad on 11 May 1941. An overall priority for the Germans was to provide the Royal Iraqi Army with a 'spine straightening.' Much of the RIrA was known to be terrified of bombing by British aircraft. In the end, *Fliegerführer Irak* failed and on 28 May Grobba sent a panicked message from Baghdad reporting that the British were close to the city with more than one-hundred tanks. By then, Junck had no serviceable Messerschmitt 110 fighters and only two Heinkel 111 bombers with just four bombs between them. Late on 29 May, Rashid Ali, several of his key supporters, and the German military mission fled under cover of darkness. On 30 May, Grobba himself fled Baghdad. In February 1942, Grobba was named foreign ministry plenipotentiary for the Arab States, a job that entailed liaison between the Nazi German government and Arab exiles in Berlin, like Mohammad Amin al-Husayni. In December 1942, Grobba was named to the Paris branch of the German archives commission. He held this post until his brief return to the foreign ministry in April 1944. In June 1944, Grobba was officially retired from the foreign ministry. At the end of the war, Grobba was captured and was kept in Soviet captivity until 1955.

6. Ghazi bin Faisal, (1912–1939). Ghazi was the King of the Hashemite Kingdom of Iraq from 1933 to 1939 having been briefly Crown Prince of the Kingdom of Syria in 1920. A pan-Arab nationalist, opposed to British interests in his country, Ghazi supported General Bakr Sidqi in his coup, which replaced the civilian government with a military one. This was the first *coup d'état* to take place in the modern Arab world. Ghazi died in 1939 in an accident involving a sports car that he was driving. Faisal, Ghazi's only son, succeeded him as King Faisal II. Because Faisal was under age, Prince Abdul Ilah served as Regent until 1953. Faisal was assassinated in a *coup d'état* in 1958.

7. Werner Otto von Hentig, (1886–1984). This is another occasion where Riess was probably wrong. Von Hentig was a critic of the Nazi regime and he intervened at great personal risk to save Jews who were in danger and was instrumental in arranging for thousands of Jews to be transferred from Germany to Palestine during the 1930s. After the anti-Jewish *Kristallnacht* of November 1938, Hentig expressed his shame and willingly used his influence at great personal risk to protest against a fresh outbreak of violence from starting. He interceded with Under-Secretary of State Ernst von Weizsäcker, pointing out the detrimental effects of the riots on German foreign policy and secured the release of many Jewish functionaries from concentration camps. Hentig held the position of the Palestine Desk in the Wilhelmstrasse at this time (1937–38), and although a critic of the Nazi regime he was a man whose foreign service expertise could not be ignored or wasted. Having said that, he may very well have been in Syria at the time and Hitler apart, he was clearly trying to further German interests.

Part VI

1. Guenther Gustave Rumrich, (b. 1911). Born in Chicago, Illinois to an Austro-Hungarian father and raised in Germany, Guenther Gustave Rumrich returned to America in 1929 and served in the U.S. Army's Medical Corps in Panama until his desertion in 1936. He became suspected in 1938 of possible spy activities because of Mrs Jessie Jordan in Dundee, Scotland. She was a woman under surveillance by MI5, who believed her to be an operative working for the Germans by acting as a mail drop, passing letters to and from a Nazi spy ring in New York City. Mrs Jordan's communications with 'Mr Crown' were intercepted by MI5. As it turned out, Crown was Rumrich's code name, and the letters were orders and instructions from his *Abwehr* handlers. The head of MI5 turned the information over to the FBI. Rumrich was put under federal surveillance, and a trap was set—but he didn't fall for it. Instead, in February 1938, he called the Passport Office in New York City. Masquerading as the U.S. Undersecretary of State, he requested thirty-five blank passports be sent to his address. The suspicious clerk he spoke to over the phone reported the incident to the authorities. Rumrich was arrested in what became America's first major pre-war espionage case. Rumrich supplied information about his fellow agents, who were also arrested. At their trials, he acted as a witness for the prosecution. For his cooperation, he was given a light sentence of two years in prison. Unfortunately, more important Nazi spies escaped the FBI's net, and the case was not considered to be a complete success. The New York spy ring case pointed out America's vulnerability to foreign espionage efforts, and prompted government action. The Rumrich case was fictionalized in the 1939 film, *Confessions of a Nazi Spy.*

2. Friedrich Ferdinand Ernest Auhagen, (b. 1899), Auhagen emigrated to the U.S. in 1923 and lived in Elmhurst, Long Island. In 1929 he applied for U.S. citizenship, and until 1935 taught German literature at Columbia University. On 16 March 1939 Auhagen founded an American Fellowship Forum (AFF). In September 1940 Auhagen was detained regarding subversive activities, but released, remaining under the observation of the U.S. Department of Justice. On 11 July 1941 he was convicted on three counts of the McCormack Act and sentenced to $1,000 and two years' imprisonment. Auhagen remained in custody until April 1947 and was then transferred to Germany, where he appeared at the Nuremberg Trials indicted as a war criminal.

3. George Sylvester Viereck, (1884–1962). Viereck was born in Germany to a German father and an American-born mother. His father Louis Viereck emigrated to the United States; his U.S.-born wife Laura and their twelve-year-old son George followed in 1897. Young Viereck soon found fame. The *Saturday Evening Post* called Viereck 'the most widely-discussed young literary man in the United States today'. For his support of Germany Viereck was expelled from several social clubs and in August 1918, a lynch mob stormed Viereck's house in Mount Vernon, forcing him to seek refuge in a New York City hotel. Viereck became a well-known Nazi apologist. His interview with Adolf Hitler in 1923 had offered hints of what was to come. In 1933, Viereck again met with Hitler in Berlin, and in 1934, he gave a speech to twenty thousand 'Friends of the New Germany' at New York's Madison Square Garden, in which he compared Hitler to Franklin Delano Roosevelt and told his audience to sympathize with National Socialism without being antisemites. In 1941, he was indicted in the U.S. for a violation of the Foreign Agents Registration Act when he set up his publishing house, Flanders Hall, in Scotch Plains, New Jersey. He was convicted in 1942 for this failure to register with the U.S. Department of State as a Nazi agent. He was imprisoned from 1942 to 1947.

4. Colin Ross, (1885–1945). Ross was born in Vienna, Austria and was a traveller and writer of Scottish descent. He studied at the Technical Universities of Berlin and Munich. He also studied economics, history and geopolitics under Professor Karl Haushofer. He first visited the U.S. in 1911 and during the 1930s he gave lectures in America on the successes of National Socialist Germany. Many of these lectures were attended by German American Bund members. On 20 September 1940 the State Department officially declared Ross to be a 'Nazi agent' although he did not become a NSDAP party member until October 1941. He was a close friend of Hitler Youth leader Baldur von Schirach. At the end of the war Ross and his wife committed suicide at the home of Baldur von Schirach.

5. Fritz Wiedemann, (1891–1970). Wiedemann was for a time the personal adjutant to Adolf Hitler, having served with him in the First World War. When Hitler came to power in 1933 Wiedemann accepted a position with Hess before taking up a new post at Hitler's side. He facilitated meetings and dealt with Hitler's correspondence. Late in 1938 he fell out of favour with Hitler and in January 1939 Hitler appointed him to be Consul General to the United States in San Francisco. In public, Wiedemann continued to support Nazism and apparently led a playboy lifestyle including a relationship with Stephanie von Hohenlohe. Allegations levelled in a case filed at the city's Federal District Court in 1941 also suggest that he worked on pro-Nazi initiatives with Henry Ford. In private, however, Wiedemann broke entirely with Nazism. He met with the British agent Sir William Wiseman, warning him of Hitler's unstable personality and urging Britain to attack Germany. He also offered to publicly denounce the German regime, but the White House at that time had no interest in such an offer. Wiedemann gave evidence at Nuremberg although charges made against him were dropped in 1948 and he subsequently returned to farming, disappearing from public life.

6. Manfred Freiherr von Killinger, (1886–1944). Killinger was a veteran of the First World War and took part in the military intervention against the Bavarian Soviet Republic. He later became an NSDAP representative in the Reichstag and a leader of the *Sturmabteilung*, before serving as Saxony's Minister-President and playing a part in implementing Nazi policies at a local level. Purged during the Night of the Long Knives, he was able to recover his status and served as Germany's Consul in San Francisco between 1936 and 1939. As Ambassador to the Slovak Republic in 1940, he played a part in enforcing antisemitic legislation in that country. In early 1941, Killinger was appointed to a similar position in Romania. He oversaw German activities in Romania but committed suicide in Bucharest a few days after the King Michael Coup toppled the Antonescu regime on 23 August 1944.

7. Edgar von Spiegel von und zu Peckelsheim, (1885–1965). Von Spiegel von und zu Peckelsheim was a German submarine commander in the First World War, but was captured and ended the war in a British POW camp. In Nazi Germany, von Spiegel served in the German diplomatic service and in 1936 and 1937 he worked at the German embassy in London under Ribbentrop. In 1937 he was appointed Consul in New Orleans. Because of suspected espionage activities the FBI investigated him and it was considered that he probably briefed German submarines in the Gulf of Mexico via radio regarding merchant vessels leaving the port of New Orleans for England. When The USA joined the War he left New Orleans and after returning to Germany he served as consul in Marseille in occupied France. In August 1944 Marseille was liberated by the Allies and von Spiegel left and joined the staff of Reichsführer SS in November 1944.

8. Herbert Wilhelm Scholz, (b. 1906). Scholz was the secretary to Ambassador Martin Luther in Washington DC from 1936 to 1940. Passenger information in the U.S. shows that he was a very regular traveller between Europe and the U.S.A.

and in particular to take up his appointment he arrived at New York on board SS *Europa* on 28 September 1936 from Southampton. He was later appointed Consul to the Boston Consular office until he was deported to Portugal in 1941 when all the consulates were closed. He was later appointed to Hungary where it is believed his duties included keeping an eye on Horthy. He probably worked in close co-operation with the SS for what turned out to be his last significant foreign policy move, *Operation Panzerfaust*, the coup that deposed Admiral Miklós Horthy, the Regent of Hungary, on 15 October 1944. Horthy was deposed because he attempted to seek a separate peace with the Allies, and was replaced with Ferenc Szálasi, who resumed the deportation of Hungarian Jews in co-operation with the SS and the *Auswärtige Amt* that Horthy had halted in July 1944.

9. George Johnson Armstrong (1902–1941). Armstrong was the first British citizen to be executed under the Treachery Act 1940. Only four other British subjects were executed under this Act; Jose Estelle Key (a Gibraltarian), Duncan Scott-Ford, Oswald John Job (born in London of German parents) and Theodore Schurch. Armstrong was tried on 8 May 1941 at the Central Criminal Court and convicted for communicating with the German Consul in Boston, Massachusetts, to offer him assistance before the United States entered the War. His appeal on 23 June 1941 at the Court of Criminal Appeal, was dismissed, and on 10 July 1941 at the age of 39 he was executed by hanging at HM Prison Wandsworth.

10. Camille Chautemps, (1885–1963). Chautemps was a Radical politician of the Third Republic, Prime Minister of France twice between 1933 and 1938. When General de Gaulle telephoned Reynaud from London to give him the British Government's offer of joint nationality for Frenchmen and Englishmen in a Franco-British Union. A delighted Reynaud put it to a stormy cabinet meeting and was supported by five of his ministers. Most of the others were persuaded against him by the arguments of Pétain and Chautemps, the latter two seeing the offer as a device to make France subservient to Great Britain. Chautemps eventually broke with Philippe Pétain's Vichy Government and after arriving in the United States on an official mission he remained, and lived there for much of the rest of his life. After the War a French court convicted him *in absentia* for collaborating with the enemy.

11. 16 June 1941—All German and Italian consulates in the United States are ordered closed and their staffs were ordered to leave the country by 10 July.

12. Frederick 'Fritz' Joubert Duquesne, (1877–1956). Duquesne, was a French national. During the Second Boer War, from 1899 to 1902, Duquesne was captured and imprisoned three times by the British and once by the Portuguese, and each time he escaped. After a failed attempt to escape prison in Cape Town, he was sent to prison in Bermuda, but he escaped to the United States and became an American citizen. In the First World War, he developed a spy ring for Germany and sabotaged British merchant ships in South America with concealed bombs and destroyed several. After he was caught by federal agents in New York in 1917, he feigned paralysis for two years and cut the bars of his cell to make his escape, thereby avoiding deportation to England where he faced execution for the deaths of British sailors. In 1932, he was again captured in New York by federal agents and charged with both homicide and for being an escaped prisoner, only this time he was set free after Britain declined to pursue the wartime crimes. The last time he was captured and imprisoned was in 1941 when he and 32 other members of the Duquesne Spy Ring were caught by William G. Sebold, a double agent with the FBI, and later convicted in the largest espionage conviction in the history of the United States. A native of Germany, William Sebold served in the Imperial German Army during the First World War. After leaving Germany in

1921, he worked in industrial and aircraft plants throughout the United States and South America. On 10 February 1936, he became a naturalized citizen of the U.S. Sebold returned to Germany in February 1939 to visit his mother in Mülheim. On arrival in Hamburg, he was approached by a member of the Gestapo who said that Sebold would be contacted in the near future. Sebold proceeded to Mülheim where he obtained employment. In September 1939, Dr Gassner visited Sebold in Mülheim and interrogated him about military planes and equipment in the United States. He also asked Sebold to return to the United States as an agent for Germany. Subsequent visits by Dr Gassner and a Dr Renken, later identified as Major Nickolaus Ritter of the German Secret Service, persuaded Sebold to cooperate with the Reich because he feared reprisals against family members still living there. Ritter was the *Abwehr* officer in charge of espionage against the United States and Britain. Since Sebold's passport had been stolen shortly after his first visit from Gassner, Sebold went to the US consulate in Cologne, to obtain a new one. While there, Sebold secretly told consulate personnel about his future role as a German agent and expressed his wish to cooperate with the FBI when he got back to America. Sebold reported to Hamburg, where he was instructed in such areas as preparing coded messages and microphotographs. On completion of training, he was given five microphotographs containing instructions for preparing a code and detailing the type of information he was to transmit to Germany from the United States. Sebold was told to retain two of the microphotographs and to deliver the other three to German operatives in the United States: Fritz Joubert Duquesne, Hermann Lang, and one other. After receiving final instructions, including using the assumed name Harry Sawyer, he sailed from Genoa, Italy, and arrived in New York City on 8 February 1940. The FBI had been advised of Sebold's expected arrival, his mission, and his intent to assist in identifying German agents in the United States. Under the guidance of special agents, Sebold established residence in New York City as Harry Sawyer. Also, an office was set up for him as a consulting diesel engineer, to be used as a cover in establishing contact with members of the spy ring. In selecting the office for Sebold, FBI agents ensured that they could observe any meetings taking place there. In May 1940, a shortwave radio-transmitting station operated by FBI agents on Long Island established contact with the German shortwave station abroad. For 16 months it served as a main channel of communications between German spies in New York City and their superiors in Germany. During this time, the FBI's station transmitted over 300 messages to and received 200 messages from Germany. After the Duquesne Spy Ring convictions, Sebold was provided with a new identity and started a chicken farm in California.

13. Herman Alexander Brassert, (1875–1961). Brassert was born in London of German parents. He graduated as a metallurgical engineer from the College of Mining and Metallurgy, Berlin, 1896. He emigrated to the U.S. in October 1896 and by 1898 he was working for the Carnegie Steel Company in Pittsburgh, PA. In 1905 he was placed in charge of the blast furnaces in the Chicago District of the Illinois Steel Company. In 1916 he joined the South Works, Illinois Steel Company as assistant general superintendent. In 1925 he organised H. A. Brassert & Company, Consulting Engineers, in Chicago which soon had offices in New York City and Pittsburgh as well as a British affiliate, H. A. Brassert & Company Ltd and he actually lived in England between 1934 and 1939, coinciding with the period when he assisted Hermann Göring; assistance which lasted right up to September 1939. In 1943 when he came under attack he put up a bland excuse—but got away with it. He said: 'When I acquired information which led me to believe that the Nazis were preparing for war, and when I learned the true

character of the Nazi movement and its leaders, I withdrew our engineers from this work, as a result of which the German government itself undertook the job of completion. For this my company and I incurred the wrath and hatred of the Nazis. In this connection I might add that to my knowledge my company was the only firm of American engineers that discontinued doing business with the Nazis prior to the outbreak of the Second World war, notwithstanding the fact that we had contracts on which we could have realized substantial profits at a time when America, England, and Germany were at peace with one another, and business with Germany was not only done by leading American companies, but was eagerly sought.'

14. The raid was *Operation Claymore* and took place in March 1941, by No. 3 and No. 4 Commandos. This was the first large scale raid from the United Kingdom during the war. Their objective was the undefended Norwegian Lofoten Islands. They successfully destroyed the fish-oil factories, petrol dumps, and 11 ships, capturing 216 Germans, encryption equipment and codebooks.